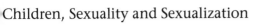

Children, Sexuality and Sexualization

Children, Sexuality and Sexualization

Edited by

Emma Renold
Cardiff University, UK

Jessica Ringrose
University College London, Institute of Education, UK

R. Danielle Egan
St Lawrence University, New York, USA

First published 2015 by
PALGRAVE MACMILLAN

Palgrave Macmillan in the UK is an imprint of Macmillan Publishers Limited,
registered in England, company number 785998, of Houndmills, Basingstoke,
Hampshire RG21 6XS.

Palgrave Macmillan in the US is a division of St Martin's Press LLC,
175 Fifth Avenue, New York, NY 10010.

Palgrave Macmillan is the global academic imprint of the above companies
and has companies and representatives throughout the world.

Palgrave® and Macmillan® are registered trademarks in the United States,
the United Kingdom, Europe and other countries.

ISBN 978–1–137–35338–2

This book is printed on paper suitable for recycling and made from fully
managed and sustained forest sources. Logging, pulping and manufacturing
processes are expected to conform to the environmental regulations of the
country of origin.

A catalogue record for this book is available from the British Library.

Library of Congress Cataloging-in-Publication Data
Children, sexuality and sexualization / edited by Emma Renold, Jessica Ringrose,
  R. Danielle Egan.
    pages   cm
  Summary: 'Offering critical response to a range of popular debates on children's
  sexual cultures, this ground-breaking volume challenges preconceived and accepted
  theories regarding children, sexuality and sexualisation. The contributions to this
  collection offer compelling accounts from a range of disciplinary fields and
  transnational contexts to present original empirical research findings, which
  offer new ways to make sense of children's sexual cultures across complex
  political, social and cultural terrains. Organised into five sections, this book
  addresses the history of young sexualities research and theory across disciplinary
  boundaries; pre-teen sexualities and a re-thinking of sexual agency and innocence;
  how space, place and history shape young queer sexualities; the representation of
  young sexualities in the popular cultural imaginary; and the role of new media
  and digital technology in the formation of children and young people's sexual
  cultures'—Provided by publisher.
  ISBN 978–1–137–35338–2 (hardback)
  1. Children and sex.   2. Children—Sexual behavior.   3. Sex in mass media.
  4. Sex in popular culture.   I. Renold, Emma, editor.   II. Ringrose, Jessica, editor.
  III. Egan, R. Danielle, editor.
  HQ784.S45C554 2015
  306.7083—dc23   2015013448

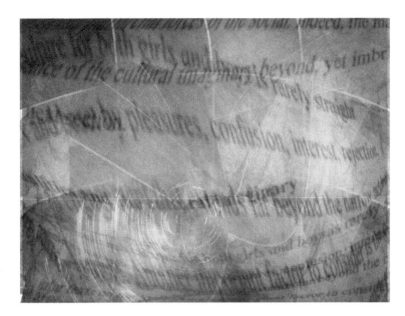

Vort(s)ex
Red Ruby Scarlet

Ode Too Scarlet Da Da La La Lolita Harlet

S/he	Four
Beamed	Him
Up	To
Scotty	Stutter
Frothy	Mutter
Potty	ShutHer
Mouth	Up
From	Little
Her	Pup
Ring	Sup?
Old	S/he
Feminist	Said
Body	As
Of	S/he
Dangerous	Bled
Knowledge	Her
Dis	Wisdom
GuySed	Filled
	Head
Dotty	Why
Scotty	Dread?
Try	He
As	Fled
He	With
May	A
Couldn't	Suitcase
Say	Diffused
In	Excuse
His	Refuse
Way	Meh'd
Sex	Meanwhile
Sexualised	S/he
Surprised	Read
Dis	
Maid	
French	
Fries	
Cock	
Eyed	
S/he	
Wrote	
Harder	
And	
Harder	
It	
Became	

RingO(l)dE Sounded by Red Ruby Scarlet (Dr Miriam Giugni)

Contents

Part V New Media, Digital Technology and Young Sexual Cultures

Figures

Acknowledgements

This collection would not have happened if it were not for the research networks made possible by the Economic and Social Research Council (ESRC), UK. The seminar series 'Pornified: Complicating debates on the sexualisation of culture' in 2011–2012 (organized with Rosalind Gill, Emma Renold, Jessica Ringrose and Meg Barker) was what enabled Emma Renold to facilitate a visit from Danielle Egan and Gail Hawkes during a seminar she led on girls' sexuality at Cardiff University. This seminar was followed by a final conference on 'pornification' at the now UCL, Institute of Education (London), organized by Jessica Ringrose, attended by many of the contributors, who subsequently submitted book chapters to this edited collection. Some of these relationships were further nurtured through a subsequent ESRC seminar series, 'Understanding the young sexual body' (organized with Lesley Hoggart, Susan Baker, Ofra Koffman, Emma Renold and Jessica Ringrose).

We would like to thank Palgrave for responding enthusiastically to the proposal and extend a heartfelt thanks to the reviewers of the book proposal whose encouraging and thoughtful comments enabled us to expand and enrich the book far beyond our original remit. Indeed, it was through a dialogue with Deborah Tolman, our most thorough and engaged reviewer, that we commissioned her chapter in the volume. We are very grateful for her continuing support throughout the process of working on the book. We would like to further thank Palgrave for their assistance and patience whilst working on the book, especially for extending the word count to make space for the wonderful chapters that we received! Indeed we would like to thank all of the authors for their thoughtful, provocative and questioning contributions which have created a truly groundbreaking collection.

We would also like to thank our wider community of academics and friends, particularly those whom we network with via social media such as Facebook and Twitter who have sparked so many conversations about the issues debated in this book. We would particularly like to acknowledge and thank our families for their support during the lengthy process of compiling the book. Emma would like to thank her partner Dean, her kids Rohen and Joss, her two English toy terriers (Sid and Nancy), her mum Jan and her Yamaha xv950! Jessica would like to say a special thanks to her partner Jose, particularly for driving her and Emma to an isolated farmhouse near Abergavenny, Wales, to put the finishing touches to the volume. Danielle would like to thank Steve, whose friendship and support she values more than he could know, and her wonder pup Milo, who is at her side when she writes; as well as the benevolent dictator that is her Maine Coon cat, Freida, who seems to love her laptop keyboard more than any other surface in the house. Finally, we would like to thank Red Ruby Scarlett whom we commissioned to create the image and ode on the inside of this book. Red's creative and collaborative process enabled us to think about key visual images that we felt captured the energetic force of the chapters, and we think she has produced a fabulous and vibrant assemblage that expresses these ideas in visual form.

Contributors

Louisa Allen is an associate professor in the Faculty of Education at the University of Auckland. She specializes in research in the areas of sexualities, young people and schooling and innovative research methodologies which seek to engage hard to reach research populations. She examines these areas through the lenses of queer, post-constructionist, critical masculinities and critical youth studies theoretical frameworks. She has written and edited four books in these fields, the latest of which is *The Politics of Pleasure in Sexuality Education: Pleasure Bound* (edited with Mary Lou Rasmussen and Kathleen Quinlivan, 2014). She has recently completed a two-year Australian Research Council Discovery Project Grant, exploring how to address cultural and religious diversity in sexuality education with a team of international colleagues from New Zealand and Australia. It epitomizes the kind of educational research she likes to do best – grappling with questions which are 'thorny' and generally avoided.

Deevia Bhana is a professor in the School of Education, University of KwaZulu-Natal. Her research interests include childhood sexualities, gender, inequalities and schooling. She is the author of *Under Pressure: Regulation of sexualities in South African Secondary Schools* (2014), a co-author of *Towards Equality? Gender in South African Schools during the HIV/AIDS Pandemic* (with R. Morrell, E. Unterhalter, D. Epstein and R. Moletsane, 2009) and a co-editor of *Babies and/or Books: Pregnancy and Young Parents at School* (with R. Morrell and T. Shefer, 2012). Her next book, *Childhood Sexuality and AIDS Education: The Price of Innocence*, will be published in 2015.

Christin P. Bowman is a doctoral candidate in critical social psychology at the Graduate Center of the City University of New York. Her research interests focus on the ways the institution of heterosexuality affects how women and girls live their lives and make meaning of their experiences. Specifically, she studies women's sexuality including women's masturbation and connections to feelings of sexual empowerment; adolescent sexuality and relationships; masculinity and femininity ideologies; and the sexualization of women and girls in society. Under the mentorship of Deborah Tolman, she has also written about sexual embodiment and engaging young women in feminist activism. She is also a research blogger and editor for the SPARK movement, which aims to push back against the sexualization of girls and women in the media and 'take sexy back'.

Sara Bragg is a senior research fellow in the Education Research Centre at the University of Brighton, UK. Her doctoral research focused on 'violent' media genres, youth audiences and media education in the UK; she has also researched debates about the 'sexualization' of childhood; youth 'voice' and participation in schools; school ethos; and 'creative' research methods. She is the co-author of *Young People, Sex and the Media* (with David Buckingham, 2004); a co-editor of *Children and Young People's Cultural Worlds* (with Mary Jane Kehily, 2013) and *Youth Cultures in the Age of Global Media* (with David Buckingham and Mary Jane Kehily, 2014). She has published in journals including *Feminist Media Studies, Gender and Education, Children & Society*, and edited collections including *Researching Creative Learning: Methods and Issues* (2011) and *The Routledge Companion to Media and Gender* (2013).

Jennifer F. Chmielewski is a doctoral student in the Critical Social/ Personality Psychology program at the CUNY Graduate Center, New York. She holds an EdM in Counseling Psychology from Teachers College, Columbia University. Her work uses critical feminist theories and methods to explore women and girls' lived experiences of gender, desire and sexual identity through an intersectional and social justice lens. She is currently examining how queer girls of colour experience their bodies and desires as policed within institutional practices of surveillance in schools and communities, with a focus on their embodied resistance. Her research has also appeared in journals including *Psychology of Women Quarterly* and *Journal of Lesbian Studies* and *Sex Roles*. She is also a research blogger for SPARK, an inter-generational feminist activist organization that works with girls to push back against the sexualization of girls and women in the media.

Diego Costa is a Luso-Brazilian PhD candidate and Provost Fellow in the Interdivisional Media arts and Practice (iMap) program at the University of Southern California. He is a film and media theorist and practitioner working at the intersection of queer theory, Lacanian psychoanalysis, new media studies, gender studies and self-ethnographic experimental filmmaking as research method. He is the co-founder of the Queer Psychoanalysis Society, a film critic for *Slant Magazine* and a contributing writer for *Brasil Post*.

Cristyn Davies is a research associate at the University of Sydney, Australia. Her areas of expertise include gendered and sexual subjectivities and citizenship; constructions of childhood and youth; sex education, health and wellbeing; sociology of medicine; neoliberalism and governmentality; cultural policy and law; regulation and moral panic; innovative pedagogies and educational practice; and narrative and (heritage and new) media. She has collaborated with academics, writers, performance artists, and digital and new media artists on a range of projects. Her research is published in *Sexualities, Cultural Studies, Feminist Media Studies, Cultural Studies Review, Contemporary Issues in Early Childhood, Australasian Journal of Early Childhood* and *Sexuality and Culture*, amongst other journals. She has co-edited several special editions of journals, and the following books: *Rethinking School Violence: Theory, Gender and Context* (2012, Palgrave Macmillan), *Queer and Subjugated Knowledges: Generating Subversive Imaginaries* (2012) and *Cultural Studies of Law* (2014).

Diederik F. Janssen is an independent researcher. He is co-founding and general editor of *Culture, Society & Masculinities* as well as *Boyhood Studies: An Interdisciplinary Journal* (2015), and a managing editor of *The Journal of Men's Studies* (2015). He holds a MD and bachelor's degree in Cultural Anthropology, both from the Radboud University, Nijmegen. His publications include 'Queer Theory and Childhood' and 'Masculinities/Boyhood', both invited contributions to *Oxford Bibliographies Online: Childhood Studies*.

R. Danielle Egan is Professor and Chair of Gender and Sexuality Studies at St Lawrence University and a psychoanalytic candidate at the Boston Graduate School of Psychoanalysis. She is the author of *Becoming Sexual: Critical Appraisal of Girls and Sexualization* (2012) and *Theorizing the Sexual Child in Modernity* (with Gail Hawkes, 2010). She has published over 25 journal articles and currently serves on the editorial boards of the journals *Sexualities* and *Sexuality and Culture*. She is also the co-editor, with Patricia Clough, of the Palgrave series *Critical Studies in Gender and Sexuality*. In addition to her academic work, Egan works with people in her clinical practice in Brookline, Massachusetts.

Laura Harvey is Lecturer in Sociology at the University of Surrey. Her work takes an interdisciplinary approach, drawing on sociology, gender studies, social psychology and cultural studies. Her interests include sexualities, everyday intimacies and inequalities, research with young people, the mediation of sexual knowledge, feminist methodologies and discourse analysis.

Lindsay Herriot is a doctoral candidate at the University of Alberta, Edmonton, Canada, in educational policy studies. Her dissertation pertains to lesbian, gay, bisexual, trans* and queer (LGBTQ) youth organizing in secondary schools. She has published in a variety of areas, including citizenship education, student voice and gay straight alliances.

Lara E. Hiseler is a doctoral candidate at the University of Alberta, Edmonton, Canada, in counselling psychology. She completed her accredited pre-doctoral internship at a psychiatric hospital in Whitby, Ontario, providing psychological treatment to adults found not criminally responsible due to mental disorder. She has experience with assessment and interventions with children and adults in a multitude of settings including student mental health, community outpatient clinics, school boards, correctional centres and inpatient psychiatric hospitals. She has particular expertise with compassion-focused approaches in treating shame and emotion dys-regulation. Her dissertation examined how incarcerated women understood and experienced self-compassion utilizing interpretative phenomenological analysis. She has published in a variety of areas, such as coping with comorbid cancer and schizophrenia, humanistic therapy, positive psychology interventions with incarcerated youth, and mentoring undergraduate students in psychology research.

Toni Ingram is a doctoral candidate in the Faculty of Education at the University of Auckland. Her research interests include girlhood, young femininities, sexualities and schooling. Her previous research has explored 11–13-year-old girls' understandings of themselves as sexual subjects. Her current research project examines the relations between girlhood, sexuality and school ball culture.

Gabrielle Ivinson is Professor of Psychology and Education, School of Education, Aberdeen University, and a social and developmental psychologist who studies gender and knowledge. She co-authored *Rethinking Single Sex Teaching* (with Patricia Murphy, 2007) and co-edited *Knowledge and Identity: Concepts and Applications in Bernstein's Sociology of Knowledge* (with Brian Davies and John Fitz, 2011). She is a co-editor of the journal *Gender and Education*. Her recent papers, 'The Body and Pedagogy: Beyond Absent, Moving Bodies in Pedagogic Practice', *British Journal of Sociology of Education* (with Jo-anne Dillabough, Maria Tamboukou and Julie McLoud) and 'Skills in Motion: Sport, Education and Society', explore relations among embodied knowledge, materiality and place.

Sue Jackson is a senior lecturer in the School of Psychology at Victoria University of Wellington, New Zealand. Much of her previous research and publication work has centred on young women's negotiation of sexuality, the ways sexuality is represented in girls' popular culture and how girls make sense of media representations of femininity and sexuality. Currently her research centres on a three-year project, 'Girls, "Tween" Popular Culture and Everyday Life' supported by the New Zealand Royal Society Marsden Fund.

Stevi Jackson is Professor of Women's Studies and Director of the Centre for Women's Studies at the University of York, UK. Among her publications are *Childhood and Sexuality* (1982), *Heterosexuality in Question* (1999), *Theorizing Sexuality* (with Sue Scott, 2010) and *Gender and Sexuality: Sociological Approaches* (with Momin Rahman, 2010). Her co-edited books include *Gender: A Sociological Reader* (with Sue Scott, 2002) and *East Asian Sexualities: Intimacy, Modernity and New Sexual Cultures* (with Liu Jieyu and Woo Juhyun, 2008). She has also published numerous articles on sexuality and intimacy.

She is currently working, with Petula Sik Ying Ho, on a book provisionally entitled *Women Doing Intimacy: Gender, Family and Modernity in Hong Kong and Britain*, which is to be published in Palgrave Macmillan's 'Studies in Family and Intimate Life' series.

Lara Karaian is an assistant professor in the Institute of Criminology and Criminal Justice at Carleton University, Ottawa, Canada. Her research interests include the legal regulation and construction of sex, gender and sexuality; feminist, queer and transgender legal theory; surveillance studies; critical/cultural/visual criminology; and porn studies. His Social Science and Humanities Research Council-funded research project 'Selfies, Sexuality and Teens: A Canadian Study' (2012–2014) examines legal and extra-legal actors' constructions of, and attempts to regulate, teenagers' digital sexual expression. She has served as an expert consultant for the Law Reform Committee of the Parliament of Victoria, Australia's International Consultation on Sexting. Her written work has been published in *Theoretical Criminology, Social and Legal Studies* and *Crime Media Culture*. She is also one of the co-editors of *Turbo Chicks: Talking Young Feminisms* (2001), the first Canadian anthology of Third Wave feminist writing.

Mary Jane Kehily is Professor of Childhood and Youth Studies at the Open University, UK. She has research interests in gender and sexuality, narrative and identity and popular culture and has published widely on these themes. Her books include *Gender, Sexuality and Schooling, Shifting Agendas in Social Learning,* (2002), *An Introduction to Childhood Studies* (2008), *Making Modern Mothers* (with R. Thomson, L. Hadfield and S. Sharpe, 2011) and *Gender, Youth and Culture, Young Masculinities and Femininities* (with Anoop Nayak, Palgrave Macmillan, 2013).

Joseph De Lappe is a doctoral researcher at CREET (the Centre for Research in Education and Education Technology) at the Open University where he conducts research based on the intersection of the sociology of social movements, the sociology of sexuality and gender, and social anthropology. Prior to this he taught in secondary schools for a decade.

Jón Ingvar Kjaran holds a PhD in educational studies from the University of Iceland and is now a post-doctoral researcher and a lecturer at the University of Iceland, School of Education. His research focus is on LGBTQ youth, queer pedagogy and the policing of masculinities in boys' and men's lives.

Maria Kromidas is Assistant Professor of Anthropology at William Paterson University in the United States. Her work revolves around issues of race, posthumanism and cosmopolitanism, and how they can be rethought with and through the critical space provided by children and childhood. She has contributed to the journals *Critique of Anthropology, Harvard Educational Review, Childhood: Global Journal of Child Research* and *Anthropological Theory*.

Anna Madill is Chair in Qualitative Inquiry, Deputy Head of the School of Psychology, and a member of the Centre for Interdisciplinary Gender Studies, University of Leeds, UK. She is a chartered psychologist, a chartered scientist, an associate fellow of the British Psychological Society, and co-founded and chaired (2008–2011) the British Psychological Society Qualitative Methods in Psychology Section. She is Associate Editor of the *British Journal of Clinical Psychology* and is on the editorial boards of the *British Journal of Social Psychology, Qualitative Psychology* and *Qualitative Research in Psychology*.

Monique Mulholland is a lecturer in the Department of Sociology and Women's Studies at Flinders University, South Australia. Her research interests include pornification, historical and contemporary constructions of normativity and perversity, critical race theory, historical sexualities, cultural studies and critical methodologies. Her most recent book is *Young People and Pornography: Young People Negotiate Pornification* (Palgrave Macmillan, 2013).

Elizabethe Payne is Founding Director of QuERI – Queering Education Research Institute©, a research and policy centre dedicated to bridging the gap between research and practice in creating more affirming schools for LGBTQ students and families. She is Interim Director of the LGBT Social Science and Public Policy Center at Hunter College's Roosevelt House, and a visiting associate professor at Hunter College, CUNY (2014–2016). As a sociologist of education, she specializes in qualitative research methodology, critical theory, youth culture, queer girlhoods and LGBTQ issues in education. Her current research addresses LGBTQ bullying, teacher experiences with transgender elementary school students, LGBTQ professional development, sex education curricula and adolescent lesbian/queer girls' gender experiences.

Emma Renold is Professor of Childhood Studies at the School of Social Sciences, Cardiff University, Wales. She is the author of *Girls, Boys and Junior Sexualities* (2005), a co-editor of *Girls in Education* (2010), and *Girls and Boys Speak Out: A Qualitative Study of Children's Gender and Sexual Cultures* (2013). Utilizing creative methodologies, her research draws on feminist, queer and post-humanist approaches to explore children and young people's gender and sexual cultures across diverse institutional sites, places and spaces. Working at the interface of policy, practice, engagement, activism and research, she is regularly consulted by government and non-governmental agencies to address sexual bullying and gender-based violence in schools (age 3–18). In 2012, she founded the national Welsh government cross-party group 'Children, Sexualities, Sexualisation and Equalities' (with assembly member Jocelyn Davies) which has become a central platform for foregrounding children and young people's voice on gender and sexual equalities.

Jessica Ringrose is Professor of Sociology of Gender and Education, at the Institute of Education. Her work develops feminist poststructural, psychosocial, 'intersectional', and new materialist approaches to understanding subjectivity, affectivity and assembled power relations. Recent research explores teens' networked sexual cultures and use of social media, and her new collaborative AHRC funded project is 'Documenting Digital Feminist Activism: Mapping Feminist Responses to New Media Misogyny and Rape Culture'. Her books and reports include: *A Qualitative Study of Children, Young People and 'Sexting'* (2012, London: NSPCC); *Post-Feminist Education?: Girls and the sexual politics of schooling* (Routledge, 2013); and *Deleuze and Research Methodologies* (EUP, 2013).

Kerry H. Robinson is Professor of Sociology in the School of Social Sciences and Psychology at the University of Western Sydney, Australia. She is a leading member of the Sexualities and Genders Research Network. Her areas of expertise include constructions of gender and sexual identities, sexual harassment, constructions of childhood and sexuality, diversity and difference, sociology of youth, sociology of education and sociology of knowledge. She has published widely in these areas, including *Innocence, Knowledge and the Construction of Childhood: The Contradictory Relationship Between Sexuality and Censorship in Children's Contemporary Lives* (2013), *Rethinking School Violence* (with Sue Saltmarsh and Cristyn Davies, 2012, Palgrave Macmillan) and *Diversity and Difference in Early Childhood Education: Issues for Theory and Practice* (with Criss Jones Díaz, 2006), which is currently being revised as a second edition publication.

Sue Scott is a sociologist who has researched and published widely in the areas of gender; sexuality, risk; the body and childhood including *Theorizing Sexuality* (with Stevi Jackson, 2010). She has held academic posts at a number of UK universities including professorships at Stirling and Durham. From 2005 to 2009, she was Executive Dean of Humanities and Social Sciences at Keele University and from 2009 to 2012 pro vice chancellor (research) at Glasgow Caledonian University. She is a fellow of the Academy of Social Sciences and a past president of the British Sociological Association. She is an honorary professor at the University of York and is an honorary professorial fellow at the University of Edinburgh and a visiting professor at the University of Helsinki. She is a co-managing editor of the online social science magazine *Discover Society*.

Anna Sparrman is Professor of Child Studies at the interdisciplinary research department, Department of Thematic Studies – Child Studies, Linköping University, Sweden. She has published on visual culture, consumption and child sexuality. Her current projects include a major study of culture for and by children, which investigates amusement parks, theme parks, science centres and children's museums. She is working on a forthcoming book, *Children, Sexuality and Visual Culture: Enacting the Paedophilic Gaze*. Among her recent books and articles are *Situating Child Consumption: Rethinking Values and Notions of Children, Childhood and Consumption* (with Bengt Sandin and Johanna Sjöberg, 2012) and 'Access and Gatekeeping in Researching Children and Sexuality: Mess in Ethics and Methods', *Sexuality and Culture* (2014).

Deborah L. Tolman is Professor of Social Welfare and Psychology at the Hunter College School of Social Work and the Graduate Center of the City University of New York. She is a developmental and critical social psychologist whose research has focused on adolescent girls' sexuality, gender development, gender equity and research methods. Her publications include edited volumes, peer-reviewed journal articles, book chapters and the award-winning book *Dilemmas of Desire: Teenage Girls Talk about Sexuality* (2002/2005). Her current research includes studies of how messages about masculinity and femininity affect boys' and girls' abilities to pursue healthy relationships, adolescent girls' experiences with oral sex and sexualization and young women's sexual well-being. She is the co-founder of SPARK, a movement building organization working with girl activists to campaign against the sexualization, objectification and violence against women present in the media.

Tina Vares is Senior Lecturer in Sociology at the University of Canterbury, Christchurch, New Zealand. Her research interests lie in the areas of gender, sexualities, the body and popular culture with a focus on the reception of popular cultural texts. She is currently working on the research project 'Girls, "Tween" Popular Culture and Everyday Life', supported by the New Zealand Royal Society Marsden Fund.

1
Introduction

Emma Renold, R. Danielle Egan and Jessica Ringrose

The entry below from 'the sex goddess blues' offers sage advice about the trials and tribulations of sociocultural and interpersonal shame and its effects on sexual expression, sexual exploration and sexual consent:

> Confidence in yourself is a lifelong process. It's sometimes a long and winding road with potholes, roadblocks, and even massive collisions. The best place to start is to know that you, as a person, are worthwhile.... You're worth fighting for; you deserve good things in your life. You deserve to set goals for yourself. You deserve healthy relationships that make you feel good. You deserve to have your voice heard. You deserve to physically present yourself however you want. You deserve to feel at peace with your body. And, if you're interested in sex, be it by yourself or with partners, you deserve pleasure and joy.
>
> 'The Sex Goddess Blues: Building Sexual Confidence and Busting Perfectionism', 2014, www.scarleteen.org

What makes the post particularly important is that it is written for a tween and teenaged cis and trans-girl audience and manages to avoid the traps of heteronormative and white privilege. If one reads Scarleteen.org – the site where this post is featured – one finds numerous pieces on consent, physiology, condoms, pleasure, sexual violence and sexual politics.

Notwithstanding, one might be wondering, why start an edited volume on children's sexuality and sexualization with a popular international sex education website? For us, Scarleteen illuminates what can go missing in policy and popular debates on sexualization – an assumption that children and young people are complex sexual subjects who are actively negotiating sexuality in their everyday lives. Indeed, this volume responds to this gap. It seeks to provide an academically situated collection that complicates and speaks back to a ubiquitous media landscape where children and young people's own experiences of doing, being and becoming sexual are often sensationalized, silenced, caricatured, pathologized and routinely undermined. Drawing together contributions from a range of disciplinary fields, across a wide breadth of regional, national and transnational contexts, the chapters offer compelling accounts of how children and young people are captured by and negotiate ideological discursive formations (sexism, racism, homophobia, to name just a few) that shape their experiences, and which often operate at the intersection of curiosity, inequality, trauma, resilience, relationality, pressure, excitement, lack of interest, ambivalence and boredom.

We begin by orienting readers towards some of the key historical ideas about child sexuality and current debates on child sexualization before offering an overview of the contributions and sections that organize the book. We conclude by posing some questions about future research on children, sexuality and sexualization.

Historicizing child sexuality

> The phenomenon of sexualisation phobia provides an excellent example of all that is irrational and ahistorical about the sexual child in our contemporary culture.
>
> (Egan & Hawkes, 2010: 147)

The social construction of the child, during the modern epoch in the Anglophone West, was inextricably tied to the education, regulation and normalization of its sexuality (Egan & Hawkes, 2010). In his first volume on the history of sexuality in Western Europe, Foucault notes that the child's sex was the object of intense scrutiny and pivotal in the deployment of a shifting disciplinary apparatus which foregrounded the project of normalization and surveillance in the late 19th century (Foucault, 1980). As with most ideas on sexuality, cultural values ebb and flow at various periods, and ideas about the sexual child are no different. For example, the assumptions at work in the discursive production of the sexual child from the 1970s stand in stark contrast to most contemporary narratives on the child and its sexuality (Angelides, 2004).

Recent scholarship reveals the particularities of how the child's sexuality was always already imbued with a particular set of socio-epistemological assumptions in order to legitimate and propagate particular conceptions of the state, the colonial project, whiteness, the family and heteronormativity, to name only a few (Stoller, 1995; Darby, 2005; Romesberg, 2008; Egan & Hawkes, 2010; Bernstein, 2011). However, the modern history of ideas on childhood sexuality is distinct in that it is more often than not plagued by fear, projection, fascination and consternation (Fahs et al., 2013). As historians and childhood studies scholars have illustrated, the history of the sexual child differs from other populations deemed sexually deviant or in need of sexual protection because of Anglophone conceptions of childhood (Males, 1992; Angelides, 2004; Darby, 2005; Robinson & Davies, 2008; Romesberg,

2008; Egan & Hawkes, 2010; Faulkner, 2011). Most dominant discourses that have emerged within the Anglophone West have, on the surface, conceptualized childhood as antithetical to sexuality (however, this tends to primarily apply to white upper-middle-class children; Egan & Hawkes, 2010).

Historically, Anglophone culture has been engrossed by the innocent or sexually endangered child and its socially pathologized counterpart, the erotic or sexually knowing child. Both operate as a barometer of social decay or progress, as a nostalgic longing for a pure past, a signal of impending societal doom or as a utopian possibility for reshaping the future as well as a site for social intervention. Nevertheless, both figures are, to use historian Robin Bernstein's term, 'imagined' children in that they are symbolic figures as opposed to material actors (Bernstein, 2011). Fears regarding sexual corruption from a variety of sexually salacious sources (comic books, television, rap music, the Internet, clothing, etc.) or deviant populations (immigrants, the poor, gays and lesbians or the paedophile) tend to gain momentum during times of social upheaval or crisis (Egan & Hawkes, 2010). To this end, the discourse on sexualization, which we outline in its contemporary shape and form below, is situated within a larger socio-historical context that has been strikingly persistent over the last two centuries (Foucault, 1980; Hunt, 1999; Mort, 2000; Egan & Hawkes, 2010; Bernstein, 2011; Faulkner, 2011).

Contemporary debates on sexualization

> Sexuality and cultural scholars have used empirical and comparative studies, as well as history and critical sociology to argue that 'sexualization' is itself a constructed and unsubstantiated concept.
>
> (Hawkes & Dune, 2013: 623)

Since the early 2000s, there has been increased public policy concern across the Anglophone West of how children and young people (particularly girls) are being 'sexualized' by the media and culture industries (Rush & LaNauze, 2006; APA, 2007; Papadopoulos, 2010; Bailey, 2011). We have seen a steady stream of sensationalist popular cultural texts purporting to illuminate the real problems of 'sexualization' as well as a range of policy and governmental responses (Egan, 2013). There has been a flurry of academic research and writing based on 'sexualization', in which there is general agreement and a strong evidence base suggesting that sexual imagery has become more ubiquitous in society, including in media and material marketed at and consumed by children (Buckingham et al., 2010). However, while attention to how changes in the significance and representation of sexuality might be shaping children and young people's sexual cultures is long overdue, the concept of 'sexualization' has been contested (see in particular Lerum & Dworkin, 2009; Albury & Lumby, 2010; Atwood & Smith 2011; Bragg et al., 2011; Duschinsky, 2013).

Indeed, a consistent theme running through both historical and contemporary discourses about the child and its sexuality is that they are rarely, if ever, about children's own social and cultural worlds. More often than not they represent adult preoccupations and anxieties about the nature, corruption and correction of the child's sex as well as the nature of society. The voices of children and how they make sense of their own lives and bodies are conspicuously absent. Indeed, relying on dubious claims and little empirical research foregrounding children's experiences of doing, being and becoming sexual, the outcomes predicted for children within the 'sexualization' literature are restrictive and frequently serve to moralize about and pathologize particular behaviours and particular children (Egan & Hawkes, 2008; Buckingham, 2009: 26). Evaluating the research evidence on the impact of 'sexualized' media and products on children, Buckingham et al. (2009: 26) summarize that 'almost all of the research on the impact of these developments relates to adults rather than children; and, insofar as it addresses children at all, to girls rather than boys' (see also Barker and Duschinsky 2012). The history of discourses on the child and its sexuality then is more accurately a narrative about adulthood (Egan & Hawkes, 2010). As such we must be careful to ground any analysis around specificities: what childhood is being addressed, who is absent and to what ends?

Renold and Ringrose have previously (2011, 2013) identified how these abstractions and generalities of child sexualization discourses have operated to define the objects and relations of scrutiny in particularly gendered ways. We draw out further below what we identify as some of the problematic effects, which include:

- Measuring harms and risks of sexual media exposure to advance protectionist agendas (Egan, 2013) that lack analyses of how children, particularly girls, make meaning of, and negotiate media in their everyday lives
- Overemphasizing the victimization and objectification of girls, thereby reducing any sexual expression as evidence of 'sexualization' (Renold & Ringrose, 2011)
- Denying girls' sexual agency, rights, pleasure and desires (Lerum & Dworkin, 2009; Tolman, 2012; Clark, 2013)
- Interpreting a range of commercial products for children as simply dangerous conduits for 'child' sexualization (Bragg et al., 2011; Kehily 2012)
- Ignoring how the eroticization of sexual objectification, including sexual innocence, features in girls' own sexual subjectification practices (Walkerdine, 1998; Renold & Ringrose, 2011; Lamb & Peterson, 2012; Bragg, 2012)
- Creating enduring binaries of passive feminine sexuality versus active, predatory masculine sexuality (Renold, 2013)

- Encouraging 'either/or' and 'polarized' position-taking among stakeholders between sexual empowerment and pleasure versus sexual danger and risk (Duschinsky, 2013; Lamb et al., 2013; Tolman, 2013)
- Promoting a linear developmental yet delayed future trajectory of 'healthy' age-appropriate non-sexual, heteronormative gender identities (Epstein et al., 2012; Holford et al., 2013)
- Mobilizing a white middle-class panic over the loss of a raced and classed sexual innocence via the Othering of working-class/racialized cultures as evidence of hypersexuality (Egan, 2013; Ringrose, 2013)
- Neglecting the wealth of cross disciplinary, theoretical, empirical, clinical and practitioner-grounded research on children, sexuality and sexualization (Atwood et al., 2013)

The aims of the collection

All these discursive effects are, in different ways and to varying extents, taken up by the chapters in this collection, with the final point on the dearth of empirical research operating as an orienting catalyst for bringing the collection together.

Our aim for this collection was to go beyond these well-worn cleavages and polarizations in the sexualization debates and profile key interdisciplinary commentators, academics, researcher and activists working in the area of children's sexuality and sexual cultures. It was imperative for us to draw together a collection that illuminates the diversity and complexity of children and young people's everyday sexual cultures, relations and subjectivities.

We begin with an important range of disciplinary chapters that situate debates in the context of particular frames of reference and meaning, showing the rich diversity of scholarship on children's sexuality. The next sections showcase a range of cutting-edge research from these various disciplinary domains that move far beyond simplistic 'telling it like it is' accounts of doing, being and becoming sexual to theoretically engaged and critical accounts of experiences and realities. The type of research we have purposefully chosen is that which is unsettling, challenging, moving beyond binaries and side-taking around a complex set of issues.

Navigating your way through the collection

Part I: Mapping the history of research and theory within the landscape of ideas

As we have noted, the child's sexuality has often served as a particularly dense site of cultural anxiety, confusion and projection. In response, a variety of disciplines have offered alternative discourses through the empirical study of the sexuality of children and its various cultural and individual manifestations. These disciplinary chapters offer unique and important contributions through an historical trajectory and assessment of ideas on children and sexuality in six different disciplinary contexts: anthropology, sociology, subcultural studies, social psychology, media studies and clinical psychoanalysis. The chapters raise questions about the impact of cultural diversity on the sexual cultures of children both within the West and outside and ask us to think about the phenomenological experience of sexuality in the lives of young people and the impact of ideological and cultural formations.

In Chapter 2, Diederik F. Janssen highlights how anthropological views on young sexualities illuminate what is specifically human, or rather culturally particular, about the induction of the young into existing mating patterns. Janssen's exhaustive review of the literature reveals a stark pattern – that children's own conceptions of intimacy remain significantly delimited by competition between and among the (adult) sexes. His contribution illustrates how young sexualities are governed in ways that illuminate significant power relations between the sexes and between generations.

In Chapter 3, Stevi Jackson and Sue Scott give readers a reflexive and critical overview of the sociological research on the sexuality of children and young people. Jackson and Scott trace the theoretical and empirical trends in sociological literature from the 1970s to today to explore the continuities and discontinuities in both sociological and public debates. They argue that adult anxieties around children and sex derive from constructions of sexuality as a special area of life and children as a special category of people, arguing against sex being seen as inevitably inimical to the well-being of children.

Mary Jane Kehily and Joseph De Lappe explore the links between youth subcultures and young people's sexual cultures in Chapter 4. Through a discussion of the concept and practice of youth subcultures, the chapter points to the continuing significance of this influential body of work on subsequent studies of young people's sexual culture. Drawing on examples from pro-ana websites and Japanese Lolita fashion, the chapter demonstrates how the study of youth subcultures and girlhood studies is marked by a distinctive set of ideas and methods that have had a generative impact upon the reconceptualization of young women as agentic, gendered and sexual subjects.

Deborah L. Tolman, Christin P. Bowman and Jennifer F. Chmielewski offer a useful overview of psychological research on sexualization in Chapter 5. As Tolman was one of the original six authors of the American Psychological Association, *Task Force on the sexualisation of girls*, the chapter provides fascinating reflections on how the report has been used (and in some cases abused) in some research, media and popular cultural debates on sexualization. They also, however, argue that accounting for the negative effects of sexual objectification, for instance, has offered powerful tools for challenging sexism and holding various media outlets and corporations responsible for their content. The authors suggest that psychological research needs to more fully explore issues of girls and women's resistance and complex relationships to sexualization and point to the need for *research-led* activist collaborations such as the organization SPARK, which empowers girls to lead an agenda for social change and challenging sexualization that is youth-driven.

Sara Bragg's contribution in Chapter 6 is unique, in that she examines the landscape of ideas on boys, masculinity and sexualization – a topic often forgotten in political discourse. Bragg renders visible how ideology, affect and culture shape a contradictory sets of responses to the issue of boys and sexualization. While popular texts argue that boys are either outside the realm of danger and/or that the concerns should be conceptualized as completely distinct, Bragg demonstrates the models of culture, media influence, learning, agency and social change that underpin these responses. She contrasts a risk model with feminist film and cultural studies' theorizations, which take popular culture seriously, emphasizing the indeterminacy of meaning, the multiple functions of fantasy genres and the fluidity of audience identifications.

In Chapter 7, R. Danielle Egan analyses the shift away from infantile sexuality in Anglophone psychoanalytical clinical literature. In the past, psychoanalysts provided a conception of the child's sexuality as active, complex and natural and offered a reasoned alternative to medico-moral perspectives. The turn towards object relations, although a welcome one in many ways, has left a blind spot in clinical literature and possibly in clinical practice. It has also meant that psychoanalysts have been absent in policy and political discussions in an increasingly anxious Anglophone discourse on girls and sexualization. This shift may have considerable implications for the ways in which diagnosis, symptom and recommendations happen in clinical work with young people.

Taken together, the disciplinary chapters offer a profound response to many of the polemical texts on child 'sexualization'. These models offer an alternative way of thinking about the child as an inherently sexual being as opposed to sexuality being a pathological outcome. In so doing, each of these literatures reviewed offer more reasoned approaches, thereby de-escalating the anxiety that can enter into conversations about the sexuality of children.

Part II: Pre-teen sexualities: Problematizing sexual agency and sexual innocence

Children's sexuality, in so many contexts, turns out to be 'more complicated than we supposed'. 'We might' – if we let ourselves explore these complications – 'find (new) stories that are not fueled by fear'.

(Kathryn Bond Stockton, 2009: 12, citing
James Kincaid, 1998: 15)

The figuration of the child 'at risk' is a luminous discourse when it comes to discussing sex and sexuality in childhood. Often the only option available when it comes to sexuality and children is within the context of sexual abuse and sexual exploitation (Holford et al., 2013). As we have outlined above, the recent and emotive discourse of sexualization continues this theme, calling up enduring anxieties over 'the spectre of adults' own unconscious desire for children's bodies; transgressing the boundaries that define how adults are supposed to look at children' (Buckingham et al., 2009: 11; see also Kincaid, 1992; Egan, 2013). This first section of empirical research chapters put children's own sexual cultures, and their messy and shifting meaning-making practices centre stage (Renold, 2005, 2013). Each chapter complicates and troubles what constitutes 'sexy' and 'sexual' in image, body, popular culture, everyday situated social practice, future imaginaries and fantasy.

Inspired by Bragg and Buckingham's (2004) study on young people, sex and the media, in Chapter 8 Anna Sparrman shares her analysis of nine-year-old Swedish children's focus-group data and multimedia scrapbooks on love, sex and relationships in visual media (e.g. advertisements, films). She highlights the stark heterogendered polarization of how boys and girls consider what constitutes a 'sexy image', with boys selecting images of nude or semi-nude images that commodify women and men's bodies (to sell products), and girls creating visual collages of couples in love and sex in relationships. Foregrounding children's enactment of sexuality through some of the contemporary theorizing of decentered subjectivity and networked agency, Sparrman argues, 'sexual agency is neither a fixed position nor a property of the individual but distributed across the material, immaterial, human and social'. This approach challenges the fixity of how sex and sexuality surfaces and mediates children's everyday social and cultural practices by making uncertain what counts as sex, sexual and sexy.

Working further with and developing the notion of sexual agency as produced in relational social-semiotic-material assemblages, in Chapter 9 Louisa Allen and Toni Ingraham examine the multiple ways in which 11- to 13-year-old Australian girls make meaning of sexuality. Drawing on visual methods, interviews and focus groups, their chapter 'critically engages with discourses of childhood innocence and sexualization investigating whether these resonate with girls' talk about themselves as sexual subjects'. Allen and Ingraham's microsocial analysis complicates any binary reading of the regulatory gendered dichotomies of contemporary Anglophone girlhood as 'innocent' (unknowing) and 'pornified' (knowing). Rather, girls' constructions of their sexual subjectivities and their investment or rejection of romantic relationship cultures and/or sexual activity are multifaceted and in constant motion.

From focus group interviews to longitudinal ethnographic data on the sexual cultures of 10- and 11-year-olds living in New York City, Maria Kromidas powerfully illustrates in Chapter 10 the gendered entanglement of race, social class and sexuality and how anxieties surface in children's negotiation of a regulatory and racialized heterosexual matrix (Butler, 1990). She argues how 'the entanglement of race and sexuality can not be understood without the notion of reproductive futurism and kids' interpellation of themselves as proper heterosexualized subjects that will one day marry someone of the "right type" and reproduce kids of their own'. However, and significantly, she stresses that not all children deferred their desires to their imagined futures, and anxiety, pleasure and desire were creatively negotiated by children in ways that traversed their futures and the here and now.

Chapter 11, the final chapter in this section, explores how heteronormativity works to regulate very young children's gender and sexual cultures. Drawing on focus group data with 3–11-year-olds, and working closely with data from 4-, 5- and 9-year-olds, Kerry H. Robinson and Cristyn Davies engage queer, feminist post-structural and post-developmental approaches to trouble the age-appropriate and heteronormative discourses embedded within many of the sexualization panics. They point to the ways in which 'children are always already sexualized through the heterosexualization of children as gendered subjects' and how for many children-ritualized 'life-markers' including 'first "special" relationships, marriage, kissing and having babies' are fundamental heteronormative citizenship practices that mediate their everyday social and cultural worlds.

The policing, shaming, violence and contextual contingency for engaging in non-heterosexual cultures focuses the next section on the significance of place and space for young queer sexualities.

Part III: Queering young sexualities: Gender, place and history

> The figure of the queer child is that which doesn't quite conform to the wished-for way that children are supposed to be in terms of gender and sexual roles (...) The term queer derives also from its association with specifically sexual alterity.
>
> (Bruhm & Hurley, 2004: x)

Each of the chapters in the previous section documented the complex ways in which heteronormativity mediates pre-teen children's peer cultures, from discourses of romance and making babies, to feeling 'sexy'. Nowhere is this presumed heterosexuality more salient than in the sexualization debates where, as we argued above, protectionist discourses surface only in relation to premature heterosexualities. While discourses of 'healthy' heterosexualities and relationships are pervasive, healthy non-heterosexualities or healthy queer relationships are notably lacking. This section is inspired by Kathryn Bond Stockton's (2009) figuration of the always already 'queer child' and her evocation of 'growing sideways' to disrupt the assumed and 'wished-for' (Bruhm & Hurley, 2004: x) heteronormative gender and sexual linearities. Such disruptions, however, are always located in place, history and space, constraining and regulating young people's capacities for any sustained rupture to heteronormative trajectories. Each chapter thus critically engages with and foregrounds the cultural and historical specificity of how queer sexualities emerge in and across gendered bodies in space and place and the everyday gender and sexual violence that permeates their lives.

Chapter 12 offers a powerful account of how the terms 'istabane' ('gay') and 'inkonkoni' ('freak of nature') travel across the everyday social and cultural worlds of young people living and growing up in the eastern Kwazulu-Natal province of South Africa. Deevia Bhana contextualizes young people's homophobic violence within current and historical legacies of structural inequalities and gendered poverty. Analysing teenagers' (aged 16) talk on gender and sexual cultures, she illustrates how male heterosexual power is valorized and gay sexuality is rendered highly visible and admonished. Indeed, publicly overt displays and/or celebrations of gay and lesbian sexualities, including non-normative gender performances, are frequently interpreted as a direct threat to the very fabric of South African society.

In Chapter 13, Jón Ingvar Kjaran takes forward the ways in which historical legacies meet and mesh with contemporary representations of Icelandic masculinities, focusing on the cultures of young men who identify as gay and bisexual. His chapter explores how male Viking culture intersects with media portrayals of young entrepreneurial bourgeois masculinities (e.g. bankers as 'Viking raiders'). Kjaran illustrates how contemporary and historical masculinities permeate boys' own accounts of how they see-saw between being 'queer' and 'real men', where hegemonic heterosexuality is assumed and privileged.

Tensions between gender, sexuality and class play out in complex ways for the young lesbian women in Elizabethe Payne's research on the experiences of white middle-class teenage lesbian-identifying young women in a major metropolitan area in Texas, USA. In Chapter 14, Payne explores the life history narratives of her participants in which they grapple with the punishing dichotomies of 'slut' and 'good girl'. Central to Payne's argument is how her participants reasserted their white middle-class privilege as a way of distancing themselves from 'the raw sexuality associated with working- and lower-class female sexualities, masculinized sexualities and the taint of lesbian desire'.

In Chapter 15, Emma Renold and Gabrielle Ivinson foreground the role of place, history, affect and culture to explore how gendered and sexual legacies of an ex-mining community surface in two teen girls' experiences of everyday gender and sexual violence. Drawing on post-queer and feminist posthuman theorizing, sexuality is opened up beyond identity and orientation, towards the more-than-human. Working creatively with interview data and historical archive, the chapter explores how the vibrancy of matter, from mud to mermaids, emerges in talk about memory books, dreams, gaming and outdoor play, and in ways that seemed to enable girls to survive and queer the often violent patriarchal forces of the social. Indeed, the materiality of culture and the significance of the cultural imaginary is the focus of the next section.

Part IV: Young sexualities and the cultural imaginary

Negotiating sexualized culture for *both girls and boys* is rarely straightforward; it is deeply complex and beset by pleasures, confusion, interest, rejection, curiosity and banality. It is an engagement that extends far beyond the narrow address of many popular texts on the topic. Another important factor to consider is the cultural context within which sexualized material culture is produced and how such products might be potent sites for a socio-historical analysis, as detailed in the previous section. More specifically, and focusing this section, is whether and to what extent sexualized material culture changes with the breeching of cultural boundaries via global consumption. This section also explores how such material may be a representation and/or re-inscription of a particular set of complex conflicts within a cultural imaginary. It further examines to what extent a set of seemingly contradictory political agendas may be constructed and deconstructed through the rhetorical and symbolic nature of documentaries of harm. Each chapter in this section complicates politico-epistemological assumptions through an analysis of popular cultural and political messages directed towards young people in three different cultural contexts.

The section begins with a psychoanalytically informed post-colonial analysis by Diego Costa. In Chapter 16, Costa's analysis focuses on Xuxa, a larger-than-life Brazilian icon in children's television between the mid-1980s and mid-1990s. Costa offers a layered account of Xuxa and her place within the socio-historical imagination of Brazil in the 1990s. For Costa, Xuxa represents a national screen memory of the (colonial) primal scene as well as a site of queer identification for one young boy. In his queering of the historical discourse of recapitulation, Costa renders Xuxa as both a failed attempt at race and class erasure as well as an evocative symbol of ambivalence in sexual(ized) identification. Xuxa is unable to upend or appease colonial legacies via displacement, but she is, nevertheless, a rich symbol, in the Brazilian cultural imaginary during a particularly important historical moment, which has since faded away.

Sexualization is often a political metonym for pornification, antipornography movements and sex trafficking of women and girls (Egan, 2013; Lerum, 2014). In Chapter 17, Anna Madill discusses the consumption of Shotocon-inspired Japanese manga and its classification within English obscenity law, which serves as a compelling case study for how globalization renders these associations even more complex. Madill offers a queer reading of this genre which often features erotic and relational exchanges between boys, as well as boys (boy-loving or BL) and non-human animals and other non-human figures. Madill shows how a paedophilic interpretation (its dominant reading under English law) ignores the transgressive ways in which these texts can be read and raises some key challenges and questions for the Anglophone West of 'how intelligible, meaningful, non-paedophilic frames are available for reading non-realistic, erotic texts involving visually young characters'.

Deconstructing the gendered and sexual messages at work in North American documentaries aimed at eradicating the sexualization of girls is the focus of Chapter 18, by Lindsay Herriot and Lara E. Hiseler. The authors demonstrate the dominant discourses of childism, historical revisionism, heterosexism and slut-shaming in the films which produce moralizing responses to the 'problem' of girl sexting by focusing on what girls should do to shield and protect themselves from digital visibility and exploitation. The dominant focus on risk for girls thus has a paradoxical effect of re-regulating girls' sexuality, rather than offering any critical intervention. The authors suggest an alternative to the tenor of moral panic in the anti-sexualization films can be found in Jessica Valenti's documentary of the same name as her book *The purity myth*, which disrupts the naturalization of girls sexual innocence, via an intersectional discussion of how prolonging virginity is a particular problem of middle-class heterosexual normativity in Western cultures.

Ultimately all the chapters in this section highlight the limits of a monolithic reading of sexualized popular cultural materials as shaping cultural imaginaries.

Part V: New media, digital technology and young sexual cultures

The final section documents the special place that digital media has occupied in relation to sexualization debates often reductively blamed for a range of ill effects in youth gender and sexual relations. Early on, Livingstone (2002) described the research field around new media and young people as a polarization between optimists who see new opportunities for creativity, community and learning and pessimists who construct media in relation to risks about the end of childhood innocence; but this is particularly heightened in relation to sexualization (Bragg et al., 2011). Rather than seeing technology as a mediator of existing social relations and cultures in contextually and historically located ways, there have been repeated calls to more heavily regulate young people's exposure to and use of sexual media imagery such as pornography, and uses of new media such as social networking. The chapters in this section all explore the representational and interpretive dilemmas of studying youth sexuality in the context of these rapidly changing media cultures and the new affordances of digital technologies.

In Chapter 19, Sue Jackson and Tina Vares explore the difficulty of adequately 'capturing' the sexual cultures of pre-teen girls in their New Zealand study, given that research encounters are weighed down with dominant discourses of girls as at risk of 'sexualized' media discourses. Although highly reflexive about the conditions of the 'male gaze' and the objectification of femininity and sexuality, the authors suggest that the video diary production offers an important range of data, including talk, gesture, movement and performance. These data offer insights into girls' everyday lives, which move in, around and beyond the assumptions of sex-saturated pre-teen media cultures. Perhaps most importantly the methodology allowed a medium for girls to create parodies of sexualized, girly femininity in ways that disrupt notions of pre-teen girls as passive recipients of sexualized media cultures.

In Chapter 20, Monique Mulholland takes a different tack on a similar problem, foregrounding the more specific notion of 'pornification'. Presenting research from 12- to 16-year-olds in South Australia, she argues that whilst young people do report on the commonplaceness of explicit representation in public spaces, they also have complex critiques, which include strategies of dealing with explicit content through humour and caricature, much like the girls in Jackson and Vares. And yet, dominant constructions of female sexual respectability and shaming of sluttiness shore up the limited range of positions and discourses available to girls to navigate the public norms of doing and living youth sexuality.

In Chapter 21, Lara Karaian documents how the sexualization and pornification panics dovetail in particularly negative ways in the Canadian legal system. She explores how youth sexters are constructed as sexually self-exploiting in Canadian legal discourses, which constructs young people (particularly girls) who create or share nude or sexually explicit images as unable to actively consent to these acts. What is critical in Karaian's exploration is the detailed mapping of how the legal discourse is connected to other neo-liberal right-wing reform in a constellation of discourses that undermine capacity to see girls as making legitimate choices or having complex sexual desires. Thus Karaian's chapter raises a whole set of important questions about what consent, exploitation and objectification mean in contemporary cultural contexts of new digital technology.

Where Karaian focuses on how girls' agency is reduced in relation to dominant sexting discourses, in Chapter 22 Laura Harvey and Jessica Ringrose seek to address the dominant constructions of masculinity and sexting. Drawing on the experience of young people from a qualitative research study in London, UK, they address the dominant international narrative of boy sexters as sexual perpetrators who pass around images to gain social currency. They situate these new media practices within a politics of recognition in performing forms of high-status masculinities within specific communities of practice, including local cultures of physical violence, ethnic conflict and school surveillance. Thus, by taking account of the complexities and nuances derived from the lived experiences of boys from their qualitative research project, the chapter serves as an important disruption of the many simplistic and common-sense notions about teen boys' sexuality in contexts of new digital technologies.

Taken together, therefore, the chapters in this section move beyond any simplistic media effects perspectives, and challenge reductive concerns about young people as the audience of risky sexual media content, by documenting what young people are actively doing to manage, create and in some cases trouble and transform their own digital media consumption and production.

What next for the field of children's sexuality studies in the social sciences?

We wish to conclude this introduction by noting what an honour it has been to work with some amazing childhood sexuality researchers in bringing together this timely collection. Their research consistently troubles our taken-for-granted ideas about children, sexuality and sexualization, offering new ways to make sense of children's sexual cultures across some complex political, social and cultural terrains. We have learned so much from each chapter about our own research practices and what it means to be doing sexuality research with children/on childhood, and at a time of ubiquitous youth sex panics and high-profile sexual abuse scandals. While problematic in their effects, the ways in which discourses of sexualization weave and weft with the rise of queer and feminist activisms seem to have created small spaces for research scholarship to make some inroads, both in the academy and beyond. Engaging directly and critically with policy and practice, however, is never straightforward or without risk. Rather, these processes are fraught, messy and sometimes dangerous (see Phipps, 2014), yet nonetheless vital. Creating ways to shift and resituate key research messages that flatten out complex intersectional power relations or braving the backlash when we endeavour to introduce notions of sexual pleasure, sexual rights or sexual citizenship is critical to the future of how critical childhood sexuality scholarship makes and creates impact.

Before we draw this introduction to a close, we would like to engage further with the problematics and challenges that this volume has raised for us, both theoretically and substantively and also methodologically. What follows are a series of questions that we might want to consider in our current and future practices when researching young sexualities. For us, each of these areas is ripe for how they might envision some of the ways in which the field of childhood sexuality research might twist, turn and evolve:

- What are the challenges of working within and beyond the social sciences and humanities for researching children, childhood and sexualities?
- How do the specificities of sociopolitical and cultural histories mediate how we come to understand and research young sexualities?
- How might we hold on to the unknown as children be and become sexual?

- What are the risks and affordances of post-developmental and non-linear approaches to researching children's sexual subjectivities?
- How might post-queer and posthuman approaches unsettle what counts as sex and sexuality?
- Which theoretical approaches enable researchers to better understand the contemporary and ever-changing landscape of digital sexual practices?
- How might inventive and creative methodologies enable us to explore what else childhood sexuality research can be and become?
- How might we create transformative, safe spaces for radical and critical sexuality pedagogy and practice?
- How can our research practices dovetail with our activisms and engagements with policy processes in ways that are sustainable and ethically viable?
- What are the opportunities and challenges for involving children and young people more directly in research, activism, practice and policy formation?

Finally, we thank all the contributors once again and hope that this book might inspire the next generation of childhood sexuality scholars to continue to ask questions that challenge and subvert what we think we know about children, childhood and sexuality, and collaborate on research projects which foreground children's own sexual experiences in all their diversity and complexity.

References

Albury, K., & Lumby, C. (2010) Too much? Too young? The sexualisation of children debate in Australia. *Media International Australia*, 135, 141–152.

American Psychological Association Task Force (2007) Report of the APA task force on the sexualization of girls. *American Psychological Association*. http://www.apa.org/pi/wpo/sexualization.html, accessed 25 April 2008.

Angelides, S. (2004) Feminism child sexual abuse and the erasure of childhood sexuality. *Gay and Lesbian Quarterly*, 10 (2), 141–177.

Atwood, F., & Smith, C. (2012) Investigating young people's sexual cultures: An Introduction. *Sex Education*, 11 (3), 235–242.

Atwood, F., Bale, C., & Barker, M. (2013) *The Sexualisation Report* 2013. thesexualizationreport.files.wordpress.com.

Bailey, R. (2011) Letting children be children. UK Department for Education, Report of an Independent Review of the Commercialisation and Sexualisation of Childhood. https://www.education.gov.uk/publications/standard/publicationDetail/Page1/CM%208078, accessed 6 July 2011.

Barker, M., & Duschinsky, R. (2012) Sexualization's four faces: Sexualization and gender stereotyping in the Bailey Review. *Gender and Education*, 24 (3), 303–310.

Bernstein, R. (2011) *Racial innocence: Performing American childhood from slavery to civil rights*. New York: New York University Press.

Bond Stockton, K. (2009) *The queer child: Or growing up sideways in the twentieth century*. Durham, NC: Duke University Press.

Bragg, S. (2012) What I heard about sexualisation: Or, conversations with my inner Barbie. *Gender and Education*, 24 (3), 311–316.

Bragg, S., Buckingham, D., Russell, R., & Willett, R. (2011). Too much, too soon? Children, 'sexualisation' and consumer culture. *Sex Education*, 11 (3), 279–292.

Bragg, S., & Buckingham, D. (2013) Global concerns, local negotiations and moral selves: Contemporary parenting and the 'sexualisation of childhood' debate. *Feminist Media Studies*, 13 (4), 643–659.

Bruhm, S., & Hurley, N. (Eds.) (2004) *Curiouser: On the queerness of children* Minneapolis, MN: University of Minneapolis Press.

Butler, J. (1990) *Gender trouble: Feminism and the subversion of identity*. New York Routledge.

Buckingham, D., & Bragg, S. (2004) *Young people, sex and the media: The facts of life?* London: Palgrave Macmillan.

Buckingham, D., Willett, R., Bragg, S., & Russell, R. (2010). *Sexualised goods aimed at children: A report to the Scottish parliament equal opportunities committee*. Edinburgh, UK: Scottish Parliament Equal Opportunities Committee.

Clark, J. (2013) Passive, heterosexual and female: Constructing appropriate childhoods in the 'Sexualisation of Childhood' debate. *Sociological Research Online*, 18 (2), 1–13.

Darby, R. (2005) *A surgical temptation: The demonization of the foreskin and the rise of circumcision in Britain*. Chicago: University of Chicago Press.

Duschinsky, R. (2010) Feminism, sexualisation and social status. *Media International Australia*, 135, 94–105.

Duschinsky, R. (2011) Ideal and unsullied: Purity, subjectivity and social power. *Subjectivity*, 4, 147–167.

Duschinsky, R. (2013) Childhood, responsibility and the liberal loophole: Replaying the sex-wars in debates on sexualisation? *Sociological Research Online*, 18 (2), 1–7.

Egan, R. D. (2013) *Becoming sexual: A critical appraisal of girls and sexualization*. Cambridge, UK: Polity.

Egan, R. D., & Hawkes, G. (2008) Endangered girls and incendiary objects: Unpacking the discourse on sexualization. *Sexuality and Culture Special Issue on Sexuality, Sexualization and the Contemporary Child*, 12, 291–311.

Egan, R. D., & Hawkes, G. (2010) *Theorizing the sexual child in modernity*. New York: Palgrave Macmillan.

Epstein, D., Kehily, M. J., & Renold, E. (2012) Culture, policy and the un/marked child: Fragments of the sexualisation debates. *Gender and Education*, 24 (3), 249–254.

Faulkner, J. (2011) *The importance of being innocent: Why we worry about children*. Cambridge: Cambridge University Press.

Hawkes, G., & Dune, T. (2013) Narratives of the sexual child: Shared themes and shared challenges. *Sexualities*, 16 (5/6), 622–634.

Holford, N., Renold, E., & Huuki, T. (2013) What (else) can a kiss do? Theorizing the power plays in young children's sexual cultures. *Sexualities*, 16 (5/6), 710–729.

Hunt, A. (1999) *Governing morals: A social history of moral regulation*. Cambridge: Cambridge University Press.

Kincaid, J. (1992) *Child loving: The erotic child and Victorian literature*. New York: Routledge.

Kincaid, J. (1998) *Erotic innocence: The culture of child molesting*. Durham, NC: Duke University Press.

Lamb, S., Graling, K., & Wheeler, E. E. (2013) 'Pole-arized' discourse: An analysis of responses to Miley Cyrus's teen choice awards pole dance. *Feminism and Psychology*, 23 (2), 163–183.

Lamb, S., & Peterson, Z. D. (2010) Adolescent girls' sexual empowerment: Two feminists explore the concept. *Sex Roles*, 66 (11–12), 703–712.

Lerum, K. (2014) Human Rights V Human Wrongs. *Contexts: Understanding people in their social worlds*. Winter edition. American Associological Association. http://contexts.org/articles/selling-people/#lerum, accessed 8 April 2015.

Lerum, K., & Dworkin, S. L. (2009) 'Bad girls rule': An interdisciplinary feminist commentary on the report of the APA task force on the sexualization of girls. *Journal of Sex Research*, 46 (4), 250–63.

Livingstone, S. (2002) *Young people and new media: Childhood and the changing media environment*. London: Sage.

Males, M. (1992). Adult liaison in the 'Epidemic' of 'Teenage' birth, pregnancy, and venereal disease. *Journal of Sex Research*, 29 (4), 525–545.

Mort, F. (2000) *Dangerous sexualities: Medico-moral politics in England since 1830*. London: Routledge.

Papadopoulos, L. (2010) *Sexualisation of young people review*. London: Home Office, UK.

Phipps, A. (2014) *The Dark Side of the Impact Agenda*. Times Higher Education. http://www.timeshighereducation.co.uk/comment/opinion/the-dark-side-of-the-impact-agenda/2017299, accessed 8 April 2015.

Renold, E. (2005) *Girls, boys and junior sexualities: Exploring children's gender and sexual relations in the primary school*. London: Routledge Farmer.

Renold, E. (2013) *Boys and girls speak out: A qualitative study of children's gender and sexual cultures* (age 10–13). Cardiff. http://www.nspcc.org.uk/preventing-abuse/research-and-resources/boys-girls-speak-out/ (accessed 20 April 2015).

Renold, E., & Ringrose, J. (2011) Schizoid subjectivities?: Re-theorising teen-girls' sexual cultures in an era of 'sexualisation'. *Journal of Sociology*, 47 (4), 389–409.

Renold, E., & Ringrose, J. (2013) Introduction: Feminisms re-figuring 'sexualisation', sexuality and 'the girl'. *Feminist Theory*, 14 (3), 247–254.

Ringrose, J. (2013) *Post-feminist education? Girls and the sexual politics of schooling*, London: Routledge.

Robinson, K., & Davies, C. (2008) Constructing the Australian child and regulating Australian children's sexual knowledge in schooling 1950s to late 1990s. *Sexuality and Culture* 12 (4), 221–239.

Romesberg, D. (2008) The tightrope of normalcy: Homosexuality, developmental citizenship, and American adolescence, 1890–1940. *Journal of Historical Sociology*, 21 (4), 417–442.

Rush, E., & La Nauze, A. (2006) Corporate paedophilia: Sexualisation of children in Australia. *Australian Institute Working Paper #90*. Australian Institute, Deakin, ACT. Viewed at http://www.tai.org.au/documents/dp_fulltext/DP90.pdf

Stoller, A. (1995) *Race and the education of desire: Foucault's history of sexuality and the colonial order of things*. Durham, NC: Duke University Press.

Tolman, D. L. (2012) Female adolescents, sexual empowerment and desire: A missing discourse of gender inequity? *Sex Roles*, 66 (11–12), 746–757.

Tolman, D. M. (2013) Insisting on 'both/and': Artifacts of excavating moral panics about sexuality: An Afterword, in B. Fahs, M. Dudy, & S. Stage (Eds.) *Moral Panics about Sexuality*. New York: Palgrave Macmillan.

Walkerdine, V. (1998) *Daddy's girl: Young girls and popular culture*. Cambridge, MA: Harvard University Press.

Part I

Mapping the History of Research and Theory within the Landscape of Ideas

2
Anthropologizing Young/Minor Sexualities

Diederik F. Janssen

Introduction

Cross-cultural studies on young sexualities have been presented since the late 19th century. Notwithstanding this, the question of how the rubrics of *youth* and *sexuality* interweave in anthropological discourse has only sporadically been considered anthropologically intriguing. Neither a comprehensive history nor a critical evaluation of anthropologies of young sexualities is currently available. Any such effort would have to wrestle with a multitude of conceptual angles and empirical inroads: 'modesty and sex training', 'Oedipal' themes in myths and parables, 'sex taboos', 'premarital freedom', 'normal childhood sexuality', 'sexual abuse'.

It pays to think about this apparent exuberance of anthropological facets as the outcome of the proliferation and consolidation of European academic disciplines at the end of the 19th century, converging as they did on interlocking questions of evolution (Darwin), development (Freud) and social progress (Marx). This convergence in the Western history of ideas made child development, and more specifically its *mise en scène* within the Victorian 'nuclear family' setting, the explanatory lynchpin to a score of 19th-century psychiatric, sexological and anthropological puzzles, from the precise aetiology of 'sexual inversion' and that of 'hysteria' to the supposed sexual 'atavisms' and backward 'promiscuities' of primitives, degenerates, neurotics and criminals. The sexual child has remained an anthropological *idée fixe* ever since, precisely such that in understanding its continued traction, one will need to centralize anthropology's and sexology's own 19th-century infancies.

From the start, ethnologists cultivated wide-angled views on childrearing and family life, but even they often turned out humble witnesses to key fascinations and preoccupations at home, some of which have long shrivelled into endearing anachronisms while the claim to usefulness of others remains on overdrive. Early discussions pertinent to sex in armchair ethnologies on childhood and womanhood by Hermann Heinrich Ploß (1887, I: 278–340; 1912, II: 519–559), for instance, offer a patchwork of ethnographically encountered attitudes and intuitions on intimacy (*tabu, defilement, desecration*) and ethnologists' own preferred moral taxonomies and rankings (*modesty, shamefacedness, promiscuity*). This admixture of exotic and domestic moral concerns characterizes all eras of anthropological commentary and remains in blatant effect, for instance, around today's globalism of *child sexual abuse* and its conceptual entanglement, particularly as of the late 19th century, with notions of *incest*.

Throughout the 20th century there were many alternative occasions for cross-cultural inquiries into young sexualities, however, with as many dimensions within which to pinpoint, correlate and evaluate cultural variability. Methodological and theoretical problems abound across the board. In anthropology's most piquant quarrel – the Mead-Freeman controversy (Shankman, 2009) – male and female authorities warred for decades over how to interpret Samoan teens' accounts of their intimate lives. As Margaret Mead was challenging the 'storm-and-stress' conception of US adolescence popular in the 1920s, pioneering anthropologist Bronisław Malinowski was challenging the universality of core elements of Freud's psychosexual theory, including the Oedipus complex. Theories concerning young sexualities, in short, animate the earliest implementations of, as well as the most protracted disputations over, anthropological methods. Though increasingly in the margins, anthropologists were consulted on many subsequent occasions to speak to Euro-American problems concerning young sexualities, from the mid-1970s US 'epidemic of teen pregnancy' to the recent proposal to have *hebephilia* (the sexual attraction of adolescents or adults to pubescent, rather than prepubescent, children) enter the 2013 *DSM-5* as a 'mental disorder'.

The latter rubric did not make the books. But ensuing discussions beg the related, anthropological question of the move of 'paedophilia' from a century-old psychiatric circumscription to an indisputably central organizing topos in Anglo-American sexual ethics today (Janssen, forthcoming). It figures prominently in increasingly globalist attempts to provide a scientific contour to 18th-century Western European notions of childhood innocence.

One would think that the recent 'sexualization of childhood' debates have done a good job in making this medicalized and psychologized topic social, historical and cultural. Fascinatingly, anthropological and cross-cultural commentary remains almost non-existent on this subject. This seems true on a broader plane. In the past decades a tradition in 'ethnographic' studies of children's gender and sexual cultures has been developed on a feminist and at times queer theoretical benchmark, but these mostly address anglophone, particularly UK, contexts. Researchers of sexualization notably restrict their scope to 'the Anglophone West' (Egan, 2013: 3), 'Western culture' (Attwood, 2009), 'dominant U.S. [pop] culture' (APA, 2010: 2n1), or else extend it, rather panoramically, to 'the global media'. In a 2008 special issue of the *Journal of Historical Sociology* on the topic of childhood and youth sexuality, its editors Egan and Hawkes signal that 'some of its most notable absences are in the area of cross cultural comparisons as well as a lack of research on race and the postcolonial' (*sic*: 265n3). Too few studies have set out to extend critical historical impressions of 'the sexual child' to the empirical domains of empire, colony and race (a pioneering text picking up from foundational work by Michel Foucault is Stoler, 1995). Still, 'even the best of recent global scholarship on sexuality and rights tends to underplay specific issues of youth, childhood and children's rights' (Waites, 2010: 972).

This is not to say that sexuality has not readily lent itself for discussion by anthropologists (e.g. Montgomery, 2009: ch. 7) or historians (e.g. Bailey, 2013) of childhood. Following either angle typically led researchers to underscore the profoundly cultural constructedness both of sexuality and childhood. One is invariably reminded of their importantly disjunctive status in the modern West. Modern 'sex' is importantly that 'adult' realm and industry where children would not, cannot, should not or shall not enter. Modern childhood, recursively, is importantly that life stage where sexuality 'develops' but never assumes a reckonable or valid form. How either may be represented is correspondingly strained. World citizens do not have to be reminded that depiction of young intimacies, even in cartoon drawings, has become one of the truly few items not protected by free speech clauses. What is often pronounced 'natural' and universal also figures as the paradigm of unsightliness, criminal to behold even where no actual children are involved. It dawns that no simple 'actuality' anchors the broad façade of upheaval around unseen images. Around related themes even social scientific discourse trades less in evidence than in inference, exemplars, morality tales, conceptual slots, stipulated entitlements and presumed interests. The child's sexual actuality lies importantly in being slotted, entitled and presumed.

Anthropologists are not known for having made much theoretical headway vis-à-vis this status quo. Pioneering cross-culturalist George Murdock (1949: 318–319) once briefly alluded to a 'positive gradient of appropriate age' – along those of propinquity and kinship – applicable to 'sexual choice' across cultures. Apropos: what makes 'age' (or the 'ages of Man') a positively core parameter of appropriate sex? Anthropologists have often dived into this question by recourse to cross-species approaches to the life-course; first, for instance, by reference to two core choreographies of intimacy, namely, mother–infant bonding and post-pubertal courtship. It is often noted that the latter appears an ethological echo of the former, that the dividing line remains culturally intriguing (note the versatile poetics of words like *baby*, *cute* and *naughty*) and that at least from the male perspective their joint appeal to the maternal body makes them rivalling forces (hence psychoanalysts' fascination by the *post-partum taboo*). Second, one could take the non-human primate record and look at the ubiquity and frequent indispensability to reproductive success of infantile and juvenile 'sex play'. Ubiquitous, but not universal and notably variable, sanctions on such play among humans would thus have to be explained.

Third, 'appropriate age' may have something to do with the biologically and culturally ubiquitous limiting of incest, or rather, with the bio-cultural principle of preferred or optimal 'outbreeding' and the concomitantly likely 'critical periods' of both sibling and parent–child closeness ('propinquity') and eventual nest-leaving by offspring. One would need to consider that the scope and spectre of incest are variably defined, construed and psychologized, and that their relation to modern understandings of 'sexuality' and 'childhood' has been complex and importantly shifting in recent decades. Moreover, what counts, or *should count*, as 'sex' is perhaps least obvious where concerning the young, invariably referring the anthropologist beyond evolutionary theory, to the wider, local – however globalized – poetics of intimacy's lore and law. What is *sex* made to mean, and which implications does this semantic overlay have for rubrics such as childhood? If sex can and increasingly may be *play*, why can't it be *child's play*? As for *childhood*, adopting an age-based definition for anthropological comparison may easily trample the typically kinship-, myth- and parable-inflected connotations of native life course terminology – and this applies unchangingly to the anglophone world.

Minor sexualities

Why these and other anthropological and historical questions remain distinctly marginal to contemporary discussions on sexuality and sexualization is itself an anthropological and historical question. As a recent *Handbook of Child and Adolescent Sexuality* (Bromberg & O'Donohue, 2013) sums up, conceptualization of young sexualities under global neo-liberalism, from the late 1970s onward, has significantly contracted around the need for the medical, forensic and legislative contouring of the child as world citizen, precisely regardless of its cultural background. The 'world society theory' proposed by Frank, Camp and Boutcher (2010) seems to apply to this promotion of developmental individuality in world sex law reform around minors (under-18s). They sketch an international policy shift around intimacy towards containment of 'risk', 'protection' of 'rights' and the securing of 'health', 'agency' and 'autonomy'. Where at the outset of the 20th century global laws protected family life from its many distractions (criminalizing adultery and sodomy, for instance), at its close they protected 'free-standing personhood' from such 'corporatist' interference (with an emphasis on criminalizing intramarital rape and child sexual abuse). From the 1960s onward, Western sexuality importantly became a matter of 'consenting adults in private'. This put 'the minor' at the administrative heart of sexual regulation.

Anthropologists have delayed studying the incipient centrality to sexual culture of this sexual persona, accompanying global impositions of 'minority status' onto 'childhood'. To what extent have children become *minors*? Do they actively ponder, obey or resist this positioning and its calculus? *Minority status* introduced specific patterns of tension between culture and administration. It still trades in *notional* dimensions of childhood (e.g. sexual/nonsexual) but along *metric* adjudications of *young* and *younger, too-young* and *too-much-younger*. Moreover, 'minority' has had a way of lumping together the otherwise richly anthropologized notions of *childhood* and *adolescence*. This is interesting, given long-standing complaints that Western 'childhood' has been 'teened', 'hurried' or is altogether 'disappearing' (e.g. Lynott & Logue, 1993). With current obscenity laws criminalizing even 'virtual' images of and risqué 'selfie' depictions by under-18s, representational dimensions are increasingly foregrounded.

Unsurprisingly, handbooks like the one cited pay only passing and paragraph-wise lip service to 'culture', and here only where culture would impede on 'diagnosis' and 'treatment' of obstacles to the proclaimed free-standing of minor persons. This puts a major stress both on wide-angled and nuanced perspectives. Anthropological sensitivity may not sit well with intentions to 'radically end' this or that harmful practice. Ethnographic observations have been increasingly offered up within purportedly 'culture-sensitive' frameworks for global citizenship: human/child rights, reproductive health, family planning, gender and development. Worthy occasions for related discussions have been legion: child marriage, genital 'mutilation', commercial exploitation, Internet pornography, HIV/AIDS. But since 'data' emerge *within* respective negative frames, it is a delicate question whether they can ever help reflecting on these frames, or only ever fortify them.

Frames and caveats

Anthropological perspectives typically take stock of extant, 'local' frames of meaning-making. To do this, however, one has to own up to some frame or another. Whether looking abroad or at home for 'anthropological data', this entails substantial risks – first, of insulting aggressively cherished constructions at home and second, of projecting theoretical hang-ups and regulatory discourses where they were never at home.

In anthropologizing minor sexualities, it pays to look at ways in which children have been both defined and raised to reflect specific notions of sexual governance and justice. Doing so, one may find cause to doubt that the move from corporatist ('traditional', privileging interests of social groups over individuals) to individualist ('modern') sensibilities around children's sexualities has been anywhere complete even in the post-millennial West. Enduringly, 'sex' acts as an all-round arbiter of sociality. However hard to pin down, it distinguishes proud subject from mere object, the initiated from the uninitiated, healthy intimacies from sickening assaults. Sexual socialization remains very much escalated to a culture-identifying significance, whether it is said to require rank-closing around 'tradition' or the mainstreaming of a modern 'awareness'.

Around issues of child and youth sexuality, at least, anthropology has been importantly at the mercy of a steady rise in theoretical belabouring over the course of the 20th century, mirrored by a marked intensification in popular meaning-making. 'Western culture' has sponsored many anthropological inroads into young sexualities, from ethnopsychoanalysis and psychohistory, culture-and-personality studies, cultural psychology and the 'anthropology of childhoods' to the metatheory of evolutionary psychology – opening out, most relevantly, onto 'evolutionary developmental psychology', 'mating psychology' and Darwinian or 'evolutionist feminist psychology'.

Mentioned shades of theory formation have spawned divergent ways to unpack, and then repackage, the conceptual baggage loaded onto 'sexuality' and 'reproduction' in the contemporary Anglo-American moment. They have divergent ways of facing the world, too. Feminist and faith-based perspectives on intimacy have had signature evangelical, indeed *ecumenical*, drives from the 18th century onward. Anthropology itself was superimposed onto centuries of colonial administration and missionary work. In the 1980s, major discussions arose about the compatibility of feminism and anthropology. Today, an anthropological focus is perhaps most useful where reflecting on residual dilemmas: how to critically reflect on the abundance, the fast internationalization and the enduring symbolic weight of today's expert and public intuitions on young sexuality's uses and abuses.

One major puzzle is why young sexualities after the circum-Atlantic sexual revolution remained aggressively circumscribed by scandal, by law and by 'reproduction' – along what seem securely interlocking tangents: *promiscuity, pornography, prostitution, sexualization, paedophilia, incest, sexual abuse*. What kind of globalizing work is done in the name of these late 20th-century 'global problems'? What are they made to mean across ethnographic settings? What are the conditions for their explosive meaningfulness? How do they impose conceptions of value, subjectivity or identity onto children? How are 'minors' inhabiting today's globalisms of risk and health management?

These questions light up variably across theoretical angles, three of which are briefly explored below. Sticking to the term *sexualization* seems productive throughout, for two reasons. First, it suitably exposes an anthropological *problem* (intimacy) as a process of *problematization*, as a *becoming-problematic*. Second, it usefully begs the anthropological question of sex as a 'symbolic economy' of *mate value*: a collective scene of moderating indiscriminate uses, unwise uses and overuse of sex as a meaningful symbol. Across cultures, the child remains both an opportune and an inevitable pivot for these moderations.

Becoming-sexual: Three approaches

Three lines of argument have been influential in locating children in and across sexual cultures. They were never cleanly separated but do illustrate varying inroads to contemporary sexualization debates.

'Psychosexual development'

Psychodynamic and *psychohistorical theories* see culture as the collective symbolization of the corollaries of parent–infant relations (e.g. Moore, 2007). Culturally particular trajectories of 'psychosexual development', or *sexuation*, would be mirrored in specific social constellations meant to deal with their psychological traces and debris. Formalized coping strategies and 'defence mechanisms' take the form of taboos and shared representations. Becoming-gendered and becoming-sexual in this literature entail the lifelong echo of parent–child intimacies on a societal, even civilizational, level. Gender, for instance, is figured as the outcome of the proper resolution of an 'Oedipal' relation of children with their mother and father. Across different kinship systems, core 'complexes' and their 'proper resolutions' would vary (Johnson & Price-Williams, 1996).

Psychoanalysis has lost most of its 20th-century primacy and is often castigated as a-cultural. Many, even central, interpretative gestures lack substantiation by research into children's lives. Psychodynamic theories remain interesting, however, where they help to reimagine the status of 'psychosexual development' across such ubiquitous conditions as single-parent, LGBT-parent and post-divorce families, in AIDS or war orphans, moreover in childhoods where family life is massively cross-cut by social media and horizontal social networks, and where man and woman, mother and father, but also parent and child, become less clearly dichotomized, demarcated and hierarchical 'roles'. 'Sexualization of childhood' and 'infantilization of women' have been tipped as the psychocultural accompaniments of such 'category crises' across post-industrial settings such as the US and Japan. To diagnose them as 'symptoms', at least, appeals to critical perspectives on such changes. Entering anglophone academic literature in the early 1990s, Japan's erratically eroticized 'cute culture' (*kawaii karucha*) and well-known 'Lolita complex' (*rorikon*) have classically lent themselves to psychodynamic interpretations of the 'mother complex' (*mazakon*) of *salari-imen*. Note that key Japanese terms were imported from the West. Sadly, comparative perspectives have been few to date.

'Politics of reproductive ritual'

Socio-political theories rather assume an organizing role for administrative strategizing within and between corporate social units at the occasion of girls' and boys' entry into reproductive maturity (e.g. Whiting et al., 1986; Barry, 2007). Related agenda (timing and arranging of marriages in relation to pubescence, honouring legitimate claims to paternity, prevention of incest and rivalries between siblings, among others) gave rise to legal frameworks to optimally capitalize on newly productive and reproductive lives. The timing of acknowledging a child's sexual status varies accordingly (Rogoff et al., 1975). Attitudes towards girls' premarital sex vary with the time gap between pubescence and marriage, the social and economic value of children and the exchange of goods accompanying marriage (Schlegel, 1995). In the absence of centralized governments, ritualized negotiations tune in on these issues (Paige & Paige, 1981). Within and beyond initiation rituals, particularly, pubescent bodies are put on display or under conspicuous surveillance, made to advertise 'nubility' or put through tests of endurance, loyalty or virility. Ornaments, magic or body modifications might be in order; veiling might have to be commenced. Concomitant politics might work smoothest where abstracted, idealized and encoded into such 'lived metaphors' as *fallen-ness, purity, virginity, chastity, purdah, virtue,* family *name* and *honour.* In fact well before puberty, along starkly gendered lines, children's intimate bodies are often understood as embodying the 'honor, reputation and morality' (Rydstrøm, 2003: 95–96) of past and future generations.

Extensive studies have been done to show such concepts' historical and regional specificities. Related themes have been probed along historical lines by Foucault (1978), describing related politics in terms of a 'symbolics of blood'. Here 'sex' referred to the privilege and duty to 'consummate' marriage – that is, to certify strategically opportune familial alliances and to produce legitimate heirs. An opportune set of rules must regulate commerce between social units, and this could centrally include an 'exchange of women', that is, marriageable and fertile daughters. If anything, 'sexuality' entailed a youth's likelihood for adherence to these rules of exchange. Across pre-industrial and premodern societies, a child was betrothed and/or married out. It mattered *whose* son or daughter (or niece or nephew) fancied *whose* son or daughter. In some societies senior and junior 'age sets' of men competed bitterly for wives, with polygynous gerontocrats depriving young men of marriage options. 'Consummation' of marriage was tied up securely, with the political scope of families, lineages, age sets or clans thus being fortified, allied, extended – or split up as the case may be.

A child's erotic escapades either conformed to or challenged its status conferred by birth, initiation or marriage. Early stirrings would be interpreted in the light of these milestones. Sex was either politically (economically) opportune, or it was 'illicit': a sin, a crime, a disrespect, a foolishness, a waste, a foregone opportunity. Rubrics including *prenuptial sex, incest, adultery, sodomy, wrongful seduction, elopement* and so on figured prominently in the policing of its 'symbolics'. They add up to a sociosymbolic structure weighing down on all intimate relations young or old. Mature sex had the capacity to honour ancestral blood and beget and correctly deploy new blood. Much depending on its latent or actual consequences for this capacity, *immature* sex could be anything from catastrophic or suspect to trivial, nameless, 'naught', cute and amusing.

Unlike psychodynamic theories, the broad frame of sociopolitical views has been useful for providing a context for understanding the encumbering of childhood and adolescence in the West with the weight of sexological and developmental sciences. After all, much of 'reproductive politics' (arranged marriage, harsh initiations, virginity inspections, dowries, bride price) has been rooted out as violations of human rights. With the rise of state bureaucracies, authority and discretion invested in clan, extended family, dynasty, 'filial interest group' or father were transferred to national and (after the Second World War) international laws on 'child protection', 'reproductive choice' and 'personal integrity'.

This entailed new ways to read, value and administer children's bodies – their work and play in a world of adult work and play. Into the 20th century, adherence to the rules of the mating game continued to fulfil a central 'task' or 'identity': it still secures substantial symbolic capital. Sex 'completes' an otherwise impoverished life. It entails 'scoring', 'marks' adulthood, certainly manhood, and so it remains a metonym for the life well lived. Likewise, sexual trespassers, spoilsports and rule-breakers are still 'beasts', 'inhuman', to be treated like the animals they are. Their crimes remain 'unspeakable', 'unthinkable', an absurdity. Their victims shall still turn out traumatized, spoilt forever, 'murdered', their souls 'scarred'.

Symbolism, in other words, remained. Talk of *murdered innocence, stolen childhood, harm, damage, trauma, scarring, healing* and *survival* is suggestive of the heavy psychologizing and medicalizing of 'lived metaphors' concerning intimacy throughout the modern West, and furthermore of the central signifying role for childhood experience to adult politics. Mentioned tropes no longer honour ancestral bloodlines or family reputations. Instead they figure what would be children's inner nature and private sense of self-worth, notably through new, quasi-scientific abstractions such as 'development', 'safety', 'mental health' and 'normality'.

How children learn to live with these core metaphors is being studied on occasion, but they are rarely fundamentally challenged. They are ascriptive: descriptive only where successfully ascribed. Politicians have a field day with them. Therapists earn their living with them. Weeping parents recite them on talk shows. How they hold up in different languages or cultural contexts often remains unexamined. Foucault identified their 18th- to 19th-century rise as the 'pedagogization of children's sex'. Regulatory conventions were now socialized and marked as the normal habitus, or emergent 'psychological functioning', of those regulated. This 'sexualized' the child in new and aggressive ways: it placed the child at the heart of a new discursive projection of 'human sexuality'. Associated metaphors attained a psychological, even neurological, urgency. For anthropologists it pays to pause on at least one cardinal implication: that this Western 'sexualization of children' did not definitively 'individualize' minor sexualities but in fact deepened their conceptual centrality to sexual politics. Perennial alarm over sex still ties children into the name, honour and reputability of family, nation and 'world community'.

'Learning the mating game'

In the mid-19th century an evolutionary, Darwinian outlook on life emerged, which had a major influence on psychoanalysis but today has gained most footing in bio-social approaches to adolescence. *Evolutionary psychologists* see in sexual culture the playing out of adaptive behavioural patterns transpiring into often collective strategies to time and balance 'mating efforts' with 'parenting efforts' – both requiring substantial investments and implying shared risks and benefits to fitness and reproductive success.

Summed up in one sentence: Human sexuality is problematic because human mating was problematic in homo sapiens' *environment of evolutionary adaptedness* (the social and ecological world of Pleistocene hunter-gatherers); and human mating remains problematic because childrearing is intensive. Human mating has universal aspects of infant altriciality (helplessness), delayed reproduction, a neurological capacity for complex social learning involving language, a 'nested family' social pattern including long-term pair-bonding with paternal and alloparental (other than parental) care, leading up to the unusual model of moderately exclusive pair-bonding in multiple-male groups (Flinn et al., 2007). Notwithstanding, males and females differ substantially in minimal investments per reproductive cycle. Mating styles differ correspondingly between the sexes; they also vary markedly along factors such as community sex ratio and long-/short-term prospects. The overall evolutionary scenario is that of deeply ingrained and gendered sexual psychologies, reflecting millions of years of adaptive problems, that over the course of a few generations, especially for the female case, have been subjected to game-changing conditions of birth control, disease control, social security, high life expectancy, low pubescence age, social media and the overriding centrality of money-making and status-enhancing (in any case not just reproductive) careers.

These and other conditions set juveniles on a course of responsive, but still markedly sex-typed (Hatfield et al., 2012), mating careers. 'Mating psychologists' assume an evolutionary, or *adaptationist*, view of many aspects of these careers, from beauty standards to sexual coercion (Geher & Miller, 2008; Geher & Kaufman, 2013; Fisher et al., 2013). It is argued that this has broad consequences for the timing of intimate life and for the socialization of 'mate choice and retention' strategies, including 'mate value' (attractiveness) assessment tactics (Sugiyama, 2005). Beyond socialization, 'life history theories' point to multiple pathways through which family relationships and family composition independently affect even girls' pubertal timing (Belsky et al., 2010).

Growing up sexually, from this perspective, entails the laborious acquisition and testing of 'mating intelligence': the ability to know, optimally display and if necessary fake one's own mate value, and to mind-read, impress, out-bargain and if necessary fool or fend off both opposite-sex mating candidates and same-sex rivals doing the same. The purported interplay of hardwired and acquired sensitivities has been tipped as particularly relevant to sexualization debates given the central role attributed to self-awareness, self-censure, cliques and mind-reading, especially in girls' peer cultures and social media. Particular emphasis has been laid recently on 'intrasexual competition' between and 'indirect aggression' among young adult women (e.g. Vaillancourt & Sharma, 2011; Benenson, 2013). Studied in these terms, both being sexy and commotion over peer sexiness ('sluts') appear responsive to a part-hereditary, part-cultivated, part-experience-borne arsenal of sensibilities that reflects women's increasingly competitive social milieus, for instance campuses with a high female to male ratio. To overestimate the degree to which the opposite sex sexualizes one's own sex turned out to be more *characteristic* of women, as indeed it would be more *adaptive* for young women to err on this side of 'commitment scepticism'. Most of the research on this 'sexual overperception bias' comes from North America, however, and its peri-pubescent development remains to be studied.

Parental moderation of sexuality's 'gamesmanship' (Eyre et al., 1998) is well theorized within evolutionary frameworks. The perennial game is to show without showing too much, to appear interested but never too interested. Children, by arguable but frequent definition, are those who cannot be expected to understand or play this subtle and critical game very well. One strategic option here is to make the playing field – indeed any aspect of the game itself – entirely off limits to those designated as children. In humans the sexual body, with the sex act it refers to, is the Great Invisible (Friedl, 1994) in the public and even the domestic space. It remains a precious good and powerful symbol primarily given its guarded unavailability to the unprivileged and undeserving eye. It remains a symbol of mature and sincere sociality primarily given its absolute dissociation from the immature. (Note the potential role for childhood innocence as a vital and necessary element in the orchestration of any symbolic economy: it is only to a truly powerful symbol that there is a class of vulnerables that would be 'harmed' by mere visual exposure to, even by mere knowledge of, its truths.) The merest allusion to sex risks not only to be *defined* as 'adult' territory, but also to be pronounced as 'harmful to minors' and thus loaded with juvenile apprehension, typically managed by jokes. (Much of 'childhood sexuality' across many contexts might derive its pleasure and formative properties from making a joke of this territorialization.) Age restriction and parental advisories indeed became the most conspicuous features of Euro-American media rating and marketing. With any introduction of a new medium (photography, cinema, TV, Internet), a managerial campaign unfolds to bluntly access-restrict, ban, bleep, block, blur, censor, cut and filter. Related is a logic and tactic to construe the young body as void of erotic appeal, and to medicalize, shame, boycott and punish any hint of such an appeal. Amazingly, today even the clothed young body itself is being experienced and regulated as pornographic where shown 'in certain contexts' and with certain 'apparent intentions'. Here, too, it has been argued that this recent scrutiny accomplishes not 'protection' but precisely a cross-culturally unprecedented eroticization. A distinctly modern, Western and scientific *erotics* came to burden the child's purported inner truth: the child has something desirable to hide, so let us all intensely focus on this colossal mystery.

Mate value into erotic capital

Negotiating this science-backed erotics requires, first, a sensitivity for the ways related terms have figured widely, and variably, in public debates throughout modernity. It seems ill-advised to try to coerce psychodynamic, sociopolitical and evolutionary perspectives into a single anthropological account of these debates. One notes that bits of all three angles can be found throughout global popular discussions on sexuality, and indeed on young sexualities. Popular culture is a potpourri of theoretical sound bites; so is much academic commentary. Exhaustive discussions of 'mating strategies' have been cardinal features of the novel, zine, blog and column spheres of public life for centuries, and much trickles down into the tween market. Around culture-defining themes of child sexual abuse, even Freudian concepts such as *repression* have been granted a rich, if embattled, afterlife.

Discussions ubiquitously reckon with the fact that 'society' changes rapidly around notions of age, sex, gender and personhood, and that such changes rekindle millennia-long animosities, for instance, between Judeo-Christian, Islamic and secular spheres of influence. 'Sexualization' discussions extend across centuries of discourse both on women's virtue and children's innocence. Historians note that the modern trajectory has been importantly that of youths' *desexualization* (Killias, 2000), and key inputs to today's debates seem to fall neatly in line. Foucault, as mentioned, alluded to the perverse scenario, that modern desexualizations accomplished precisely the opposite, and that they have been producing their own nightmare.

From this perspective, many anti-sexualization proponents may seem to be more interested in articulating their stakes in nightmarish terms than in actually ending any purported nightmare. So which needs may lie behind this perennial articulation?

This question has us return to the anthropological question about what women's and children's bodies are 'worth' and to whom, within which cultural framework of valuation and exchange. It is a question that increasingly refrains from presupposing the heterosexual dyad but that still finds itself reckoning with the many stone-age – hetero, male, dyadic, post-pubescent – imprimaturs of 'sex'. Fitting today's free market economies, an economistic view of sex would highlight sexuality's overriding cultural construction as a scarce female resource over which men compete. Sexuality's politics are concomitantly wedged between women's rivalries at the heterosexual marketplace and women's collusion in the negotiation of a collective bargaining position vis-à-vis men over resources including 'sexual access'. Baumeister and Vohs' (2004) theory of 'sexual economics', Green's 'sexual fields framework' (Green, 2008) and Hakim's (2011) notion of 'erotic capital' are attempts to describe in general terms this gendered social exchange view of heterosexuality in contemporary global economies. Many cross-cultural reviews as well as evolutionary perspectives indeed argue against male, and in favour of female, stakes in sexual restraint. 'Thus, essentially, the cultural suppression of female sexuality can best be understood as a process by which women pressure each other to restrain their sexuality and make sex less available to men, so that price of sex is high, which benefits women in general' (Ainsworth & Baumeister, 2012: 37).

Implications for the status and understanding of childhood are extensive. But it seems key to male–female strategizing that many of these remain encoded in metaphor, correctness and silence. Let me explain this point below. Economistic models can be found at the heart of unending discussions from pornography and prostitution to homosexuality, paedophilia, incest, even sex education. Until recently all prominently figured as assaults on good morals. They would 'trivialize', 'sell out', 'cheapen', 'pervert' or 'make a joke of' the exchange function of sex, upsetting the delicate balance between female supply and male demand. Where religious commentaries foretell their catastrophic effects on divinely sanctioned family life and its reproduction, feminist commentaries foretell the destruction of female bargaining positions, especially within families (regarding this 'discursive coalition', compare Duschinsky, 2013). In the US, especially, these two condemnations coalesced to form a global vista of 'abuse prevention'. A major keyword for late modern sexual culture, 'sexual abuse' spells out the wrong use of sex as an exchange function: too much, too early, too flagrant, too easy, too cheap and too casual. In Anglo-American discourses from the late 1970s onward, these injunctions attained Victorian levels of alarm. Small incidents are figured as 'assaults' on society itself that speak to all women (to 'feminist' or maternal sensibilities), all children (assaulting 'childhood'), all men (to 'patriarchy'), finally to all 'human' dignity.

Although sexual economics theorists reckon with a multifactorial model including erotic 'plasticity' and biological differences in sex drive, they place a heavy emphasis on female-to-female complicity (feminism) and mother–daughter socialization. Contemporary with the late 19th century and late 1970s feminist waves, one indeed sees a modern pedagogical preponderance of especially religious spokeswomen, feminists, mothers, female politicians, women-dominated service sectors and pro-feminist men to monitor, 'protect' and problematize female sexuality at the level of daughters and sons. Resolutions were hardcoded in laws and minds. Children's 'agency' often means their being implicated in totalizing appeals, made on their behalf, to the winning codes. With the global accreditation of 'consenting adults in private' and feminism's fragmentation along lines of sex-positivity and sex-negativity, the best bet for *any* regulation of sex were discourses of child protection. Note that even today and on a worldwide scale, homosexuality remains figured a 'threat to society' through time-honoured slogans of 'child recruitment', 'propaganda to minors' and (around issues of same-sex parenthood) 'normal child development'. Where all this has been marked as 'homophobia', an epochal focus on 'paedophilic grooming' ensued, indeed almost overnight.

The narrowing of 'healthy sexual development' against this background seemingly closely inflects with shifting adult negotiations over what sex means and what it is worth to whom, now problematized by a 'sexual revolution' that threatened to throw many established meanings and economies of intimacy into doubt, especially its marital and familial imprimatur. More radically put, observing the extensive metaphorical work they are still made to perform, one must ask to what extent colourful discourses about 'childhood sexuality' have ever really been about any such thing as 'childhood' or, indeed, any such thing as 'sexuality'.

A theme anthropologists would be likely to offer up for consideration at this point is the tabooing of incest. Prohibitions of incest were syntactically critical to kinship-centred societies, and incest's impossibility was an unquestioned societal condition for 'individuation' in psychodynamic theories. What anthropologists found varying is the specific social unit to which these taboos pertained. Throughout human history families were often extended and complex, and so were incest taboos. In the modern West, households contracted into emotionally close mother-father-child units, if not single-parent-child dyads. This effectively transfigured incest taboos into strong intergenerational taboos. Around the early 1980s these hastily took on a scientific, medical face where conceptualized through the trope of 'sexual trauma'. Incest importantly became 'a type of child abuse'. Specifically psychiatric models of abuse as involving 'traumatic sexualization', 'eroticization' and 'sexualized behaviours' were seen in Anglo-American literature from the early 1980s onward. The great human universal of tabooed incest became importantly contained by a new scientific framing of guilty offenders and innocent victims. But the spectre of incest can be seen to extend way beyond this frame. 'Special friendships' would interfere with the administrative task of all education, and education is key. Student sexualities therefore figure diffusely – taboo-like – as 'dangerous', 'unhealthy' or 'inappropriate' across educational institutions. Pedagogical and domestic intuitions readily interweave into the working hypothesis that they are pristinely delicate and incongruent 'onto themselves', indeed in all cultures alike. Consider that both intrafamilial and school sex education remain rhetorically tied to inarticulate 'problems' in many post-millennial contexts. Parents enduringly report their relation to the topic through such glosses as 'uncomfortable', 'embarrassed', 'awkward', 'dangerous', 'delicate', 'tricky', 'sensitive', 'nervous', 'uneasy', 'guarded', 'conflicted', 'hesitant' and 'hardest thing I ever had to do as a father'. An apparent tightrope is being walked, but over which unspoken abyss?

Conclusion

Through the prism of three anthropological models, the neo-liberal figure of the sexualized child can be seen to point to major shifts in the domestic competition between and among the sexes. Ensuing debates remain staged and experienced as part of the kernel value structure of personhood, family and nationhood alike. Problematizations of sex animated the operational face of Abrahamic religions, greasing interdenominational animosity. They went on to have a major impact on late 19th-century sexological, developmental and medical forensic sciences which are still very much with us. Medico-moral demarcations of childhood innocence remain central to these sciences as it is here, in the absence of myth, totemic lore or scripture, that past valuations of sex might be retrialled, contemporary valuations moderated and new valuations monitored. Signature notions such as 'innocence' and 'sexual development' remain suspended halfway between managerial shorthand and deep identification.

'Child sexual abuse' echoes 19th-century figurations of 'corruption', 'spoiling' and 'brutalization' of children's innocence, but it attained a revitalized sense of alarm. Consider that the figure of the sexualized or sexually mistreated child today is being successfully levelled against any plane of cultural authority up to the King of Pop and the Catholic Church – an extraordinary landslide in power configurations unseen in world history and brought about securely within a generation's time. Today's stern focus on kings and Church fathers seems metaphoric of the ongoing recalibration of male and female power in today's 'post-feminist', particularly white, families (compare Borneman, 2012). With a sexuality of its own, the child risks being offered up for male sexual demand, and the lowest standards for women's prime bargaining power, risk becoming those of the smallest, gullible child. To eroticize the boy-child would problematically both mobilize and expose to 'seductions' his presumed heterosexuality, and thus his privilege and power. To eroticize the girl-child would do the same and have the complicating potential to undercut women's coalitional deployment of sex as bargaining tool. Sexualization of girlhood is figured as the universal insult (to Woman, to the child, to childhood, to society, to humanity) because it disturbs and destabilizes the already and increasingly delicate bond between emancipated mothers and humbled *patres familias*. It would unsettle the already increasingly less – and never truly – settled convention of 'sex' as a critical interface between 'the sexes'.

That interface ('sexuality') therefore became and remains heavily developmentalized and qualified – by whatever theory may do the job. Young sexualities remain massively problematic at a gut level from the perspective of parents, who must oversee their child's increasingly delicate entry into intimate relations from the vantage point of their own increasingly delicate and divorcive intimate relations. Where *incest* may have figured as the unspeakable catastrophe across kinship-centred societies, in late 20th-century kinship-*de*centred societies it is 'paedophilia' – the sick sexualization of *anyone's* child – that is unanimously figured as 'the nightmare of every parent', 'the death of childhood' and 'society's biggest evil'. To contemporary interpreters, this apocalyptic figuration remains suspended between feminism's flagship victory and society's most pathetic moral panic. How children grapple with it will be an accordingly tricky question.

References

Ainsworth, S. E., & Baumeister, R. F. (2012) Changes in sexuality: How sexuality changes across time, across relationships, and across sociocultural contexts. *Clinical Neuropsychiatry*, 9 (1), 32–38.

American Psychological Association (APA), Task Force on the Sexualization of Girls (2010) *Report of the APA task force on the sexualization of girls*. Retrieved from http://www.apa.org/pi/women/programs/girls/report-full.pdf.

Attwood, F. (2009) *Mainstreaming sex: The sexualization of western culture.* New York: I.B. Tauris.

Bailey, B. (2013) The vexed history of children and sex, in P. S. Fass (Ed.) *The Routledge History of Childhood in the Western World.* New York: Routledge.

Barry, H., III. (2007) Customs associated with premarital sexual freedom in 143 societies. *Cross-Cultural Research*, 41, 261–272.

Baumeister, R. F., & Vohs, K. D. (2004) Sexual economics: Sex as female resource for social exchange in heterosexual interactions. *Personality and Social Psychology Review*, 8, 339–363.

Belsky, J., Houts, R., & Fearon, R. M. P. (2010) Infant attachment security and timing of puberty: Testing an evolutionary hypothesis. *Psychological Science*, 21, 1195–1201.

Benenson, J. F. (2013) The development of human female competition: Allies and adversaries. *Philosophical Transactions of the Royal Society B*, 368. doi:

10.1098/rstb.2013.0079. Retrieved from http://rstb.royalsocietypublishing.org/content/368/1631/20130079.short.

Borneman, J. (2012) Incest, the child, and the despotic father. *Current Anthropology*, 53 (2), 181–203.

Bromberg, D. S., & O'Donohue, W. T. (Eds.) (2013) *Handbook of child and adolescent sexuality*. Oxford: Academic Press.

Duschinsky, R. (2013) The emergence of sexualization as a social problem: 1981–2010. *Social Politics*, 20 (1), 137–156.

Egan, R. D. (2013) *Becoming sexual: A critical appraisal of the sexualization of girls*. Malden, MA: Polity Press.

Eyre, S., Hoffman, V., & Millstein, S. (1998) The gamesmanship of sex: A model based on African American adolescent accounts. *Medical Anthropology Quarterly*, 12, 67–489.

Fisher, M., Garcia, J. R., & Sokol Chang, R. (Eds.) (2013) *Evolution's empress: Darwinian perspectives on the nature of women*. Oxford: Oxford University Press.

Flinn, M. V., Quinlan, R. L., Ward, C. V., & Coe, M. K. (2007) Evolution of the human family: Cooperative males, long social childhoods, smart mothers, and extended kin networks, in C. Salmon & T. Shackelford (Eds.) *Family Relationships*. Oxford: Oxford University Press, pp. 16–38.

Foucault, M. (1978) *The history of sexuality. vol. 1: An introduction*. New York: Pantheon.

Frank, D. J., Camp, B. J., & Boutcher, S. A. (2010) Worldwide trends in the criminal regulation of sex, 1945 to 2005. *American Sociological Review*, 75, 867–893.

Friedl, E. (1994) Sex the invisible. *American Anthropologist*, 96, 833–844.

Geher, G., & Kaufman, S. B. (2013) *Mating intelligence unleashed: The role of the mind in sex, dating, and love*. New York: Oxford University Press.

Geher, G., & Miller, G. F. (Eds.) (2008) *Mating intelligence: Sex, relationships, and the mind's reproductive system*. New York: Lawrence Erlbaum.

Green, A. I. (2008) The social organisation of desire: The sexual fields approach. *Sociological Theory*, 26, 25–50.

Hakim, C. (2011) *Erotic capital: The power of attraction in the bedroom and the boardroom*. New York: Basic Books.

Hatfield, E., Hutchison, E. S. S., Bensman, L., Young, D., & Rapson, R. L. (2012) Cultural, social, and gender influences on casual sex: New developments, in J. M. Turn & A. D. Mitchell (Eds.) *Social Psychology: New Developments*. Hauppauge, NY: Nova Science, pp. 1–38.

Janssen, D. F. (forthcoming) 'Chronophilia': Entries of erotic age preference into descriptive psychopathology. *Medical History* (Cambridge UP).

Johnson, A. W., & Price-Williams, D. R. (1996) *Oedipus ubiquitous: The family complex in world folk literature*. Stanford, CA: Stanford University Press.

Killias, M. (2000) The emergence of a new taboo: The desexualization of youth in western societies since 1800. *European Journal on Criminal Policy and Research*, 8 (4), 459–477.

Lynott, P. P., & Logue, B. J. (1993) The 'hurried child': The myth of lost childhood in contemporary American society. *Sociological Forum*, 8 (3), 471–491.

Montgomery, H. (2009) *An introduction to childhood: Anthropological perspectives on children's lives*. Malden, MA: Wiley-Blackwell.

Moore, H. L. (2007) *The subject of anthropology: Gender, symbolism and psychoanalysis*. Cambridge, UK: Polity.

Murdock, G. (1949) *Social structure*. New York: Macmillan.

Paige, K., & Paige, J. M. (1981) *The politics of reproductive ritual.* Berkeley: University of California Press.

Ploß, H. H. (1887) *Das Weib in Natur – und Völkerkunde.* Vol. 2, 2nd edn. Leipzig: Th. Grieben.

Ploß, H. H., & Renz, B. (Eds.) (1912) *Das Kind in Brauch und Sitte der Völker.* Vol. 2, 3rd edn. Leipzig: Th. Grieben.

Rogoff, B. et al. (1975) Age of assignment of roles and responsibilities to children: A cross-cultural survey. *Human Development*, 18 (5), 353–369.

Rydstrøm, H. (2003) *Embodying morality: Growing up in rural Northern Vietnam.* Honolulu: University of Hawaii Press.

Schlegel, A. (1995) The cultural management of adolescent sexuality, in P. R. Abramson & S. D. Pinkerton (Eds.) *Sexual Nature, Sexual Culture.* Chicago, IL: University of Chicago Press, pp. 177–194.

Shankman, P. (2009) *The trashing of Margaret Mead: Anatomy of an anthropological controversy.* Madison, WI: University of Wisconsin Press.

Stoler, L. (1995) *Race and the education of desire: Foucault's history of sexuality and the colonial order of things.* Durham, NC: Duke University.

Sugiyama, L. S. (2005) Physical attractiveness in adaptationist perspective, in D. M. Buss (Ed.) *The Handbook of Evolutionary Psychology.* New York: Wiley, pp. 292–343.

Vaillancourt, T., & Sharma, A. (2011) Intolerance of sexy peers: Intrasexual competition among women. *Aggressive Behavior*, 37 (6), 569–577.

Waites, M. (2010) Human rights, sexual orientation and the generation of childhoods: Analysing the partial decriminalisation of 'unnatural offences' in India. *The International Journal of Human Rights*, 14 (6), 971–993.

Whiting, J. W. M., Burbank, V. K., & Ratner, M. S. (1986) The duration of maidenhood across cultures, in J. Lancaster & B. Hamburg (Eds.) *School-Age Pregnancy and Parenthood.* New York: Aldine de Gruyter, pp. 273–302.

3
A Sociological History of Researching Childhood and Sexuality: Continuities and Discontinuities

Stevi Jackson and Sue Scott

Both public and academic debates on the sexualization of culture and its impact on children and young people have a history. In this chapter, we locate current concerns about children and sex in historical context through a retrospective engagement with our own work, set against the backdrop of wider social changes since the 1970s. We write as feminist sociologists who have been actively engaged with the sociology of sexuality for four decades both separately and together. We reflect on our motivations for becoming and remaining academically interested in this area based on our own experience of changing sexual mores over time. We map changes but also highlight continuities in relation to the ways in which sexuality was, and continues to be, seen as a danger to children and especially to girls. Underlying our analysis is the argument that anxieties around children and sex and the challenges this poses for children and young people derive from constructions of sexuality as a special area of life and the child as a special category of person; we will argue for the need to question and disrupt the ways in which the former is seen as inimical to the well-being of the latter. This has been a recurrent theme in our work and, despite changes in the sexual landscape, remains relevant to contemporary critical analysis.

Feminist and sociological beginnings

For both of us, our interest in debates about sexuality derived from feminist concerns and involvement in the women's liberation movement. Like many feminists in the 1970s we were engaged in politicizing the personal and making sense of our own experience, past and present, in political terms. We had been teenagers in the 1960s when, despite the hype to the contrary, girls were expected to guard their 'reputations' and remain virginal and when there was little information available on female desire and pleasure.[1] Each of us, in different ways, had to negotiate the double standard and tensions between our own desires on the one hand and fears of pregnancy and damage to 'reputation' on the other, while also managing pressures from boyfriends to 'go all the way' – and we were both acutely aware of the injustice of this situation. Feminism gave us a means of making sense of this in political terms, the knowledge that we were not alone in our experiences; it offered us an analysis of how women's sexuality had historically been policed and regulated in a way which (heterosexual) men's had not. This understanding was later to motivate us to think critically about the gendered ways in which children and young people learn about sex and become sexually active.

The politics of sexuality that emerged within second wave feminism should, then, be understood in the historical context of the 1960s and 1970s. At this time there was a resurgence of Left politics in Europe and North America and it was largely from among the ranks of this 'New Left' that the new generation of feminist activists came. New Left political ideas were far more libertarian than more traditional and established forms of left-wing politics. These ideas included a vision of individual sexual freedom as a legitimate revolutionary goal. A further influence at this time was the so-called 'sexual revolution'. The extent to which this was actually a revolutionary change has been called into question (Weeks, 1990), but ideas of sexual liberation were prevalent in some left-wing, largely middle-class, circles and in various counter-cultural movements in the late 1960s and the 1970s, where 'sexual radicals' such as Reich (1951) and Marcuse (1964) were widely read. In these contexts 'free love' was promoted while marriage and monogamy were condemned as bourgeois institutions that reduced people to property (e.g. Red Collective, 1973). These ideas offered a challenge to the old double standard, but in practice they had different consequences for women and men. In retrospect many women felt that 'sexual liberation' meant greater access for men to women's bodies and the removal of their right to say 'no' to sex, lest they be damned as 'unliberated' (Piercy, 1970; Snitow et al., 1984). This, combined with the marginalization of women, and women's issues, within Left organizations, provided the impetus for feminist critique.

While some of the effects of the so-called sexual revolution can be seen as problematic for women, it did open up sexuality as a political issue. Many feminists tried to preserve what they saw as the positive elements within the libertarian ideas of the New Left – the dissociation of sex from reproduction, the emphasis on sexual pleasure and freedom – while also challenging the coercive and predatory aspects of male sexuality (Greer, 1970; Millet, 1971; Boston Women's Health Collective, 1973). Feminists continued to attack the double standard, to demand the right to define their own sexuality, to see themselves as sexually active rather than passive objects of male desire and to seek forms of sexual pleasure not constrained by the set heterosexual pattern of foreplay (if you were lucky) followed by penetration (Lydon, 1970; Koedt, 1972; Whiting, 1972). At the same time, women's shared experiences of pressured sex with men led to new analyses of sexual coercion and violence (Griffin, 1971; Medea & Thompson, 1974; Brownmiller, 1975).[2]

One immediate difficulty when we began academic work in the 1970s was in establishing sexuality as a legitimate object of sociological enquiry. Studying sexuality was simply not taken seriously. When Stevi began research on teenage girls and sex in 1973, academics in her department reacted with either bemusement or ribald comments – and one told her that this topic was the province of psychology and not sociology. Sue's experience a few years later was not so different; she was told that the study of sexuality was 'pop sociology', fun for undergraduates but not fit for serious academic enquiry. A further issue was the lack of existing work on which to draw. There was already a great deal of polemical writing circulating among feminists, much of it unpublished, but little academic research. We were both looking for explanations of the development of female sexuality from childhood onwards that would explain girls' and women's experience of the sexual as socially mediated rather than naturally given or explicable in purely psychological terms. Anthropological work made the most sense in that it revealed the diversity of human sexual relations and practices and therefore their sociocultural origins (e.g. Mead, 1935; Ford & Beech, 1951). Psychoanalysis was the only large body of work explicitly addressing the constitution of sexuality; both of us read a great deal of Freud but found it literally incredible. It had no resonance at all with our own experience or with our sociological imaginations. The feminist exposé of 'the myth of the vaginal orgasm' (Koedt, 1972) further fuelled our scepticism about Freud, as well as making us wonder how generations of women could have been so successfully deceived about their own physiology.

It was our discovery of the work of Gagnon and Simon that provided the major breakthrough (Gagnon, 1965, 1973; Simon & Gagnon, 1969; Gagnon & Simon, 1974). They were 'truly the first sociologists to radically question the biologism, the naturalism and the essentialism that pervaded most existing research and study' (Plummer, 2001: 131). They also made it possible to think about childhood and sexuality in new ways. Rather than simply asserting the pre-eminence of the social over the natural, they critiqued the idea of repression, thus allowing for a positive conception of the social as *producing* sexuality rather than moulding or modifying inborn drives. As a consequence of this they challenged both the Freudian idea of children's innate sexual desires and the common-sense view of children as asexual. From Gagnon and Simon's perspective, children are neither intrinsically sexual nor intrinsically asexual – how sexual they can be is a product of the social ordering of sexual knowledge and conduct. For Gagnon and Simon acts, feelings and body parts are not sexual in themselves, but only become so through the application of sociocultural scripts that imbue them with sexual significance. Since nothing is sexual in itself, children do not begin to construct a sense of themselves as sexual beings until they have gained access to sexual scripts.

Gagnon and Simon initially identified two, and later three, levels of scripting that interact with each other in shaping everyday sexuality (Gagnon & Simon, 1974; Simon & Gagnon, 1984): cultural, interpersonal and intrapsychic. Cultural scenarios are the 'cultural narratives' constructed around sexuality, 'what the intersubjective culture treats as sexuality' (Laumann et al., 1994: 6), which also provide 'instructional guides' for sexual conduct (Simon, 1996: 40). These are mediated through interpersonal scripting, which emerges from and is deployed within everyday interaction, both in negotiating sexual activities and in talking about sex with others. In negotiating sexual relationships and activities, wider cultural scenarios are interactively shaped 'into scripts for behaviour in specific contexts' (Simon, 1996: 41). Intrapsychic scripting occurs at the level of our individual desires and thoughts, the internal reflexive processes of the self. Unlike the psychoanalytic psyche, where desires originate largely in our unconscious, intrapsychic scripting is a process through which we reflexively interpret material from cultural scenarios and interpersonal experience through internal conversations with ourselves.

The interaction between these levels means that scripts are not fixed: this is not a deterministic perspective, although the concept of scripts is open to this misinterpretation. As Gagnon and Simon themselves note, while the dramaturgical analogy is appropriate for understanding human sexuality – we *act* sexually – 'the conventional dramatic form' is 'more often than not…inappropriate' (1974: 23), since even the most conventional of erotic sequences 'derives from a complicated set of layered symbolic meanings' which might not be the same even for participants in the same sexual 'drama' (1974: 23). Scripts are, therefore, fluid improvisations involving ongoing processes of interpretation and negotiation. Individual sexual histories are also subject to interpretation and reinterpretation. Gagnon and Simon suggest that rather than the past determining the present, 'the present significantly reshapes the past as we reconstruct our biographies to bring them into greater congruence with our current identities, roles, situations and available vocabularies' (Gagnon & Simon, 1974: 13). So, when we remember 'sexual' events in our own childhood they are filtered through the lens of adult sexual understanding and would have had quite different meanings for us at the time. Moreover, what adults see as 'sexual' behaviour in children is also a product of the application of adult sexual scripts, and may not have the same meaning for children themselves.

It was Stevi who first applied this perspective to women's and children's sexuality (Jackson, 1978a, 1978b, 1982), arguing that children only appear to be asexual because adults seek to block their access to crucial aspects of sexual scripts, thus making the acquisition of sexual knowledge and coming to terms with their own sexuality far more problematic than it might otherwise be. This argument was most fully developed in *Childhood and Sexuality* (1982), which begins by drawing attention to the ways in which children are regarded as a special category of person and sexuality as a special area of life – with the latter being seen as inimical to the well-being of the former – hence the idea of childhood 'innocence'. As was argued in Stevi's early work, children are not totally excluded from adult sexual scripts: they learn a great deal about heterosexual romance and marriage, gender and conventions of bodily modesty that are informed by adult understandings of sexuality. They are also often aware when adults are keeping secrets from them. This was cast in terms of the metaphor of a jigsaw from which crucial pieces are missing – notably those relating to desire, pleasure and physical sexual acts – and therefore children have no way of knowing that the pieces they have 'belong to the same puzzle or how they fit together until the missing portion is supplied' (Jackson, 1978b: 342). This idea has underpinned the work we have done together since the early 1990s and was further developed in later publications (e.g. Scott et al., 1998).

We have never denied that children do need protection from potentially predatory adults; the point we have consistently made in our earlier and more recent work is that keeping children in ignorance does not protect them effectively. One illustration of this used in *Childhood and Sexuality* was a story told by one young woman:[3]

> When I was about eight a man called me over to his car and he didn't have any trousers on and that came as a shock . . . I didn't really understand, you know. I didn't think it was wrong or anything – I thought he'd get a cold sitting there without any trousers on, you know – it just didn't seem like anything.
>
> (Jackson, 1982: 61)

Two points were drawn from this. First, had this situation turned threatening, the girl's inability to recognize it as a sexual advance meant that she would have been ill-prepared: her 'innocence' may have put her in potential danger rather than protecting her from it. Secondly, she was not, in fact, in any way upset about it and it did not seem to have had any lasting consequences for her, in part because she told no one about it. It may therefore be that adults overestimate the traumatic effects of such experiences for children and, indeed, may contribute to them by over-reacting. Where children lack knowledge about sex 'they are unlikely to attach the same significance to such encounters as adults would'; if they can interpret such an event only in terms of the horrified responses of their elders, 'it may be made to seem more terrifying than it actually was' (Jackson, 1982: 62).

This second point was somewhat controversial at a time when feminists were working hard to put sexual violence against women and children on the academic and political agenda (Rush, 1980; Herman, 1981; Kelly, 1988). It was not intended to underplay the seriousness of child sexual abuse but to highlight possible unintended consequences of potential adult reactions to it, often fuelled more by the idea that sex in itself was a threat to children rather than the abuse of adult power. In the climate of the 1980s, it became more difficult to argue for this kind of approach (and, arguably, has become increasingly difficult). Although the study of sexuality was becoming more established, it was still marginal within sociology and among feminists it was becoming increasingly contentious as a result of the so-called 'sex wars'. At issue in this context was the tension between the pursuit of sexual autonomy and pleasure on the one hand and the increasing awareness of sexual violence and exploitation on the other. These two concerns are not, of course, mutually exclusive: it would seem self-evident that to enjoy sexual autonomy, women had to be free from the threat of violence and exploitation. In the context of differing feminist positions, what should merely have been a question of priority became instead a polarity, expressed in the title of one of the key texts of the time as between 'pleasure and danger' (Vance, 1984).

A gulf developed between those who defined themselves as 'sex-positive' and were keen to explore all imaginable possibilities for pleasure and to counter all attempts to censor any erotic representations or censure any consensual sexual practices on the one hand and those campaigning against pornography and sexual violence on the other. Our perspective differed from both sides. The 'sex-positive' libertarians seemed to want to argue that children were intrinsically sexual (possibly because of the influence of psychoanalysis) and therefore were against the denial of their sexuality. For example, Gayle Rubin's (1984) argument for a politics of sexuality distinct from a politics of gender includes, among those outlaw sexualities she deems worthy of protection from oppression and opprobrium, 'cross-generational' sex. This stance takes no account of the relative size, experience and power of those involved in such encounters: there is a great deal of difference between an adult man having penetrative sex with a three-year-old (who is unable to consent and unlikely to understand what it is s/he would be consenting to) and the same act between, say, a sexually savvy 15-year-old and an adult – even if, in the latter case, there would probably still be a power relationship. On the other side of the argument, those concerned with the abuse of children wanted to deny, or at least ignore, the possibility of children ever being sexual. For example, one prominent anti-violence feminist took us to task for suggesting that a pre-pubescent girl could masturbate, stating that this would not occur unless she had been abused. Our point was, and is, that a child without access to sexual scripts will not, of course, be able to label this activity as masturbation or even connect it with the pieces of the sexual puzzle she has, but she can nevertheless discover for herself the pleasures of manipulating her own genitals (see Jackson, 1982: 69–70). Our views on childhood and sexuality, then, did not fit with those of either side in the sex wars, and were unacceptable to both.

Nor did our perspective fit well with the dominant theoretical positions of the time. Some feminists were sceptical of a perspective seen as placing too little emphasis on male domination, while most Marxist feminists still tended to think of the social ordering of sexuality in terms of its repression in the interests of capitalism. This latter view was lampooned by Foucault, who argued that that aligning the age of repression with the rise of capitalism helped to perpetuate the repressive hypothesis, a process whereby the 'minor chronicle of sex and its trials is transposed into the ceremonious history of the modes of production' (Foucault, 1981: 5). Prior to the widespread appreciation of Foucault's work, our insistence that sexuality was not constituted through repression was frequently met with incredulity. Foucault changed this, through his understanding of power as productive:

> Sexuality must not be thought of as a natural given which power tries to hold in check, or as an obscure domain which knowledge tries gradually to uncover. It is the name that can be given to a historical construct.
> (Foucault, 1981: 105)

There are obvious resonances here with Gagnon and Simon's critique of the concept of repression and the idea that sexuality is not pre-given and extra-social. The idea that sexuality has been historically constituted as an object of discourse is in many ways compatible with the notion of scripts, particularly at the level of cultural scenarios. Foucault made questioning the idea of repression acceptable within the academic circles we inhabited, but also eclipsed the more interactive focus of Gagnon and Simon. Foucault did, however, provide some new conceptual tools in historicizing the way that sexuality is 'known' and categorized. He also gave some attention to the 'pedagogization of children's sex' from the eighteenth century onwards, characterizing this in terms that still ring true today: 'parents, families, educators ... would have to take charge ... of this precious and perilous, dangerous and endangered sexual potential' (1981: 104). Foucault's work added another element to our critical thinking about childhood and sexuality. It also, of course, became the basis of a much wider growth of theorizing around sexuality in the 1980s and 1990s (Weeks, 1981; Heath, 1982; Butler, 1990; Bell, 1993).

Politics, public health and sex education

The political climate of the1980s presented challenges, with a marked shift to the right in mainstream politics on both sides of the Atlantic and a general weakening of the Left in Britain. The combination of neo-liberal economic policies and moral conservatism that characterized the Thatcher government was particularly bad news for both policy and research on sexuality. Emblematic of this was the infamous 'Section 28' of the Local Government Act 1988, which prohibited local authorities from 'promoting' homosexuality and 'pretended family relationships'. Since schools came under local authority control, this placed restrictions on what could be taught as sex education. Sex education was already limited and patchy, hedged around by the anxiety of revealing 'too much' to children 'too soon' and the difficulties teachers had in talking about sex in the classroom. There had, however, been signs of more relaxed attitudes in some schools, which the 1988 legislation curbed. The irony was that the 1980s was also the era of the AIDS crisis. Because of this, AIDS education became compulsory while teaching about homosexuality was effectively outlawed, and sexuality education in general was squeezed both by the introduction of the national curriculum and the perception of it as a minefield that schools preferred not to risk navigating.

Paradoxically the AIDS crisis did open up the agenda for research into young people's sexual knowledge and practices. It had become apparent that medical and epidemiological research was insufficient in terms of understanding the complexity of what was happening and that social scientific work was essential. Sue (with Janet Holland and Caroline Ramazanoglu) gained funding for research entitled the 'Women Risk and AIDS Project (WRAP)'.[4] For the young women in this study lack of any detailed sexual knowledge prior to engaging in sexual activity was a common factor, as was lack of confidence and therefore a tendency to defer to their male partners. When the young women spoke about their sex education, it was recounted in terms of a 'protective discourse', alerting them to the dangers of sex, and of men, but not equipping them to deal with the challenges of male power or encouraging them to develop any sense of their own sexuality – and certainly not encouraging them to expect sexual pleasure (Thomson & Scott, 1991). Many of the young women spoke in terms of the gendered language of love in that they tended to justify having sex in terms of being in love and to speak of 'going on the pill for him' as a gesture of love. The study illustrated very clearly the complex nature of gendered power relations and the ways in which these were played out in the context of early sexual relationships to the systematic disadvantage of the young women involved (Holland et al. 1990).

In 1993 Sue and Daniel Wight began working together to develop evaluation research on sex education in schools which drew on the WRAP findings and Daniel's earlier work on young men (Wight, 1994), and aimed to utilize an interactionist perspective. This was at a time when sex education was highly contested terrain with a widespread view that too much information would only encourage young people to have sex too soon (Thomson, 1994). However, there was also a high degree of anxiety about what were perceived to be high (and rising) teenage pregnancy rates, relative to the rest of Europe, as well as continuing concern about the risk of STDs. Working with the Health Education Board for Scotland, and an educational consultant, they developed the SHARE programme of sex education lessons for 13–15-year-olds which took as their starting point the need for interaction and negotiation between sexual partners as well as a commitment to focusing on gendered power relations. In 1996 the project received funding from the MRC for a randomized control trial evaluating the impact of SHARE on the recipients' sexual experience and behaviour.[5] There were a number of challenges in carrying out this research, not least the general climate of anxiety about teaching young people about sex; many teachers found it difficult to move away from the still standard biological/reproductive format of sex education (Buston et al., 2001) and there were also concerns that parents would withdraw their children. In fact this was not an issue, and later research (Scott & Botcherby, 2004) reinforced the view that parents were in the main happy for schools to take responsibility for sex education. A more crucial problem was that it had been decreed, during the fieldwork period, that if a teacher was told about instances of under-age sex then they were obliged to report it to social services, thus removing an important avenue of support for young women in particular. This illustrates the ongoing anxiety about young people's sexual behaviour, which was being dealt with in increasingly formalized and bureaucratized ways.

The findings from the initial sweeps of the SHARE evaluation showed that, while those who had undertaken the programme were significantly more likely to feel positive about sex and relationships, they were no more likely to have reduced their risk-taking behaviour than the control group (e.g. their use of condoms was no greater) (Wight et al., 2002). This, rather than simply being a result of the failure of what was the most developed and sustained sex education programme available at the time, is likely to be indicative of a wider cultural negativity about young people's sexuality as well as the embeddedness of gendered power relations.

Risk anxiety and sexualization

We began writing together in the early 1990s, at a time when issues around childhood and sexuality, and increasingly the idea of sexualization as a threat to children, came to the fore. During the mid-1990s there was much public debate about the sexually explicit content of teenage girls' magazines and an attempt, in Britain in 1996, to introduce legislation on providing a minimum age recommendation on the covers of these publications. There was also extensive coverage of the child beauty pageant phenomenon after the murder of a US child beauty queen, JonBenet Ramsay, in December 1996, ensuring that media coverage of sexualized girlhood continued well into 1997. Unsurprisingly public debate was framed in terms of the threat such phenomena posed to childhood, and especially to childhood 'innocence', a concept already the subject of critique by feminists (Ennew, 1986; Kitzinger 1988).[6] This furore was all about girls, with hardly any public discussion about gender as such – and none about what boys might be reading (see Jackson, 1996, 1999; Scott et al., 1998).

Another event had occurred in 1996 which, while not self-evidently sexually motivated, focused attention on risks to children: the killing of 16 children and a teacher at a primary school in Dunblane, Scotland. The perpetrator's homosexuality figured in the tabloid press as part of the characterization of him as a mad beast preying on innocents. The homophobia evident in some of the reportage gave the story a sexual subtext, eliding homosexuality and paedophilia and, in turn, paedophilia and murder. This fed into the stereotype, widespread at the time, of the homosexual as child molester (Scott & Watson-Brown, 1997). This was occurring in a climate of increased concern about child sexual abuse and a generalized risk anxiety about children (Jackson & Scott, 1999, 2013), one manifestation of which was the ramping up of 'stranger danger' education in schools – despite wide acknowledgement that most sexual abuse of children involved known individuals (see Scott et al., 1998).

These events and trends led us to enquire further into the risk anxiety surrounding children and childhood and we successfully applied for funding, along with Katherine Backett-Milburn, for a project investigating this phenomenon (Backett-Milburn et al., 2000).[7] While sexual risk was not the sole focus of the research, it loomed large in the wider landscapes of risk inhabited by our participants. Our data confirmed that keeping sex from children did not protect them from sexual risk – children of nine, ten and eleven tended to equate strangers with strangeness, leading them to fear anyone odd or different. Older children in their early and mid-teens were able, retrospectively, to put the pieces of the puzzle together and link stranger danger to sex, often commenting that they had not been able to do so when they were younger (Backett-Milburn et al., 2000). Most parents were disproportionately worried about sexual risks to children – in particular they were haunted by the image of the paedophile who might abduct and inflict unspeakable things on their children. Even those aware that the actual risk of such events was inflated expressed such anxiety, to the extent that one mother told us that she experienced 'emotional terror' at the prospect of this happening to her children. Externalizing these threats onto the mythic figure of the predatory paedophile was common, expressed forcefully by one father who said:

I think the overwhelming threat is from strangers. Weirdos and creeps, for want of a better word. Weirdos. I mean that is the biggest threat as far as the kids going to play in a play park, is all these pervos that are kicking around.

These anxieties do not seem to have diminished since we conducted this research. Indeed they may have increased, since the imagined 'pervert' is no longer only to be found lurking around parks, but also in cyberspace, ready to invade the supposed safety of the home. In recent years there has been a great deal of concern around the 'grooming' of underage girls for sex with older men. This was brought into sharp focus in 2012 with revelations about the past conduct of the late British media personality, Jimmy Savile, who has been accused of 'grooming a nation' (Cree, 2014). Although the sexual abuse perpetrated by Savile (and other celebrities subsequently accused or convicted of similar acts) spans decades, in the ensuing media frenzy all sense of history has been lost – time is collapsed so that hundreds of offences appear as though they are happening in the here and now – thus exacerbating public anxiety about 'the paedophile' as a threat to children's safety.

The early 21st century has also witnessed increasing public concern about the sexualization of children. In this context, the potential accessibility of pornography to children has provoked outrage: the BBC in covering a report on this issue on 28 March 2014 quoted a spokesperson for the National Society for the Prevention of Cruelty to Children as saying 'even six year olds are accessing porn'. This is one issue among many, from children's clothing to raunchy music videos, that are held to be responsible for the sexualization of children, particularly girls – and sexualized girls are deemed to be at risk of sexual exploitation. Girls are thus seen as requiring protection from sexualization and this is framed in terms of preserving their childlike 'innocence', drawing on the same tropes and mantras evident in the 1990s debates about teen magazines. While there is more discussion about boys and pornography than in previous decades, largely because of the rise of Internet porn, gender hierarchy is still rarely addressed explicitly.

In 2007 the American Psychological Association published a report on the dangers of early sexualization for young girls. Media reportage, in tones of shock and horror, played up the sexualization of children who 'ought' to be innocent. More recently the British government commissioned two reviews on sexualization. One was for the Home Office, focusing on young people (Papadopoulos, 2010); the other, on children, was for the Department for Education, authored by the Chief Executive of the Mothers' Union (Bailey, 2011). Both called for greater protection of children and young people from sexualization, both constructed sexualization as a threat to 'healthy' sexual development and to the very essence of childhood, summed up by the title of the Bailey report: 'Letting Children Be Children'. While there are, of course, grounds for concern about the ways in which women (and girls) are represented in much of the sexual imagery available today, presenting the problem as one of 'lost childhood innocence' misses the point, as many feminist critiques have noted (see Introduction and Chapter 5 in this volume). The effort to keep children ignorant of sex prevents them from being able to make adequate sense of the sexual representations which they will inevitably see around them. Adult anxieties about these issues can serve to render children less safe by potentially depriving them of the knowledge they need to interpret the sexual mores of the world in which they must make the transition to adulthood (see Jackson & Scott, 2010). As numerous feminist critics have noted, there is little or no recognition in these reports of young people's sexual desire, no sense of them as embodied sexual subjects – the focus is on sexual objectification. Good sex, where it is defined, is that based on mutual respect between consenting adult partners, but with no sense of it involving embodied practices and pleasures. The 'missing discourse of desire', noted in critical approaches to sex education (Fine, 1988; Fine & McClelland, 2006), is also evident in these reports on sexualization and in public discourse around it. Somehow young people who are innocent of desire are expected suddenly to become functioning adult sexual actors engaged in 'healthy' sexual practices.

There has been considerable feminist engagement with the issue of sexualization, both in terms of critiquing mainstream interpretations of the phenomenon and in providing alternative perspectives. In particular attention has been drawn to the 'limited and commodified vision of active female sexuality' in the media (Attwood, 2006: 83), the reinforcement of normative heterosexuality, the classed and racialized dimensions of the imagery and so on (e.g. Tolman, 2002; Attwood, 2006; Gill, 2009; Faulkner, 2011; Renold & Ringrose, 2013). This matters because the representations of sexuality available to children and young people are part of the discourses or cultural scenarios on which they draw in making sense of their own sexuality and locating themselves as competent sexual actors. If these are limited in terms of their representation of gendered sexual practices, this potentially also limits the resources young people can access in constructing a sense of sexual selfhood and in developing sexual practices.

It is important, however, not to locate children and young people as cultural dopes, as passive recipients of media messages (Buckingham & Bragg, 2004). It is equally important in recognizing children's agency not to equate it with resistance. If we see girls as either 'brainwashed' by the media or as in rebellion against dominant discourses, we lose sight of the actualities of their everyday experience and practices. As Danielle Egan says: 'In the end, we may demonize, exoticize, or canonize the girl' as 'only a victim' or as 'an agentic warrior' so that 'either way, she becomes a figure frozen in the amber of adult projection' (2013: 135). Feminists, in particular, should know to be wary of homogenizing girls in any way since we have long critiqued the notion of 'the woman' as a monolithic category and would not have wanted our younger selves to be subjected to such stereotyping.

Our objection to the stereotyping conceptions of children, especially girls, as innocent victims, as 'bad girls' (sluts and proto-criminals) or as proto-feminist rebels resisting dominant discourse is one reason for our continued allegiance to the interactionist perspective of Gagnon and

Simon. Developing their perspective allows for a nuanced understanding of the relationship between cultural scenarios, interpersonal interaction and intrapsychic self-reflexivity through which sexual selves are constructed and sexual practices learnt and enacted. It enables us to conceptualize agency not as resistance to social forces but as a product of social interaction, involving active intersubjective interpretation of cultural scenarios (such as sexualized imagery). It is this understanding of children as active interpreters of their social worlds, as engaged in making sense of it with their peers, that is missing from most of the public debate around sexualization. Feminist researchers, as this volume demonstrates, are engaged in constructing alternative approaches and, in our view, the interactionist perspective has much to offer here.

In particular, Gagnon and Simon's perspective might enable us to think about the ways in which changing cultural scenarios in Western societies are affecting the process of becoming sexual. In all the public controversy about the sexualization of girls, what goes unnoticed or unsaid is the reverse process – the desexualization of girls. Not only do efforts continue to be made to keep children asexual, but also the supposed sexualization of girls in particular is very much focused on a surface commodification of young women's bodies (as sexual objects), not on their lived embodied experience of themselves as sexual subjects. Young women are thus deprived of space to develop an autonomous sexuality – and this is becoming increasingly problematic given the contradictions of contemporary Western sexual culture. In the relatively recent past, the process of developing from asexual childhood to adult femininity was assumed to be a transition to a passive sexuality in which women were recipients of men's sexual activity. Our memories of our own teenage years in the 1960s were that all the discussion among girls was about what we were willing to 'let' boys do to us; we were not expected to be active initiators of sexual practice, nor to demonstrate sexual expertise, except possibly in relation to kissing. While double standards certainly persist, and young women may still be expected to be sexual gatekeepers, what is expected in terms of sexual practice has changed. As some commentators have noted, young adult women are now addressed in popular media as active desiring subjects – within certain limits (e.g. Attwood, 2006). Performance anxiety is no longer reserved for men; in heterosexual relations women are exhorted to develop expertise in techniques designed to 'please your man' and also to be 'in touch' with their own bodily pleasure. Thus the transition from asexual child to sexually competent adult woman has become more complex. We need to know more about how this transition is managed, how young women negotiate becoming sexual in the context of their everyday lives. Gagnon and Simon's focus on the everyday can illuminate the ways in which sexuality is intertwined with other aspects of life.

A feminist sociological understanding of children, young people and sexuality should also attend to the material social and political contexts in which everyday sexual lives are lived and which constrain choices and opportunities available to young people. In many ways contemporary Western sexual mores have been liberalized, with increasing openness about sexuality, the availability of more information, greater opportunities for women's sexual and social autonomy and increased tolerance of sexual diversity (Weeks, 2007). Yet this is occurring in a climate of widening gaps between rich and poor and a neo-liberal agenda that places more emphasis on individual and family responsibility and accommodates diversity only insofar as it does not disrupt this familial focus (Richardson, 2005; Heaphy, 2014). The category of 'the child' or 'children' held to be at risk from a sexualized culture has little to do with actual children; it is constructed in terms of an idealized notion of childhood (of children shielded from the world within happy families). Inflating the dangers of sexualization conceals more significant everyday threats to children's well-being that derive from gender, class and racialized inequalities (Cree et al., 2014) as well as specific forms of sexual and other risks to children from abusive adults.

Notes

1. These conditions were, in part, documented in Schofield's pioneering study (1965) and changed little for most young women in the following two decades (Jackson, 1980; Lees, 1986).
2. While we have cited published sources, most of the writing on the politics of sexuality in the early 1970s was circulated in pamphlets and newsletters produced in mimeographed form – this was long before personal computers existed or even photocopiers. Much has therefore been lost, though some is preserved in feminist archives and libraries.
3. She was one of those interviewed by Stevi in 1973 and 1974.
4. The WRAP project, which was funded by the UK Economic and Social Research Council, ran from 1988 to 1991 involved 148 in-depth interviews with young heterosexual women aged 16–21 in London and Manchester, exploring their understandings and experience of sex and relationships in general and in the context of the risk of HIV infection.
5. The research involved 7,600 young people, in East and Central Scotland, half of whom were attending schools in which the SHARE programme was delivered and half were in control schools receiving the standard sex education lessons.
6. There have, of course, been a number of publications since that time critiquing the public deployment of the concept of innocence, for example, Kincaid (1998); Egan & Hawkes (2010); Faulkner (2011); Egan (2013).
7. Funding came from the ESRC for the Children and Risk Anxiety (CARA) project in which, between 1997 and 2000, we interviewed both parents and children.

References

Attwood, F. (2006) Sexed up: Theorizing the sexualization of culture. *Sexualities*, 9 (1), 77–94.

Backett-Milburn, K., Scott, S., Jackson, S., & Harden, J. (2000) Scary faces, scary places: Children's perceptions of risk and safety. *Health Education Journal*, 59, 12–22.

Bailey, R. (2011) *Letting children be children – Report of an independent review of the commercialisation and sexualisation of childhood*. London: Department for Education.

Bell, V. (1993) *Interrogating incest: Feminism, Foucault and the law*. London: Routledge.

Boston Women's Health Collective (1973) *Our bodies ourselves*. Boston, MA: Boston Women's Health Collective.

Brownmiller, S. (1975) *Against our will: Men, women and rape*. London: Secker and Warburg.

Buckingham, D., & Bragg, S. (2004) *Young people, sex and the media: The facts of life?* Basingstoke: Palgrave Macmillan.

Buston, K., Wight, D., & Scott, S. (2001) Difficulty and diversity: The context and practice of sex education. *British Journal of the Sociology of Education*, 22 (3), 353–368.

Butler, J. (1990) *Gender trouble: Feminism and the subversion of identity*. New York: Routledge.

Cree, V., Clapton, G., & Smith, M. (2014) Moral panics, Jimmy Savile and social work: A 21st century morality tale. *Discover Society*, 5. www.discoversociety.org

Egan, D. R. (2013) *Becoming sexual: A critical appraisal of the sexualization of girls*. Cambridge: Polity.

Egan, D. R. & Hawkes, G. (2010) *Theorizing the sexual child in modernity*. Basingstoke: Palgrave Macmillan.

Ennew, J. (1986) *The sexual exploitation of children*. Cambridge: Polity.

Faulkner, J. (2011) *The importance of being innocent: Why we worry about children*. Cambridge: Cambridge University Press.

Fine, M. (1988) Sexuality, schooling and adolescent females: The missing discourse of desire. *Harvard Educational Review*, 58 (1), 29–51.

Fine, M., & McClelland, S. (2006) Sexuality education and desire: Still missing after all these years. *Harvard Educational Review*, 76 (3), 297–338.

Ford, C., & Beach, F. (1951) *Patterns of sexual behavior*. New York: Harper and Brothers.

Foucault, M. ([1978] 1981) *The history of sexuality volume one*. London: Pelican.

Gagnon, J. (1965) Sexuality and sexual learning in the child. *Psychiatry*, 28, 212–228.

Gagnon, J. (1973) The creation of the sexual in early adolescence, in S. Groubard (Ed.) *From Twelve to Sixteen*. New York: W. W. Norton.

Gagnon, J., & Simon, W. (1974) *Sexual conduct*. London: Hutchinson.

Gill, R. (2009) Beyond the 'sexualization of culture' thesis: An intersectional analysis of 'sixpacks', 'Midriffs' and 'hot lesbians' in advertising. *Sexualities*, 12 (2), 137–160.

Greer, G. (1970) *The female Eunuch*. London: Paladin.

Griffin, S. (1971) Rape: The all-American crime. *Ramparts*, 10 (3), 2–8.

Heaphy, B. (2014) Same-sex marriage: Time to celebrate? *Discover Society*: 6. Retrieved from: www.discoversociety.org

Heath, S. (1982) *The sexual fix*. London: Macmillan.

Herman, J. L. (1981) *Father-daughter incest*. Cambridge, MA: Harvard University Press.

Holland, J., Ramazanoglu, C., Scott, S., Sharpe, S., & Thomson, R. (1990) *Don't die of ignorance – I nearly died of embarrassment: Condoms in context*. London: Tufnell Press.

Jackson, S. (1978a) *On the social construction of female sexuality*. London: Women's Research and Resources Centre.

Jackson, S. (1978b) How to make babies: Sexism and sex education. *Women's Studies International Quarterly*, 1 (4), 341–352.

Jackson, S. (1980) Girls and sexual knowledge, in D. Spender & E. Sarah (Eds.) *Learning to Lose*. London: The Women's Press.

Jackson, S. (1982) *Childhood and sexuality*. Oxford: Blackwell.

Jackson, S. (1996) Ignorance is bliss when you're just seventeen. *Trouble & Strife*, 33, 50–60.

Jackson, S. (1999) *Heterosexuality in question*. London: Sage.

Jackson, S., & Scott, S., (1999) Risk anxiety and the social construction of childhood, in D. Lupton (Ed.) *Risk and Sociocultural Theory: New Directions and Perspectives*. Cambridge: Cambridge University Press.

Jackson, S. & Scott, S. (2010) *Theorizing sexuality*. Maidenhead: Open University Press.

Jackson, S. & Scott, S. (2013) Childhood, in G. Payne (Ed.) *Social Divisions*, 3rd edn. Basingstoke: Palgrave Macmillan, pp. 182–199.

Kelly, L. (1988) *Surviving sexual violence*. Cambridge: Polity.

Kitzinger, J. (1988) Defending innocence: Ideologies of childhood. *Feminist Review* 28, 77–87.

Kincaid, J. R. (1998) *Erotic innocence: The culture of child molesting*. Durham, NC: Duke University Press.

Koedt, A (1972) The myth of the vaginal orgasm, in A. Koedt (Ed.) *Radical Feminism*. New York: Quadrangle, pp. 198–207.

Laumann, E., Gagnon, J., Michael, R. T., & Michaels, S. (1994) *The social organization of sexuality. Sexual practices in the United States*. Chicago, IL: University of Chicago Press.

Lees, S. (1986) *Losing out: Sexuality and adolescent girls*. London: Hutchinson.

Lydon, S. (1970) The politics of orgasm, in R. Morgan (Ed.) *Sisterhood Is Powerful*. New York: Vintage Books, pp. 210–227.

Marcuse, H. (1964) *One dimensional man*. London: Routledge & Kegan Paul.

Mead, M. (1935) *Sex and temperament in three primitive societies*. London: George Routledge and Sons.

Medea, A., & Thompson, K. (1974) *Against rape*. New York: Farrer, Strauss and Giroux.

Millet, K. (1971) *Sexual politics*. London: Rupert Hart-Davis Ltd.

Papadopoulos, L. (2010) *Sexualisation of young people*. London: Home Office.

Piercy, M. (1970) The grand coolie damn, in R. Morgan (Ed.) *Sisterhood Is Powerful*. New York: Vintage Books.

Plummer, K. (2001) In Memoriam: William Simon (1930–2000). *Sexualities*, 4 (2), 131–134.

Red Collective ([1973]1978) *The politics of sexuality in capitalism*. London: Red Collective/Publications Distribution Cooperative.

Reich, W. (1951) *The sexual revolution*. London: Vision Press.

Renold, E., & Ringrose, J. (Eds.) (2013) Feminisms, 'sexualisation' andcontemporary girlhoods. *Feminist Theory* (special issue) 14 (3).

Richardson, D. (2005) Desiring sameness? The rise of a neoliberal politics of normalisation. *Antipode* 37 (3), 515–535.

Rubin, G. (1984) Thinking sex: Notes for a radical theory of the politics of sexuality, in C. Vance (Ed.) *Pleasure and Danger*. London: Routledge & Kegan Paul, pp. 267–319.

Rush, F. (1980) *The best kept secret*. Englewood Cliffs, NJ: Prentice Hall.

Schofield, P. (1965) *The sexual behaviour of young people*. London: Longmans.

Scott, S., & Botcherby, S. (2004) *Parents as sex educators*, Report for Durham Education Authority.

Scott, S., Jackson, S., & Backett-Milburn, K. (1998) Swings and roundabouts: Risk anxiety and the everyday worlds of children. *Sociology*, 32 (4), 689–705.

Scott, S., & Watson-brown, L. (1997) The beast, the family and the innocent children. *Trouble and Strife*, 36, 36–40.

Simon, W. (1996) *Postmodern sexualities*. New York: Routledge.

Simon, W., & Gagnon, J. (1969) On psychosexual development, in D. A. Goslin (Ed.) *Handbook of Socialization Theory and Research*. Chicago, IL: Rand McNally, pp. 733–752.

Simon, W. & Gagnon, J. (1984) Sexual scripts: Permanence and change. *Archives of Sexual Behavior*, 15 (2), 97–120.

Snitow, A., Stansell, C., & Thompson, S. (1984) 'Introduction', in *Desire: The politics of sexuality*. London: Virago.

Thomson, R. (1994) Moral rhetoric and public health pragmatism: The recent politics of sex education. *Feminist Review*, 48, 40–60.

Thomson, R. & Scott, S. (1991) *Learning about sex*. London: Tufnell Press.

Tolman, D. (2002) *Dilemmas of desire*. Cambridge, MA: Harvard University Press.

Vance, C. S. (Ed.) (1984) *Pleasure and danger*. London: Routledge & Kegan Paul.

Weeks, J. (1981) *Sex politics and society*. London: Longman.

Weeks, J. (1990) *Sex politics and society*, 2nd edn. London: Longman.

Weeks, J. (2007) *The world we have won the remaking of erotic and intimate life*. London: Routledge.

Whiting, P. (1972) Female sexuality: It's politics implications, in M. Wandor (Ed.) *The Body Politic*. London: Stage 1, pp. 189–213.

Wight, D. (1994) Boys' thoughts and talk about sex in a working class locality of Glasgow. *The Sociological Review*, 42 (4), 703–737.

Wight, D. et al. (2002) The limits of teacher-delivered sex education: Interim behavioural outcomes from a randomised trial. *British Medical Journal*, 324, 1430–1435.

4
Reappraising Youth Subcultures and the Impact upon Young People's Sexual Cultures: Links and Legacies in Studies of Girlhood

Mary Jane Kehily and Joseph De Lappe

Introduction

In this chapter, we aim to consider the links between youth subcultures and young people's sexual cultures and particularly how the concept of youth subcultures has had an impact upon the study of young people's sexual cultures, leaving a distinguished legacy of ideas and methods that have had a generative impact upon the fields of education and childhood studies. Studies of youth subcultures burgeoned in the post-war period as a way of making sense of the self-generated activity of young people in broader terms than the pathologizing themes of deviancy or youthful rebellion that permeated prior studies (Hall & Jefferson, 1976). Largely associated with the disciplines of sociology and cultural studies in the US and the UK, youth subcultural studies, at their most persuasive, provide compelling accounts of youthful expression: reading and interpreting what young people say and do in the collective stylization of subgroups such as teddy boy, mod, punk, skinhead or goth. Since the high-water mark of subcultural research in the 1970s, the concept of subculture has been subject to successive waves of critique, the most recent questioning its explanatory power in a changed environment that can be described as post-subcultural (Muggleton & Weinzier, 2004). While recognizing the salience of much critical commentary, this chapter argues for an acknowledgement of its rich heritage, revisiting youth subcultures as a generative approach to understanding children and young people as social actors in the present. Contrary to debates suggesting that the concept of subcultures has outlived its usefulness and in need of radical revision (Maffesoli, 1995; Bennett, 1999, 2001; Hesmondhalgh, 2005), we argue for the renewed recognition of subcultural ideas and methods as part of an intellectual legacy that can be seen in contemporary studies of girlhood, gender and sexuality. The chapter is divided into five sections. Beginning with a discussion of youth subcultures as a concept characterized by the distinctive approach pioneered at the Centre for Contemporary Cultural Studies at the University of Birmingham, the body of the paper considers the influence of the subcultural in contemporary research on girlhood in sections on the links between youth subcultures and a case study of the Lolita subculture in Japan. A final section extends earlier discussions into an account of the impact of subculture as a concept that is now dispersed across many spheres of experience, carrying ideas into different sociocultural and geographic locations.

Conceptualizing youth subcultures

Reflecting on being in London in 1988 just as the rave music scene exploded in what became known as the second 'summer of love', Spaceman says:

> It was brilliant. Brilliant. And then I met this gang of guys, and this is where my descent, my climb into the big league of pissheads and fucking scammers and working-class yobbos really started. I started knocking round with them.
>
> (quoted in Williamson, 2004: 58)

Williamson's serial ethnography of the Milltown Boys, a group of working-class young men he first met in the 1970s, presents an insider account of youth subculture within the context of deindustrialization and a shrinking labour market. Williamson's work can be placed within a tradition of subcultural studies defined in the1940s as:

> a subdivision of a national culture, composed of a combination of factorable social situations such as class status, ethnic background, regional, rural or urban residence, and religious affiliation, but forming in their combination a functioning unity which has an integrated impact on the participating individual.
>
> (Gordon 1947, in Gelder & Thornton (Eds.)
> *The Subcultures Reader,* p. 41)

This early definition allowed sociologists and cultural anthropologists to look at aspects of difference and diversity within Western societies. Foreshadowing Street's idea of culture as a verb, A. K. Cohen (1947) explored subcultural formations as a way of understanding and explaining what people *do*. In Cohen's analysis subcultures arise when people with similar problems get together to look for solutions; however, achieving status within a subculture may entail a loss of status in the wider culture. Classic studies of subcultures during this period elaborated upon Cohen's analysis by seeking to explain the contrast between the dominant values of society and the values of marginal groups, as in William Whyte's study (1943) *Street Corner Society: The Social Structure of an Italian American Slum* and Jock Young's later study (1971) *The Drugtakers*. These studies illustrate respectively the subcultural connection to place, in Whyte's case the youth of Boston's North End, as well as to particular practices such as drug use or hanging out.

The cultural studies approach to youth subcultures

The cultural studies approach to youth subcultures is largely associated with the Centre for Contemporary Cultural Studies (CCCS) at the University of Birmingham, UK (1964–2002). CCCS researchers focused upon subcultural formations among young people in 1970s and 1980s Britain. In an influential collection, *Resistance through Rituals, Youth Subcultures in Postwar Britain* (Hall & Jefferson 1976), CCCS researchers trace their interest in youth subcultures as expressive forms of resistance that make connections between everyday experience, social class, culture and the wider society. Engaging in subcultural activity involves young people in acts of 'articulation' – the bringing together of different elements in particular contexts, in ways that make sense to the individuals concerned. Hall and Jefferson (1976) suggest that working-class youth subcultures involve young people in a 'double articulation' firstly with their parents' culture and secondly the broader culture of post-war social change. Skinhead subculture, for example, is theorized as seeking a 'magical solution' to the decline of traditional working-class communities in the UK. Skinhead style can be seen as an embodied response to the emasculating affect of unemployment and immigration, made visible through the enactment of an aggressive and exaggerated whiteness that parodied the look of a manual worker (Clarke, 1976). To view youth subcultures as adolescent rebellion is to underestimate the extent to which young people seek to speak to and comment upon generational change and social structures.

From a cultural studies perspective, youth subcultures appear as purposeful interventions, imbued with meaning. This perspective has had a generative impact upon subsequent studies of skinhead culture. Demonstrating the fluidity of subcultural signifiers, Healy (1996) documents the experiences of working-class gay men in Europe and the US who adopt the skinhead look to assert their homosexual masculinity. Keen to distance themselves from middle-class gays and stereotypical embodiments of 'camp' style, skinheads in Healy's study sought to demonstrate that being gay did not necessarily involve a compromise with the 'hardness' associated with white, class-coded masculinity. Further studies of skinhead culture build upon Clarke's early work to explore the performativity of whiteness as an ethnicity in suburban locations (Nayak, 1999) and the appropriation of skinhead identity among young people in post-Soviet Russia (Pilkington et al., 2010). While the meaning of Skin is subject to flux and change, the CCCS approach to understanding young people through subcultural activity remains a productive, adaptable and much-utilized method.

School-based subcultures

Of all the work to emerge from the Birmingham School in the 1970s, the publication of Willis's *Learning to Labour* (1977) casts the longest shadow over contemporary studies of young people's sexual cultures. Willis's compelling school-based ethnography of a working-class peer group in the English West Midlands focuses on the high jinks and anti-school antics of the 'lads', a group of nonconformist boys who achieve their status through dominance over the other less rebellious boys, the 'ear'oles'. The focus on student experience, the identification of intra-group differences within the school population and the relationship between informal student cultures and leaning processes highlight key features of the text that have had an influential and enduring impact upon school-based work. Subsequent studies documenting the gendered, sexualized and racialized nature of student culture such as, cool guys, swots and wimps (Connell, 1989), kazzies, DBTs and try hards (Nilan, 1992) macho lads, academic achievers, new entrepreneurs and real Englishmen (Mac an Ghaill, 1994), gang girls, faith girls, survivors and rebels (Shain, 2003) can be seen as part of a rich tradition of educational research that builds upon and elaborates Willis's creative approach.

Willis observes how achieving and maintaining within student culture lies in the ability of 'the lads' to milk every moment for humour. Ridiculing teachers and other students, fooling around and finding ever more creative ways of "aving a laff" becomes the lads' main reason for attending school. This accomplished comedic repertoire, Willis argues, serves as preparatory work for the trickery and subversion needed to survive the manual labouring and factory work that await the lads on leaving school. In this sense, the self-styled culture of the lads enacts the significance of the book's subtitle, 'how working class kids get working-class jobs'. Willis's study has been much critiqued for the treatment of unheard and marginal voices embedded in the text. The absence of teachers', ear'oles' and girls' perspectives places the lads at the centre of the ethnographic gaze as class-based rather than gender-located subjects. Rereading *Learning to Labour* through the lens of recent work on young people's sexual cultures, it is interesting to trace the muted presence of the girls in intermittent cameo appearances as girlfriends or as the object of sexual jokes and boasts:

> It was in the sexual realm especially that 'the lads' felt their superiority over the 'ear'oles' . . .

Joey: We've [the lads] all bin with women and all that (…) we counted it up the other day, how many kids had actually been with a woman like, how many kids we know been and actually had a shag…

Lascivious tales of conquest or jokes turning on the passivity of women or on the particular sexual nature of men are regular topics of conversation. Always it is their own experience, and not that of the girl or their shared relationship, which is the focus of the stories. The girls are afforded no particular identity save that of their sexual attraction:

X: I was at this party snogging this bird, and I was rubbing her up and suddenly felt a hand on my prick, racking me off…I thought, 'Fucking hell, we're in here', and tried to put my hand down her knickers, but she stopped me…I thought, 'That's funny, her's racking me off but won't let me get down her knickers'. Anyway we was walking home and Joe said to me, 'How did you get on with that bird, was she racking you off?'. I said, 'Yeah, how do you know?'. He said, 'It warn't her, it was me behind you putting my hand up between your legs!' (pp. 15–43).

While the sexism and homosociality of 'the lads' is much commented on, the desire and erotic charge that may exist *between* lads is largely unscrutinized. The lads themselves are quick to disavow any affiliation with homosexuality; same sex attraction commonly featuring in the slap-stick routines of 'the lads' as an object of ridicule and disgust that is further animated by the fear of contagion (Nayak & Kehily, 1996). Running in parallel with homophobic rituals and everyday sexism is a desire to achieve the heteronormative ideal – to find the right girl and settle down. Willis's respondent Spike expresses the pleasure of serious courtship as:

I've got the right bird, I've been going' out with her for eight months. Her's as good as gold. She wouldn't look at another chap. She's fucking done well, she's clean. She loves doing fucking housework…She's as good as gold and I wanna get married as soon as I can. (p. 45)

Beyond the Birmingham School

Within the context of the exaggerated heteronormativity of working-class youth in the 1970s, it is perhaps unsurprising that the heaviest critique of Birmingham subcultural studies has focused on gender (Griffin, 1985). Early studies profiled/celebrated young men's dominance of public space and viewed the street as a backdrop for the unfolding of male subcultural activity (Corrigan, 1979). Girls and young women were often invisible in these studies or occupied marginal positions in the home and the bed-room (McRobbie & Garber, 1976; Canaan, 1991). This was, at least in part, a reflection of the gendered social relations of the time; subsequently challenged and reconfigured through processes of feminist struggle and social change in the intervening decades. A less commented upon absence in early CCCS studies of subculture is sexuality itself. While most subcultures developed a distinctive approach to the sexual, sexuality was rarely a defining feature of the subculture or its participants. Rather, sexuality remained a trope within the wider expression of subculture style, signalling a particular approach or attitude congruent with the group's shared values. In what has become part of subcultural mythology, hippies famously advocated free love and permissiveness largely within heterosexual norms amid an abundance of hair, velvet and cheesecloth (Green, 1999). By contrast, and in a self-conscious inversion of hippy values, punks reputedly hated sex. Punk style incorporated the accoutrements of pornography – bondage gear, fetish garments, chains, leather and rapist's masks. The provocative look declared that sex had little to offer beyond the shock value generated by the displacement of its signs – and romantic love was out of the question. In keeping with punk sensibility of the time, in 1976 John Lydon commented, 'By the time you're 20 you just think – yawn – just another squelch session' (quoted in Savage, 1991: 189), while Boy George famously claimed he would rather have a nice cup of tea.

How has the experience of being a girl changed since the 1960s and 1970s? Contemporary research on girlhood indicates that there are different ways of being a girl and that femininity is no longer so rigidly defined or hinged to the domestic. The embracing of pleasure by young women in the 1990s and 2000s through leisure spheres such as rave/club culture, television, magazine readership and fashion and beauty has been observed by feminist scholars as the emergence of new forms of femininity marked by moments of celebration, freedom and fun (McRobbie, 1996; Brunsdon, 1997; Hermes, 2006). Terms such as 'post-feminism', 'third wave feminism' and 'new femininities' have been deployed to characterize the changes in young women's experiences and their engagement with the social world. The terms themselves are open to contestation in different contexts, signalling both an anti-feminist backlash and new ways of understanding feminism in contemporary times (Hollows and Moseley, 2006).

At one level, the 'post' of post-feminism signifies a way of thinking and acting beyond the rubric of feminism and may imply some critique of former orthodoxies. However, as with other terms such as post-colonialism or postmodernism the new moment cannot fully escape the shadow of the past, but grows out of it. As Sonnett (1999: 170) declares, 'The current post-feminist "return" to feminine pleasures (to dress, cosmetics, visual display, to Wonderbra "sexiness") is "different" because, it is suggested, it takes place within a social context fundamentally altered by the achievement of feminist goals'. In this respect, gender in late-modernity is characterized by a blurring of boundaries between the feminine and feminist. Young women's presence in the night-time economy is equally as visible as young mens' as the girls' night out, birthday celebrations and hen parties become a high-profile feature of the city centre pub and club scene. The contemporary moment appears to further enhance the emergence of new femininities in its appeal to subjects as agentic controllers of their own destiny (Beck, 1992). This poses complex issues for sexual politics when girls and young women's participation in the sex industry and employment in gentlemen's clubs may also be claimed as an expression of autonomous girlhood. Like feminist subjectivities, this 'active girlhood' places an emphasis on the rights of the individual to be an active sexual subject without recourse to moral judgement from patriarchal or feminist discourse.

Enduring themes

An obvious link between youth subcultures and young people's sexual cultures can be found in the way both bodies of work locate themselves within the cultural sphere. Culture can refer to the traditions of a particular society or community, but it can also be used more narrowly to refer to artistic forms and practices, in the sense of 'high culture'. From a cultural studies, perspective culture is defined more inclusively as everyday social practice in which no distinction is made between 'high' and 'low' culture and their associated practices. The idea of culture is extended to include the commonplace routines and practices that characterize and bind together a particular group or community. Culture, in this sense, can be observed and studied in day-to-day engagements with the social world, drawing upon the work of Raymond Williams (1961, 1989) who insisted that *culture is ordinary*. Williams refers to the everydayness of culture as a *way of life* that makes sense to individuals involved in a particular community. This perspective also sees culture as a form of action: it is not just something that people have, it is also what people *do*. Street (1993) suggests that 'culture is a verb', indicating that it can be seen as a dynamic process rather than a fixed entity. Culture is something that people actively produce in their day-to-day activities. Applying these ideas to children and young people has important consequences for understandings of gender and sexuality. Working within the lineage of culture as everyday social practice, viewing the activities of young people as a way of making sense of the world and taking their place within it establishes a way of looking that can be applied to children's self-activity and particularly the idea of young people's sexual cultures.

Many contemporary studies of girlhood generatively explore earlier subcultural themes: culture; style; meaning – using familiar methods of ethnographic observation and semiotic analysis. The following case study provides a rich example of this fusion, using subcultural analysis to make girls visible in ways that highlight the playful negotiation of gender and sexuality in a specific cultural context.

Lolita: Case study of a contemporary youth subculture

In 21st-century Japan, youth cultures often revolve around a constantly evolving set of very distinctive 'street fashions'. Yuniya Kawamura (2006) explains that these fashions are not produced or controlled by professional fashion designers, but by teenage girls who rely on their distinctive appearance to produce a subcultural identity. Lolita or 'Loli' is a particular subcultural aesthetic, which is often associated with the Harajuku area of Tokyo where many Lolis gather to socialize and to pose for photographs. Although the subculture is not exclusively female, there are far more female Lolis than male.

In the Western world, the term Lolita is likely to evoke the eponymous heroine and sexually precocious girl of Vladimir Nabokov's 1955 novel. Yet, while the subculture does reference this character in its name, Lolita takes on a completely different meaning in the context of Japanese youth culture. The roots of the Loli subculture can be traced back to the kawaii or cute trend in 1970s and 1980s Japan. In the 1980s, band members within the newly emerging visual-kei (or visual style) music scene began to wear elaborate costumes and make-up which explored what has become known as the Lolita aesthetic. This very distinctive style of dress draws upon and adapts a wide range of influences, including British Victoriana, particularly porcelain dolls and Lewis Carroll's *Alice in Wonderland* books, and Japanese popular cultural forms. In addition to visual-kei bands and celebrities, the style is influenced by characters from anime and manga (Japanese animation and comics).

By the beginning of the 21st century, the Lolita subculture had grown in popularity within Japan and internationally. A wide variety of Lolita-style clothes and accessories can be bought in specialist boutiques and, increasingly, in mainstream shops. The Lolita aesthetic centres round an idealized image of Victorian childhood. Lolis wear clothes designed to de-emphasize the features of an adult female body; they use flattened bodices, high waists and full skirts with voluminous underskirts in order to conceal their bust and hips. They often wear their hair in ringlets with a bonnet, and make use of a range of accessories, including aprons, small bags, stuffed animals or parasols. This style of dress is complemented by striking poses intended to evoke the illusion of a very young girl or of a porcelain doll. When posing for photographs, Lolis often stand with their knees together and toes pointed inwards and their head inclined to one side; a stylization that embodies a regressed state of girlhood that is both innocent and knowing at the same time.

This 'classic' or 'traditional' Lolita aesthetic has diversified into a wide range of different subgenres. 'Sweet Lolitas' emphasize the kawaii (or cute) aspects of the style and incorporate overtly Romantic or Rococo elements, and 'Gothic Lolitas' incorporate influences from Victorian mourning dress

into the overall aesthetic and make use of a range of cute yet macabre acces
sories (such as coffin-shaped bags or injured teddy bears). Indeed, the Gothic
Lolita look is so popular that it is often said to have produced its own sub
genres, such as Elegant Gothic Lolita or Elegant Gothic Aristocrat Lolita, who
wear longer dresses and use different accessories.

Kawamura (2006) argues that Lolita identities are resolutely not politica
or ideological; Lolita is primarily an aesthetic and the subculture is con
cerned with the production and display of innovative fashion. Despite this
claim, she argues that Japanese street fashions are a way for young people to
express shifting cultural values in contemporary Japanese society. The Lolita
subculture challenges traditional Japanese values. For Osmud Rahman and
colleagues (2011) the Lolita subculture in Japan, and in South East Asia more
generally, is as much a way of reacting to societal pressures as it is an expres
sion of their dreams and fantasies. The subculture provides young Lolitas
with a way to escape from their immediate realities and to express their
feelings about their lives and experiences as young women. Far from being
resolutely a-political, then, the Lolita subculture is intricately interwoven
with contemporary Japanese sexual and gender politics.

Winge (2008) argues that the Lolita subculture in Japan is a combina
tion of both distinctive dress and what she calls 'ritualised performance'
in particular public spaces. She describes the experience of these perfor
mances in terms of the 'carnivalesque' insofar as they allow Lolitas some
release from the usual norms of Japanese society. By performing as part o
this subcultural community, Lolitas are able to assert their difference from
mainstream society without entirely abandoning the collectivism privileged
in Japanese culture. Winge explains that Lolitas attempt to prolong child
hood through the use of extensive use of kawaii or cuteness. As a result, the
Lolita subculture may appear to be anti-feminist because it portrays an idea
of feminine passivity by valorizing the image of virginal youth. However
Winge argues that the doll-like Lolita aesthetic creates a safe space for young
women to perform their sexuality.

The Lolita subculture has caused controversy both within Japan and
internationally. Much of this controversy centres around issues of female
sexuality and sexualization, particularly surrounding lolicon (a Japanese
portmanteau of 'Lolita complex') or sexual attraction to prepubescent girls
Winge argues that the Lolita subculture is entirely separate from lolicon as
a sexual fetish. She explains that although Lolitas attempt to prolong child
hood through the use of kawaii, they are striving to create the appearance
of living dolls, rather than young girls. In contrast, Mackie (2009) argues
that the Lolita aesthetic and lolicon are different manifestations of the same
anxiety about female sexuality: Lolitas are attempting to escape from the
pressures within Japanese society by prolonging their girlhood, while adul
men choose to focus on the image of young girls which they find less
threatening than adult women.

Since its emergence as a subculture some decades ago, the Lolita subculture has grown in popularity and influenced popular culture both within Japan and internationally. A range of dedicated fashion labels and accessory boutiques have emerged to supply the subculture, although many Lolitas continue to adapt these items or make their own. The subculture has also been commodified for consumption within Japanese popular culture more generally, particularly in manga, anime and video game franchises. As a result, the Lolita aesthetic has been embraced outside the subculture, particularly among cosplayers (fans who choose to dress up as characters from their favourite anime, manga or video game). Winge explains that cosplayers are not really considered to be part of the Lolita subculture; even though they share the same aesthetic, Lolitas feel that cosplayers do not really understand Lolita culture.

Aided by the global export of Japanese media products, the Lolita subculture has begun to circulate globally, and dedicated boutiques and fashion labels have emerged in Australia and in the UK. Mackie (2009) explains that Lolita brands are not designed for export; they are intricately linked with the dreams and frustrations of young women in Japan, and with rebellion against Japanese society. This means that the Lolita aesthetic rarely reflects the Japanese subculture when it is adopted for global consumption. For example, the American singer, Gwen Stefani, incorporated a group of female dancers known as the Harajuku Girls into her act. In doing so, she removed the subculture from its original performative context, and adapted it to the norms of Western music videos. The overt sexualization of the aesthetic in the Harajuku Girls was the source of much discontent within the Japanese subculture (Winge, 2008). Stefani has also further commodified the Lolita subculture through a range of perfumes called Harajuku Lovers. Stefani's engagement with the Lolita subculture has brought accusations of Orientalism – the exoticization and fetishization of non-Western cultures. Yet, Mackie reminds us that the Lolita subculture is itself a bricolage of different international factors, which have been redefined into something uniquely Japanese. In this sense, '[t]he exoticisation of the European past in the adoption of the Gothic Lolita style in Japan is paralleled by the Orientalist exoticisation of the "Harajuku Girls" in the United States' (2009).

Subcultural ideas as a diaspora

> Contrary to youth subcultural ideologies, "subcultures" do not germinate from a seed and grow by force of their own energy into mysterious 'movements' only to be *belatedly digested* by the media. Rather, media and other culture industries are there and effective right from the start. They are central to the process of subcultural formation.
>
> (Thornton, 1995, our italics)

In this final section, we consider the ways in which the idea of subculture has extended beyond the Birmingham School and the academy to become part of popular discourse and lived experience more generally. Descriptions of groups and groups within groups abound in all spheres of experience – work, leisure, neighbourhood and family life – as individuals act upon late modern imperatives to forge a reflexive project of self (Giddens, 1991). Affiliation to a group or, more commonly, several groups creates opportunities for identity-work across a range of sites. Since electronic communication allows for the reformulation of various kinds of cultural activity, subcultures do not need to be face-to-face or local. Aided by the diversity of digital culture, points of identification and forms of belonging available online appear to offer indeterminate possibilities for the crafting of self-hood through reflexive identity tags and/or aspirational projects. Viewed through the lens of girls and subculture, the absence of girls on the street in the 1970s is temporally disrupted by the proliferation of girl culture and the presence of girls online in the 1990s. Girl power, Riot Grrrls and zine culture all flourished during this period as subcultural forms expanded into the cyberspace afforded by new technologies. Recognizing the significance of digital culture in young women's lives, we focus on pro-ana websites as an illustrative example of a contemporary subculture. Organized by and for girls to promote anorexia nervosa as a lifestyle choice and support those with the condition, pro-ana sites share ideas through blogs and chat rooms, tips on diet, exercise and food products and, controversially, 'thinspiration' images of emaciated bodies that profile extreme weight loss as a state to aspire to. We ask, what happens when we view the pro-anorexia movement (sometimes termed the pro-ana or ana-mia, anorexia-bulimia movement) as a sexual and gender youth subculture affecting mainly, though not exclusively, teenage girls?

The pro-ana movement, largely accessed online, has been written about as a subculture mostly from within the field of social psychology (Giles, 2006; Pascoe, 2007; Sheppird, 2007; Casilli, 2010). It should be noted that the term 'subculture' is used uncritically in most of this literature to denote a group of young people who have a shared social characteristic. This is further complicated by the fact that anorexics aren't necessarily deviant or delinquent figures of the type that characterized Chicago School research into youth cultures and particularly street gangs. Nor are they necessarily oppositional or resistant types such as the Birmingham CCCS choose to explore, largely focusing on the interaction of race and class in a post-war, post-Empire Britain. Nor are the practices of anorexia expressed by pro-ana advocates analogous to a euphoric hedonism that merited the explosion of research into global club cultures in the late 1980s (Thornton, 1995). And yet, the pro-ana movement contains traces of all three of these shifts in subcultural theory. Anorexics who engage with the pro-ana movement are both identifiable, however anonymously, and involved in collective problem-solving – a key characteristics for Chicago School theorists in defining subculture as discussed above. Moreover, the questions raised by pro-ana and its members are not isolated from larger questions concerning body image, advertising, the fashion industry, the pressure of aspiration, the pressure to be normal/perfect, the role of parenting and so on; different in specifics but not in type from the large representational issues CCCS sought to explore for two decades.

'Anas' believe themselves to occupy a higher moral ground within the pro-ana community, defining themselves *as against* those with other forms of eating distress. Such a belief is frequently reinforced on a casual basis in postings on the sites. 'Mia' is commonly constructed as an easy option or a fallback position for failed anas:

> I always found something pure about ana, but mia I think would be easier: but then again they both leave messy emotional scars.

> When I was mia I intentionally switched to ana because mia is so disgusting: Just look at all the anas who have a slip and end up asking mias for advise (sic) on how to purge.

> > (Giles, 2006)

It is within the context of what Sara Thornton has termed 'the sub-cultural capital' or 'taste cultures' for young people in Britain (Thornton, 1995), that pro-ana as a sexual and gender youth subculture comes into view. Building on the work of Bourdieu (1984) on taste and distinction, Thornton views subcultural capital as the signifying discourses of 'cool' young people in subcultures apply to key subcultural practices (in her research, dance music) to distinguish the cool from the uncool, the authentic from the fake, the subcultural from mass culture. As Thornton notes, these distinctions are arbitrary, which is not to say that they are without meaning. They are part of what we now recognize as the performative nature of identity (Butler, 1993).

Conclusion

In this chapter we have explored the links between youth subcultures and subsequent studies of young people's sexual cultures, particularly in relation to girlhood studies. Contrary to the suggestion that the concept of subcultures is no longer relevant or useful, we argue for the renewed recognition of subcultural ideas and methods as part of an intellectual legacy that can be seen in contemporary studies of girlhood, gender and sexuality. Through the use of illustrative examples, the Lolita subculture in Japan and the transnational 'pro-ana' Internet sites, we demonstrate the ways in which key features associated with the study of youth subcultures have been drawn upon to explore emergent gender and sexual identities. The recurrent themes of a subcultural analysis manifest in a distinctive approach to culture, style and symbolic meaning, combined with the use of ethnographic methods, highlight the points of continuity between past and present work. Viewed from this historical vantage point, research on youth in the present owes an often-unacknowledged debt to subcultural studies of the past. Finally, we suggest that the idea of subculture has enduring significance as a concept that has been dispersed across academic fields of enquiry and now has a presence in popular discourse more generally.

References

Beck, U. (1992) *Risk society, towards a new modernity*. London: Sage.
Bennett, A. (1999) Subcultures or neo-tribes? Rethinking the relationship between youth, style and musical taste. *Sociology*, 33 (3), 599–617.
Bennett, A. (2001) *Cultures of popular music*. Buckingham: Open University Press.
Bourdieu, P. (1984) *Distinction*. London: Routledge.
Brunsdon, C. (1997) *Screen tastes, soap opera to satellite dishes*. London: Routledge.
Butler, J. (1993) *Bodies that matter, on the discursive limits of sex*. London: Routledge.
Canaan, J. (1991) Is 'doing nothing' just boys' play? Integrating feminist and cultural studies perspectives on working-class masculinities, in S. Franklin, C. Lury, & J. Stacey (Eds.) *Off-Centre: Feminism and Cultural Studies*. London: Routledge.
Casilli, A. A. (2010) Studying eating disorders in the social web. New methods, new questions, *Institute of Social Psychology SSS*, London School of Economics and Political Science, 11 May. Retrieved from http://www.bodyspacesociety.eu/2010/05/12/studying-pro-ana-communities-in-the-social-web-lse-seminar
Clarke, J. (1976) The skinheads and the magical recovery of community, in S. Hall & T. Jefferson (Eds.) *Resistance through Rituals, Youth Subcultures in Postwar Britain*. London: Hutchinson.
Cohen, A. K. (1947) *Delinquent boys: The culture of the gang*. New York: Free Press.
Connell, R. W. (1989) Cool guys, swots and wimps: The interplay of masculinity and education. *Oxford Review of Education*, 15 (3), 291–303.
Corrigan, P. (1979) *Schooling the smash street kids*. London: Macmillan.
Giddens, A. (1991) *Modernity and self identity: Self and society in the late modern age*. Cambridge: Polity.
Giles, D. (2006) Constructing identities in cyberspace: The case of eating disorders. *British Journal of Social Psychology*, 45, 463–477.
Gordon, M. (1947) The concept of the subculture and its application, in K. Gelder & S. Thornton (Eds.) *The Subcultures Reader*. London: Routledge.
Green, J. (1999) *All dressed up, the sixties and the counterculture*. London: Pimlico.
Griffin, C. (1985) *Typical girls? Young women from school to the job market*. London: Routledge.
Hall, S., & T. Jefferson (Eds.) (1976) *Resistance through rituals, youth subcultures in postwar Britain*. London: Hutchinson.
Healy, M. (1996) *Gay skins, class, masculinity and queer appropriation*. London: Cassell.
Hermes, J. (2006) 'Ally McBeal', 'Sex in the City' and the tragic success of feminism, in J. Hollows & S. Moseley (Eds.) *Feminism in Popular Culture*. Oxford: Berg.
Hesmondhalgh, D. (2005) Subcultures, scenes or neo-tribes? None of the above. *Journal of Youth Studies*, 8 (1), 21–40.
Hollows, J., & Moseley, S. (Eds.) (2006) *Feminism in popular culture*. Oxford: Berg.

Kawamura, Y. (2006) Japanese teens as producers of street fashion. *Current Sociology*, 54 (5), 784–801.

Mac an Ghaill, M. (1994) *The making of men*. Buckingham: Open University Press.

Mackie, V. (2009) Transnational bricolage: Gothic Lolita and the political economy of fashion, intersections: Gender and sexuality in Asia and the Pacific 20. Retrieved from http://intersections.anu.edu.au/issue20/mackie.htm#n47.

McRobbie, A. (1996) More! New sexualities in girls and women's magazines, in J. Curran, D. Morley, & V. Walkerdine (Eds.) *Cultural Studies and Communications*. London: Arnold.

McRobbie, A., & Garber, J. (1976) Girls and subcultures, in S. Hall & T. Jefferson (Eds.) *Resistance through Rituals, Youth Subcultures in Postwar Britain*. London: Hutchinson.

Maffesoli, M. (1995) *The time of the tribes: The decline of individualism in mass society*. London: Sage.

Muggleton, D., & Weinzier, L. (2004) *The post-subcultural reader*. New York: Berg.

Nayak, A. (1999) Pale Warriors: Skinhead culture and the embodiment of white masculinities, in A. Brah, M. Hickman, & M. Mac an Ghaill (Eds.) *Thinking Identities: Ethnicity, Racism and Culture*. Basingstoke: Macmillan.

Nayak, A., & Kehily, M. J. (1996) Playing it straight: Masculinities, homophobia and schooling. *Journal of Gender Studies*, 5 (2), 211–230.

Nilan, P. (1992) Kazzies, DBTs and tryhards: Categorizations of style in adolescent girls' talk. *British Journal of Sociology of Education*, 13 (2), 201–214.

Pascoe, C. J. (2007) No Wannarexics allowed: An analysis of online eating disorder communities, *Digital Youth Project*. Retrieved from http://digitalyouth.ischool.berkeley.edu/, University of California, Berkeley.

Pilkington, H., Omel'chenko, E., & Garifzianova, A. (2010) *Russia's skinheads, exploring and rethinking subcultural lives*. London: Routledge.

Rahman, O., Wing-sun, L., Lam, E., & Mong-tai, C. (2011) 'Lolita': Imaginative self and elusive consumption. *Fashion Theory*, 15 (1), 7–28.

Savage, J. (2002) *England's dreaming, anarchy, sex pistols, punk rock and beyond*. London: St Martin's Griffin.

Shain, F. (2003) *The schooling and identity of Asian girls*. Stoke on Trent: Trentham Books.

Sheppird, S. (2007) Dangerous inspiration: A subculture that supports anorexia nervosa. *The Los Angeles Psychologist*, May/June, 12–13.

Sonnett, E. (1999) Erotic fiction by and for women, the pleasures of postfeminist heterosexuality. *Sexualities*, 2 (2), 167–187.

Street, B. (1993) Culture is a verb: Anthropological aspects of language and cultural process, in D. Graddol, L. Thompson, & M. Bryam (Eds.) *Language and Culture: British Studies in Applied Linguistics 7*. Clevedon: Multicultural Matters.

Thornton, S. (1947) Introduction to subcultures, in K. Gelder & S. Thornton (Eds.) *The Subcultures Reader*. London: Routledge.

Thornton, S. (1995) *Club cultures: Music, media, and subcultural capital*. Cambridge: Polity Press.

Whyte, W. F. (1943) *Street corner society: The social structure of an Italian American slum*. Chicago, IL: University of Chicago Press.

Williams, R. (1961) *The long revolution*. London and New York: Columbia University Press.

Williams, R. (1989) *Resources of hope: Culture, democracy, socialism*. R. Gale (Ed.) London: Verso.

Williamson, H. (2004) *Milltown boys revisited.* Oxford: Berg.

Willis, P. (1977) *Learning to labour, how working class kids get working-class jobs.* Farnborough: Saxon House.

Winge, T. (2008) Undressing and dressing loli: A search for the identity of the Japanese Lolita, *Mechademia,* 3, 47–63.

Young, J. (1971) *The drugtakers: The social meaning of drug use.* London: Paladin.

5
Anchoring Sexualization: Contextualizing and Explicating the Contribution of Psychological Research on the Sexualization of Girls in the US and Beyond

Deborah L. Tolman, Christin P. Bowman and Jennifer F. Chmielewski

In the US, psychological researchers have been at the forefront of establishing and contributing to a public discourse on sexualization that holds responsible the media and corporations for using sexualization for profit. A growing body of knowledge produced by psychologists asks a particular set of research questions: What are the negative effects of sexualization on girls and women? How can we understand girls' and women's 'participation' in sexualization practices while maintaining the perspective that external forces are ultimately responsible and should therefore be called out and redressed? In the US public discourse, sexualization is understood as perhaps an unfortunately simplistic word for two distinct phenomena: (1) the sexualization of culture, which is an intensified presence and infusion of often uncalled-for sexuality into products, media and norms; and (2) the sexualization of individuals, meaning both the process and the effects of living within this sexualized context particularly on girls and women. This includes how girls navigate these pervasive representations of women and girls as sexual objects and introduces the psychological phenomena of self-sexualization and overt resistance to sexualization and being sexualized. Consistent with much of mainstream psychology, the behaviour of girls and women in relation to sexualization is studied with the assumption that this process is a response to the cultural omnipresence of sexualized imagery.

This chapter is part recent history of sexualization in US psychology and part (critical) review of the psychological literature and reflections on differences in how US and UK feminists are working with and against the process of sexualization, as both an individual and a social phenomenon. We first provide an 'insider' history of the APA Report (Deborah Tolman was one of the six authors), which is so often referenced by both conservative protectionists and progressive feminists alike in the UK and the US. We then review a sampling of the psychological research literature that for the most part, including the work of feminists, fits within the parameters of mainstream psychology. We write this chapter to convey some highlights of the social psychological research on the sexualization of girls – and how it and the APA Report have been parlayed in both the US and UK contexts. Many of us in the US who draw deeply on the insightful UK feminist analyses and commentaries are puzzled by fissures that we have experienced and perceived between feminist scholars in the US and the UK regarding sexualization. We take this chapter to try to unpack and understand the genesis of this divide to open dialogue about how we might work more collaboratively to better understand sexualization and disrupt protectionist interpretations and consequences in our distinct national public discourses about them.

The history of sexualization in US psychology: The brinkmanship of pathology

One of the key distinctions between academic understanding of sexualization in the UK and US is that US feminists are more often embedded in psychological (rather than sociological or cultural) study, which positions the individual-in-context as the unit of analysis. While we will trouble this particular strain of psychological research, we also suggest that research questions posed about the impact of external, particularly oppressive, phenomena on (groups of) individual girls are important to ask. The research itself neither assumes nor concludes that girls are positioned as empty vessels into which sexualization is poured, that all are equally vulnerable to or resilient against negative outcomes or that sexualization is the only factor salient in how girls learn to navigate their sexuality, subjectivity and sense of self and connections with others. What matters are the actual research questions posed – and those not posed. We argue that the goal of US feminist psychological literature on sexualization is to understand the ways in which sexualization can shape or predict negative outcomes for girls, while still positioning girls as capable of and interested in resistance. We also recognize that this literature has left important questions unasked, thus knowledge unknown.

For this chapter, our conception of sexualization in the US is based on the literature stemming from the theoretical development of *objectification theory* (Fredrickson et al., 1998). This feminist social psychological theory is unusual in that it sits squarely within mainstream psychology. It explains how some girls and women learn to internalize a *sexually objectifying* gaze and thereby develop an outsider view of themselves or self-objectification. Even *without the presence of others*, many girls and women experience internal as well as external pressure, and learn to assess their self-worth based on impossible (and elite) physical standards of beauty, focused continually on the appearance of their bodies, often to the exclusion of their other qualities. This social psychodynamic theory offers a framework for explicitly understanding women's experiences in a sexually objectifying society in which women and girls are often treated as bodies for others' sexual consumption. Our understanding of sexualization and self-sexualization in US psychological research and discourse is embedded in this framework's definitions of sexual and self-objectification and conception of the individual-in-context. That objectification theory is the key anchor for the subsequent research on this subject is important, as it pre-dates the 2003–2005 emergence of feminist media discourse (Duschinsky, 2013).

The 2007 *Report of the APA Task Force on the Sexualization of Girls* was commissioned in 2005 by the professional organization for US psychologists to review the *psychological* literature – and explicitly *not* the literature from all disciplines, for which it has often been called to task (see Else-Quest & Hyde, 2009) – on the topic for use by a range of stakeholders, especially policymakers. To anchor this project, the Task Force elaborated the current terms *sexualization* and *self-sexualization*. Based on objectification theory, the Report defined sexualization and summarized the psychological research, documenting what we found: its negative effects on girls in response to a growing public concern that girls were being increasingly sexualized in media and marketing. This assessment reflects how sexualization is understood by US psychology as a process that engages *individuals*. While the Report has been taken up inappropriately and often inaccurately for nonresearch purposes, the authors of the Report were clear that sexualization is not about the process of girls becoming *sexual* (in whatever way that might be) but by which girls are viewed and/or treated in purely sexual terms rather than as fully functioning persons. Rather than positioning sexualization as a counterpoint to sexual innocence, the Report underscored how this process can challenge or interfere with girls' ability to feel comfortable with, own or even experience their own embodied sexuality.

As Fredrickson and Roberts (1997) argued when they articulated objectification theory, the authors of the APA Report proposed that this sexualization could occur through living in a sexualized society, through interpersonal encounters, as well as through self-sexualization. Although when the Report was published most of the psychological research was on women, it spurred public conversations and activism, as well as a wealth of research, on the sexualization *of girls* in particular. This work has yielded knowledge about the ways in which sexualization may have negative effects on girls, and the processes and mechanisms by which those effects may ensue.

We offer a brief review of some of this US research on sexualization that documents the answers to questions posed about negative effects of sexualization on girls and on society. This research has in large part focused on three themes: sexualization and (1) women's and girls' psychological health, (2) women's and girls' physical and cognitive functioning, and (3) perceptions of women and girls. As the authors were psychologists, the Report was written in the careful language that represents the kinds of claims that are possible using different methodologies in psychology. This body of research also marks the *variability* of the associations between and impacts of various forms of sexualization and the problematic outcomes studied. We suggest that an outright rejection of measures of various real psychological, cognitive and physical phenomena does not serve girls, though a measured and tempered understanding of the shortcomings of this approach as one piece of the puzzle rather than definitive and exclusionary of other forms of knowledge is equally necessary (see Moscovici, 1984 for discussion of potential and limitation of such measures).

We focus on the question of negative effects, because these questions comprise the psychological literature on sexualization – and mainstream psychological literature in general. As loud critics of this shortcoming of psychology as a discipline, we will conclude by problematizing this focus, the research questions that derive from it and those that are not asked within this epistemology. We concur with the critique of the APA Report that, in lieu of other questions about how girls navigate and negotiate sexualization, in particular the kind of nuanced and complex understanding of girls' lived experience that qualitative research and questions premised on resilience and agency raise (i.e. Ringrose & Renold, 2011; see also Tolman, 2002), the psychological literature to date can be cannibalized to serve an individualizing, pathologizing conception and discourse, as well as a profoundly limited and erroneously targeted response to sexualization that blames girls (and their mothers) and can yield protectionist policies and slut shaming practices. Yet even as we problematize the deployment of the psychological literature, used by both the conservative political forces and feminist scholars, we urge resistance to throwing out the baby with the bathwater, in part by recognizing the power and limitations of claims made in the psychological literature within a framework that recognizes what kinds of knowledge the discipline enables, as well as how the conventions of mainstream psychology dampen the production of other forms of psychological knowledge.

Sexualization and women's and girls' psychological health

Research has consistently demonstrated that sexualization of women's bodies can impact and be associated with girls' and women's psychological health. Sexualization among women, working through the psychological mechanism of self-objectification, has been *associated* with increased body shame (Fredrickson et al., 1998; Grabe et al., 2008; Mercurio & Landry, 2008; Calogero & Thompson, 2009; Carr & Szymanski, 2011), decreased sexual self-esteem (Calogero & Thompson, 2009), increased depression and anxiety symptoms (Carr & Szymanski, 2011; Erchull et al., 2013), increased substance abuse (Carr & Szymanski, 2011) and increased disordered eating (Fredrickson et al., 1998; Calogero & Thompson, 2009a).

Experimental research that poses the questions 'What, if any, are negative *effects* on young girls of sexualization?' and 'What characterizes the *contexts* of girls for whom those effects pertain?' has documented specific ways that sexualization can have damaging effects on young girls. Girls as young as six have been shown to internalize a sexualized ideal (Starr & Ferguson, 2012). In their experimental study, Starr and Ferguson (2012) showed six- to nine-year-old girls paper dolls wearing sexualized clothing and non-sexualized clothing. The girls were asked to choose which doll looked most like their 'actual' selves, their 'ideal' selves and 'the most popular' girl. Overwhelmingly, girls chose the sexualized doll as their ideal self and as the most popular, and chose the non-sexualized doll as their actual self. Though this study provides evidence of early internalization of sexualized norms, it also suggests that mothers can play a vital role in *buffering* against the negative effects of media sexualization. This research was framed to illuminate how mothers (or other important female adults) can enable a nuanced and collaborative path of resistance by providing alternative conceptions of what women's bodies are like, inviting resistant readings and interpretations of whatever sexualizing media or toys girls may be encountering. Mothers who discussed sexualizing images as unrealistic with their daughters reduced the incidence of girls sexualizing themselves. While it is the case that these findings could lead to parent-blaming, the actual research does not yield that conclusion. As carefully articulated by the researchers, whose explicit stance is querying the effects of corporate contexts of production of goods, these findings highlight the role parents can play in fostering critical media-viewing skills in their daughters – rather than just saying 'no' to sexualized clothing or toys or taking girls (or themselves) to task for engaging in these practices – as well as how important these skills may be for psychological well-being. This is a prime example of how regressive actors misuse and abuse psychological research.

As young girls grow into adolescence, the psychological consequences of a culture saturated with sexualization follow them. Research with adolescent girls has shown that self-objectification is associated with increased depression and anxiety symptoms (Grabe & Hyde, 2009) and increased disordered eating (Grabe & Hyde, 2009; Petersen & Hyde, 2013). In particular, the ways in which sexualization can undermine girls' ability to become sexually agentic have been identified: decreased sexual self-efficacy (Schooler et al., 2005; Impett et al., 2006) and increased body shame (Lindberg et al., 2007; Grabe & Hyde, 2009). Negative psychological effects of sexualization can persist into adulthood. Self-objectification has been shown to decrease women's overall life satisfaction (Mercurio & Landry, 2008), sexual satisfaction (Sanchez &

Kiefer, 2007; Calogero & Thompson, 2009b) and increase inappropriate feel-ings of responsibility for being sexually objectified (Chen et al., 2013). Chen and colleagues (2013), for example, asked women to write about a time in which they interacted with a man who either focused only on their physi-cal appearance or *did not objectify them*. Women who recalled an objectifying experience reported feeling more responsible for being sexually objectified in general than women who recalled a more neutral experience, whereas this association was not found for women who recalled a non-objectifying experience.

Sexualization and women's and girls' physical and cognitive functioning

Sexual objectification has also been shown to impair cognitive and physical functioning (Fredrickson et al., 1998; Quinn et al., 2006; Gay & Castano, 2010). In their classic foundational experiment, Fredrickson and colleagues (1998) asked undergraduates to try on either a sweater or a bathing suit while alone in a dressing room with a mirror. The swimsuit condition was *designed to trigger* self-objectification, while the sweater condition was the control condition. While wearing the sweater or bathing suit, the participants took a challenging maths test. Women who tried on the bathing suit performed significantly worse on the maths test than women who tried on the sweater. The researchers postulate that self-objectification triggered by internalizing sexualization draws cognitive resources away from women's mental capac-ity, negatively impacting maths performance. This study, as well as research that has subsequently replicated its results among women and men of var-ied ethnicities (e.g. Hebl et al., 2004), is important in demonstrating the tangible cognitive consequences of a culture of sexualization above and beyond the psychological impact, underscoring that this body of research neither can nor should be characterized as pathologizing girls and women. This experiment was done to demonstrate objectification theory in action; thus its design was to test for negative effects. A few later experiments have been conducted to demonstrate that alternatives to sexualizing experiences, in particular in relation to sexualized versus non-sexualized representa-tions, have shown that self-objectification is not inevitable but an effect of 'uninterrupted' sexualizing practices or lack of presence of non-sexualizing, including competent female, body images (Daniels, 2009).

Just as self-objectification siphons cognitive resources for intellectual tasks, the mental energy used to pay attention to one's body also drains focus away from performing physical tasks (Fredrickson & Harrison, 2005). Fem-inist philosophers have long believed it to be the case (e.g. Beauvoir, 1952; Young, 1990), and in a recent empirical study researchers demonstrated that girls with higher rates of self-objectification showed poorer throwing per-formance (Fredrickson & Harrison, 2005). This study provides evidence that when girls take the outsider perspective on the appearance of their bodies that social norms and practices pressure them to do, they have less cognitive energy available to fully immerse themselves in the capacities of their bodies, thereby undercutting those capacities. Studies that illuminate whether resistance to sexualizing representations and processes might enable girls to focus more on their physical competence have yet to be conducted.

Sexualization and perceptions of women and girls

Alongside psychological research that aims to determine how unreflective or uncritical consumption of sexualized imagery can have negative impacts on women and girls, another fruitful collection of recent experimental work illuminates how consumption of sexualized imagery affects people's perceptions of women and girls as a class. Psychologists contributing to this line of research are instrumental in holding the media and corporations responsible for changing attitudes and sexualizing behaviours.

Researchers have consistently found that when people are exposed to sexually objectifying media, they are more likely to demonstrate acceptance of rape myths and violence against women (Aubrey et al., 2011; Beck et al., 2012; Burgess & Burpo, 2012; Loughnan et al., 2013). For example, Aubrey and colleagues (2011) had undergraduate men view either highly sexualized music videos or non-sexualized music videos. In their experimental study, men who were exposed to the sexualized media more frequently believed that women tend to be sexually manipulative and were more accepting of violence against women than men in the control condition. Furthermore, the researchers demonstrated that this relationship was mediated, meaning that exposure to sexualized media led to an increase in beliefs that women are sexually manipulative, which in turn led to more acceptance of violence against women.

Sexualization also causes people to perceive women more like objects, and therefore, as less than fully human. Experimental research has shown that people perceive sexualized women as less cognitively and physically capable (Behm-Morawitz & Mastro, 2009; Harrison & Secarea, 2010), and as lacking human characteristics such as thoughts, emotions and morality (Loughnan et al., 2013). For example, Loughnan and colleagues (2013) presented participants with an image of either a non-sexualized or sexualized woman and asked them to rate her mental ability and the extent to which they felt moral concern for her. Those shown the sexualized woman rated her as having less mental ability, and they also reported less moral concern for her, while the participants who rated the non-sexualized woman did not report these reactions.

The increase in sexualized representations of women's bodies (Hatton & Trautner, 2011, 2013) coincides with an increase in sexualized depictions of girls in the past several decades (Graff et al., 2013). Several recent studies have begun to demonstrate that sexualized media can change people's perceptions of girls as well (Machia & Lamb, 2009; Graff et al., 2012). Graff and colleagues (2012) showed undergraduate women and men a photo of a pre-teen girl wearing childlike clothing, somewhat sexualized clothing or definitely sexualized clothing. The girl depicted wearing the definitely sexualized clothing was judged to be less capable, competent, determined and intelligent than the girls depicted wearing childlike or somewhat sexualized clothing, and also as having less morality and less self-respect than the girls in the other conditions. Experiments that flip this comparison towards an evaluation of positive responses to non-sexualized and/or competent, smart and innovative images of pre-teen girls could complement the finding of an absence of negative response to sexualized depictions.

Gaps in and guidelines for the psychological literature

The APA Report recognized critical gaps in the research literature on the sexualization of girls. It is in the nature of inferential statistics and experimental design that results do not generalize to all girls. In fact, variability is required – the findings in the report do not pertain to all girls by any stretch of the imagination but report associations between high and low scores, such that interpretations could also be made that girls who are less self-sexualizing are less likely to be depressed – depending on how the research question is articulated. While the report does include some studies of sexualization among girls and women of colour, it also notes that the research literature has a paucity of studies on women and girls of colour and class, sexual orientation and ability differences; thus, the findings are primarily about white, heterosexual, middle-class girls. This shortcoming remains persistent in much US research. The outcome can be unfortunate and problematic: to conclude that the only girls who experience sexualization are white, heterosexual and middle class, and that the only way girls respond are the patterns that the extant research has identified, which also has the effect of resonating with hypersexualizing discourses about these populations of girls (Collins, 1990). However, some critics of the report fail to recognize that this research was in fact included. Sexualization is part of the landscape of all girls' lives and psychology's lacklustre record diversifying samples constitutes a kind 'false positive' as if only one group of girls matters.

Importantly, as feminists outside psychology both in the UK and the US have noted, the questions that have been posed in this body of research produce knowledge about what they address; that is, negative outcomes. Other questions have yet to be asked that can enable a fuller picture of the ways in which girls (and women, men and boys) respond to sexualization in a variety of forms. Much of the research to date has evaluated the potential negative impact of sexualized images and toys, as reviewed above. There have yet to be studies about girls' resistance to or resilience in the face of sexualized images or sexualizing experiences or that compare differences in outcomes in conditions that prime resistance versus prime self-sexualization. Most importantly, there is a dearth of qualitative psychological research on how girls navigate sexualization that can capture the contradictions, nuances, complexities and various venues in which girls engage with sexualizing processes. The voices of girls themselves are disturbingly absent in the US psychological literature to date – but UK researchers have begun to redress this (i.e. Ringrose, 2010; Renold & Ringrose, 2011).

While Egan (2013) states that disciplinary conventions and practices are not relevant to problematizing this literature, we suggest that they do matter. Psychological research on sexualization has been conducted in several ways. Not all psychological findings are causal, in particular using inferential analyses to illuminate associations between various dimensions of sexualization and various outcomes that are explicitly non-directional and thus do not allow for claims of causality versus experimental designs, by which causality can be claimed. In inferential statistics, as in all knowledge production, interpretation is powerful. While feminist researchers pose these research questions from theoretical and political positions that hold commodification, commercialization and corporate interests responsible for the costs to girls' mental and other forms of health and capacity, an unfortunate risk of mainstream inferential and experimental research is that it can set up a straw woman or girl and be parlayed to pathologize girls or 'the (iconic, monolithic, elite) Girl Child', in particular by those with protectionist and neo-liberal agendas.

Reflections on the APA Report on sexualization: Querying deployments of psychological research

Without question, sexualization is, like any umbrella term, problematic for lacking nuance or complexity and for suggesting a singular, monolithic process or outcome. We recognize that it is flimsy (Attwood, 2006) and obfuscates salient processes, such as how media is consumed, embodied and reproduced, not just what it contains. We have been asking ourselves and those who engage in this practice: Why does 'sexualization' invariably appear in quotes in the feminist literature from the UK? As we will articulate below, for place-specific and disciplinary reasons, feminists in the UK seem to have found this representation of 'sexualization' an effective way to communicate to policymakers and in public discourse that it is not an inevitable societal ill emanating from "bad" girls or that girls are corrupted by a sexualized social landscape. Yet for many psychologists in the US, this signification reads completely differently from how it is intended; it reads as a derision of the concept itself, implying that it does not exist, or that at the very least the construct must at all times be somehow denigrated. For many of us in the US who are hungrily reading the smart, insightful and savvy work of UK feminists, what sounds to us to be a rhetorical strategy of mini-mization is puzzling and troubling. Yet some UK feminists may understand this US interpretation of 'sexualization' as a projection or pathologization. All of these perceptions are both accurate and inaccurate. We propose that it is the different origins and trajectories of the history of sexualization (Duschinsky, 2013), how it has been circulated, leveraged and addressed in the US and the UK, that underpins our distinct strategies for discussing and addressing it.

Governmental bodies in the UK have responded to the increasing sexu-alization of culture by institutionalizing policies that are predicated upon and contribute to pathologizing and limiting girls themselves. Girls are seen as the problem – they are overly sexualized or sexual and therefore in need of protection or punishment (*Papadoulos Review on the Sexualization of Young People (2010)*, *The Bailey Review (2011)*). UK feminists' use of 'sexualization' in quotes, then, seems meant to counter these oppressive responses and per-haps resist the actual term and reject it as a viable concept for discussion. Critical feminists in the UK have to carefully engage in an inflammatory pol-icy and media terrain around these issues. The UK media plays an enormous role in fanning the flames, known for its sensationalism and moral panic ten-dencies around any issues of child sexuality and sex (Ringrose, 2010; Egan, 2013). Problematizing sexualization manifests in 'sexualization' in quotes much as 'race' has been put in quotes to signify a contested category of social identity. Perhaps sexualization, however, needs to be recognized as a legiti-mate social concern without quotations, much as racialization as a process is investigated beyond the essentialized category of 'race'.

In contrast, the history of sexualization as a concept has a different tra-jectory in the US, notably lacking the intense governmental intrusion into people's lives in the UK. As we look back on the influence of the APA report in the light of the current public and academic conversations about sexu-alization and girls' sexuality today, we see several profoundly different and unintended ways in which it has been deployed in the US and in the UK. The APA report had a strong role in shaping the US public discourse on sexual-ization just as it gained momentum, as well as on subsequent psychological research, to sharpen the focus on challenging society and institutions – corporate and otherwise – rather than blaming girls for self-sexualization. In particular, moral panics around sexualization serve as lightning rods for a full array of discourses that include those deployed to surveil and constrain girls via their right to develop into full sexual beings. These discourses may blame girls for particular instantiations of sexual expression (Egan & Hawkes, 2008; Egan, 2013). However, as the report incited widespread recognition of sexualization as an issue for society to redress, US feminists – tied to the gravitas of the APA – have also been able to leverage this privileged status to influence primary public discourse and policy recommendations, thereby intervening in such panics. Mainstream media and feminists can and do call on the report to underscore that sexualization needs to be redressed to enable girls to be more rather than less free, more rather than less embodied, more rather than less able to develop and access their own sexual agency (whatever that may be) as they develop into young women. The loss of an innocent (read desexualized) childhood or girlhood is certainly a trope among handwringers and naysayers of various stripes.

As a policy document, the report has, as is inevitable, also taken on a life of its own, with statements often taken out of context and misrepresented, and has been utilized by a plethora of interest groups, perhaps most vocally by those with power whose practices regarding girls are more protectionist than critical. Reading the UK literature, we understand how the APA report has been (mis)appropriated by conservative governmental bodies to position girls as in need of protection from an evil force or their pathological selves. The subsequent policies and discourses that constrain and contain girls and those who care for them (Rush & La Nause, 2006; Papadopoulos, 2010; Bailey, 2011) – a kind of blaming of the victim that does and should raise the UK feminist community's hackles about blame and victimhood (i.e. Ringrose & Renold, 2012; Bragg & Buckingham, 2013) – is equally appalling to us.

The specific US context moderated the ways in which the report was taken up in the US, including such US particularities as the profound protection of free speech (Fiss, 1985), a highly diverse population and strong states' rights. Legislation or governmental policy regulating parents, children and those who work and care for young people was an unlikely avenue for addressing sexualization in the US. While there have been some attempts at high-level policy change, these efforts are the work of US feminists and allies rather than the unholy alliances of the Left with the Right that characterized efforts such as pornography censorship in the 1980s (Ferguson, 1984). A caveat to this assertion is the taking up and inappropriate hyperbolizing deployment of the psychological research literature by a small group of feminist scholars and activists who are not psychologists, who are fuelling renewed anti-pornography efforts in the wake of new technologies by which it is now circulated (e.g. Dines, 2010). We are also aware of how the report has been deployed by some in the US feminist community out of context, yielding readings that take us aback even as we apprehend that they are decontextualized.

Did the APA report sound a panicky alarm about sexualization? In some sense, it did. As Duschinsky (2013) noted, the report yielded unintended consequences, such as the right-wing leveraging discourses of sexualization as a symbol of moral decline, calling for protectionist policies focused on preventing children from becoming *sexual*. In the US academic psychology community, research on sexualization in particular is predicated on the assumption that the process of becoming an agentic sexual (and gendered) adult – however that sexuality is expressed (i.e.

sexual minorities, transgendered young people) – is to be expected into and through adolescence (Tolman, 2012), and that for girls in particular, in the context of an intersectional understanding of patriarchy, this process should incorporate learning both about pleasure and about risk management (McClelland & Fine, 2008; Tolman & McClelland, 2011). Girls have an inalienable right to experience and enjoy the pleasures of sexual embodiment, and this right is not predicated on being or becoming a sexual object of another's desires; in fact, it defies such positioning of girls by others. Thus such misinterpretations call for a stronger response from feminist psychologists and even possibly the APA. In particular, we should reinforce our underlying commitments to girls and young women's right to sexual subjectivity, self-determination and expression, and underscore the ways that sexualization impedes what the report (strategically) called healthy sexuality, a somewhat ambiguous term that allows for the corralling of concerns with public health and feminist propositions of entitlements to pleasure, freedom and rights to diverse expressions.

Yet we are also concerned that critics of the 'anti-sexualization literature' have lumped together carefully interpreted psychological research with deployment of it and ideologies around childhood innocence in popular culture (Egan, 2013). We share the scepticism of many UK feminists about governments' capacities to meaningfully improve the experiences of girls and women regarding sexualization without addressing broader social contexts. Thus we argue that social psychological research can contribute to social change through how it is utilized to exert public pressure and practices rather than government interventions and policies, and that in the US we have had the freedom to proceed in this way. Expanding the scope of this research to incorporate qualitative studies will add fuel to this power.

Derailing moral panics over sexualization: Replacing either/or with both/and

As in the UK, sexualization often emerges in US public discourses as moral panics over girls' sexuality. Public outcries (often paradoxically both *from* parents and *towards* parents) over consumer events of sexualization are common. Companies such as Aerie or Victoria's Secret market risqué knickers to teenage and tween girls, video games show extremely sexualized violence, and Barbie's ever skinnier, larger-breasted body sports less and less clothing. Public conversations about young girls' and teens' self-sexualization also pervade the landscape. As a prime example, one need only Google 'girls dancing to single ladies' to find a 2013 viral YouTube video of elementary school girls dancing to Beyoncé's 'All the Single Ladies' – and the accompanying moral outrage. And when it comes to teenage girls using technology, the public is increasingly concerned that teens are engaging in harmful self-sexualization via sexting and social media sites (Koefed & Ringrose, 2012).

When these events enter public discourse, we witness a wide range of responses: blaming corporations, blaming parents, blaming patriarchy, and slut-shaming and blaming girls. In the US, these panics are consistently in conversation with, and somewhat tempered by, the academy and, as noted below, girls themselves; the government is rarely involved in legislating responses, though institutions, particularly schools, have promulgated restrictive policies, such as dress codes in schools limiting girls' attire to the 'non-provocative' (see teen SPARK blogger Izzy Labbe's (2013) commentary).

An important question that we need not only ask but emphasize is distinguishing between morally driven cries for protection and an understanding of how sexualization is in fact a problem for girls and women that can and needs to be addressed. Girls and women are not *tabulae rasae*, and often are not simply drinking the Koolaid (or not drinking it to save on calories). Yet girls do have to navigate pervasive and largely uninterrupted sexualized products and images. In the face of emerging research (much of it from the UK) illuminating the complexity of how young girls and teens are in fact engaging with their own bodies and the various pressures and options for representing them (Ringrose, 2010; Renold & Ringrose, 2011), the either/or positioning – either sexualization is everywhere, it's frightening and impacting girls as a class or monolithic group (or, even worse, only some (privileged) girls), or sexualization is an overblown entrenched moral panic that is not reflective of a real issue – calls for a forthright conversation that feminists working in very different contexts should have to enable us to support one another more effectively. It behoves us as feminists to start to listen to one another more deeply about how sexualization can be *both* recognized *and* problematized as a driving force in the US and UK social and political, as well as material and cultural contexts. We have seen how 'the quotes' have signalled both these differences and their roots, with the effect of mutual misunderstanding and therefore diminishing coordinated efforts in the academy and beyond.

Even as the APA report has been misquoted and misused, and despite its shortcomings, it has helped give rise to activism around sexualization by teens, adults, collectives and intergenerational groups. Some evidence-based activist organizations have embraced this both/and strategy of resisting sexualization while acknowledging girls' right to an embodied and agentic sexuality. This has been perhaps most meaningfully accomplished when organizations build their momentum upon the solid foundation of feminist psychological research and deploy the APA report findings to bolster resistance and push back. The organization SPARK (Sexualization Protest: Action, Resistance, Knowledge; co-founded by Tolman and Lyn Mikel Brown in 2010), which is girl-driven, supports girls as activists to push back against sexualization with the goal of social and material change in how girls are represented, including concerns about race, sexual orientation, gender, and class (see Ali et al., 2014; Jones et al., 2014). Within three years of its formation, SPARK has become a go-to organization by mainstream media for commentary on sexualization concerns (i.e. moral panics that erupt). Because SPARK is grounded in empirical feminist psychological research, the media's reliance on the organization has provided an alternative venue for feminist psychologists and girls themselves to continually weigh in on the complexity of these concerns. In this way, SPARK is able to mindfully interject a both/and perspective into moral panics, reminding the public again and again that sexualization can be harmful to girls, but that girls have the capacity and will to challenge sexualization (rather than be passive 'empty vessels' for corporate representations, events, processes and products), and that girls still have the right to live freely in their bodies and to develop as sexual agents (see www.sparkmovement.org's media tab). More research that supports this stance of resistance would bolster this effort. Even within this kind of feminist organizing with girls, the complexities of sexualization are visible in the contradictory positions and self-constructions that the girls themselves take, navigating pressures to produce particular kinds of identities, practices and performances that constitute complex critiques even as they reproduce elements of this process (Edell et al., 2013).

The psychological contribution to debates on sexualization of girls, activism and advocacy

What *sexualization/'sexualisation'* really means remains shaky within and across disciplines and nations. By providing a critical review of the psychological literature, along with trying to delineate the different contexts in which UK and US feminists have developed scholarship about sexualization, we hope to take a step towards opening discussion across disciplines that can see the usefulness of psychological research discussed along with its shortcomings. Egan and Hawkes (2008; Egan, 2013) provide an insightful analysis of how the sexualization of girls – and the sexualized girl, in particular the white, heterosexual, middle-class girl – functions as a monstrosity upon whom the anxious public can project its fears and ignorance. These scholars remind us that the sexualization of girls produces and fuels discourses that assuage and obfuscate the social inequities resulting from the increasingly unchecked forces of commodification and capitalism. We believe that the threat of misuse and abuse of inferential and experimental research on negative outcomes using measures of harm in the policy and media domains, which ultimately are out of our control and our careful explanations of the limits of measurement and how findings should be reported, does not mean that feminist psychologists – mainstream or critical – should sidestep this research agenda. Of course ultimately, research and theory, feminist and otherwise, is often misappropriated in the service of the very concern we are seeking to redress.

Sexualization is not simple. It is not an individual woman or girl making a simple choice to wear revealing clothing or send a sext, though neo-liberal discourses might try to pathologize those girls and those choices and deploy the psychological research literature to buttress this argument. It is also not simply a terrifying force of culture from which women and girls must be constantly protected. Sexualization is real, and its psychological effects are real.

But girls and women are also resilient and intelligent and capable of sexual agency. Girls are entitled to a sexuality development that *both* acknowledges them as sexual subjects with an array of sexual subjectivities, desires and embodiments *and* recognizes the difficult sexualized terrain that normalizes a profoundly narrow and problematic construction of young women's sexuality premised on becoming 'good sexual objects' even as they risk punishment for doing so as they come of age. We are hopeful that feminists across continents can use their collective energies to support each other moving forward in a fight we can all support: girls' rights to healthy, agentic and embodied sexuality development and social change that renders sexualization unacceptable and not profitable. Working together, we can explore sexualization as it intersects with other dynamics, such as the marginalization of specific groups of girls, the undermining of parental confidence and commitment, and the proliferation of sexualization in commercial practices.

References

Ali, S., Wong, C., & Slobe, T. (7 February 2014) Trans people speak their own truths – and that scares Piers Morgan. [Weblog post]. Retrieved from http://www.sparksummit.com/2014/02/07/trans-people-speak-their-own-truths-and-that-scares-piers-morgan/

American Psychological Association (2013) Experts available to discuss Halloween costumes, body image, sexualization of girls. [Press release]. Retrieved from http://www.apa.org/news/press/releases/2013/10/costumes-sexualization.aspx

American Psychological Association, Task Force on the Sexualization of Girls. (2007) *Report of the APA task force on the sexualization of girls.* Washington, DC: American Psychological Association. Retrieved from www.apa.org/pi/wpo/sexualization.html

Attwood, F. (2006) Sexed up: Theorizing the sexualization of culture. *Sexualities, 9,* 77–94.

Aubrey, J., Hopper, K., & Mbure, W. G. (2011) Check that body! The effects of sexually objectifying music videos on college men's sexual beliefs. *Journal of Broadcasting & Electronic Media, 55,* 360–379.

Bailey, R. (2011) *Letting children be children: Report of an independent review of the commercialisation and sexualisation of childhood.* London: Department of Education.

Beauvoir, S. (1952) *The second sex* (H. M. Parshley Trans.). New York: Knopf.

Beck, V. S., Boys, S., Rose, C., & Beck, E. (2012) Violence against women in video games: A prequel or sequel to rape myth acceptance? *Journal of Interpersonal Violence, 27,* 3016–3031.

Behm-Morawitz, E., & Mastro, D. (2009) The effects of the sexualization of female video game characters on gender stereotyping and female self-concept. *Sex Roles*, 61, 808–823.

Bragg, S., & Buckingham, D. (2013) Global concerns, local negotiations and moral selves: Contemporary parenting and the 'sexualisation of childhood' debate. *Feminist Media Studies*, 13, 643–659.

Burgess, M. R., & Burpo, S. (2012) The effect of music videos on college students' perceptions of rape. *College Student Journal*, 46, 748–763.

Calogero, R. M., & Thompson, J. K. (2009a) Sexual self-esteem in American and British college women: Relations with self-objectification and eating problems. *Sex Roles*, 60, 160–173. doi: 10.1007/s11199-008-9517-

Calogero, R. M., & Thompson, J. K. (2009b) Potential implications of the objectification of women's bodies for women's sexual satisfaction. *Body Image*, 6, 145–148.

Carr, E. R., & Szymanski, D. M. (2011) Sexual objectification and substance use in young adult women. *The Counseling Psychologist*, 39, 39–66.

Chen, Z., Teng, F., & Zhang, H. (2013) Sinful flesh: Sexual objectification threatens women's moral self. *Journal of Experimental Social Psychology*, 49, 1042–1048.

Daniels, E. (2009) Sex objects, athletes, and sexy athletes: How media representations of women athletes can impact adolescent girls and college women. *Psychology of Women Quarterly*, 24 (4), 399–422.

Dines, G. (2010) *Pornland: How porn has hijacked our sexuality*. Boston, MA: Beacon Press.

Duschinsky, R. (2013) The emergence of sexualization as a social problem: 1981–2010. *Social Politics*, 20 (1), 137–156. doi: 10.1093/sp/jxs016.

Edell, D., Brown, L. M., & Tolman, D. (2013) Embodying sexualisation: When theory meets practice in intergenerational feminist activism. *Feminist Theory*, 14 (3), 275–284.

Egan, R. D. (2013) *Becoming sexual: A critical appraisal of the sexualization of girls*. Cambridge, UK: Polity Press.

Egan, R. D., & Hawkes, G. L. (2008) Endangered girls and incendiary objects: Unpacking the discourse on sexualization. *Sexuality & Culture*, 12, 291–311.

Else-Quest, N. M., & Hyde, J. S. (2009) The missing discourse of development: Commentary on Lerum and Dworkin. *Journal of Sex Research*, 46, 264–267.

Erchull, M. J., Liss, M., & Lichiello, S. (2013) Extending the negative consequences of media internalization and self-objectification to dissociation and self-harm. *Sex Roles*, 69, 583–593.

Ferguson, A. (1984) Sex war: The debate between radical and libertarian feminists. *Signs*, 10 (1), 106–112.

Fiss, O. M. (1985) Free speech and social structure. *Iowa Law Review*, 71, 1405–1425.

Fredrickson, B. L., & Harrison, K. (2005) Throwing like a girl: Self-objectification predicts adolescent girls' motor performance. *Journal of Sport and Social Issues*, 29, 79–101.

Fredrickson, B. L., & Roberts, T. (1997) Objectification theory: Toward understanding women's lived experiences and mental health risks. *Psychology of Women Quarterly*, 21, 173–206.

Fredrickson, B. L., Roberts, T., Noll, S. M., Quinn, D. M., & Twenge, J. M. (1998) That swimsuit becomes you: Sex differences in self-objectification, restrained eating, and math performance. *Journal of Personality and Social Psychology*, 75, 269–284.

Gay, R. K., & Castano, E. (2010) My body or my mind: The impact of state and trait objectification on women's cognitive resources. *European Journal of Social Psychology*, 40, 695–703

Grabe, S., & Hyde, J. S. (2009) Body objectification, MTV, and psychological outcomes among female adolescents. *Journal of Applied Social Psychology*, 39, 2840–2858.

Grabe, S., Ward, M. L., & Hyde, J. S. (2008) The role of the media in body image concerns among women: A meta-analysis of experimental and correlational studies. *Psychological Bulletin*, 134, 460–476.

Graff, K. A., Murnen, S. K., & Krause, A. K. (2013) Low-cut shirts and high-heeled shoes: Increased sexualization across time in magazine depictions of girls. *Sex Roles*, 69, 571–582.

Graff, K., Murnen, S., & Smolak, L. (2012) Too sexualized to be taken seriously? Perceptions of a girl in childlike vs. sexualizing clothing. *Sex Roles*, 66, 764–775.

Harrison, L., & Secarea, A. M. (2010) College students' attitudes toward the sexualization of professional women athletes. *Journal of Sport Behavior*, 33, 403–426.

Hatton, E., & Trautner, M. (2011) Equal opportunity objectification? The sexualization of men and women on the cover of Rolling Stone. *Sexuality & Culture*, 15, 256–278.

Hatton, E., & Trautner, M. (2013) Images of powerful women in the age of 'choice feminism'. *Journal of Gender Studies*, 22, 65–78.

Hebl, M. R., King, E. B., & Lin, J. (2004) The swimsuit becomes us all: Ethnicity, gender, and vulnerability to self-objectification. *Personality and Social Psychology Bulletin*, 30, 1322–1331.

Hill Collins, P. (1990) *Black feminist thought*. New York: Routledge.

Impett, E. A., Schooler, D., & Tolman, D. L. (2006) To be seen and not heard: Femininity ideology and adolescent girls' sexual health. *Archives of Sexual Behavior*, 35, 131–144.

Jones, M., Nesbitt, M., Gujral, M., Evans, L., Luckhurst, G., & Ubiñas, B. (14 February 2014) Real girls, real talk: 'I'd give #AerieReal a B'. [Weblog post]. Retrieved from http://www.sparksummit.com/2014/02/14/real-girls-real-talk-id-give-aeriereal-a-b/

Kofoed, J., & Ringrose, J. (2012) Travelling and sticky affects: Exploring teens and sexualized cyberbullying through a Butlerian-Deleuzian-Guattarian lens. *Discourse*, 33 (1), 5–20.

Labbe, I. (17 June 2013) Ugh, dress codes. [Weblog post]. Retrieved from http://www.sparksummit.com/2013/06/17/ugh-dress-codes/

Lindberg, S. M., Grabe, S., & Hyde, J. S. (2007) Gender, pubertal development, and peer sexual harassment predict objectified body consciousness in early adolescence. *Journal of Research on Adolescence*, 17, 723–742.

Loughnan, S., Pina, A., Vasquez, E. A., & Puvia, E. (2013) Sexual objectification increases rape victim blame and decreases perceived suffering. *Psychology of Women Quarterly*, 37, 455–461.

Machia, M., & Lamb, S. (2009) Sexualized innocence: Effects of magazine ads portraying adult women as sexy little girls. *Journal of Media Psychology: Theories, Methods, and Applications*, 21, 15–24.

McClelland, S. I., & Fine, M. (2008) Writing on cellophane: Studying teen women's sexual desires, inventing methodological release points. *The Methodological Dilemma: Creative, Critical and Collaborative Approaches to Qualitative Research*, 232–260.

Mercurio, A. E., & Landry, L. J. (2008) Self-objectification and well-being: The impact of self-objectification on women's overall sense of self-worth and life satisfaction. *Sex Roles*, 58, 458–466.

Moscovici, S. (1984) The phenomenon of social representations, in R. Farr & S. Moscovici (Eds.) *Social Representations*. Cambridge: Cambridge University Press.

Papadopoulos, L. (2010) *Sexualisation of young people review*. London: Home Office. Retrieved from http://webarchive.nationalarchives.gov.uk/+/http://www.homeoffice.gov.uk/documents/Sexualisation-of-young-people.html

Petersen, J. L., & Hyde, J. S. (2013) Peer sexual harassment and disordered eating in early adolescence. *Developmental Psychology*, 49, 184–195.

Quinn, D. M., Kallen, R. W., Twenge, J. M., & Fredrickson, B. L. (2006) The disruptive effect of self-objectification on performance. *Psychology of Women Quarterly*, 30, 59–64.

Renold, E., & Ringrose, J. (2011) Schizoid subjectivities? Re-theorizing teen girls' sexual cultures in an era of 'sexualization'. *Journal of Sociology*, 47, 389–409.

Ringrose, J. (2010) Sluts, whores, fat slags and playboy bunnies: Teen girls' negotiations of 'sexy' on social networking sites and at school, in C. Jackson, C. Paechter, & E. Renold (Eds.) *Girls and Education 3–16: Continuing Concerns, New Agendas*. Basingstoke: Open University Press, pp. 170–182.

Ringrose, J., & Renold, E. (2012) Slut-shaming, girl power and 'sexualisation': Thinking through the politics of the international SlutWalks with teen girls. *Gender and Education*, 24, 333–343.

Rush, E., & La Nauze, A. (2006) *Corporate paedophilia: Sexualisation of children in Australia*. Canberra: The Australia Institute.

Sanchez, D. T., & Kiefer, A. K. (2007) Body concerns in and out of the bedroom: Implications for sexual pleasure and problems. *Archives of Sexual Behavior*, 36, 808–820.

Schooler, D., Ward, L. M., Merriwether, A., & Caruthers, A. S. (2005) Cycles of shame: Menstrual shame, body shame, and sexual decision-making. *The Journal of Sex Research*, 42 (4), 324–334.

Starr, C., & Ferguson, G. (2012) Sexy dolls, sexy grade-schoolers? Media & maternal influences on young girls' self-sexualization. *Sex Roles*, 67, 463–476.

Tolman, D. L. (2002) *Dilemmas of Desire: Teenage Girls Talk about Sexuality*. Cambridge, MA: Harvard University Press.

Tolman, D. L. (2012) Female adolescents, sexual empowerment and desire: A missing discourse of gender inequity. *Sex Roles*, 66 (11–12), 746–757.

Tolman, D. L., & Brown, L. M. (2010) *Halloween and the sexualization of girls*. Retrieved 24 July 2014 from http://www.huffingtonpost.com/deborah-l tolman/halloween-and-the-sexuali_b_769891.html

Tolman, D. L., & McClelland, S. I. (2011) Normative sexuality development in adolescence: A decade in review, 2000–2009. *Journal of Research on Adolescence*, 21(1), 242–255.

Young, I. M. (1990) Throwing like a girl: A phenomenology of feminine body comportment, motility, and spatiality, in *Throwing Like a Girl and Other Essays in Feminist Philosophy and Social Theory*. Bloomington: Indiana University Press, pp. 141–159.

6
What about the Boys?: Sexualization, Media and Masculinities

Sara Bragg

Familiar responses to the issue of boys and sexualization lead in opposite directions. Some suggest that we really don't need to worry about them at all, as a mother in my earlier research argued: 'Well, you don't need to worry about a wee boy dressing to look older and looking tarty or anything' (Buckingham et al., 2010). Others, such as those below, suggest that we do need to worry about them (sometimes, in fact, we need to be extremely concerned indeed, as the last quotation from Bronwyn Davies implies), but in a very different way from how we worry about girls.

> [G]irls are sexualised to a much greater degree than boys...That children themselves are now being sexualised in...ways that emphasise male domination seems likely only to increase the risk that the ethical values that foster healthy relationships will be undermined, in particular for boys.
>
> (Rush & La Nauze, 2006: 5, 46)

> The belief that girls are sexual objects may be related to boys' tendency to sexually harass girls in school and in this way could affect girls adversely.
>
> (APA, 2007: 32)

> Boys who are exposed to sexualised media are likely to perceive women to be sex objects.
>
> (Coy, 2009: 373)

> In developing the character of Lisa they [primary school children] find it difficult to find an alternative to sexy, pretty and scared. If she cannot be these, she must be 'fat and ugly', even 'fuckin' ugly'. This aggressive description from Brian is evocative of an attitude I encountered when counselling an adolescent boy involved in gang rape...
>
> (Davies, 2003: 110)

These responses, or affects, are embodied indicators of what moves, fascinates or unsettles us; they appear spontaneous and immediate but are inevitably socially shaped. 'Follow the affect' – your feelings and visceral reactions to a topic, analysing critically where they come from – is one of Danielle Egan's very useful precepts for gaining greater insight into the sexualization debates (Egan, 2013: 136–137). I try to do this here, arguing that our affects about boys, media and sexualization might be produced in part at least by the theories or models of culture, learning and individual agency embedded in them, which also restrict and limit strategies for change. I then go on to explore how feminist media and cultural studies has long since challenged their core suppositions and thereby brought issues of masculinity and male audiences into a different kind of view in the sexualization debate. I draw these together with recent work on theories of social practice (Shove, 2010; Shove et al., 2012) to suggest how we might re-conceptualize the politics of sexualization.

I will also be following my own affects: remembering my partner's nephew Jozef, then aged about 17, quipping (in a context I now cannot recall) 'bros before hos', and my response (something like amusement, immediately followed by guilt at my feminist lack). During the research on 'sexualized' goods that generated the first quotation of the chapter, many parents had told us that what they saw as such relatively trivial items weren't 'worth the battle', and indeed, I have myself argued for bringing a more benign gaze to bear on the issue (Bragg & Buckingham, 2013). But I did so as part of opposing the anti-sexualization position's often punitive approach to (particularly, working-class) girls and their mothers and victim-blaming in relation to sexual violence. It was not intended to laugh off women's experiences, as detailed for instance on the Everyday Sexism blog (everydaysexism.com). Was finding 'bros before hos' funny part of our culture's general inability to take sexism seriously? What should I have said to Jozef? But equally, why do I worry so much about that question, as if the whole of my feminist politics hangs on getting it right?

Culture and audience in anti-sexualization discourse

The anti-sexualization position repeatedly indicts popular, commercialized culture, targeting advertisements, magazines, TV, films, music videos and consumer goods. Consider these examples:

> The world is *saturated* by more images today than at any other time in our modern history. *Behind* each of these images lies *a message* about expectations, values and ideals. Women are revered – and rewarded – for their physical attributes and both girls and boys are under pressure to emulate polarised gender stereotypes from a younger and younger age.... [T]hese developments are having a profound *impact*, particularly on girls and young women.... [I]t is important to look at the social scripts children are being influenced by and what makes children *susceptible* to them....

The predominant message for boys is to be sexually dominant and to objectify the female body.... Sexualised ideals of young, thin, beauty...[and]
'airbrushing' photographs...can lead people to believe in a *reality that
does not exist.*

(Papadopoulos, 2010: 5, 7–8, my emphasis)

A content analysis of...Barbie Magazine [demonstrates that] fully three
quarters...is *sexualising* material....[the authors] noted that the *'clear
message*...is that...a girl needs products, products, products'...that
'each issue is a large and *clever* advertisement which uses development
and psychological knowledge to market products to young and *vulnerable* children'....[particular poses] can have *a sexualising effect*....they
are now being replicated by children, who have not yet developed the
adult physical features such poses are *calculated* to show off.... For girls,
examples include...the demure pose (*downcast eyes, which have the effect
of drawing attention to the body*).

(Rush and la Nauze, 2006: viii & 24 my emphasis)

Last summer, sick of the pocket money-stealing, overly sexy and ridicu-
lously similar role models on offer in pop music, [performance artist]
Bryony Kimmings and [her niece] Taylor Houchen decided to play the
global Tween machine at its own game by inventing a new type of
pop star...the dinosaur-loving, bike-riding, tuna-pasta-eating Catherine
Bennett...[who] sings songs about things other than love, fame and
money.

(publicity for That Catherine Bennett Show aka
Credible Likeable Superstar Role Model, 2014)

Typically in the sexualization debate, as here, media are described in
metaphors that suggest they are not so much a cultural expression or a language, but a form of (damaging) social action, a homogenous, negative and
coercive force that 'bombards', 'saturates' and 'dominates', that is at worst
invasive, 'other' and alien, at best an unavoidable but highly problematic
environment, the 'wallpaper of our lives' as it is referred to in the 2011 UK
government review (DfE, 2011).

Meanings are singular, not to mention simple. One 'clear' or 'predominant' message can be identified in texts, not multiple or ambiguous ones.
These meanings are located in, or even more insidiously 'behind', single
texts in stable ways – that is, they can be identified in isolation from
their generic, narrative or viewing contexts. They are efficacious in and of
themselves; that is, they alone are able to have 'effects' and to act – to 'sexu-
alize' for instance. Identifying those meanings, and whether they are 'objectionable', falls to those with particular authority or expertise, who can also
define what genres and cultural fields should (or should not) guide our interpretation. In content analysis, to which Rush and La Nauze refer, researchers

Buckingham, 2013; Buckingham, 2003). At times the insistence that it can be administered by the otherwise untrained becomes laughable, as when mothers are encouraged to spend 'two minutes' showing their daughters how images are airbrushed in order to teach them 'not to try and live up to an image of perfection that doesn't exist' (see Bragg, 2012). In a more sophisticated and developed account, Davies (2003) describes working with a female researcher, Chas, and groups of Australian primary school children to raise their awareness of the 'constitutive force' of gender representations in popular media and fairy tales. Children are taught about the 'dominant discourse' of male/female dualism, learn to 'disrupt the familiar patterns of gender relations' and create alternative storylines that also open up a 'different kind of agency' (201).

Such strategies for change operate within a dominant psychological paradigm that emphasizes the significance of human behaviour, and intervenes at this individual level. Elizabeth Shove and colleagues have highlighted its inadequacy in relation to climate change. Shove shows (2010) how current policy-making is predicated on an 'ABC' model in which social change is said to depend on values and attitudes (A), which drive the kinds of behaviour (B) that individuals 'choose' to adopt (C). Analyses of sexualization frame the problem similarly: wrong (sexist) attitudes and beliefs lead to wrong actions. Thus in the quotations at the start of the chapter, Rush and La Nauze assume that behaviours such as 'healthy relationships' rest on 'values' that are 'undermined' by media misconceptions about male domination, and the APA asserts that boys' *belief* that girls are sexual objects may explain their *actions* towards (harassment of) girls. Change attitudes and beliefs (either by changing the media content that shapes them, or directly by pedagogical strategies), and behaviours will change – as will, ultimately, society.

Shove contends that such framing both obscures the role of institutions including governments in perpetuating unsustainable practices, and 'marginalises and excludes serious engagement with other possible analyses included those grounded in social theories of practice' (2010: 1274). Her arguments help explain why it comes to be seen as so important that individuals do not appear to express sexist 'attitudes' (because these are considered to be external drivers that shape their behaviours), whilst also, perhaps, illuminating why such monitoring seems so inadequate as a response to the scale of the issues.

It is worth lingering a while on the 'mode of address' of the pedagogies mentioned above – that is, who they think young people are, who they want them to be and what ways of 'reading' the world they construct for them (Ellsworth, 1997). While apparently benign and liberal, they leave little space for young people's perspectives (unlike, say, Renold, 2013). In the sexualization literature, children are occasionally cited if their views align with campaigners' and policy-makers'. For instance, Papadopoulos cites uncritically a girl reflecting that 'I've started worrying a lot more about my weight and body image. That could be caused by all the magazines I read in a week' (59); Davies reports the claims of some (white, middle-class) girls to have been enlightened and 'amazed' by Chas. However, when children resist such adult 'ventriloquism', their views are discounted, used as evidence of how they have been deceived and misled, or worse. Papadopoulos argues that 'while children themselves *may believe* that they can understand and contextualise, say, a Playboy logo on a pencil case... such encounters may be having a profound impact on attitudes and behaviour at an *unconscious* level' (29, my emphasis). Davies's gloss on 'Brian' is even more judgemental. In the exchange on which the quotation at the start of the chapter is based, Chas asks a group of (working-class and aboriginal) children to develop the character of a 'woman victim' in their story in a way that is 'completely different' from the 'dominant discourse' of 'sexy and pretty'. This is why Anna proposes 'fat and ugly' (but this is merely a logical reversal of the terms) and Brian's 'fuckin' ugly' then plays on and twists her words. Both suggestions, that is, are responses to how the teacher addressed and positioned them in the first place, and while Brian does mobilize sexist discourse, this does not necessarily indicate a commitment to an oppressive world order beyond the classroom. To read a pun – the return of a sound that is almost but not quite 'fat and ugly' – by a 10- or 11-year-old boy as suggesting that he is like a rapist is psychologically crude. This is not to condone Brian's remark; but it is to suggest the importance of examining the disciplinary power relations of critical pedagogies and media literacies.

Feminist scholars have repeatedly returned to 'Girl Number 20', a metaphor for the problem of classroom strategies that encourage critique of gendered subjectivities, but which, by assuming that the subject position of autonomous, distanced viewer is equally available to all, often have the effect of silencing (particular) girls' voices (Williamson, 1981/1982; Turnbull, 1998; Gonick, 2007). In relation to working-class boys and young men, I would argue that often the psychodynamics of the encounter with 'otherness' (Bhabha, 1994) meshes with what Pearson (1983), in his study of 'hooligans', terms the history of 'respectable fears'. When those 'others' do not echo adults' own words, but instead respond in ways that displace and challenge adults' identities as imparters of knowledge and truth, (middle-class) adults tend to find in their words menace and aggression (cf. Young, 1990: 47; see also Bragg, 2000).

Media and audience in feminist and cultural studies

Cultural and feminist studies approaches have long challenged the kinds of assumptions about culture and agency made in arguments about media violence as well as sexualization. The necessarily schematic account below indicates briefly how this work insists on the ambiguity and complexity of popular cultural texts; considers pleasure to be potentially radical rather than/as well as problematic; views audiences as active; and insists on the performativity of textual analysis and method.

Rather than a form of social action, as above, media texts are taken to be a language or form of cultural expression, whose meanings are necessarily ambiguous and open-ended. Popularity is taken to indicate not successful manipulation of a gullible audience, but that a text resonates with the contemporary moment: thus the relevant question is not one about effects, but about the nature of the society in which these media make sense. Intertextual approaches move beyond the analysis of single texts as self-contained objects, to their accompanying texts and practices, such as the star/celebrity system, publicity, censorship, exhibition and reviewing (Mayne, 1993). These are seen as actively working to fragment and pluralize the text in order to maximize its audience and to create 'divergent' readings (Klinger, 1989: 7). They therefore dispute that mainstream commercial products have limited polysemy compared to 'open' alternative or avant-garde texts (or, to put it another way: Taylor Swift is at least as interesting as 'Catherine Bennett'). Tony Bennett's concept of 'reading formation' explains how meaning is 'activated' by readers according to the cultural sources available to them (Bennett, 1983: 7), displacing the privilege granted to academic interpretations whilst noting that different institutions (schools, the press etc.) may 'superintend' readings in particular ways. The notion of distorted or inaccurate readings or texts thereby becomes irrelevant: meaning and impact derive from texts' relation to other texts rather than to an external reality, while any interpretation is valid if we aim to explore how it came about, rather than to evaluate its truth.

Lumby and Albury's (2010) response to Rush and La Nauze is a contemporary example of contextualized arguments about meaning. They survey contemporary Australian girls' popular culture and representational traditions, from media to family photography, arguing that set in this broader context rather than against earlier soft porn, the kinds of poses and clothing Rush and La Nauze condemn are in fact commonplace, and this alters the 'cultural messages' they can be said to carry (145). While they try to limit interpretation by referring to the gaze of 'reasonable adults', I like Simpson (2011) have argued that acknowledging ambiguity may allow us to tolerate the anxiety of thinking about childhood sexuality in terms of both agency and abuse, without one excluding the other, which may open new possibilities for conceptualizing children's sexuality (Bragg, 2014).

Cultural studies perspectives identify realism as one historically specific set of generic conventions with no automatic superiority. They consider the pleasures of 'low' cultural forms and re-evaluate the question of fantasy. As Linda Williams remarks, circular and repetitive narratives, improbability, lack of psychological depth, infantile emotions and spectacular excesses are 'moot as evaluation points if such features are intrinsic to their engagement with fantasy' (1991: 9). Pleasures have been perceived as a potential source of alternative political imaginings (Dyer, 1977); as that which can move us and deliver the unexpected (Mercer, 1986), and thus provide a basis for disruption rather than stabilization of meaning. Psychoanalytically informed work has drawn (for instance) on Laplanche and Pontalis (1986 (1964)) to see cinema as the *mise en scène* or setting of desire – one in which the subject is 'caught up in the sequence of images', rather than in pursuit of a definite object or content.

Audiences have generally been seen as active meaning-makers rather than passive receivers or cultural dupes, not least because the latter view is politically paralysing. As such, the media act as resources – essential, constitutive elements in our capacities to make sense of the world, 'tools to think with' about self and other, for making sense of cultural space and identity, in specific contexts (e.g. Buckingham & Sefton-Green, 1994; Silverstone, 1994, 1999). Empirical studies of audiences emphasize the varied meanings and uses they make of texts, often against expectations. For instance, in relation to video games such as *Grand Theft Auto*, some young players prove uninterested in their most controversial features, such as murderous 'mission structures' and misogynist 'hacks' (DeVane & Squire, 2008), while others use them in ways that connect to their own life experiences of violence (Renold, 2013); elsewhere young people refuse to define their online sexual experimentation as victimization (Brodala, 2014). Studies also emphasize social context: the processural, domestic and everyday nature of media reception, for example, challenges claims about effects that attempt to separate texts from the far broader patterns of social interactions in which they are embedded (Morley, 1986). Fan studies commonly stress the 'insider knowledge' of conventions acquired by seasoned audiences, which enables them to read and play with the different levels of meaning in the text. At its most sophisticated, this literature interprets gender and other social categories, not as stable a priori variables generating different interpretations, but instead as the historically and culturally specific *effect* of technologies of subjectivity, such as viewing practices and indeed research methods (Harbord, 2002).

Feminist media scholarship from the 1980s onwards increasingly described genres, forms and fantasies as gendered – referring partly to textual processes (narrative structure, for example), but also to the significance of a sexed audience for, and sexed authorship of, particular cultural forms. Initially many feminist critics ignored 'male' genres, instead focusing on women's forms such as magazines, soap opera and romantic fiction (Ang, 1985; Radway, 1987; Winship, 1987; Geraghty, 1991). Their aim was to redeem their aesthetic, moral and other qualities from the disparagement commonly targeted at them and by extension their audience; and in the process to instantiate new understandings of femininity.

However, this criticism also arguably involved a polarizing construction of the feminine and the masculine. For instance, analyses of soap opera stressed the open and process-centred nature of its narratives, which were also argued to be qualities of 'feminine desire'. But in order to do this, masculine desire (as in crime fiction or classic Hollywood narrative) had to be constructed as closed, goal-centred and so on. 'Thus a fit is established between the narrative patterns, the thematic content of these shows, particular qualities associated with masculinity/femininity, and finally, male and female viewers' (Tasker, 1991: 89). In the process, there is a slippage between notions of sex (of the audience, or characters) and gender (as a subject position or set of cultural competences). The ignoring of men as audiences for 'women's genres' tended to fix 'the feminine' with women, and crucially, notions of identification were considerably simplified in order to sustain the argument.

Subsequent work, notably 'bad girl' feminism and queer theory, rejected visions of women as inherently nurturing and paid increasing attention to 'nonconformist' media consumption by women and 'male' popular cultural genres such as action, horror and pornography. One particularly influential example is the work of Carol Clover on horror, in *Men, Women and Chainsaws* (1992). Her work is most appropriately read as a contribution to the psychoanalytically informed debate about the gendered cinematic gaze that Laura Mulvey had initiated in 1975 (Mulvey, 1989). Clover challenges key aspects of psychoanalytic film theory, especially its assumption of a sadistic male spectator identifying with a star of the same gender. In an argument with much resonance for contemporary debates about sexualization, she calls this a 'status-quo supportive cliché of modern cultural criticism' that has not served 'real life women and feminist politics' well (1992: 226). She explores the textual processes that force an identification between young male audience members and female characters, especially the masochistic (victim-identified) or passive viewing positions the films set up. Highlighting the instability and fluidity of masculine identities, aligning male audiences with an unstable rather than a powerful gaze, aims to forge new political alliances. She even reads young male audiences' preparedness to identify with female victims as a promising 'visible adjustment in the terms of gender representations' (127). Such work challenges mimeticism and insists on the fluidity of spectatorial identifications.

Subsequent work has been even more radical in, for instance, exploring the pleasures of violent fantasy for women (Hart, 1994) and the 'queering' of spectator positioning through the monstrous 'reconfiguring' of gender in more recent horror films, such as *Texas Chainsaw Massacre 2* (Halberstam, 1995). Meanwhile Penley's analysis of the homoerotic 'slash fiction' produced by heterosexual women fans of *Star Trek* showed that fantasies can be written across the bodies of male characters. Although they do not represent women or call themselves 'feminists', imagining Kirk and Spock as both heterosexual and homosexual means the women can identify with – *be* – them as phallic and powerful, but at the same time still *have* them as sexual objects, since as heterosexual they are still available to them (Penley, 1992). The demand for a broader range of representations to be made available in popular culture is important politically, but Penley's work challenges the idea that only *then* can they be useful for audiences. Walkerdine's work on the meanings of *Rocky* was an early (and still rare) example of an analysis that allows a mainstream film to serve metaphorical functions for a white working-class man (Walkerdine, 1986).

Textual analysis of these kinds can be seen as a 'performative act' or 'active intervention in meaning-making' that does not 'discover' pre-existing meanings in texts, but enacts creative interpretations with the potential to bring new meanings, identities and possibilities into being – and indeed to close down others. In relation to sexualization, Duschinsky observes the inconsistency with which images of women are described as 'hypersexualized', but equivalent images of men merely 'hypermasculinized', reinforcing the gender-specific effects ascribed to girls versus boys (Duschinsky, 2013). In general the complacent assumption that men adopt only the 'masterful' position as viewers enacts masculine subjectivity in specific and limited ways, as I note below.

These perspectives relate to Shove's in their displacing of individual human agency as the driver of change. In Judith Butler's more Foucauldian and discourse-oriented account, human subjects are conceptualized as 'interpellated kinds of being, dependent on ... a language we never made in order to acquire a tentative ontological status' (Butler, 1997: 26). She emphasises the ambivalence of our 'linguistic vulnerability', our reliance on meanings that we borrow but cannot control. Subjectivity is performatively enacted rather than pregiven; and agency derives from within language rather than from without. In this sense it 'sustains as well as threatens' (27), Butler argues, not in its content, but through the address that brings us into being and thereby gives us the possibility of both speaking (agency) and answering back (resistance). Our responsibility lies in our 'repetition' rather than 'origination' of language, for what meanings we sustain or challenge when we use it (ibid.). But this is more a question of context (time, place and audience) than intention. If some speech acts can be unhappy or infelicitous, then none are necessarily efficacious as hate speech theory – or, here, anti-sexualization discourse – suppose. Taking up Derrida's work on the inevitable iterability of language, Butler argues that each new utterance performs a 'break' with context that allows for reinscription and misappropriation rather than simple reproduction of meanings (Butler, 1997: 147). In effect she argues for the strategy of resistance that Bronwyn Davies uses – although Davies might not recognize it as such. Davies cites Brian's pun, breaking with the context in which it was uttered, giving it a new meaning by placing it in her feminist academic textbook and relating it to the words of a rapist. Similarly, by re-citing it myself I hope to have again shifted how we read it.

We might consider this also in relation to 'Blurred Lines'. The controversy around this hit song centred on both the video (which, directed by a woman, in its 'unexpurgated' form showed topless women with the three fully clothed male performers) and the violent and non-consensual overtones of lyrics such as 'you know you want it' and 'I'll give you something big enough to split your ass in two'. The public debate interestingly demonstrated the reach of (feminist-inflected) 'media literacy' skills, considering for instance whether the women gazing directly into the camera rather than adopting the conventional 'eyes-down demure' pose (described by Rush & La Nauze, above) represented their 'empowerment' or their availability to the male gaze. Describing it as 'objectionable', however, calls to mind Butler's suggestion that 'hate speech' theory might be displacing fears about how all language 'injures' us by disallowing our fantasies of 'radical autonomy' and self-creation. The video is certainly seductive: I find myself desirous, 'caught up in the sequence of images', wanting both to be and to have the beautiful women. The idea that boys and men watching the video would only ever identify with the subject position of 'having' the woman as object, never with 'being' themselves sexually passive, in my view says far more about our culture's homophobia than about masculine fantasy. While the video's playful tone should not allow it to avoid responsibility for its meanings, censorship seems to me less relevant than the many subsequent feminist parodies of the video that appeared online. Geraldine Harris, reviewing these, notes how the 'feminist blogosphere' has helped reinvigorate feminist debate, whilst the web in general simultaneously accommodates proliferating misogynistic sites and practices such as trolling or 'slut-shaming'. As she argues, the web 'provides a fascinating contemporary example of Michel Foucault's analysis of the complexity of the relationship between power and resistance' (Harris, 2014). It cannot easily be said to be the location of either empowerment or oppression. Nonetheless, the parodies represent an ethical manoeuvre, exploiting fault lines and aporia in representations in order to return meaning in a different form; in so doing, they promote reflection and resistance within the discourses and practices of everyday life, rather than relying on a gesture of censorship or critique delivered from above. The kind of politics and pedagogy my arguments envisage here are not a brief stop to hand over our adult tools of reason and knowledge *about* texts or institutions to arm children against influence, but an ongoing struggle, focused more on 'social self-understanding' (Richards, 1998) and on 'reflecting back a difference that makes a difference' (Ellsworth, 1997) to give young people new relationships to what they 'already' know.

There is further room to connect these arguments to social theories of practice, which similarly displace attention away from individuals to consider how practices persist or decline, how they 'recruit' individuals to carry them and how individuals might 'defect' (Shove et al., 2012). One example is that of 'lad culture' in universities, which the 'Blurred Lines' controversy served to highlight. While there are continuities with earlier practices of masculine competitiveness and harassment, Alison Phipps argues that lad culture needs to be set in the context of the commodification of higher education in the UK and the aggressively individualistic and consumerist practices that this promotes (Phipps & Young, 2014). Likewise, we might read the growth of sex industry work in the light of austerity policies that have disproportionately affected women's public sector employment and education opportunities (or, as a protester against student fees expressed it eloquently on her placard: 'ok, I'll be a stripper then').

Conclusion

In general the postmodern perspectives on which I have drawn in the second part of this chapter involve giving up on certainty. And this, of course, is difficult, because it involves not knowing what someone or something means, whether an image is positive or negative, what the effect of our well-intentioned pedagogical and campaigning efforts will be, accepting that we may not liberate, empower, deliver critical audiences, or oblige young people to abandon their fascination with the media. It means being reflexive about the performative impact of our textual analyses and our constructions of gendered audiences, about the power relations of pedagogical addresses that vainly seek only to hear our own words reflected back to us.

On the other hand, it doesn't mean giving up on any of these either. Interrupting dominant discourses about the male sex drive or girls and women 'asking for it', challenging everyday sexism and demanding resources for survivors of sexual abuse and violence are all still as important and necessary as ever. Some of our critical categories and concepts, our analyses and reflections, will offer useful resources for young people, help them think about themselves and society in new and radical ways; but – so too will the media themselves. And perhaps we need to be more ambitious in identifying what elements of sexist *practices* might be disrupted, how to force discontinuities and defections, rather than monitoring *individuals*.

So finally, back to 'bros before hos'. When I asked Jozef if I could cite it, he responded 'Hearing that feels like seeing a Facebook photo from years ago and seeing a terrible haircut and wondering why it ever happened.' The comparison to a haircut seems apposite, in the light of my comments above about the 'triviality' of the objects that are so often the focus of anti-sexualization campaigners' energies. But now I can be clearer about what taking a statement like 'bros before hos' seriously (or not) might involve. It is not trivial or insignificant. There is much to say about what it encodes: a rich history of relations and borrowings between black and white, urban and suburban youth cultures, a repressed-in-plain-view homo-eroticism/homosociality, for example. It is also witty, poetic and vivid. More locally, I was intrigued by its capacity to shed a different light on Jozef's more visible identity at that time, at least in the family contexts where I encountered him, as a pro-Tory, church-going teenager. All this is interesting, in my view. But what we cannot do is to peer through language into Jozef's originating intention; we cannot say once and for all what it means and what it tells us about him, his attitudes, values or beliefs. He, like all of us, is constituted in language but not determined by it; we cannot predict his future, as Davies threatens to do for Brian. Thus it is important to me that in this chapter I have also cited Jozef's final-year undergraduate paper on sexualization (Brodala, 2014). His journey to writing it showed me that young people, men as well as women, are not as lost as we seem to fear; that they may find their way through the maze of contemporary culture – with or without input from the inadequately feminist adults around them.

References

Ang, I. (1985) *Watching Dallas: Soap opera and the melodramatic imagination*, D. Couling (Trans.). London and New York: Methuen.

APA (2007) *Report of the American psychological association task force on the sexualization of girls*. Washington, DC: American Psychological Association. Retrieved 04042011, from http://www.apa.org/pi/women/programs/girls/report.aspx

Bennett, T. (1983) Texts, readers, reading formations. *Bulletin of the Midwest Modern Language Association*, 16 (1), 3–17.

Bhabha, H. K. (1994) *The location of culture*. London and New York: Routledge.

Bragg, S. (2000) *Media violence and education: A study of youth audiences and the horror genre*. Unpublished PhD. London: Institute of Education University of London.

Bragg, S. (2012) What I heard about sexualisation: Or, conversations with my inner Barbie. *Gender and Education*, 24 (3), 311–316.

Bragg, S. (2014) 'Shameless mums' and universal pedophiles: The sexualization and commodification of children, in C. Carter, L. Steiner, & L. McLaughlin (Eds.) *The Routledge Companion to Media and Gender*. London and New York: Routledge, pp. 321–331.

Bragg, S., & Buckingham, D. (2013) Global concerns, local negotiations and moral selves: Contemporary parenting and the 'sexualisation of childhood' debate. *Feminist Media Studies*, 13 (4), 643–659. doi: 10.1080/14680777.2012.700523.

Brodala, J. (2014) *How do young people experience sexualisation based on their gender? How has the rise of instant messaging services, in particular MSN impacted on these differences?* Political Science BA (Hons), University of Birmingham, Unpublished undergraduate dissertation.

Buckingham, D. (2003) *Media education: Literacy, learning and contemporary culture*. Cambridge: Polity.

Buckingham, D. (2014) *Objectionable content? Young people, censorship and pornography*. Unpublished. Retrieved from https://http://www.academia.edu/7453955/Objectionable_content_Young_people_censorship_and_pornography

Buckingham, D., Bragg, S., Russell, R., & Willett, R. (2010) *Sexualised goods aimed at children: A report to the Scottish parliament equal opportunities committee*. Glasgow: Scottish Parliament.

Clover, C. (1992) *Men, women and chainsaws: Gender in the modern horror film*. London: British Film Institute.

Buckingham, D., & Sefton-Green, J. (1994) *Cultural studies goes to school*. London and Bristol, PA: Taylor and Francis Ltd.

Butler, J. (1997) *Excitable speech: A politics of the performative*. London and New York: Routledge.

Coy, M. (2009) Milkshakes, lady lumps and growing up to want boobies: How the sexualisation of popular culture limits girls' horizons. *Child Abuse Review*, 18 (6), 372–383. doi: 10.1002/car.1094.

Davies, B. (2003) *Shards of glass: Children reading and writing beyond gendered identities*. NSW, Australia: Hampton Press.

DeVane, B., & Squire, K. D. (2008) The meaning of race and violence in Grand Theft Auto San Andreas. *Games and Culture*, 3 (3–4), 264–285.

DfE (2011) *Letting children be children: Report of an independent review of the commercialisation and sexualisation of childhood*. London: Department for Education.

Duschinsky, R. (2013) Sexualization: A state of injury. *Theory & Psychology*, 23 (3), 351–370.

Dyer, R. (1977) Entertainment and Utopia. *Movie*, 24, 2–13.

Egan, R. D. (2013) *Becoming sexual: A critical appraisal of the sexualization of girls*. Cambridge: Polity Press.

Ellsworth, E. (1997) *Teaching positions: Difference, pedagogy and the power of address*. New York: Teachers College Press.

Garner, M. (2012) The missing link: The sexualisation of culture and men. *Gender and Education*, 24 (3), 325–331. doi: 10.1080/09540253.2012.670392.

Geraghty, C. (1991) *Women and soap opera: A study of prime time soaps*. Cambridge: Polity Press.

Gonick, M. (2007) Girl number 20 revisited: Feminist literacies in new hard times. *Gender & Education*, 19 (4), 433–454. doi: 10.1080/09540250701442625.

Halberstam, J. (1995) *Skin shows: Gothic horror and the technology of monsters*. Durham, NC, and London: Duke University Press.

Harbord, J. (2002) *Film cultures*. London: Sage.

Harris, G. (2014) Parodying 'blurred lines' in the feminist blogosphere. *Contemporary Theatre*. Retrieved from http://www.contemporarytheatrereview.org/2014/parodying-blurred-lines/

Hart, L. (1994) *Fatal women: Lesbian sexuality and the mark of aggression*. Princeton, NJ: Princeton University Press.

Klinger, B. (1989) Digressions at the Cinema: reception and mass culture. *Cinema Journal*, 28 (4), 3–19.

Laplanche, J., & Pontalis, J.-B. (1986 (1964)) Fantasy and the origins of sexuality, in V. Burgin, J. Donald, & C. Kaplan (Eds.) *Formations of Fantasy*. London: Methuen, pp. 5–27.

Lumby, C., & Albury, K. (2010) Too much? too young? The sexualisation of children debate in Australia. *Media International Australia*, 135, 141–152.

Mayne, J. (1993) *Cinema and spectatorship*. London and New York: Routledge.

Morley, D. (1986) *Family television: Cultural power and domestic leisure*. London: Comedia.

Mulvey, L. (1989) *Visual and other pleasures*. Basingstoke and London: Macmillan.

Papadopoulos, L. (2010) *Sexualisation of young people review*. London: Department for Education and Employment.

Pearson, G. (1983) Ḥooligan: A history of respectable fears. London and Basingstoke: Macmillan.

Penley, C. (1992) Feminism, psychoanalysis, and the study of popular culture, in L. Grossberg, C. Nelson, & P. Treichler (Eds.) *Cultural Studies*. New York and London: Routledge, pp. 379–400.

Phipps, A., & Young, I. (2015) Neoliberalisation and 'lad cultures' in higher education. *Sociology*, 49(2), 305–32, doi: 10.1177/0038038514542120.

Radway, J. A. (1987) *Reading the romance: Women, patriarchy and popular literature*, British edition. London and New York: Verso.

Renold, E. (2013) *Boys and girls speak out: A qualitative study of children's gender and sexual cultures (age 10–12)*. Cardiff: Cardiff University.

Richards, C. (1998) *Teen spirits: Music and identity in media education*. London and Bristol, PA: UCL Press.

Rush, E., & La Nauze, A. (2006) *Corporate paedophilia: Sexualisation of children in Australia, working paper no. 90*. Canberra: ACT: Australia Institute. Retrieved from http://www.tai.org.au/documents/dp_fulltext/DP90.pdf

Shove, E. (2010) Beyond the ABC: Climate change policy and theories of social change. *Environment and Planning A*, 42 (6), 1273.

Shove, E., Pantzar, M., & Watson, M. (2012) *The dynamics of social practice: Everyday life and how it changes*. London: Sage.

Silverstone, R. (1994) *Television and Everyday Life*. London and New York: Routledge.

Silverstone, R. (1999) *Why Study the Media?* London, Thousand Oaks, New Delhi: Sage.

Simpson, B. (2011) Sexualizing the child: The strange case of Bill Henson, his 'absolutely revolting' images and the law of childhood innocence. *Sexualities*, 14 (3), 290–311. doi: 10.1177/1363460711400809.

Tasker, Y. (1991) Having it all: Feminism and the pleasures of the popular, in S. Franklin, C. Lury, & J. Stacey (Eds.) *Off-Centre: Feminism and Cultural Studies*. London: Harper Collins Academic, pp. 85–96.

Turnbull, S. (1998) Dealing with feeling: Why girl number twenty still doesn't answer, in D. Buckingham (Ed.) *Teaching Popular Culture: Beyond Radical Pedagogy*. London and Bristol, PA: UCL Press, pp. 88–106.

Walkerdine, V. (1986) Video replay: Families, films and fantasy, in V. Burgin, J. Donald, & C. Kaplan (Eds.) *Formations of fantasy*. London: Routledge, pp. 167–199.

Williamson, J. (1981/1982) How does girl number 20 understand ideology? *Screen Education*, 40(Autumn/Winter), 80–87.

Winship, J. (1987) *Inside women's magazines*. London: Pandora.

Young, R. (1990) *White mythologies: Writing history and the west*. London and New York: Routledge.

7
Desexualizing the Freudian Child in a Culture of 'Sexualization': Trends and Implications

R. Danielle Egan

Introduction

American schoolteacher Jessica Lahey published 'A Dress-Code Enforcer's Struggle for the Soul of the Middle-School Girl' in the popular North American publication *The Atlantic* on Valentine's Day in 2013. In her call for proper comportment she states,

> [W]hen I worry about students, it tends to be the girls. They are the ones I lose sleep over. I am not just worried about inches of exposed anatomy: I am concerned for their souls, their being, and their sense of self.... I don't blame them completely – it does happen fast... sixth graders are mere children, while eighth graders are burgeoning adults; their minds and bodies change more rapidly than they realize. During these chaotic middle years, they evolve from carefree kids to body-obsessed teenagers almost overnight. One day they can't pay attention in class because they're thinking about ponies and their pet guinea pigs, and the next they're incapacitated by daydreams about the opposite sex.
>
> (Jessica Lahey, 2014, accessed 10 November 2014)

In her plea, Lahey equates clothing choice with self-respect, intellectual promise and a good future. In contrast, sexualized clothes are said to lead to sexual behaviour, to anorexia and to portend a future of mental illness and, quite possibly, even death. Lahey views her fight over hemlines as a battle worth fighting because she wants to ensure a future of 'strong minds, kind hearts and unlimited potential' (Lahey, 2013). Lahey also cautions readers about the consequences of failure:

> Some hated themselves and loathed their bodies; they wanted to shrink down and disappear from notice. Others plucked out their eyebrows and

stopped eating. Years after she was my student, one made it out of law school before she lost her battle with depression in a motel room in North Carolina.

Lahey knows many girls who could 'change the world if they would only give themselves a chance' – a chance that only seems possible if a girl eschews her sexy displays in the classroom.

As I have noted, at length, elsewhere, narratives forwarding the cause of respectable comportment (as opposed to sexualized display) rely upon long-standing classist assumptions and, disturbingly, too often dovetail with a subset of claims found in some feminist anti-sexualization rhetoric (Egan, 2013). Sexualization literature, like many of the narratives forwarded by sexual reformers of the past, argues that (girl) child's sexuality is quiescent until puberty (Egan & Hawkes, 2006; Egan, 2013). As Foucault notes in his introductory volume on *The History of Sexuality*, in modernity, the child's sexuality has was conceptualized as physiologically present (in that everyone is born with sex organs), but experienced as subjectively and phenomenologically absent until puberty (Foucault, 1980). In my research I have shown the trenchant nature of this presumption. As such, any manifestation becomes proof that sexualization has occurred (Egan, 2013; Egan & Hawkes, 2006). Once tainted, girls become 'body obsessed' almost 'overnight', their sexuality is almost preternaturally compulsive and incapacitating. Once sexualized, innocence is lost and, as a result, so is her status as a child. Reading Freud's 1907 essay on *The Sexual Researches of Children* could not be more different. In it, he notes:

> The new-born infant brings sexuality with it into the world; certain sexual sensations attend to its development while at the breast and during early childhood, and only very few children would seem to escape some kind of sexual activity and sexual experiences before puberty.
>
> (Freud, 1907: 222)

Freud's conception of psychosexual development states that the child, from birth, is a sexual being. This does not mean that the subjective experience of the child is the same as the adult, but that rather the child is autoerotic, curious and that sexuality extends far beyond a reproductive or heteronormative imperative.

During his life, Freud actively critiqued moralizing discourses regarding masturbation and spoke against the various movements espousing moral rather than scientifically based sexual education (Gay, 1999; Egan & Hawkes, 2006). In his essay, 'Civilized Sexual Morality and Modern Nervousness' he argued that cultural double standards and cultural dictates against masturbation were particularly deleterious for women (Freud, 1908b). Examining cultural contradictions through the lens of psychoanalysis did not stop with

Freud (Samuels, 2007). In the 1940s and 1950s, Anglophone social workers, teachers and activists, inspired by Freud's early writing on the sexual life of children, crafted alternative sex education curriculums and called for more measured thinking about children, masturbation and sexual knowledge (Burston, 1994; Burstein & Gillian, 1997; Egan & Hawkes, 2006). They feared that imposing anxiety and fear into discussions about sex with children would create negative associations and inspire shame (Burston, 1994; Berstein & Gillian, 1997; Egan & Hawkes, 2006). In the 1980s psychoanalysts challenged the dominant clinical discourse that sexual expression in children (a.k.a. precocious sexuality) was always already a marker for sexual molestation. At base, Freud's conceptualization of infantile and childhood sexuality has long served as an alternative model to the presence and absence model outlined above. Starting from the assumption that sexuality is not, per se, pathological opens up a more nuanced set of questions around the sexual expression and exploitation of children. However, unlike their predecessors, psychoanalysts in the Anglophone West have been conspicuously absent from more recent discussions of sexualization and its harms. Why?

After reviewing the literature, I have found that a funny thing has happened in the century since *Three essays on the theory of sexuality* was published in 1905 – infantile sexuality has faded from prominence within Anglophone Western clinical literature. In contrast, psychosexual development is increasingly equated with gender development (as opposed to a model for gender and sexuality as it was earlier); and, paradoxically, although an increasing interest in 'pre-Oedipal conditions' dominates much of the literature, the pre-Oedipal phases which formerly stressed a set of autoerotic aims (oral, anal, phallic) have been effectively desexualized and linked with aggression (Green, 1997; Laplanche, 2011; Celezena, 2014). Prior to exploring the desexualization of childhood within Anglophone psychoanalytic literature, it is important to understand Freud's contribution to the history of ideas on the child and its sexuality.

Freud's sexual child

Although Freud is often credited with 'inventing childhood sexuality', he was not alone in his desire to decipher the phenomenological, biological and cultural implications of sexuality and eroticism in the life of child (Egan & Hawkes, 2010). His theories were part of a larger discursive constellation including paediatric medicine, sexology, pedagogy, child development and social reform written in the late 19th and mid-20th century in the Anglophone West (Egan & Hawkes, 2010). The impetus driving psychoanalytic discourse was not an attempt to unravel the 'problem', 'danger' or 'damage' caused by childhood sexuality – rather it was a desire to understand its 'nature' (1905b: 8). Unlike many of his contemporary counterparts who argued that sexuality was a physiological presence which, under normal circumstances, was dormant until puberty, Freud asserted that the manifestation of sexuality in the life of the child was a normal rather than pathological predicament (Freud, 1905c, 1907; Egan & Hawkes, 2010). In fact, he believed that the child engages in fantasies, wishes and actions that stem from an *active* erotic impulse *that is self and other directed* (at least until latency); and, moreover, that such fantasies may involve masochistic and sadistic longings (Freud, 1905a, 1905b).[1]

Sexuality, according to Freud, is an evolving subjective experience that begins in earliest infancy and is formed at the intersection of the cultural, biological and biographical. He argued that sexual instincts were situated at the nexus of the mental and the physical – that they were the psychical representation of a continuously flowing source of stimulus – as opposed to the response to a singular source of excitation (1905c). Sexuality, he wrote, 'consists of many single component-impulses' and is evidenced long before puberty (1908b: 16). As such, eroticism is the result of a complex amalgamation of aims, objects, bodily pleasure, scopic registers, sexual curiosity (what Freud terms sexual researches), as well as the desire for mastery and surrender (Freud, 1905a, 1905c, 1908b, 1928). The search for pleasure is apparent 'in infancy, when it attains its aims of pleasurable gratification not only in connection with genitalia, but also in other parts of the body (erotogenic zones), and hence is in a position to disregard any other than these easily accessible objects' (Freud, 1908a: 16–17). This can be seen in children tugging earlobes or rubbing their cheeks. Pleasure is sensual, autoerotic and not simply located in genitalia.

Freud suggested that the sexual constitution of the child is more 'variegated', 'polymorphously perverse' and autoerotic than that of its adult counterparts (Freud, 1905). Infantile sexuality emerges from and in relation to 'one of the vital somatic functions' (1905: 48). As a result, it is the pleasurable feeling the child receives from the satiation of its basic needs, such as hunger, that it later seeks to reproduce on its own. Moreover, a child's sexual aim and its search for a sexual object are formed in an analogous fashion; both are created 'in connection with the bodily functions necessary for self-preservation' (1912: 50). In her daily care of the infant, the mother produces a continuous source of excitation and pleasurable feelings in the various erotogenic zones of her child's body (1905c). While some regions of the body are 'predestined' to provide pleasure (such as the oral and anal orifices and later the genitals), any 'part of the skin or mucous membrane can function as an erotogenic zone' (1905a: 49). Primary sexual experiences are 'naturally passive in character' during the oral phase (because it is the mother who 'suckles, feeds, cleans and dresses' the child) (ibid.). However, during infancy 'active' characteristics also come to the fore and are manifested during the anal phase (for example, the child's ability to withhold faeces) (Freud, 1905).

The prolific and non-genital constitution of the child's sexual impulse, within Freudian psychoanalysis, displaces the otherwise taken-for-granted assumption of models of adult sexuality which may foreground the primacy of genitalia and during her lifetime a reproductive imperative. As I noted at the outset, sexualization literature in its conceptualization of the child assumes that sexuality is dormant until puberty and that sexual expression in children must be the outcome of a sexualized culture. Freud, in contrast, paints a picture of childhood where sexuality is active and marked by a host of contradictory features. For example, Freud underscores that the emergence and stimulation of the erotogenic zones in the child has 'more to do with producing a pleasurable feeling' than with 'the nature of the part of the body concerned' (1905c: 49). The psychosexual life of the child is further complicated by its 'component instincts' that come to the fore during the child's pursuit of sexual pleasure (1905c: 58). Devoid of shame and empathy, children are driven by a quest for mastery and sadistic cruelty (ibid.). Scopophilia, exhibitionism and cruelty are not only present, according to Freud, but are also universally expressed in children. When reviewing popular antisexualization texts, one sees rather quickly that sexy dress, consumption of sexual material and/or 'phallic displays' of bawdy behaviour are conceptualized as proof positive of sexualization and are believed to be portents of dangerous sexual behaviour in the near future (Papadopoulos, 2010). Freud's model, in contrast, examines fantasy, identification, the unconscious and the self. Fantasy and action are not corollary.

Unlike other theorists, Freud believed that pre-Oedipal eroticism was gender neutral – in that it was polymorphously perverse, autoerotic, bisexual and primarily compelled by the pleasure principle (1905c, 1908a). As Freud states in his 1913 essay on 'The Predisposition to Obsessional Neurosis', gender difference does not influence 'pre-genital object choice' (1913: 82). In the early life of children, sexuality is conceptualized as primarily active; unfortunately Freud equates this term with masculine, but as others have noted, this is more cultural than biological. Masculine subjects were allowed to pursue sexuality, whereas cultural dictates demanded passivity in the feminine (an equation Freud felt was unequal and pathological) (Freud, 1908b). Nevertheless, what is important to keep in mind is that, for Freud, *the child experiences its sexuality long before it comes to see itself as masculine or feminine*. In this way, the awareness of one's gender is secondary. The increasing importance placed on the pre-genital phase in Freudian psychoanalytic discourse is evident in his 1915 revision of *Three essays on the theory of sexuality*, in which he states that a child's pre-genital sexual organization 'constitutes a regime of a sort' in its life and when passed through normally offers 'only a hint' of its prior existence (1905c: 64). The sexual impulse during the pre-genital phase becomes almost analogous to its manifestation in puberty. For Freud, the only distinction is that in childhood 'the combination of the component instincts and their subordination under the primacy of the genitals has been effected only very incompletely or not at all' (1905c: 65). As he further articulates in 1919, it is in 'the years of childhood between the ages of two and four or five that the congenital libidinal factors are first awakened by actual experiences and become attached to certain complexes' (1919: 102).

As Jessica Benjamin and Patricia Gherovici have noted, it is only after Oedipalization and the castration complex that eroticism becomes confined and bifurcated by the dictates of civilization and plagued by a kind of haunting absence for what one had to give up (Benjamin, 1998; Gherovici, 2010). For Freud, Oedipalized gender and sexuality is a melancholic formation; this means they are plagued by what must be surrendered (masculinity must refute femininity and vice versa) in order to conform to the often rigid dictates of masculinity or femininity (Freud, 1928). Notwithstanding, part of the pleasure of early life is the more open terrain of bodies and pleasures that are transformed in later life.

Freud's pre-genital organization is radical in one sense because it foregrounds the universal and polymorphous nature of sexuality in early life and in so doing uncouples the association of sexuality with corruption and/or pathology. To this end, the eroticism of childhood is not something to correct (unless it becomes dangerously intertwined with the instinct to cruelty); rather it is a foundational instinct in the child. Nevertheless, Freud's conception of latency ultimately undercuts the potential of his theory by consigning the child's sexuality back into a 'dormant state' and once resuscitated, one that was more conscripted towards heteronormative confines. Laplanche and others note that Freud's latency may be more about hormonal quietude that is an absence of fantasy or sexual curiosity (Laplanche, 2011). In other words, a lack of hormones before puberty may mean that children are less interested in erotic play, but it does not mean that they are not actively negotiating a set of fantasies about self and others in terms of sexuality and the culture at large. Given the centrality sexuality played within Freud's thinking, the transition away from his explanatory framework within the Anglophone clinical literature over the past 60 years is particularly interesting.

Some 110 years since the publication of *Three essays on the theory of sexuality*, the psychoanalytic literature in the Anglophone West has witnessed a significant decrease in clinical investigations into or theoretical extensions of Freud's thinking on infantile sexuality and, some would argue, on discussions of sexuality in general (Green, 1997). When reviewing the Psychoanalytic Electronic Publishing (hereafter referred to as the PEP) which houses psychoanalytic journals from around the globe, one can examine the shift in publications on various topics over time. When searching the term 'infantile sexuality' one will find that there were 2,443 articles on the topic between 1955 and 1994, and of said publications, 1,993 were published by analysts practising in the Anglophone West. Using the same search parameters shows that between 1995 and 2014, there were 903 articles published. However upon closer examination, one finds that 689 of these publications were clinical, and of those, only 498 were published by individuals practising in Britain or North America. Searching for the term 'childhood sexuality' shows that 387 articles have focused on this as a key term between 1955 and 1994, and that of those articles, 300 were authored by analysts located within the Anglophone West. In the years since, 204 articles have been published; however, almost half (85 of the 204) of them were focused on the humanities (literature and film). Of the remaining 119 articles, only 42 were written by clinicians in Britain or North America. Infantile eroticism, as a search term, yields the lowest number of results across the years. Between the years of 1955 and 1994, only 17 articles were written on the topic, and since that time there have been only five published pieces. What is notable is that all five of them are either reviewing clinical debates of the past or are about adult conditions.

It is the case that earlier publications tended to focus on drive theory (also known as the classical Freudian perspective), while later ones are more diverse in terms of theoretical perspective. However, with few exceptions, attempts at extending or reviewing theories of children's sexuality are increasingly rare in the Anglophone psychoanalytic literature. Unlike other concepts which have undergone scrutiny and revision, child sexuality has not undergone theoretical reconsideration for quite some time. As a consequence, an evaluation of the contemporary cultural beliefs or experiences of young people and sexuality is outside the ways in which analysts are talking about psychoanalytic practice. One reason for this transition may be the turn towards object relations theory in the Anglophone West. In the next section, I spell out what object relations says about child sexuality and how this differs from the classical Freudian account.

The object relations turn, maternal bodies and pre-Oedipal aggression

It would be impossible to create any definitive statement about psychoanalysis in the singular when one speaks of the Anglophone West. Whether one is discussing North America or Britain, it is important to emphasize that psychoanalysis is always practised in the plural. Although there has been a decline in the practice and acceptance of psychoanalysis within the Anglophone West, one can still find a number of Freudian, Kleinian, Bionian, Lacanian, Relational/Intersubjectivist, Jungian and Independent institutes in Canada, Britain and the US. Given this variance of practice, I decided that publication trends might offer the best marker of popular and/or dominant explanatory schools of thought; reviewing the PEP's most cited articles allowed me to explore consumption and citation patterns over the past 20 years.[2] I found a striking turn towards what some would call an object relations and/or intersubjective framework (www.pep.org accessed 20 November 2014). Klein, post-Kleinians such as Winnicott and Bion, as well as intersubjectivists such as Benjamin and Ogden occupy much of the top 30 list. Pre-Oedipal anxiety, rage, narcissism, autism, attachment, attunement and transference and counter-transference are the primary foci in the articles listed (see Appendix A for the chart). Only one article examines issues of the erotic and attends to infantile sexuality in some sense, Emmanuel Ghent's 'Masochism, submission, surrender – Masochism as a perversion of surrender' (Ghent, 1990). Otherwise, the topics of sexuality in general and infantile sexuality more specifically are absent. Articles in the most cited and read category have tended to offer object-relational theoretical suppositions on the early psychic life of the infant, anxiety, aggression and the underpinnings of pre-Oedipal conditions.

It is my supposition that Anglophone schools have (inadvertently or unconsciously) desexualized the child in an attempt to understand attunement/mis-attunement, anxiety, love and attachment (what Freud termed the affective current) within the caregiver/baby dyad. With this shift in emphasis, theorists have illuminated what happens when caregiving is good enough in the life of the child as well as how its lack can impact pre-Oedipal conditions such as psychosis (Winnicott, 1945; Klein, 1952). It is important to note that a similar trend can be seen in much of the recent Anglophone literature on psychosexual development literature – infantile sexuality is more often than not replaced with discussions of gender development (Benjamin, 1998). When reviewing the literature one finds that authors have become primarily concerned with how children become gendered and tend to steer away from discussions of polymorphous perversity, sexual research and/or erotic fantasy. While I am very interested in this transition, I focus on the object relations turn owing to its pre-eminence in the PEP which, I believe, makes it more reflective of what clinicians in practice and training are reading.

In order to contextualize some of this transition, it is important to note some key developments in the early part of the 20th century within psychoanalytic practice. One of the ways in which the literature on the child shifted was with the emergence of psychoanalysis and observational research with children (Holder, 2006). Through analysis of children's play, Melanie Klein painted a picture of the complicated phantasies infants create in order to grapple with the needs, anxieties and desires of dependence (Hinshelwood, 1994). The Kleinian oeuvre revolves around the following three suppositions: that (part) object awareness happens at birth; a theoretical emphasizes the primacy of the maternal (in contrast to Freud's Oedipal father or Lacan's symbolic phallus); and that Oedipalization happens in the first year of life (Henchelwood, 1994). Klein asserted that 'the infant has an innate unconscious awareness of the existence of the mother' and 'experiences, both in the process of birth and in the adjustment to the post-natal situation, anxiety of a persecutory nature' (Klein, 1959: 248) Phantasies for Klein take place at the intersection of the soma and the object – they are, at base, responses to (and defences against) the corporeal experiences of earliest infancy and the ways needs are met (or not) by the object (Isaacs, 1952). There is an innate connection to the object which is guided by somatic impulses, unconscious phantasies and both the 'libidinal and aggressive' drives (Klein, 1952: 62). However it is infantile fears of annihilation and persecutory anxiety which predominate early life (Klein, 1952: 61). To this end, Klein and her followers depart from the classical Freudian definition of instinct as autoerotic discharge based on pleasure and un-pleasure (Grotstein, 1980). Unlike Freud who wrote extensively about the ways in which the mouth becomes the site of autoerotic pleasure via the need to feed and even forwarded a connection between a baby's post-breastfeeding repose and post orgasmic bliss, Klein emphasized the desire to feed, love and, when denied, devour and destroy the breast (Klein, 1952). Instincts, for Klein, are 'always object-seeking primarily in the nutritive [as opposed to an erotic] mode' which represents a 'holistic urge or need on the part of the whole infant' (Grotstein, 1980: 378–379). In Freud's early work, libidinal energy was synonymous with the erotic – it was conceptualized as an energetic force that fuels our connection to ideas (e.g. sublimated curiosity), our sexual aims (what we want to do sexually) as well as our fascination with particular objects of desire (who we want to do it with) (Freud, 1905c). It was not until his dual drive theory that Freud used the term life drive, which he equated with the concept of an energy that created a tension which brought things together and could be used for sex (e.g. the moment that builds erotically as one moves towards orgasm) or achievement (art, scholarship, gardening, etc.); however, libido is just one aspect of the life drive (Freud, 1905c).

Klein's 'nutritive' object-seeking model resonates with what Freud describes as the 'affectionate current', a concept he developed in 'On the universal tendency toward the debasement of women' (Freud, 1912). Freud argues that the sensual and affection currents are unfused in the lives of men who must debase women in order to have sex. Accordingly, the sensual current is related to, but not synonymous with, libido and is more akin to adult sexual lure or attraction, whereas the affectionate current happens in earliest life and helps forge the primary attachment between baby and caregiver (1912). It is not that affection is anti-libido or untethered from the erotic; rather it is, for Freud, comprised of a much smaller portion of the component instincts which make up the erotic. As I noted earlier, for Freud 'sexual instinct' is not a singular or monolithic imperative, rather it is a series component instincts that fuse together in idiosyncratic ways in the lives of individuals (Freud, 1905). Klein takes this a step further. She equates the affectionate current with attachment (Grotstein, 1980). Klein is more interested in attachment, anxiety and rage in earliest life (Klein, 1952). As a result, she evacuates most of the libidinal energy from the mother/child dyad (Klein, 1959, 1952). Klein's epistemological pivot towards de-eroticizing the child transforms the ways in which the child and her or his relationship to the caregiver is conceptualized within theory and thus as an explanatory frame within the clinic.

D. W. Winnicott was also deeply interested in the anxiety or ruthlessness of earliest life (Winnicott, 1945, 1950, 1974). He theorized that prior to object awareness, infants move through a phase of pre-concern and experience a kind of rage and destructive impulse towards deprivation (Winnicott, 1945, 1950). Within such states, part objects behave as if by magic, to this end:

> it exists when desired, it approaches when approached, it hurts when hurt. Lastly, it vanishes when not wanted. This last is most terrifying and is the only true annihilation. To not want, as a result of satisfaction, is to annihilate the object.
>
> (Winnicott, 1945: 153)

This is not about the desire to destroy, rather it is a reaction to frustration. The phantasy of retaliation occurs as both a defence against the material loss of the object in the external world or as a reaction to the loss of control of the body and/or the internalized object within the psyche (Winnicott, 1945: 156). In a move away from Freud's thinking on the binding nature of libidinal cathexses, Winnicott believed it was frustration and aggression that spurred movement away from the self and towards the object. It was the need to fulfil some sort of privation (hunger, wetness, etc.) that makes the baby move towards the other for amelioration. The oral phase is so intertwined with aggressive components that Winnicott claims that in ' health *it is oral love* that carries the basis of the great part of actual aggressiveness' – that is, aggression intended by the individual and felt as such by the people around (Winnicott, 1950: 205, emphasis added). Simply stated, aggression is central to primitive forms of love and a cornerstone for maturation (Winnicott, 1974, 1950). *As in Klein it is love not eroticism that is foregrounded.*

Wilfred Bion, like Klein and Winnicott, was also interested in the earliest phase of infant life and was invested in understanding the process of mentalization, which he viewed as the building of mind and the cultivation of feelingful thinking (Bion, 1962). Over the course of his career, Bion offered provocative conceptual frameworks to help analysts illuminate how trauma or deprivation may impede, rupture or outrightly destroy psychic structure and thus close off a rich emotional life (Bion, 1962). Drawing on a digestion model, Bion theorizes that it is the mother's capacity for containment and reverie that helps transform a baby's 'uncooked' sensory elements into cooked digestible morsels capable of mentalization (Bion, 1962). Bion argues that, 'the mother's capacity for reverie is the receptor organ for the infant's harvest of self-sensation gained by its consciousness' (Bion quoted in Brown, 2012: 1203). With maturation the baby introjects the mother's capacity for symbolization which fosters the capacity to handle and mentalize new experiences – at base it is the intersubjective space developed between caretaker and child that helps build mind and think. While Bion's work, much like Winnicott's, emphasizes the vitally important place of unconscious communication and care between the caretaker and child, the libidinal erotic aspect of that dynamic, on the part of both parties, has been evacuated.

As I noted earlier, consumption and citation trends illuminate that the work of Klein, Bion and Winnicott has been highly influential over the past 20 years. This is for good reason: each of these theorists sheds light on the formation of psychosis, unconscious communication between caretakers and infants as well as much-neglected aspects of early psychoanalytic literature – aggression in the pre-Oedipal life of the infant and its place in symptomology. Given this, one might argue that the desexualization of the infant is simply an effect of a shift in clinical emphasis and a broadening of the horizon of the 'analyzable'. Or, one could ground this transformation in the historical context of a post-Second World War Anglophone West and the desire for analysts to understand the roots of such atrocities.

Both of these are certainly the case, but when one begins to examine the psychoanalytic clinical literature from another European country such as France, which has a similar historical context and has witnessed a corollary shift in clinical interest, these explanations begin to fall short (see MacDougall, 1992, 1995; Green, 1995; Eshel, 2005; Laplanche, 2011). French analyst Andre Green raised this very issue in his provocatively titled article 'Has sexuality anything to do with psychoanalysis?', in which he argues for a re-emphasis of the sexual within psychoanalytic theorizing (Green, 1995). While Green takes issue with the limits of Freud's ideas on femininity and female sexuality, it is his contention that there is still much to be discovered about the place of sexuality in earliest object relations (Green, 1995). MacDougall pushes psychoanalytic theorizing on sexuality with her conceptualization of neo-sexuality, infantile eroticism and the reconceptualization of 'perversion' in the life of children and adults (MacDougall, 1995).

Jean Laplanche's most recent writing offers a deeply important analysis of attachment and the erotic in the life of the child and its relation to objects (Laplanche, 2011). For Laplanche, the infant and child come into contact with the culture's vision of gender and sexuality through the ways in which it has been incorporated and unconsciously transmitted by the parents (Laplanche, 2011). It is the exchange of affect and these messages that form the basis of identification and shapes the baby's vision of gender and sexuality. Drawing on the work of Lacan, Laplanche argues that the baby's reception of those messages is inevitably subject to mistranslations, because of the enigmatic quality of the parents (a child can no more understand the motivations of its parents than the parents can fully know their child). Sexuality and gender emerge, for Laplanche, at the intersection of child, parent and culture. This is due to the complex exchange that unfolds with the baby's reception of impressions and inevitable mistranslations of parental fantasy (which Laplanche terms 'leaning on'). To this end, the sexual life of children is less about hormonal changes and far more about psychic formation. Laplanche problematizes the concept of component instincts with a discussion of the erotic's connection to fantasy and unconscious communication (Laplanche, 2011). This is a significant departure from the ways in which the mother/child dyad has been theorized by Klein and post-Kleinian thinkers.

The anglophone epistemological shift towards conceptualizing the early psychic and somatic life of the child as an attempt at managing the struggles of dependency in a sea of anxiety is significantly different from Freud's conception of the machinations of the autoerotic and polymorphously perverse child. By keeping this epistemological turn in mind, a different set of questions begin to emerge about the impact of the Anglophone cultural imaginary on the psychoanalytic clinical imagination and/or cultural pressures on its practice. As I have chronicled in my research with Gail Hawkes, the Anglophone West has a long history of adult anxiety regarding sexuality and the child (Egan & Hawkes, 2010). Within the history of ideas, the child's sexuality has often been a proxy or displacement for other cultural insecurities within many discourses (Egan & Hawkes, 2010). Is this simply a case of Anglophone sexual hypocrisy or sexual repression seeping into the Anglophone Object Relations School? I would argue this reading would be too simplistic and not particularly compelling.

Is it possible that there may be an unconscious defence, owing to the Anglophone cultural imaginary, against conceptualizing the erotic aspects of unconscious communication, care and the intersubjective space between mother and baby? Is this particularly gendered? In other words, is there something about the social construction of the maternal body and the child's body (both deemed in dominant discourse as inherently asexual) that makes such a conceptualization too hard to imagine? Could it be that within Anglophone culture the relationships between caregivers and children are devoid of libidinal exchange? If so, this might tell us something more about the cultural specificity of psychosexual development. Could it be that the extreme anxieties surrounding children and sexuality have made analysts shy away from this topic in an attempt to remain viable within a mental health landscape that is less than welcoming of psychoanalytic perspectives? Is it that we still have not fully taken heed of the important insights of Salvador Ferenczi's essay, *The confusion of tongues*, which would allow for eroticism that is both adult- and child-centred (Ferenczi, 1951)? Ferenczi warns that it is the adult-centred nature of conceptualizing the child's body and sexuality that often leads to deeply problematic projections (Ferenczi, 1951).

Ferenczi does not conceptualize this as an intersubjective or object-related model; however, he offers a provocative thesis that could be examined in this regard. How can his work influence thinking on the exchanges between mother and child that involve anxiety, frustration, dread, aggression and eroticism? For example, within a cultural context where the maternal body is often desexualized – how might a woman's sensual response to breast-feeding cause a level of anxiety and guilt in her and her baby? How might Anglophone anxieties regarding the child and its sexuality shape the communication, touch and engagement of a parent with a child who is curious about his or her body? Jean Laplanche argues that ideologies of gender and sexuality are translated via messages, overt and unconscious, through parents and family (which he conceptualizes as the social with a small s) (Laplanche, 2011). If this is the case, how might this shape the ways in which a caregiver is able to contain or refuse to contain any sexual expression of her or his child? Does taking the libidinal into account speak to some of the ways in which unconscious communication is either cultivated or refused within part object relations? Taking this seriously might help us think through how guilt, attunement and mis-attunement might be interlaced with the erotic current in early bonding. And, equally important, it might help Anglophone analysts develop better ways of understanding the phenomenology of that for infants, adults and in the space between them. These are open questions that I hope will cultivate more questions and research in the future. I will end this chapter by returning to the example I brought up in the introduction to think through some of the potential implications of the current conceptual blindspot surrounding the child and its sexuality within Anglophone clinical literature.

Conclusion

As I have chronicled extensively elsewhere, a cornerstone of many popular treatises and policy reports on sexualization within the Anglophone West focuses on the potential contagion of phallically oriented desires and behaviours in tween-aged girls (Egan & Hawkes, 2010; Egan, 2013). Exhibitionism, public drunkenness, premature intercourse, the rise of oral and anal sex, and the desire for a future in the sex industry are just a few that have been mentioned in the particularly hyperbolic publications and documentaries on the topic (Dines, 2010; Papadopoulos, 2010; Bailey, 2011). Revisiting the cautionary narrative offered by Jessica Lahey on why the dress of tweenage girls needs to be managed, we see a similar set of assumptions: 'I hate having to worry that being able to see a girl's underwear will so addle the boys' brains that they will be unable to concentrate in science class' (Lahey access 14 November 2014). Instead of worrying about underwear, she wants to worry about helping girls change the world. The affective nature of her plea makes the critique of her ideas far more challenging. Who, after all, could be against the achievement of girls? It is important to point out, however, the key assumptions at work in her article: girls are passive in their orientation towards sexualization, but once sexualized girls become hyper-compulsive, and finally, they are at fault for addling the brains of their male counterparts. As I have chronicled, at length, elsewhere, and as many of the chapters in this book reveal – this discourse does not accurately reflect the complicated ways in which girls and boys negotiate the sexual cultures within which they find themselves. However, given the hegemony of this perspective and its place within many government policy papers, its potential for shaping policy and mental health criteria is cause for great concern.

Clinicians, unlike many others, have access to the complicated ways in which culture and family dynamics intersect in the lives of young people and their families. Revisiting psychoanalytic ideas regarding the sexual life of the child seems particularly pressing in the midst of our current cultural climate. Taking the idea of childhood sexuality seriously might allow psychoanalytical clinicians to offer a new approach to seeing how a child's sexuality might be impacted by a set of adult projections in deeply complex ways (which might include sexualization, containment, care, desexualization or pathologization, to name only a few). They might be able to offer another window into the ways in which young people who are suffering and come into session may be negotiating, among other things, culture, family and sexuality, and how these change and transform over time. Analysts could offer a nuanced picture of how young people identify, disidentify or partially identify with culture, family, peers, and how this shapes perceptions of self. Ultimately, it is my hope that clinicians will begin to refocus on the place of sexuality within the life of the child in order to offer a reasoned counter-narrative to the current popular discourse on sexualization.

Notes

1. Sexologists such as Havelock Ellis, Magnus Hirschfeld and Albert Moll were also deeply interested in the topic, and most used adult memories of childhood as the primary data upon which they drew their conclusions – albeit in different ways and for a variety of motives (Egan and Hawkes 2006).
2. The PEP cannot offer insight into the countries of where the consumption of particular articles is taking place.

References

Bailey, R. (2011) Letting children be children. *UK Department for Education, Report of an independent review of the commercialisation and sexualisation of childhood.* Retrieved 6 July 2011 from https://www.education.gov.uk/publications/standard/publicationDetail/Page1/CM%208078

Benjamin, J. (1998) *Shadow of the other: Gender and intersubjectivity in psychoanalysis.* New York: Routledge.

Bion, W. R. (1962) *Learning from experience.* London: Tavistock Press.

Brown, L. (2011) *Intersubjective processes and the unconscious: An integration of Freudian, Kleinian and Bionian perspectives.* The New Library of Psychoanalysis. London: Routledge.

Burstein, A. G., & Gillian, J. (1997) Teaching Freud: A lesson. *Psychoanalytic Psychology,* 14, 457–473.

Burston, D. (1994) Freud, the serpent and the sexual enlightenment of children. *International Forum of Psychoanalysis,* 3, 205–219.

Celezena, A. (2014) *Erotic revelations: Clinical applications and perverse scenarios.* New York: Routledge.

Dines, G. (2010). *Pornland: How porn has hijacked our sexuality.* Boston: Beacon Press.

Egan, R. D. (2013) *Becoming sexual: A critical appraisal of girls and sexualization.* London: Polity.

Egan, R. D., & Hawkes, G. (2010) *Theorizing the sexual child in modernity.* New York: Palgrave Macmillan.

Egan, R. D., & Hawkes, G. (2006) *Theorizing the sexual child in modernity.* New York: Palgrave.

Eshel, O. (2005) Penthus rather than Oedipus: On perversion, survival and analytic presencing. *International Journal of Psychoanalysis,* 86, 1071–1097.

Ferenczi, S. (1951) Confusions of the tongues between adult and child. *Psychoanalytic Quarterly,* 20 (2), 641–642.

Foucault, M. (1980) *History of sexuality: Vol. 1.* New York: Vintage Press.

Freud, S. (1928). Fetishism. *International Journal of Psychoanalysis,* 9, 161–166.

Freud, S. (1905a/2006) Fragments of an analysis of hysteria (Dora), in S. Whiteside (Ed. and Trans.) *The Psychology of Love.* London: Penguin, pp. 11–100.

Freud, S. (1905b/1997) My views on the part played by sexuality in the aetiology of the neuroses, in P. Reiff (Ed.) *Sexuality and the Psychology of Love.* New York: Touchstone Press, pp. 1–9.

Freud, S. (1905c/2000) *Three essays on the theory of sexuality.* James, S. (Trans.). New York: Basic Books.

Freud, S. (1907) On the sexual theories of children, in *The Standard Edition of the Complete Psychological Works of Sigmund Freud, Volume IX (1906–1908): Jensen's 'Gradiva' and Other Works,* pp. 205–226.

Freud, S. (1908a) 'Civilized' sexual morality and modern nervousness, in P. Reiff (Ed.) *Sexuality and the Psychology of Love.* New York: Touchstone Press, pp. 10–30.

Freud, S. (1908b/2006) On the sexual theories of children, in S. Whiteside (Trans.) *The Psychology of Love.* London: Penguin, pp. 221–238.

Freud, Sigmund (1912/1997) The most prevalent form of degradation in erotic life, in P. Reiff (Ed.) *Sexuality and the Psychology of Love.* New York: Touchstone Press, pp. 48–59.

Freud, S. (1913/1997) The predisposition of obsessional neurosis, in P. Reiff (Ed.) *Sexuality and the Psychology of Love.* New York: Touchstone Press, pp. 81–86.

Freud, S. (1919/1997) A child is being beaten, in *On Freud's 'A Child Is Being Beaten'* series. Contemporary Freud: Turning points and critical issues. New Haven, CN: Yale University Press.

Gay, P. (1999) *Freud: A life for our times.* New York: W. W. Norton.

Ghent, E. (1990) Masochism, submission, surrender – Masochism as a perversion of surrender. *Contemporary Psychoanalysis,* 26, 108–136.

Gherovici, P. (2010) *Please select your gender: From the invention of hysteria to the democratizing of transgenderism.* New York: Routledge.

Green, A. (1997) Opening remarks to a discussion of sexuality in contemporary psychoanalysis. *The International Journal of Psychoanalysis*, 78, 345–350.

Green, A. (1995) Has sexuality anything to do with psychoanalysis? *International Journal of Psycho-Analysis*, 76, 871–883.

Grotstein, J. (1980) The significance of Kleinian contributions to psychoanalysis, Kleinian instinct theory. *International Journal of Psychoanalysis*, 8, 375–392.

Hinshelwood, R. D. (1994) *Clinical Klein: From theory to practice*. New York: Basic Books.

Holder, A. (2006) *Anna Freud, Melanie Klein and the psychoanalysis with children and Adolescents*. London: Karnac.

Isaacs, S. (1952) The nature and function of Phantasy, in J. Riviere (Ed.) *Developments in Psychoanalysis*. New York: Da Capo Press, pp. 67–121.

Klein, M. (1959) Symposium on 'depressive illness'. V. A note on depression in the schizophrenic. *The International Journal of Psycho-analysis*, 41, 509–511.

Klein, M. (1952) Some theoretical conclusions regarding the emotional life of the infant. *The Writings of Melanie Klein*, 3, 61–93.

Klein, M. (1946) Notes on some Schizoid mechanisms, in *Envy and Gratitude and Other Works 1946–1963: The Writings of Melanie Klein Vol. III*. New York: Free Press.

Lahey, J. (2013) A dress code enforcers struggle for the soul of the middle school girl. *Atlantic Monthly*. Retrieved 11 November 2014 from http://www.theatlantic.com/sexes/archive/2013/02/a-dress-code-enforcers-struggle-for-the-soul-of-the-middle-school-girl/273155/

Laplanche, J. (2011) *Freud and the sexual*. London: The Unconscious in Translation.

MacDougall, J. (1995) *The many faces of Eros*. New York: W. W. Norton.

McDougall, J. (1992). The 'dis-affected' patient: Reflections on affect pathology. *From Inner Sources*, 4, 251–273.

Papadopoulos, L. (2010) *Sexualisation of young people review*. UK, London: Home Office.

Samuels, A. (2007) *Politics on the couch: Citizenship and the internal life*. London: Karnac.

Winnicott, D. W. (1945) Primitive emotional development, in D. W. Winnicott (Ed.) *Through Pediatrics to Psycho-analysis: Collected Papers*. New York: Basic Books, pp. 145–156.

Winnicott, D. W. (1950) Aggression in relation to emotional development (1950–1955), in D. W. Winnicott (Ed.) *Through Pediatrics to Psycho-analysis: Collected Papers*. New York: Basic Books, pp. 204–218.

Winnicott, D. W. (1974) The fear of breakdown. *The International Review of Psychoanalysis*, 1, 103–107.

Part II

Pre-teen Sexualities: Problematizing Sexual Agency and Sexual Innocence

8
Seeing (with) the 'Sexy' Body: Young Children's Visual Enactment of Sexuality

Anna Sparrman

Introduction

Across the Western world, a great deal of effort is being put into regulating and constituting laws against adults' possession and use of images of nude and half-nude prepubescent children.[1] In parallel, research on children, sexuality and visuality mainly focuses on how children are sexualized in images (e.g. Higonnet, 1998, cf. Sparrman, 2013b). Less research has been conducted on children's looking at images of nude or half nude bodies beyond the moral panics concerning their surmised distorted identification with celebrities, which tends to pathologize child sexuality (for an exception, see Sparrman, 2002a, 2002b, 2013a, 2014; Buckingham and Bragg, 2004; Egan 2013, Ringrose and Coleman 2013; Egan & Hawkes, 2008). This chapter explores the close connection between visuality, sexuality, children and adults. The focus is on how children look at images of nude and half-dressed adults and how this raises questions about how child and adult bodies, child and adult gazes, and child and adult sexualities connect with and also *enact* one another. The theoretical emphasis is on *sexuality as enactments*.

Jeffrey Weeks (2003) proposes that we live with different versions of what we mean by sex and sexuality. He argues that the term has multiple meanings and refers to an act, a category applied to a person, practices, gender and 'having a sexuality', and that it is valued as either perverted or 'normal' (Weeks, 2003). As a topic, it is also closely connected to politics and social and cultural relations as well as to having a vocabulary with which to talk about it (see also Foucault, 1978; Plummer, 1995). Weeks's open and inclusive take on sexuality raises the questions of where, when, by whom and what sexuality is produced? These questions need to be explored especially in relation to the topic of children and sexuality.

Using Weeks's conceptual openness as a springboard, this chapter explores the idea that sexuality is *enacted*; that is, sexuality is viewed as being

dependent on and produced through practices, rather than as a possession of either human or material entities. The concept of enactment derives
from Science Technology Studies (STS) (Mol, 2002; Law, 2004). While Michel
Foucault's (1978) studies on sexuality established that, for example, child
sexuality was socially and culturally constructed, enactment theory tries to
push the argument further. An enactment has powerful productive consequences, meaning that 'reality' is subject to constant negotiation rather
than being made once and for all (Mol, 2002; Law, 2004). This means that
sexuality, for example, comes into being through social, cultural, material,
political and personal relations, just as Weeks argues (see also Foucault, 1978;
Plummer, 1995). The difference regarding the enactment of sexuality is that
this concept allows us to explore what sexuality is made up of instead of
using as our starting point the notion that sexuality is, for example, gendered
or political. The focus is instead on *how* it is made gendered or political.
In Annemarie Mol's words (2002):

> (...) there is no longer a single passive object in the middle [child or sex-
> uality], waiting to be seen from the point of view of seemingly endless
> series of perspectives. Instead, objects come into being – and disappear –
> with the practices in which they are manipulated. And since the object
> of manipulation tends to differ from one practice to another, reality
> multiplies.
>
> (Mol, 2002: 5)

The plurality of practices opens up different multiple 'realities' of sexualities.
A practice-based enactment approach investigates how, for example, children and adults enact sexuality, but also how they enact and are enacted as
sexual agents, in this case through visuality.

The theoretical approach developed in this chapter suggests that, when
studied as situated practices in children's everyday lives, child and adult
sexuality are complex, 'messy' and enacted (Law, 2004; see also Sparrman,
2013a). The analyses in this chapter give insight into this messiness, thereby
challenging stereotypical notions of child and adult sexuality – this time
from the point of view of children's own interpretations of 'sexy' images in
practice (Egan & Hawkes, 2008). Staying with, as opposed to avoiding, ambiguity and paradoxes as they are seen in practice can, in the long run, offer a
more nuanced template for policy and sex education curricula, for example.

This chapter is divided into five sections. Following this introduction, the
second section critically reviews the key concepts involved in understanding children and sexuality. The third section looks at the theoretical and
practical status of images in understanding children's own meaning-making.
The fourth section presents the empirical study and the methodological consequences of researching 'mess' and ambiguity. The fifth and last
section, before concluding, presents analyses of how children's focus group

discussions about 'sexy' images enact sexuality, the connectedness between child and adult sexuality and the issue of sexual agency.

Children and sexuality

Research into younger children's (age 6–12 years) meaning-making regarding sex and sexuality is today a lively and expanding field. It is situated in educational practices focusing on sexuality, gender and heterosexuality among children themselves (e.g. Thorne, 1993; Sparrman, 2002a; Epstein et al., 2001; Epstein et al., 2003; Renold, 2005) as well as in children's views on sexualized media, literature and popular culture (e.g. Walkerdine, 1997; Davies, 2003; Buckingham & Bragg, 2004; Renold, 2013; Sparrman, 2013a). As pointed out by Mary Jane Kehily (2010) in her overview of research on children and sexuality, the field of child studies has great potential for approaching childhood innocence critically by, for example, questioning the notion that sexuality is a universal biological norm. One important theoretical standpoint in child studies is to approach children as social actors *in* society, who are situated through gender, class, ethnicity and age (James & Prout, 1990; James et al., 1998). This means approaching children as active agents who produce and reproduce the social and cultural worlds they live in. Saying that children are agentive and actors is not synonymous with saying that children per se are competent, mature and rational, which is a risk when children are concerned.

Nick Lee (1998, 2001) describes how the sociology of childhood, when it was established during the 1990s, simply fitted children into standard forms of sociological theory. As a consequence, children were situated in an adult discourse of independency and maturity. Lee advances an alternative discourse for theorizing child and adult agency: 'immature sociology'. 'Immature sociology' locates agency as a property of networks of dependency rather than as possessions of individuals. This means that children's agency is distributed in networks of materials, texts, bodies and persons, which suggests incompleteness rather than completeness. It proposes that children, but notably adults as well, are always beings *and* becomings – in other words, both categories are immature and incomplete. The 'immature sociology' not only questions the ontology of the child, but it also throws new light on what it is to be an adult. Lee's concepts of being *and* becoming also opens up for the intermingling of the child–adult relation in multiple and complex ways, thus creating what could be called a pluralism of dependencies or assemblages such as: a sexual-child-adult or an adult-sexual-child or a childish-child (cf. Plummer, 1991; Walkerdine, 1997; Sparrman, 2009; Ringrose & Coleman, 2013).[2] Children's and adults' agency are, as Lee (1998: 459) puts it, 'an emergent property of patterns of dependency' rather than personal essential properties. From this follows a view of subjectivity as decentred, as it re-enacts the 'I' through the practices that enact both materials and humans as subjects (Mol, 2008). It is a 'shared activity all round' (ibid. 31). The subject in the theory is not the human child but the *relation* or, as Lee (1998, 2001) calls it, the network of relations, between children, bodies, imagination and images. This raises the question of what happens if we explore children's sexual agency as enacted as a property of codependency.

Seeing (with) the body: Enacting 'sexy' images

Images are central to this chapter as is the body, which is why it is appropriate to linger a bit on how we can understand the relationship between looking, image and body. It is no understatement to say that we live with images, we understand the world as images, and that images both shape and are shaped by the world. In this way, images are important in determining how notions such as sexuality are shaped and reproduced in our societies. Hans Belting (2005, 2011) has established an *anthropology of the image*, arguing that images never exist in themselves but *happen* or *take place* in a medium-body-image interaction (Belting, 2005). He also argues that mental (internal) and physical (external) images are two sides of the same coin, as the mental is inscribed in the physical and vice versa, and that together they perform an absent presence.

The body is the locus of images in Belting's (2011) theory, because the body is a living medium that perceives, remembers and projects images. In our bodies, he argues, the personal (gender, age, biography) and the collective (environment, historical time, education and upbringing) intermingle to form our reactions just as the beholder exercises her/his imagination in relation to the perceived images (Belting, 2005, 2011). Even though Belting (2005) talks about the 'living body', he still seems to equate body only with cognitive processes, as pointed out by Melinda Hinkson (2009). By holding on to the performativity of images, Hinkson argues that Belting's theory of the body can have much greater implications, because his dispositions of the body can mean 'person', that is the whole living body, without differentiating between eye, mind and image (see also Ringrose & Coleman 2013).

John Law (2004) argues that the concept of enactment is more open than that of performance. The latter has a tendency to favour human behaviour, while enactment comprises both the human and the material. In this way, the enactment of the image takes place in the *relation* between bodies, images, materiality and the social (Law, 2004). From this it follows that images have no essential meaning (Bal, 2003). Meanings are continuously negotiated through the relations with which they are interwoven or intertwined. This focus on the 'relation' goes beyond the contextualization of images, as the image simultaneously enacts and is enacted through practices. The body in turn becomes a body enacted in practice by intermingling bodily aspects such as seeing, thinking, verbal expressions and gestures (see also Ringrose & Coleman, 2013). The practice-based view of understanding images presented here is highly relevant to understanding how sexuality is enacted.

My argument is that images do not just happen in interaction, but that they are, just like sexuality and agency, *enacted* (creating reality) or *being done* by and through their relations. This means that images comprise a single entity in larger systems of activity (Law, 2004). The argument brought forward in this chapter is not one concerning whether children are or are not sexual. In sum, drawing on the existing literature, I suggest a complex, practice-based approach to children, adults, sexuality and images, and portray children's sexual agency as a property of networks of co-dependency. Given these arguments, one needs to ask the following questions. How and in what ways are child and adult sexuality, as well as images and bodies, enacted by children? What versions of sexuality do the children enact? How in practice do children see that something is sexual? And how is children's agentive dependency expressed? Thus, the focus here is not on children's inner cognitive processes, but on their practice-based enactments. In the next section, I address these questions using empirical material on children's appreciation of images of nude and half-nude bodies.

The study

The following analysis of children's discussions of images and sexuality is based on focus group discussions about advertising and images on the topic of love, sex, relationships and gender in the visual media.[3] In total, 27 children (age 9–12 years) from the US and Sweden participated: two focus groups in the US and four in Sweden.[4] The US groups conducted a single session per group, while the Swedish children met twice, and one group three times at their own request. The Swedish children were also invited to make a scrapbook diary over a period of one week. All discussions took place inside the children's schools, either during regular school hours or during after-school hours.

All focus group sessions were video recorded to enable a review of which image was being discussed and when. Moreover, all groups were gender mixed. This was a conscious choice, as I wanted to find out how boys and girls approached the topic of sexuality together (Sparrman, 2013a).

The focus groups discussed 16 visual images,[5] all of which had been reported to Sweden's Trade Ethical Council against Sexism in Advertising (ERK) for being sexist or gender stereotyping.[6] The images focused on sexuality and technology, food, and clothing/underwear. As ERK is a self-regulating organization, it can take its own actions against advertisements. However, most complaints reach ERK through private persons. One complaint is sufficient for the board to decide on actions (Dahlberg, 2011). Even though the focus group discussions were framed by me as being partly about sex, I as a researcher had not decided what constituted a 'sexy' image (see also Buckingham & Bragg, 2004). Time was spent in the focus groups to articulate whether and why the images were sexy and how that could be seen.

The assignment for the Swedish children making the scrapbook diaries was to collect, draw, cut out and paste in images on the topic of visual media, love, sex, relationships and 'boyish, girlish' (gender) issues that they experienced during an ordinary week. Perhaps a bit naively, I thought the scrapbooks would generate a more diverse set of images than the focus group images, as those were images that I, the researcher, had brought along.[7]

The scrapbook assignment was voluntary and 9 of the 17 Swedish children participated.[8] In one of the focus groups, all children handed in a scrapbook. This group consisted of three boys and two girls, all aged nine and ethnically white. The main focus of analysis in this chapter is on this focus group and the children's scrapbooks. They were all from the same primary class and were put together as a group on a random basis, though making sure the group included both boys and girls.

It turned out that the majority of the images the children collected or made were of nude or half-nude adults, and fewer images showed themes of love and relationships. As mentioned by the boys themselves, Stefan, Pelle and Simon,[9] they had mainly focused on images of nude women in popular culture, while the girls, Astrid and Hedda, it turned out, had focused on all the aspects of sex, gender, love and relationships, including love between children and parents and between animals. Stefan had collected 12 images, both girls had nine, while Pelle and Simon had settled for one each.

Qualitative research methodologies have lately become more specialized and differentiated (Atkinson et al., 2008). This becomes problematical when complexities such as the ones presented in this chapter are to be analysed. The theoretical framework calls for a reintegration and mixing of different analytical methods such as discourse analysis, visual analysis and ethnographic analysis. No natural analytical order is to be revealed, talk is not superior to imagination, bodily actions or the symbolic, and the human is not superior to materiality (Atkinson et al., 2008). My endeavour is to try to engage with what is taken for granted about children and sexuality by attempting to open the topic and reflect on it through the relational work taking place between talk, social interaction, visuality and fantasies; that is based on the material and immaterial at the same time. Thus, the focus of the analyses is on unmaking certainty by focusing on ambiguity, connectedness, the imaginary and fluidity (Law, 2004; Atkinson et al., 2008; Sørensen 2009), while investigating the becoming of sexuality in practice. This means unpacking and interpreting the complex using methodological tools that enable us to stay with complexity.

Children looking at adult sexual bodies

Three analyses of images enacted by the children follow. The analyses of (Figure 8.1) draw on all focus groups, both from the US and Sweden, focusing on how 'sexiness' can be seen in an advertisement reported to the ERK. Figures 8.2 and 8.3 are from Astrid's scrapbook, showing a half-nude man, an ad for underwear and a drawing. The different examples present different ways in which children, images, the very act of looking, bodies, language, love and sexuality enact one another when children, together with a researcher, explore images of 'sexy' adult bodies.

Seeing 'sexiness' in images

In the first focus group conducted in the project, one boy had already said about an ad for Lavazza coffee (Figure 8.1): 'That's not so much nudity but it's just sexy' (US focus group). I took this as a reason to ask all focus groups, when they did not take up the topic themselves, how one can see that an image is sexy. All groups, except one, collectively identified the woman as looking sexy by verbally and physically pointing out: 'the

Figure 8.1 Ad for Lavazza coffee
Convicted by ERK 2006. Lavazza coffee International Campaign 'The First Class Espresso Experience' 2006. Photographer Ellen von Unwerth. Downloaded from Sweden's Trade Ethical Council against Sexism in Advertising (ERK) webpage in 2008.[6]

crooked clothes', 'the visibility of the bra', 'the spoon in the mouth', 'the grip on the cup', 'long eyelashes', 'the smile', 'the make-up', 'nail polish', 'self-confidence', 'her gaze', 'blonde hair' and finally 'being good-looking'. No group mentioned just one thing, but presented a combination of details. Arguably when pinpointing the complexity of what sexy looks like, it is not enough, according to the children's comments, if a woman has nail polish or a spoon in her mouth. It instead has to do with the combination of *how* she has the spoon in her mouth and the relationship with other things inside the image. The children talk about the 'hows' of sexiness without making any intervisual connections (Mirzoeff, 2000). Thus, they did not connect to or draw on other images or situations in life to explain to one another what they meant. None of the children questioned any suggestions of details presented by others in the groups. Instead they verbally filled in for one another in calm and often thoughtful ways. As the children did not challenge one another in these specific situations, it suggests that the looks of 'sexiness' are enacted as a possible shared visual cultural attitude (Hinkson, 2009), or at least a shared attitude to how a female adult looks 'sexy'. The children's enactments point to how children's sexual agency is distributed between the children and the image, between the details in the image, between the children themselves, the enactment of the word 'sexy', the atmosphere in the focus group and the children's collaborative work. Sexual agency is not located to any of the individual children, but enacted in and through interrelations and dependencies between the different entities at work in the practice (Lee, 1998, 2001; Mol, 2008). In this case, the individual subjectivity is decentred, as the potential subjective 'I' in sexual agency is re-enacted in and through the multiple flows of subjects – material, human and immaterial (i.e. collective collaboration) – in practice (Mol, 2008). The example illustrates how sexual agency is enacted as a property that belongs to the relational work taking place in the situation, rather than to the individual child (Lee, 1998, 2001). Sexual agency could thereby be said to be enacted as 'owned' by external visual and textual entities (Lee, 1998).

Seeing the 'sexy' body

The atmosphere and the discussion in the Swedish focus group is hectic. The boys especially are visibly excited to see all the images. Everyone interrupts one another and few topics are elaborated on extensively. When Astrid turns her page, showing a glossy image of a man with a 'six pack' (Figure 8.2), I ask whether or not the man is 'sexy'. The question is asked following an extensive discussion about images of 'sexy' women and a not-commented-upon image of a man with a naked upper body. In this way, the discussion is framed by a 'sexiness' discourse.

Before I ask my question, Stefan has already commented on the image, stating that 'it is only a little bit of muscles'. Simon then says 'I wish I had a body like that', to which Stefan agrees. Further on in the discussion, Simon's

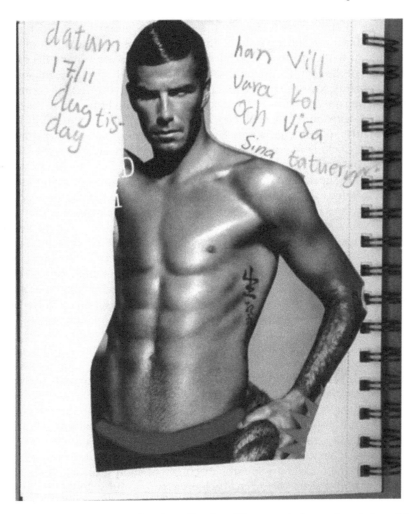

Figure 8.2 Astrid. Date: 17/11. Day: Tuesday. 'He wants to be cool and show his tattoos'

answer to my question is that the man is 'somewhat sexy'. He also replies, when asked, that the man is quite good-looking, something with which the girls neither agree nor fully disagree. When I ask what makes the man good-looking, the children state that it is neither the hair nor the tattoos that do it. Simon's contribution to the discussion is that he 'likes the muscles'. Simon says this with a dreamy voice, leaning over the image with his cheeks in his hands. There is no full or explicit rejection of the sexiness or good looks of the man in the image; the girls settle for a quiet 'maybe' or a 'little' good-looking. Still, Simon's wish enacts different possible relations and combinations between muscles, sexiness and good looks.

In one of the earlier focus group sessions, the group had looked at a cartoon image of Superman and discussed the possible 'sexiness' of his muscles. At that time, the group rejected Superman as sexy, saying his muscles were needed for his strength (see also Renold, 2013 for boys' investing in muscularity for strength and particularly for surviving violent community relations). When later in the discussion, I compared the man in Astrid's scrapbook with Superman's muscles, all participants in the group loudly disagreed with me. This enacts muscles as dependent on, among other things, whom they belong to and possibly in what mode they are expressed – cartoon or photograph. None of the boys said they wanted to look like or have muscles like Superman. However, all three boys, on their own initiative, agreed to some extent that they would like muscles like the man in Astrid's image. This was most explicitly expressed by nine-year-old Simon.

When Simon looked at the image and wished he had the body depicted in the image, it can be argued that the image looks back at him as it makes him think about himself (Rossi, 1993–1995). The relational work being done involves words, image, bodies, the very act of looking and imagination, and support rather than challenge from his classmates, enacting numerous relational connections. By trying to disentangle all the relations involved in his enactment of the image and himself, Simon moves in time and space, imagining himself in the future with muscles and a 'sexy' body.

Simon's own enactment of the image also creates a multitude of possible ways of understanding the image. He intermingles an external image with an internal one, connecting his own 'real' child body (external) with an image of an adult body (external) and a future imagined adult body (internal) (Belting, 2005, 2011). The relational work between Simon's 'real' body, the body on display, the image, imagination, the situation and the wish intermingle the child and adult body. As Simon enacts the image of the man as somewhat sexy, it also intertwines child and adult sexuality. By seeing sexiness in the male body, Simon's enactment of adult sexuality also enacts Simon as both a sexual being *and* becoming (cf. Lee, 1998, 2001).

The 'wish' to have the adult body could of course also be an expression of wanting to have that muscly body now, at this moment, rather than in the future. This makes the process even more complex, as it means that nine-year-old Simon is also enacting himself as wishing to be sexy at the age of nine. Enacting himself as sexual now, at this moment, means he elaborates on his sexual agency. However, it should be mentioned that he does this in collaboration with the other boys. Sexual agency is in this way situated and relational work. The wish to have firm, large and possibly sexy muscles 'locates' the sexuality in his own body (cf. Mol, 2008: 32), and in the wish, imagination and the shared wording at the same time. It is more or less impossible to disentangle the process, especially because Simon and the rest of the children enact both the 'sexiness' and good looks of the man as fluid and in motion. It is not as easily disentangled as the image of the Lavazza advertisement. Instead sexuality moves around without having a firm location; it is decentred and, importantly, never fully rejected. The image and the uncertainty in the group enable Simon to elaborate around his own body, its present constitution, what it lacks at the moment and what he can enact in the future.

Simon's wish shows the complex work involved in the enactment of a 'sexy' image. Simultaneously it shows how sexuality is sustained as an activity, as something personal and yet still impersonal. It challenges the presumed hierarchical relations between children and adults and between child and adult sexualities as Simon blurs the present with the future and his own wishes with the adult body. Weeks's (2003) broad definition of sexuality is both confirmed and challenged through this example. It creates a multiple and complex view of sexuality and it questions the aspect of 'having sexuality', as sexuality seems to be in constant motion, thus multiplying in its meanings. Simon, it can be argued, is enacted and enacts himself as a sexual agent through this example expressed best as sexual agency in motion. His enactments show that sexual agency is not a fixed position but a motion of moving in and out of concepts and connections between entities, and the dependency on group dynamics. The enactments are also made possible through the textual mediation of the question from the researcher: 'Is he sexy?' Simon 'has' neither sexuality nor sexual agency. His independence as a person emerges from the fundamental dependency of the situation. From this it follows that there is no authentic place for him to speak from, as sexual agency is not enacted as a property (Lee, 1998).

Seeing with the body

The next image for discussion is a drawing created by Astrid. The image shows two persons lying on a bed, from a bird's-eye view. The image is in red and blue with red heart-shaped bows in each corner of the bed. In red and blue over the image, Astrid has written: 'they are sexing', perhaps indicating that the couple are 'making love'. The two people on the bed are smiling, framed by loving heart-shaped bows, something Astrid says she really likes. They are so close that one can hardly distinguish one limb from the other. One of the characters has somewhat longer hair than the other, which might indicate that it is a man and a woman, as hair length in children's drawings can indicate gender (Aronsson, 1997; Sparrman, 2002a, 2014) (Figure 8.3).

Drawing an image is a bodily activity involving the eyes, hands, bodily postures and feelings intertwining and simultaneously enacting internal and external images (Belting, 2005, 2011; Hinkson, 2009). The image tells us something about one possible image Astrid can and wants to enact of 'sexing'. She enacts 'sexing' as a smiley, happy (colours) loving (heart-shaped bows) event. While the boys mainly cut out images of women, which excited or disgusted them, Astrid uses a more elaborate rhetoric that intertwines

Figure 8.3   Made by Astrid, nine years old. 'They are sexing'

the sexual act with possibly heterosexual love. I say possibly, as she has not gendered the bodies except by the length of the hair. She has, for example, left out genitals, not because she cannot draw them, as she has drawn a penis on another page. She could have chosen to make a drawing without red heart-shaped bows, which would have focused the image more on the sexual act. The children even discuss whether the couple is dressed or naked, which is a bit unclear. The sexuality in the image is enacted through the relation between the words – 'they are sexing' – the image, the topic of the scrapbooks and the topics under discussion in the focus group.

The process of imagining and imaging the adult sexual act enacts Astrid as a subject with sexual fantasies expressed through her body and the drawing (cf. Mol, 2008). She enacts sexuality as located in her *and* in the adults, and adult sexuality as enacted 'in' her and she 'in' the adults on the paper. This means that Astrid's sexual agency does not have to do with the practice, experience or inexperience of a sexual act; rather it is about the resources she enacts when externalizing internal images on paper. It can be argued that Astrid enacts the image of sexual intercourse as a symbol for sexuality itself.

My assumption that the people on the bed are adults and not children is based on the classmates' enactment of the image as adult sexual intercourse: the image generated a discussion about whether or not the children wanted to 'do it' when they are 'older'. Older here thus indicates that 'sexing' is not for children their age. Pelle and Stefan vacillate between wanting and not wanting to, while Simon says he wants to 'do it'. The girls are very quiet. Pelle, however, lets the discussion feed into an elaboration of how it can feel in one's own body when watching a film of people involved in a sexual act, and how looking at such sequences makes it 'feel as if I'm doing it myself'. I ask Pelle to explain how it feels:

Pelle: There's a tingling in my body when I watch sex, then it feels as if
 I'm doing it myself
Stefan: yes but then my willie tightens and
Simon: I know I know
Pelle: and then it tickles there [the penis]
Anna*: Yeah
Pelle: and then you think it should do that when you're sexing
Anna: Yeah
Pelle: and then it feels like you're doing it
Anna: Okay, do you agree girls?
Astrid: Yeah
Anna: Yeah

*Focus group discussant

It is not clear exactly which film Pelle is referring to. However, earlier in the discussion the boys have mentioned the thrill of watching James Bond films with adults 'making out'. This example takes the enactment of sexuality one step further, making it even more complex, as it also involves subjective bodily feelings. Still, as will be shown, these feelings are not all together only subjective.

The relational work carried out by Pelle involves the enactment of Astrid's drawing of 'sexing', its intervisual (Mirzoeff, 2000) connections to films showing adults having sex, the very act of looking, images of bodies, bodily (tingling) feelings, tightened penises, shared verbal description and imagination. Pelle connects the bodily feelings he can feel in his own body when looking at images of adults having, or pretending to have, sex with how he thinks it actually feels to 'do it'. In this way, he enacts a very close connection between adult sexuality and his own. He intermingles the very act of looking, bodily experiences, feelings and imagination. He thereby enacts child (his bodily feelings) and adult sexuality (how they feel in their bodies when sexing) as occupying the same space. At the same time, he is sharing his feelings with the rest of the group. Stefan and Simon support Pelle's feelings. They say they 'know' and even expand on how the bodily tingling goes along with 'tightened' penises. Also the girls, after some questioning from me, the researcher, agree on there being a connection between looking at a film and one's own bodily sexual feelings.

Sexuality in this example is physically located in the child body but simultaneously also in the imagination. Pelle knows what he feels, but he does not exactly know what other physical sexual experiences he can relate it to. He enacts his own bodily feelings as part of a child innocence discourse produced in practice with the other children, and as connected to adults' feelings. In this way, he enacts adult sexuality as part of children's sexual feelings. This blurs the child and adult sexuality at the very core of personal individual experiences. But, as I started out by saying, Pelle's feelings are not only subjective. The example and the analyses show that Pelle's subjective feelings are enacted through the relational work taking place in the situation. Also his subjective feelings are shared, not just with the boys but with the girls in the focus group. They are not a possession of his, but a shared 'property of networks of dependency' (Lee, 1998). It can be argued that both Pelle's and adults' sexuality are enacted as 'immature', 'incomplete' and co-dependent (Lee, 1998, 2001).

Concluding discussion

This chapter has proposed a complex and practice-based framework for exploring children's own enactments of sexuality and images, children's sexual agency as a property of networks of dependency, as well as child and adult sexuality as relational and codependent.

The three empirical examples point in different ways to how nine-year-old children in practice enact and are enacted by sexuality. The process is relational and involves physical and imagined bodies, internal and external images, details in images, language, wishes, imagination, trust, time, the very act of looking and creative processes. It is also shown that children, when looking at adult bodies, enact both adults and themselves as sexual subjects. A simple conclusion could therefore be that moral panic discourses claiming that sexy advertising demoralizes and pathologizes children and makes them sexually precocious are true (cf. Egan & Hawkes, 2008). But as I say, that is a simple conclusion. Looking at 'sexy' images does not per se lead to negative outcomes as images are enacted in and through cultural, social and material practices. An image can of course enact strong emotions of disgust or discomfort (Sparrman, 2013a). However, what the children's own enactments demonstrate is that their relations and enactments of and through visuality and sexuality give a much more complex view of what is going on. Their enactments illustrate that what counts as child and adult sexuality is contingent and that sexual agency is neither a fixed position nor a property of the individual, but distributed across the material, immaterial, human and social.

Where does this leave us? First of all it questions predetermined views of how 'sexy' images enact and are enacted by children; secondly it questions the location of the sexiness; thirdly it challenges the dichotomy between child and adult sexuality, and fourthly it calls into question the politics behind established discourses of sexuality and sexual agency. The rationale behind the politics of, for example, separate sex education for girls and boys, of schools waiting until the age of 12–13 before introducing sex education, or for that matter of adults having the preferential right of interpretation of children's sexual knowledges are cast into doubt. This brings us back to Michel Foucault's (1978) point that sexuality must be understood through the politics of talk and the spatial and material organization of sexuality. In this chapter, Foucault's point appears to be at the heart of children's own meaning production! Children themselves question the politics that sustain the dichotomy between child and adult sexuality. So, the question is who or what gains from maintaining this dichotomization? Who loses if it becomes blurry (Mol, 1999)? Children's enactments of 'sexy' images, and their own enactment by 'sexy' images, demonstrate that the politics could be different.

Notes

1. The Data Protection Act 1998, UK. Child Anti-pornography Law CODE Title 18, Part 1, Chapter 71 Obscenity, §§1466A. *Obscene visual representations of the sexual abuse of children* (and §2252A&B), USA. The Penal Code > Chapter 16 > On Crime Against Public Order > Section 10a, Sweden.
2. Lee (1998, 2001) draws on Deleuze and Guattari's theory of assemblage (1972, 1980).
3. The research project is inspired by David Buckingham and Sara Bragg's (2004) research project 'Young people sex and the media, the facts of life?'
4. Altogether, 2 schools, 8 classes, and 175 children were asked to participate in the project. Twenty-seven children (US = 10, Sweden = 17) consented to participate in the study and 23 of them actually attended the focus groups. In total 10 girls and 13 boys participated. All together there were 11 focus group sessions. The small number of participants has been discussed by Sparrman (2013a).
5. The same material was used in the Swedish and American focus groups. Most of the ads contained texts written in English, which is why the American children

were sometimes able to interpret the pictures at multiple levels while the Swedish children at times needed help in translating the English.

6. Etiska rådet för könsdiskriminering (ERK) has since 2009 been merged with the Swedish advertising ombudsman established by the markets as a self-regulating organization. Before the merger, all ERK cases were public and could be found and read online.

7. Focus group one concerned the ERK images, while focus group two focused on images from children's own cultures chosen by me but also based on information generated from the first focus group session.

8. All of the children came from the same school situated in a middle-size city (approximately 150,000 inhabitants). The part of the city where the study took place consists of a 50/50 mix of single homes and multiple unit dwellings; 6% of the inhabitants are foreign born, 5.3% unemployed and 47% of the adults have a post-secondary education.

9. All names of the children are anonymized.

References

Aronsson, K. (1997) *Barns världar – barns bilder [Children's worlds – children's images]*. Stockholm: Natur och kultur.

Atkinson, P., Delamont, S., & Housley, W. (2008) *Contours of culture: Complex ethnography and the ethnography of complexity*. Walnut Creek, CA: Altamira Press.

Bal, M. (2003) Visual essentialism and the object of visual culture. *Journal of Visual Culture*, 2 (1), 5–32.

Belting, H. (2005) Image, medium, body: A new approach to iconology. *Critical Inquiry*, 31 (2), 302–319.

Belting, H. (2011) *An anthropology of images: Picture, medium, body*. Princeton, NJ, Oxford: Princeton University Press.

Buckingham, D., & Bragg, S. (2004) *Young people, sex and the media: The facts of life?* New York: Palgrave Macmillan.

Dahlberg, C. (2010) *Picturing the public: Advertising self-regulation in Sweden and the UK*, (Diss.). (Acta Universitatis Stockholmiensis). Stockholm: Stockholms universitet.

Davies, B. (2003) *Frogs, snails and feminist tales: Preschool children and gender*. New York: Hampton Press.

Egan, D. R. (2013) *Becoming sexual: A critical appraisal of the sexualisation of girls*. Cambridge: Polity Press.

Egan, D. R., & Hawkes, G. (2008) Girls, sexuality and the strange carnalities of advertisements: Deconstructing the discourse of corporate paedophilia. *Australian Feminist Studies*, 23 (57), 307–322.

Egan, D. R., & Hawkes, G. (2010) *Theorizing the sexual child in modernity*. Basingstoke: Palgrave Macmillan.

Epstein, D., Kehily, M. J., Mac An Ghaill, M., & Peter, R. (2001) Boys and girls coma out and play: Making masculinities and femininities in school playgrounds. *Men and Masculinity*, 4 (2), 158–172.

Epstein, D., O'Flynn, S., & David, T. (2003) *Silenced sexualities in schools and Universities*. London: Trentham Books.

Foucault, M. (1978) *The history of sexuality: An introduction*. New York: Vintage Books.

Higonnet, A. (1998) *Pictures of innocence: The history and crisis of ideal childhood*. London: Thames & Hudson.

Hinkson, M. (2009) Australia's Ben Henson scandal: Notes on the new cultural attitude to images. *Visual Studies*, 24 (3), 202–213.

James, A., Jenks, C., & Prout, A. (1998) *Theorizing childhood*. Cambridge: Polity Press.

James, A., & Prout, A. (1990) *Constructing and re-constructing childhood: Contemporary issues in the sociological study of childhood*. London: Falmer Press.

Kehily, M. J. (2010) Children and sexuality, in H. Montgomery (Ed.) *Oxford Bibliographies in Childhood Studies*. New York: Oxford University Press.

Law, J. (2004) *After method: Mess in social science research*. London, New York: Routledge.

Lee, N. (1998) Towards an immature sociology. *The Sociological Review*, 46 (3), 458–482.

Lee, N. (2001) *Childhood and society: Growing up in an age of uncertainty*. Maidenhead: Open University Press.

Mirzoeff, N. (2000) Introduction, in N. Mirzoeff (Ed.) *Diaspora and Visual Culture*. London: Routledge, pp. 1–18.

Mol, A. (1999) Ontological politics: A word and some questions, in J. Law & J. Hassard (Eds.) *Actor Network Theory and After*. Oxford, UK., Malden, USA: Blackwell Publishers/The Sociological Review, pp. 74–89.

Mol, A. (2002) *The body multiple: Ontology in medical practices*. Durham, NC, London: Duke University Press.

Mol, A. (2008) I eat an apple: On theorizing subjectivities. *Subjectivity*, 22, 28–37.

Plummer, K. (1991) Understanding child sexuality. *Journal of Homosexuality*, 20 (1–2), 231–249.

Plummer, K. (1995) *Telling sexual stories: Power, change and social worlds*. London: Routledge.

Renold, E. (2005) *Girls, boys and junior sexualities: Exploring children's gender and sexual relations in the primary school*. London: Routledge.

Renold, E. (2013) *Boys and girls speak out: A qualitative study of children's gender and sexual cultures (age 10–12)*. Cardiff: Cardiff University.

Ringrose, J., & Coleman, R. (2013) Looking and desiring machines: A feminist Deleuzian mapping of bodies and affects, in R. Coleman & J. Ringrose (Eds.) *Deleuze and Research Methodologies*. Edinburgh: Edinburgh University Press, pp. 124–144.

Rossi, L-M. (1993/1995) Att re-turnera blicken [To re-turn the gaze], in A.-L. Lindberg (Ed.) *Konst, kön och blick: Feministiska bildanalyser från renässansen till postmodernism* [Art, gender and gaze: Feminist image analyses from Renaissance to postmodernism]. Stockholm: Norstedt, pp. 211–227.

Sørensen, E. (2009) *The materiality of learning: Technology and knowledge in educational practice*. Cambridge, New York: Cambridge University Press.

Sparrman, A. (2002a) *Visuell kultur i barns vardagsliv – bilder medier och praktiker* [Visual culture in children's everyday lives – Images, media and practices] (Diss.). (Linkoping Studies in Arts and Science, 250). Linkoping: Univ.

Sparrman, A. (2002b) Spectatorship in a visual world – Sexuality in children's interactions, in R. Grankvist (Ed.) *Sensuality and Power in Visual Culture*. (Department of Modern Languages, Umeå University). Umeå: Univ, pp. 110–119.

Sparrman, A. (2009) Ambiguity and paradoxes in children's talk about marketing breakfast cereals with toys. *Young Consumers*, 10 (4), 297–313.

Sparrman, A. (2013a) Access and gatekeeping in researching children's sexuality: Mess in ethics and methods. *Sexuality and Culture*. doi: 10.1007/s12119-013-9198-x.

Sparrman, A. (2013b) Visual representations of childhood, in H. Montgomery (Ed.) *Oxford Bibliographies in Childhood Studies*. New York: Oxford University Press.

Sparrman, A. (2014) Barn tecknar nakenhet – och sexualitet? [Children draw nudity – And sexuality?], in Y. Eriksson (Ed.) *Barn tecknar världen [Children Draw the World]*. Lund: Studentlitteratur, pp. 49–78.

Thorne, B. (1993) *Gender play.* New Brunswick, NJ: Rutgers University Press.

Walkerdine, V. (1997) *Daddy's girl: Young girls and popular culture.* Basingstoke: Macmillan.

—— (1990). *Schoolgirl fictions.* London: Verso Books.

Weeks, J. (2003) *Sexuality*, 2nd edn. London: Routledge.

9
'Bieber Fever': Girls, Desire and the Negotiation of Girlhood Sexualities

Louisa Allen and Toni Ingram

Introduction

Girls' sexuality is often the focus of intense public debate and concern. Anxieties over 'raunch culture' (Levy, 2005) and premature 'sexualization' of girls are currently at a premium in the media and popular literature. This public interest has been accompanied by an array of international and governmental reports documenting the 'sexualization' of culture as an area of major social concern (Rush & LaNauze, 2006; American Psychological Association, 2007; Papadopoulos, 2010; Bailey, 2011). These reviews describe the negative effects contemporary sexualized culture is believed to have upon (particularly) girls, such as 'body dissatisfaction', 'poor self-esteem', 'depression' and 'promiscuous behaviour'. While finding many sympathetic ears, these documents have met with critical debate within academia (Lerum & Dworkin, 2009; Smith, 2010; Atwood & Smith, 2011; Barker & Duschinsky, 2012). Critics have highlighted concerns over the corporate sexualization of young people, while others draw attention to the under-theorized and often overly simplistic and generalized nature of aspects of some reports. Use of the term 'sexualization' as '*a non sequitur* causing everything from girls flirting with older men, to child sex trafficking' has been a point of exegesis (Egan & Hawkes, 2008: 297).

Feminist analyses have offered critical commentary on the implications of this 'sexualization' panic for girls. The reach and damage of sexualization is conceptualized as universal and reproducing a moral framework that renders understanding girlhood sexuality beyond sexualization untenable (Egan & Hawkes, 2008). Duits and van Zoonen (2011) view positioning girls as 'vulnerable to' or 'at risk of' today's sexualized culture denies them agency. Others argue that concerns over girls and sexualization maintain classed and raced moral boundaries and work to regulate appropriate heteronormative female sexuality (Ringrose, 2013). Sexualization discourses serve to construct girls as inherently vulnerable and in need of protection, thus diminishing the possibility of actively negotiated lived realities (Egan and Hawkes, 2009).

Embedded in current 'moral panics' surrounding girlhood and sexuality is the idea that childhood is a time of presumed sexual innocence (Renold, 2005). A deluge of popular books detail sexualization's perils for girls by invoking arguments based on notions of childhood innocence (see Hamilton, 2008; Oppliger, 2008; Durham, 2009). While this literature conceptualizes sexualization as a 'new danger' for girls and young women, Egan and Hawkes (2012) suggest current discourses draw on problematic assumptions pertaining to children and sexuality from the Social Purity Movement over a century ago. While themes of sexual corruption and innocence cohered around 'the child' during the late 19th century, current sexualization debates have shifted to 'the girl'. This new focus is evidenced in popular titles such as 'Girls gone skank: The sexualisation of girls in American culture' (Oppliger, 2008), as well as media commentary and education programmes labelling girls the primary 'victims' of the sexualization 'epidemic'. Critics argue that ideas of childhood innocence construct girls' sexuality as potentially 'dangerous', 'vulnerable' and 'in need of protection', and profoundly endanger them by denying their sexual knowledge, desire and a sense of agency (Robinson, 2008).

This chapter critically engages with discourses of 'childhood innocence' and 'sexualization', investigating whether these resonate with girls' own talk about themselves as sexual subjects. Through narratives concerning relationships, liking and loving people and attraction, we reveal how some 11–13-year-old girls' talk constitutes desire as a normal and everyday expression of their sexuality. Although desire has been theorized previously (Allen et al., 2013) across a myriad of disciplinary realms such as psychology (Tolman, 2002; Fine, 2005), psychoanalysis (Walkerdine, 1997) and sociology (Hawkes, 2004), it is the way girls' talk in this study conceptualizes it, which forms our point of departure. Rather than placing our emphasis on what desire is, and in this way contributing to the literature above, our task is to understand talk about desire as a site of potential agency in relation to discourses of sexualization and childhood innocence. We are concerned with understanding agency's shape at the intersection of these discourses and posing the question of how girls' talk configures desire and with what possibilities there are for agency in relation to discourses of sexualization and childhood innocence. In the current study, girls conceptualized desire as sexual feelings projected towards others (i.e. typically celebrities, boyfriends, other boys) that they may, or may not, intend acting upon.

A theoretical aim of this chapter is to examine the potential for agency in girls' desiring talk and map its shape. At first glance, girls' desiring talk appeared lacking in agency. To discern what were almost imperceptible movements, a way of reading data which illuminated the smallest of micro-movements was needed. We draw on the theorizations of Renold and Ringrose (2008, 2011), who work with Deleuze and Guattari's concepts of 'lines of flight' and Braidotti's (2006) 'schizoid double pull' (detailed below) to delineate what agency's movements might look like.

Within mainstream media and public discourses, acknowledging girls as positively desiring sexual subjects is controversial. Adult acknowledge-ment of girls' desire as an expected and positive part of adolescence is rare (Tolman, 2002). Conventionally, female sexuality is constituted in opposi-tion to the virility of male sexual desire, as muted and receptive (Holland et al., 1994). Feminists document how within normative discourses of heterosexuality, women and girls must navigate a sexual reputation requir-ing them to be sexually desirable yet avoid expressions of active sexual desire (Holland et al., 1994). These dominant discourses surrounding girl-hood and sexuality preclude positive understandings of them as actively desiring sexual subjects.

Acknowledging 11–13-year-olds as legitimately sexual, that is, as having a right to experience and express their sexuality and for these practices to be viewed positively (Allen, 2005, 2011), also troubles discourses of childhood innocence. Within the regulating dyad of 'good' and 'bad' girl sexuality (Griffin, 2004), girls who experience and express desire are understood as displaying sexuality that is premature, precocious and consequently 'bad'. Caught at the intersection of discourses of childhood innocence and sexu-alization, desiring girls are often positioned as vulnerable to, and in need of protection from, adult commodified configurations of sexuality. They are constituted as innocent dupes of a process of sexual objectification they do not fully comprehend and are therefore impotent to negotiate. A counter-narrative is offered by contemporary 'girl power' discourses (Harris, 2004), where femininity is associated with a 'new' agency that positions young women as equally sexually desiring and demanding as young men. Within this discourse, girls are rendered powerful by an exercise of agency conferred and constrained by neo-liberal notions of individualism.

Refusing dichotomous depictions of 'girls as powerful' or 'girls as vic-tims', our aim is to rethink girls and agency at the specific intersection of discourses of childhood innocence and sexualization. This location is cho-sen because both discourses inspire what Kehily (2012) drawing on Egan and Hawkes (2008) identifies as a 'paradoxical logic' of assuming girls ' . . . as asexual or innocent while introducing strategies for the regulation of prema-ture expressions of sexual knowingness' (Kehily, 2012: 256). Both discourses also constitute dichotomous positions for girls as either 'sexually inno-cent' or 'sexually corrupted' (i.e. 'good girls' or 'bad girls'). We argue girls' talk negotiates this sexual dichotomy in ways that reveal potentially more complex and nuanced understandings of sexual self. Our contention is, for many girls in the current study, sexual desiring talk is understood as 'normal' at 11–13 years – not as premature/sexualized/bad/wrong. Rather, sexual desire, regardless of intention to act upon it, is conceptualized as 'commonplace' and a potential source of delight and pleasure.

Although girls articulate their desire in relation to what have been identified as adult-constructed discourses of sexualization (Kehily, 2012) and childhood innocence, their reading and mobilization has different inflections. Our contribution to a theorization of girlhood agency is to highlight its non-linear exercise by drawing on Renold and Ringrose's (2008, 2011) work which 'brings together Butler, with Deleuze and Guattari to...reconfigure resistance' (Renold & Ringrose, 2008: 316). Our aim in this chapter is specific and modest. We seek to characterize agency's movements as constituted in girls' talk about desire at the intersection of discourses of sexualization and childhood innocence. Drawing on Renold and Ringrose's (2008, 2011) explication of schizoid subjectivities, we illustrate the ways in which girls' desiring talk is characterized by contradiction and multiplicity so that agency may be fleeting. In this sense, agency does not equate with historical notions of feminist empowerment as something which once attained is more or less secured (Gavey, 2012). Instead, agency is conceptualized as more fleeting and can be quickly reterritorialized (Renold & Ringrose, 2008) within normative rules of femininity (Harris et al., 2000) and heteronormativity (Warner, 1993). While analysing girls' agency utilizing some of Deleuze and Guattari's toolkit is not new, the site of this mapping – girls' talk about desire at the intersection of discourses of sexualization and childhood innocence (in a New Zealand context) is.

The concept of schizoid subjectivities builds on post-structural understandings of a fractured subject in its acknowledgement of the contradiction and multiplicity of subjectivity. Within this paradigm girls are not positioned *either* within discourses of sexual innocence *or* discourses of sexualization, but rather they experience 'multiple pushes and pulls' (Renold & Ringrose, 2011: 392). Renold and Ringrose (2008) draw these ideas into articulation with Butlerian (1990) notions of 'performativity', where the subject is always in process, so girls are seen to navigate intersections of these discourses, as perpetual moments of 'becoming' via non-linear movements. Rather than replicating regulating subjectivities constituted by these discourses as 'pornified' or 'sexually innocent', girls may engage in a performance of norms that is not an exact replica. That is, girls' talk may constitute a performance of desiring that 'echoes the master discourse' (Renold & Ringrose, 2011: 401) but somehow distorts its previous form. Using Deleuze and Guattari (2004), these digressions might be conceptualized as 'lines of flight' or micro-practices of agency operating at an 'imperceptible' level (Deleuze, 1995). When these deterritorializations occur they can be quickly reterriorialized in a simultaneous manifestation of 'push pull' (Braidotti, 2006). As the discussion below indicates, intersection of discourses of childhood innocence and sexualization offered girls in this study opportunities for lines of flight, which were quickly recuperated via other normative discourses.

Research methodology

Data is drawn from a two-year New Zealand-based study examining how girls aged 11–13 understand themselves as sexual subjects. Twenty-eight girls were recruited from two state-funded intermediate schools in urban locations in the North Island. Both schools were co-educational and comprised diverse socio-economic and ethnic populations. All participants were volunteers, in Year Seven or Eight and represented a variety of ethnicities including: New Zealand Pakeha (non-Maori New Zealander of European descent), Maori, Samoan, Tongan, Chinese, Cambodian, Pilipino and South African Indian. Each school was designated a decile six rating by the Ministry of Education. Decile ratings indicate the extent to which a school draws its pupils from low socio-economic communities; decile one schools have the highest proportion of students, while decile ten have the least (Ministry of Education, 2011). Ethics approval was granted by the University of Auckland Human Participants Ethics Committee.

A multi-method approach involving visual methods (Rose, 2007) individual interviews and focus groups was employed. This multi-method design enabled the complexities and contradictions inherent in girls' constitution as sexual subjects to be captured (Allen, 2005). Firstly, girls participated in focus group discussion to garner a 'public' presentation of their thoughts concerning clothing, media, crushes and expectations of being a girl. Composition of focus groups was determined by the girls and was primarily friendship-based, engendering a comfortable space for enthusiastic and candid discussion around attraction and relationships. Next, participants engaged in an activity to collectively decide whether a series of statements were 'true' or 'false'; for example: 'Lots of girls our age have crushes or fancy other people' and 'It's normal for people to fancy or have crushes on people from both genders'.

Following focus groups, participants created a collage in their own time, responding to the question, 'What does sexuality mean to you?' Participants were encouraged to access images and words from sources they chose including magazines, newspapers and photos. Magazines aimed at girls aged 10–18 years, such as *Crème* and *Girlfriend*, were a popular imagery source. In addition, girls also added their own personal embellishments such as writing or hand-drawn pictures. This visual method provided girls with alternate means of articulating their thoughts and desires.

Individual interviews (undertaken by the second author) were conducted approximately two weeks later and involved participants presenting their visual collage and discussing what sexuality meant to them. Many

Figure 9.1 Hand-drawn 'Boyfriends' and 'holding hands' on Roxy's collage

participants included words and images on their collage that conveyed (hetero)sexual desire; for example, 'hot boys', 'kiss' (written next to an image of a male) and 'boyfriends'. Several words were embellished with hand-drawn illustrations such as hearts, lips and holding hands (see Figure 9.1). As girls explained the meanings, they attached to these visual representations, a desiring sexual subject emerged via their talk. Several images from participant collages and their related narratives are included below and form the basis for the following discussion around girls' articulations of desire.

'He's hot': Girls' expressions of celebrity desire

Previous school-based studies exploring girls' sexuality note that girls often don't spontaneously talk about their own desire. Reiterating this point, Tolman (2002) remarks girls are unlikely to raise sexual desire as a topic within research contexts unless specifically asked. In the current study, girls raised the topic of desire and 'liking' people unprompted and early, in many focus group discussions and individual interviews. It was frequently mentioned in response to the question, 'What is it like being a 11–13-year-old girl?'; suggesting expressions of desire or what we conceptualize below as 'crush talk' were noteworthy, as a usual occurrence in their lives. Open-ended questions such as this sparked enthusiastic discussion about their lives and experiences; topics such as boys, crushes and current and past relationships were peppered throughout these narratives.

A common way girls articulated desire was through their 'he's hot' talk. Girls' collective and individual celebrity 'he's hot' talk was directed either at someone they knew personally or celebrities from pop music, television and film. Popular male celebrities during the research period were Taylor Lautner and Robert Pattinson from the *Twilight* saga, Zac Efron, famous for his role in *High School Musical*, and singer Justin Bieber. Girls who professed liking or loving Justin Bieber affectionately described this experience as Sophia [12 years, Roseview Intermediate] does here as, '*We've kind of gone through ... Bieber fever'*.

When asked what made someone 'hot', girls' variously responded 'being a good singer or actor', although overwhelmingly 'hot' status was earned via physical appearance. This is articulated in the following extract typifying what girls admired about Taylor Lautner.

Toni: So what makes Taylor Lautner hot?
Layla: His face and his hair.
Sophia: And his abs.
Layla: His abs, everything.
Sophia: Abs.
Venessa: If we had our phones I have a picture on there ...
(Girls aged 12 years, Roseview Intermediate)

Taylor Lautner's 'abs' were a common point of focus group conversation; being 'hot' meant having a face and body girls found attractive and that equated with notions of hegemonic masculinity (Connell, 2005). What made Taylor Lautner attractive for these girls was his embodiment of corporeal features of esteemed masculinity (Morrell et al., 2012), such as his chiselled face and muscled stomach.

Girls' collages contained images of 'hot' male celebrities configured in ways which illustrated subtle differences in their articulations of desiring. Many girls made declarations of desire by handwriting the words 'c[e]leb crush' (celebrity crush) with an arrow pointing at the image of a male celebrity (see Figure 9.2). Others included pictures of their desired celebrity, adding hand-drawn hearts or cutting and pasting the words 'Hot' and 'Cute Boy' next to his visage (see Figure 9.3).

Some girls went a step further, offering depictions of more self-actualized desire. These girls included image embellishments (hand-drawn and/or cut

Figure 9.2 'Cleb Crush' handwritten on Drew's collage

Figure 9.3 'Hot' and 'Cute Boy' placed next to celebrity images on Ashley's collage

Figure 9.4 'Me and Justin at the movies' on Drew's collage

from mainstream magazines) placing them in a fantasy romance with a celebrity. Drew (Pakeha, Year Eight), for instance, included a picture of Justin Bieber with the words 'my boyfriend' scrawled across his head. Similarly, Drew made a cut-out-head of herself and stuck it over the original figure standing next to Justin Bieber in a magazine. The result, consolidated with a handwritten descriptor, was to make it look like, 'me and Justin at the movies' (see Figure 9.4). These kinds of practices suggest a strongly articulated notion of desiring, as girls not only identified who they thought was 'hot', but also positioned themselves in relation to this figure. In these instances, girls acknowledged and depicted themselves as embodied sexual subjects who could legitimately express desire.

Erotic attachments to celebrities, teachers and male classmates have been described as a resource for girls' friendship talk and a fantasy space where different forms of desire can be articulated (Kehily et al., 2002). These kinds of preoccupations have been conceptualized as preparatory, 'inducting pre-teenage girls into the meanings of heterosexuality in anticipation of their practice' (Kehily et al., 2002: 174). The insinuation here is that girls are not yet practising desire, only preparing for its future expression. Below, girls' talk depicts an array of relationships which imply another story.

Constituting a desiring sexual subjectivity through relationships

The constitution of girls as sexually desiring subjects was also communicated via talk about current and past relationships. Typically these relationships were referred to as 'going out' and pertained to boyfriend and girlfriend (i.e. heterosexual) couplings, illustrating the documented heteronormative nature of schooling (Ferfolja, 2007; DePalma and Atkinson, 2009). Almost half of participants had previously had, or were currently in, these relationships. Existing research documents the average age of first dating in New Zealand as 13 years (Allen, 2005). Narratives from girls in this study about previous and current relationships corroborate this finding.

As it is rarely positively acknowledged that girls aged 10–13 years can be in relationships, little is known about them. To convey a more nuanced understanding of girls' desiring talk, a brief description of types of relationships girls narrated is offered. Four girls' relationships have been selected as they exemplify the breadth and diversity of 10–13-year-old girls' relationship experience in this study.

Debra, who was Pakeha and in Year Eight, had been in a relationship with Chris for six months. They met through friends on the social networking site bebo, and communicated via phone, text and online. Debra and Chris had not yet met in person, but they were making plans to meet face to face in the upcoming school holidays. Debra's friend Drew (Pakeha, Year Eight) was also in a relationship and had been going out with Jay, a fellow Year Eight student, for around nine months. Drew spent time with Jay at school and during the weekends, when they would go to such places as the pools or movies. Min (Pilipino, Year Eight), who was in a five-month relationship with a Year Seven student (Luke), primarily conducted this relationship at school. Although Min talked to her boyfriend outside school hours, she was not allowed to go anywhere with him, a rule she attributed to her mum being 'too strict'. When asked what she liked about Luke, Min's response was, 'oh his personality and I like how the way he makes people laugh and stuff'. Lastly, Maia (Maori, Year Eight) had been going out with a Year Nine student whom she had met via her cousin for two months. When asked what she liked about her boyfriend, Maia stated his 'personality' and 'looks'. Maia and her boyfriend communicated through text, phone and bebo, and sometimes met as part of a group of Maia's closest friends.

These four examples reveal the diverse nature of relationships described by girls aged 11–13 years. This diversity was apparent in how partners met, communicated and socialized. While some girls initially met boyfriends through school or friends, as with Drew and Min, others did so outside school via family (Maia) or through social networking sites such as bebo (Debra). Girls communicated with their boyfriends through a plethora of means including in person, text, phone and online. Previous research (Renold, 2000, 2005) conducted with children in Year Six (age 10 and 11) indicates boyfriend and girlfriend relationships are predominantly school-bound. For the Year Seven and Eight girls in this study many relationships extended, or in some cases were exclusively conducted, outside school. Some relationships were purely telephone-, online- and text-based (e.g. Debra's). Described relationships exhibited no prescribed 'formula', and it was evident from girls' talk they were considered equally valid. Through the girls' talk (both those in relationships or not), engagement in relationships was constituted as a legitimate expression of their desire.

Heterosexuality and the regulation of desire

Girls whose talk constituted a desiring sexual subjectivity actively positioned themselves within heterosexual relations of desire. This does not necessarily imply their heterosexual identity, but rather demonstrates their engagement in performances of heterosexual desire. The institution of heterosexuality is considered a key social process that shapes young people's lives (Ingraham, 2005). Heterosexuality is deeply embedded within hegemonic discourses of female sexual maturity, where it is deemed normal, natural and inevitable for healthy growing children (Stockton, 2009). Primary schools are a major site for the (re)production of sexual and gender identities where dominant notions of heterosexuality underscore much of children's identity work and peer relationships. Renold (2000) demonstrates how both boys and girls resist and reinforce heteronormative gender and sexual identities. While some girls in her study worked to challenge hyperfeminine discourses and practices, by refusing investment in fashion and cosmetic culture, the construction of alternative femininities appeared only possible when performed in conjunction with heterosexuality.

The current findings resonate with Renold's work (2000), where participants' talk demonstrates moments of simultaneous resistance and accommodation of heteronormativity. While many girls confidently stated it was normal to be attracted to the same or both genders, they concurrently highlighted it would be very difficult for someone their age to project anything but a heterosexual identity. This sentiment is expressed in the following focus group prompted by the statement card: 'Girls are expected to have crushes on boys'.

> Justine: I think it's true. Well no I take that back, does it mean like they have to? I don't think so. I think girls can have crushes on girls and boys can have crushes on boys.
> Toni: OK, yeah.
> Justine: It doesn't mean...
> Toni: So you think there's that freedom?

Justine: Yeah I don't think anyone should tell them that they have to be like gay or straight or something.
Toni: What do you girls think about that one?
Kendra: I think it's false.
Toni: How come?
Kendra: Cause like um, you should be able to kind of like, like who you want to like. Not be told if you've got to like a guy if you're a girl or like a girl if you're a guy.
Justine: It's just more of who you're attracted to.

(Girls aged 13 years, Leighvale Intermediate)

This narrative demonstrates girls' critical engagement with discourses of compulsory heterosexuality through asserting their right to choose which gender to have a crush on. When pressed further, however, several divulged that they felt same or both sex attracted girls their age would 'keep it to themselves' because of the risk of being teased and bullied. Previous research (Adler & Adler, 1998; Renold, 2002) documents bullying behaviours such as exclusion and ridicule perpetuated against primary aged children who do not conform to hegemonic gender forms. This may explain why no girls in the current study identified as same or both sex attracted (see also Renold, 2013). Girls' assertion that it is normal to be same or both sex attracted, coupled with reluctance to identify themselves or others as lesbian or bisexual, illustrates a simultaneous resistance to, and accommodation of, dominant discourses of heterosexuality. Below we outline micro-movements of agency at work here in more detail.

'Non-desiring' talk: Constituting sexual subjectivity differently

While many girls' talk positioned them as desiring sexual subjects, this was not deemed a compulsory position. A significant minority of girls constituted their sexuality in ways that were non-sexual. In characterizing these girls' talk as 'non-desiring' we do not place them in a binary with 'desiring' girls, or view this constitution of sexual subjectivity as lacking agency. On the contrary, we indicate below, being 'non-desiring' was a position actively undertaken. While these girls acknowledged it was common for peers to talk about attraction and crushes, they themselves did *not* engage in 'he's hot' talk. Similarly, their collages were devoid of boy celebrities designated 'cute' or any kind of references to love, desire or romance.

Girls who did not speak about desire (hetero or otherwise) indicated during their interview they were either 'not interested' or had 'no time for boys' or crushes. Some drew upon a 'plenty of time later' discourse in positioning themselves as desiring. For example, Katy felt high school would be a more suitable context for crushes and relationships, as seen here.

Katy: But I don't even like anybody here, because like the thing I've had in my head, like I see people going out with people this year, and they're only 12. I mean when you get to college you're going to find so many people that you like, and we're still in intermediate and eventually they're going to dump that person and yeah.

(12 years, Roseview Intermediate)

Katy also exhibited talk of latent desire when explaining her self-professed 'hate' for romance, and aversion to the (then) popular romantic movie *Twilight*. The mere mention of *Twilight* during focus groups elicited bored groans from Katy, marking her out from other girls. During her interview she was asked if she disagreed with anything mentioned during the focus group.

Katy: Um I do not like *Twilight*, like the whole saga, I don't like it. I'm probably the first girl that you've heard that doesn't like it, cause like everybody is like, in the school 'are you going to see Eclipse tonight?', and it's like 'no' cause I hate *Twilight*.

(12 years, Roseview Intermediate)

Elaborating further on her dislike of romantic movies, Katy indicated she saw no point in them, preferring action movies instead.

Katy: Yeah I don't like the romance, I don't like it because I don't see a point in romance. Like because everybody knows in the movie some-body is going to love somebody else, and fall in love, so I don't really like romance movies.
Toni: You can't sort of identify with it?
Katy: No, not really.

(12 years, Roseview Intermediate)

Katy's narratives demonstrate her difference from the talk of desiring girls whose interest in romance fuelled their enthusiasm for *Twilight*. Legitimacy of a non-desiring position was consolidated by desiring girls such as Sophia, who explained it was fine not to be interested in boys or have crushes:

Toni: Is it quite common do you think, amongst friends to have crushes?
Sophia: Yeah we, most of us have started liking boys now, but there's a couple of us that aren't interested yet.
Toni: That aren't?
Sophia: No, but that's OK.
Toni: Which one would you be – crushes or no crushes?
Sophia: Ah, crushes.
Toni: And the ones that don't, does that matter?

Sophia: No, cause you can talk about other stuff, you don't always have to talk about boys, can talk about like I said school, and flashbacks and stuff, or movies and music or whatever.

(12 years, Roseview Intermediate)

Although Sophia's talk positions her as desiring, she acknowledges it is 'OK' for girls not to have crushes. While being desiring was certainly a popular way of 'doing' girl, clearly there was some leeway in the constitution of different subjectivities. This space was not unbridled, however, and its regulatory features are visible when Sophia states these girls 'aren't interested yet'. Sophia's talk positions girls whose talk negates desire on a heterosexual trajectory where they are destined for latent heterosexual futures. A future that is not heterosexual is not entertained, because not desiring boys is only a 'temporary' situation.

Girls, desire and mapping agentic movements

In this section we analyse findings for nuances of girl's sexual subjectivities as constituted within their desiring talk. We also interrogate this talk for signs of possible agency as performed at the intersection of discourses of sexualization and childhood innocence. Here we endeavour to contribute to Renold and Ringrose's (2011) theorization of schizoid subjectivities by locating talk about desire as a site for recognizing girls' agency. In terms of global reach of these ideas, we extend this analysis to a group of girls in one regional locality in New Zealand. Our aim is to map the movements of this agency by showing how girls' desiring talk negotiates schizoid sexual subjectivities in a process of 'anti-linear becoming' (Renold & Ringrose, 2011: 392).

In narratively asserting that experiencing desire was normal for their age, these 11–13-year-old girls can be seen to deterritorialize discourses of 'childhood sexual innocence'. This positioning as actively sexually desiring may be recognized as constituting lines of rupture from ideas that girls are *naturally sexually unknowing*. This position might be opened by the space discourses of sexualization offer in their positioning of girls 'as sexual' (albeit suspiciously/negatively). Yet, girls in this study did not replicate discourses of sexualization as typically constituted. In a 'failure' to exactly replicate this discourse, girls did not understand the expression of their 11–13-year-old sexuality as 'premature', or their sexuality as 'corrupted'. As girls' narratives above reveal, it was entirely legitimate not to desire boys and not be 'into' romance. Simultaneously, sexually desiring talk has a multitude of configurations that may have little to do with actually engaging in relationships and/or sexual activity. As explicated, girls' sexual desire is constituted in nuanced ways: declaring a boy 'hot' (and nothing more), placing themselves in a fantasy relationship with a celebrity boy, going out with someone online, going out with someone face to face in and/or outside school.

These possibilities are configured by girls' talk as legitimate, positive and commonplace manifestations of sexual desire.

In what Renold and Ringrose drawing from Braidotti conceptualize as the 'schizoid double-pull' (393), girls' expressions of sexual desire offer lines of flight which are simultaneously reterritorialized. At the same time as girls' narratives of desire position them in ways that disrupt notions of childhood innocence, this talk reappropriates regulating norms. For instance, girls expressed desire for boys who exhibited conventional features of esteemed masculinity (e.g. muscled abs and chiselled faces). While their active sexual desire might be read as agentic in the face of its refusal of sexual innocence, its form was conventional in scaffolding heteronormativity and hegemonic masculinity. Similarly, the refusal of girls such as Katy to situate themselves as sexually desiring might be read as an exercise of agency in relation to discourses of sexualization or traditional notions of romance-focused female sexuality. However this positioning was also quickly recuperated by a latent heteronormativity – while girls like Katy didn't desire boys now, they would in the future. Such reterritorializations were also evident in girls' declarations that 11–13-year-olds could have crushes on both genders. This position was maintained as girls simultaneously rendered it unlikely that those their age would be 'out' and no participants identified as lesbian or bisexual.

Concluding thoughts

Acknowledging 11–13-year-old girls' talk as sexually desiring is controversial in the light of current discourses of sexualization. Our aim has not been to reinforce these discourses by suggesting that girls' narration of sexual desire is premature or in some way bad for them (i.e. girls in this study are promiscuous exceptions to the majority). We have endeavoured to reveal girls' constitution of their sexual subjectivities as more complex and nuanced than those of 'corrupted innocence'. The intention is to refuse to position girls in a dyad of 'sexually innocent' or 'pornified'. To do this we have drawn on girls' own narratives, interweaving a theory of agency which refuses binaries of empowered/disempowered subjectivity, instead teasing out complexity in girls' narrative negotiations of these positions.

Some readers will have interpreted the 'non-desiring' girls as 'sexually innocent'; that is, displaying the kind of disinterest in romance and desire designated the hallmark of childhood. However, we have tried to demonstrate that such girls are not oblivious to romance and/or sexual desire – they are just not interested in it. They lack 'innocence's' traditional character by recognizing it is legitimate for other girls their age to be sexually desiring and interested in romance; it is just not for them ('yet' – their word). Although our methodology did not enable this form of analysis, it is also likely that religion, faith and/or race play a part here (see Renold, 2013). This is a more complex negotiation of discourses revealing possibilities engendered at the intersection of discourses of 'sexual innocence' and 'pornification'.

Such anti-linear movements reveal a display of agency that is perhaps 'crueller' in its optimism (Berlant, 2006) than feminist notions of empowerment (Gavey, 2012). Yet, it is still, we would argue, an exercise of agency.

References

Adler, P. A., & Adler, P. (1998) *Peer power: Pre-adolescent peer culture and identity*. New Brunswick, NJ: Rutgers University Press.

Allen, L. (2005) *Sexual subjects: Young people, sexuality and education*. Houndmills: Palgrave Macmillan.

Allen, L. (2011) *Young people and sexuality education: Rethinking key debates*. Houndmills: Palgrave Macmillan.

Allen, L., Rasmussen, M.-L., & Quinlivan, K. (2013) *The politics of pleasure in sexuality education: Pleasure bound*. New York: Routledge.

American Psychological Association (2007) *Report of the APA task force on the sexualisation of girls*. Washington, DC: APA.

Atwood, F., & Smith, C. (2011) Lamenting sexualisation: Research, rhetoric and the story of young people's 'sexualisation' in the UK Home Office Review. *Sex Education*, 11 (3), 327–337.

Bailey, R. (2011) *Letting children be children: The report of an independent review of the commercialisation and sexualisation of children*. London: Department of Education.

Barker, M., & Duschinsky, R. (2012) Sexualisation's four faces: Sexualisation and gender stereotyping in the bailey review. *Gender & Education*, 24 (3), 303–310.

Berlant, L. (2006) Cruel optimism. *Differences: A Journal of Feminist Cultural Studies*, 17, 20–36.

Braidotti, R. (2006) *Transpositions: On nomadic ethics*. Cambridge: Polity Press.

Butler, J. (1990) *Gender trouble: Feminism and the subversion of identity*. New York: Routledge.

Connell, R. W. (2005) *Masculinities*. Sydney: Allen and Unwin.

Deleuze, G., & Guattari, F. (2004) *Anti-Oedipus: Capitalism and schizophrenia*. Minneapolis, MN: University of Minnesota Press.

Deleuze, G. (1995) *Difference and repetition*. P. Patton (Trans.). New York: Columbia University Press.

DePalma, R., & Atkinson, E. (2009) 'No outsiders': Moving beyond a discourse of tolerance to challenge heteronormativity in primary schools. *British Educational Research Journal*, 35 (6), 837–855.

Duits, L., & van Zoonen, L. (2011) Coming to terms with sexualisation. *European Journal of Cultural Studies*, 14, 491.

Durham, M. G. (2009) *The Lolita effect: The media sexualisation of young girls and what we can do about it*. London: Gerald Duckworth Press.

Egan, R. D., & Hawkes, G. (2008) Engendered girls and incendiary objects: Unpacking the discourse of sexualisation. *Sexuality and Culture*, 12, 291–311.

Egan, R. D., & Hawkes, G. (2009) The problem with protection: Or, why we need to move towards recognition and the sexual agency of children. *Continuum: Journal of Media and Cultural Studies*, 23 (3), 389–400.

Egan, R. D., & Hawkes, G. (2012) Sexuality, youth and the perils of endangered innocence: How history can help us get past the panic. *Gender & Education*, 23 (4), 269–284.

Ferfolja, T. (2007) Schooling cultures: Institutionalizing heteronormativity and heterosexism. *International Journal of Inclusive Education*, 11 (2), 147–162.

Fine, M. (2005) X. Desire: The morning (and 15 years) after. *Feminism & Psychology*, 15 (1), 54–60.

Gavey, N. (2012) Beyond 'empowerment'? Sexuality in a sexist world. *Sex Roles*, 66, 718–724.

Griffin, C. (2004) Good girls, bad girls: Anglocentrism and diversity in the constitution of contemporary girlhood, in A. Harris (Ed.) *All About the Girl: Culture, Power and Identity*. New York: Routledge, pp. 29–44.

Hamilton, M. (2008) *What's happening to our girls? Too much, too soon. How our kids are overstimulated, oversold and oversexed*. Victoria: Viking (Penguin Group).

Harris, A. (Ed.) (2004) *All about the girl: Culture, power and identity*. New York: Routledge.

Harris, A., Sinikka, A., & Gonick, M. (2000) Doing it differently: Young women managing heterosexuality in Australia, Finland and Canada. *Journal of Youth Studies*, 3 (4), 373–388.

Hawkes, G. (2004) *Sex and pleasure in western culture*. Cambridge: Polity Press.

Holland, J., Ramazanoglu, C., Sharpe, S., & Thomson, R. (1994) Power and desire: The embodiment of female sexuality. *Feminist Review*, 46, 21–38.

Ingraham, C. (2005) *Thinking straight: The power, the promise and the paradox of heterosexuality*. New York: Routledge.

Kehily, M.-J. (2012) Contextualising the sexualisation of girls debate: Innocence, experience and young female sexuality. *Gender & Education*, 23 (4), 255–268.

Kehily, M.-J., Mac an Ghaill, M., Epstein, D., & Redman, P. (2002) Private girls and public worlds: Producing femininities in the primary school. *Discourse: Studies in the Cultural Politics of Education*, 23 (2), 167–177.

Lerum, K., & Dworkin, S. L. (2009) 'Bad girls rule': An interdisciplinary feminist commentary on the report of the APA task force on the sexualisation of girls. *Journal of Sex Research*, 46 (4), 250–263.

Levy, A. (2005) *Female chauvinist pigs: Women and the rise of raunch culture*. New York: Free Press.

Ministry of Education (2011) Retrieved 7 April 2011 from http://www.minedu. govt.nz/NZEducation/EducationPolicies/Schools/SchoolOperations/Resourcing/ ResourcingHandbook/Chapter1/DecileRatings.aspx

Morrell, R., Jewkes, R., & Lindegger, G. (2012) Hegemonic masculinity/masculinities in South Africa: Culture, power and gender politics. *Men and Masculinities*, 15 (1), 11–30.

Oppliger, P. A. (2008) *Girls gone skank: The sexualization of girls in American culture*. Jefferson, NC: McFarland & Company, Inc.

Papadopoulos, L. (2010) *Sexualisation of young people review*. UK: Home Office.

Renold, E. (2000) 'Coming out': Gender, (hetero)sexuality and the primary school. *Gender and Education*, 12 (3), 309–326.

Renold, E. (2002) Presumed Innocence: (Hetero)sexual, heterosexist and homophobic harassment among primary school girls and boys. *Childhood*, 9 (4), 415–434.

Renold, E. (2005) *Girls, boys and junior sexualities: Exploring children's gender and sexual relations in the primary school*. London: RoutledgeFalmer.

Renold, E. (2013) *Boys and girls speak out: A qualitative study of children's gender and sexual cultures (Age 10–12): An exploratory research project to inform the National Assembly for Wales Cross-Party Group on Children, 'Sexualisation', Sexualities and Equalities*. Wales: University of Cardiff.

Renold, E., & Ringrose, J. (2008) Regulation and rupture: Mapping tween and teenage girls' resistance to the heterosexual matrix. *Feminist Theory*, 9 (3), 313–338.

Renold, E., & Ringrose, J. (2011) Schizoid subjectivities?: Re-theorizing teen girls' sexual cultures in an era of 'sexualisation'. *Journal of Sociology*, 47 (4), 389–409.

Ringrose, J. (2013) *Postfeminist education?: Girls and the sexual politics of schooling*. Abingdon: Routledge.

Robinson, K. (2008) In the name of 'childhood innocence': A discursive exploration of the moral panic associated with childhood and sexuality. *Cultural Studies Review*, 14 (2), 113–129.

Rose, G. (2007) *Visual methodologies: An introduction to the interpretation of visual materials*, 2nd edn. London: Sage.

Rush, E., & La Nauze, A. (2006) *Letting children be children: Stopping the sexualisation of children in Australia*. Australia Institute Working Paper No. 93. Australia Institute, Deakin, ACT.

Smith, C. (2010) Sexualisation of young people review. *Participants*, 7 (1), 175–179.

Stockton, K. B. (2009) *The queer child, or Growing sideways in the twentieth century*. Durham, NC: Duke University Press.

Tolman, D. (2002) *Dilemmas of desire: Teenage girls talk about sexuality*. Cambridge, MA: Harvard University Press.

Walkerdine, V. (1997) *Daddy's girl: Young girls and popular culture*. Cambridge, MA: Harvard University Press.

Warner, M. (1993) *Fear of a queer planet*. Minneapolis, MN: University of Minnesota Press.

10
'He's Cute, for Her': Kids' Entangled Pedagogies of Sexuality and Race in New York City

Maria Kromidas

Through their analysis of various foundational discourses concerning sexuality in modernity, Egan and Hawkes argue that discourses on child sexuality have rarely been about children themselves. Rather, 'childhood sexuality and the desire to bring it under control provided an avenue for addressing other cultural anxieties (e.g., racial purity, affirming the institution of marriage, and constructing more rigid gender boundaries)' (2010: 155). Indeed, the taboo nature of children's sexuality and their presumed innocence amplifies many of the general anxieties surrounding sexuality, particularly the vexed concerns about the maintenance of racial and gendered differences and of childhood itself. Various institutions codify rules, prescriptions and assumptions about child sexuality and its stakes. Thus part of being a child today means being entangled in a thicket of discourses and regulations from multiple sources on multiple scales. While recent scholarly literature has begun to explore how primary school children navigate discourses of gender, class, age, heteronormativity and the sanctity of marriage and how they are productive of children's sexualities, very little research has explored how race intersects with sexuality in children's everyday lives (for notable exceptions see Connolly, 2002; Ali, 2003; Bhana, 2005). The innocent child construct that inhibits our understanding of children's sexualities also plagues our understanding of children's racial subjectivities. But if we dispense with faulty constructs of the innocent child or a bounded children's culture and begin instead with the understanding that children are indeed both sexual and racial (as well as gendered, national, classed, religioned) subjects, then new questions are opened for exploration. How are race and sex productive of each other? How is sexuality a site for racial (trans)formation? And how does learning race and becoming a racial subject inform sexual desires and experiences? What does it 'feel' like to experience desire within these raced, classed, gendered structures? What emotional and interactional responses do they oblige? This chapter will explore these

159

questions through analysis of talk and interactions of 9-, 10- and 11-year-old children in a 'superdiverse' school in NYC, illustrating how the domain of sexuality is a productive site for the (trans)formation of race.[1]

The research context: Sexualities amidst cosmopolitan sociabilities

The material in this chapter is based on a 14-month ethnographic explo-ration, conducted in 2006–2007, of kids' contributions to everyday processes of racial formation and transformation in New York City (NYC). Participant observation was the major method used, along with unstructured interviews of individual and small groups of kids. The bulk of material was collected in two classrooms within one primary school, Public School AV.[2] I spent 10 months with 10 and 11-year olds in one Fifth Grade classroom (Year Six in the UK), two months with another classroom and two months conducting research in the surrounding neighbourhood of Augursville. Augursville is a neighbourhood that contains various axes of difference, with no numerical racial or ethnic majorities. When considering that NYC has the most segre-gated school system in the US (Kucsera & Orfield, 2014), Augursville's public schools are unique. Augursville kids represent all defined races as well as some that defied racial categorization, and the kids or their parents hailed from various parts of the world, from Algeria to Albania. I contend that the unique demographics of Augursville is one of the main factors in the kids' cosmopolitan sociability, a structure of feeling in the sense defined by Williams (1977): a moral, affective, aesthetic and political perspective relating to difference and belonging; a type of civility defined by one's relations with Others. I have explored the kids' emergent cosmopolitanism elsewhere, arguing that these kids, through their interactions and social rela-tions, offered a compelling model of how to live with and beyond difference (Kromidas, 2011, 2012).

Friendship was arguably the most important site for creative and counter-hegemonic racial meaning-making. Although I did not set out to explore the kids' sexual attractions, behaviour or talk, it became increasingly apparent that the domain of sexuality was another important site for the transforma-tion of racial meanings. This did not so much entail a shift in the focus of research, as a realization of the imbrication of sexuality with race, along with gender and class in the kids' lives. As Kath Weston noted in her exhortation to 'unbound' sexuality studies, 'one cannot "just" study sexuality because sexuality is [...] embedded in any and every topic constituted as an object of research' (1998: 3–4), and this inevitably includes childhood. Childhood scholars relying on the inherent flexibility and reflexivity of ethnographic methods (Renold, 2000: 310) have thus often 'discovered' childhood sexualities through their studies of children's friendships, gendered, raced or classed subjectivities (Hey, 1997; Connolly, 2002; Ali, 2003).

Despite the theoretical productivity of sexuality studies within anthropology, gender and queer studies, sexuality is still an ambiguous concept (Lyons & Lyons, 2011), and the question 'what is sexual' is still relevant (Freeman & D'Emilio, 2005: 168). This is especially the case for childhood sexuality. While Herdt could remark in 2004 that little had changed since Money's claim that childhood sexuality was the last taboo in sexuality research in 1967 (2004: 40), since then, many path-breaking researchers have begun to incorporate kids' own perceptions of sexuality and their understandings of themselves as sexual subjects into reconceptualizations of sexuality (L. Allen, 2005; Renold, 2005; Bhana, 2007; Renold, 2013; Renold & Ringrose, 2013). Enabled by these recent conversations, I borrow from scholars who conceive sexuality in a broad and open-ended manner and refuse simple definitions that reduce sexuality and sexual meanings to behaviour, practices or identity (Lyons & Lyons, 2004; Vance, 2005; Donnan, 2010). Arguing for the inclusiveness of the concept, Jafari Allen affirmed that talking about sexuality 'is to talk not only about the everyday lived experience of the sexual(ized) body, but also about the imagination, desires and intentions of the sexual(ized) subject' (2009: 83). In this way, I consider encounters, emotions and talk to fall under the rubric of sexuality when they expressed the desires of sexual subjects. Current scholars have also argued for conceptualizing desire as a complex of intersubjective and embodied experiences that include race, gender and class (J. Allen, 2012: 326). This moves sexuality into the public realm, entailing a 'whole assemblage of heterogeneous practices, techniques, habits and dispositions' (Epstein et al., 2003: 3). Indeed, I focus on talk, practices and emotions that are embedded within everyday processes within schools. Centring the most mundane aspects of sexuality has the added advantage of writing children's experiences in ways that are not 'eaten up and spat out in hollow and caricature forms' (Epstein et al., 2012: 253). Wary of the risk of inadvertently conscribing children further to the gaze of surveillance, it is a response to the moral panics concerning children's purported hypersexualization, a phenomenon not nearly as salacious as the current discourse implies (see Egan's [2013: 35–42] summary of empirical research from the US, UK and Australia). It is thus one aspect of an overall politics of representation, one that I believe reflects the way in which these particular kids experienced sexuality, although it differs markedly from how adults perceive of sexuality in general and children's sexuality specifically.

Within the school, sexuality was a thoroughly public text that was fully pedagogical. That is, it was subject to observation, analysis, scrutiny and debate. A large bulk of time and energy within the kids' informal interactional structures (in the playground, staircases, in 'free time' in the classroom) concerned sexuality. This included but was not limited to: expressing sexual desire and responding to others, talk devoted to 'who likes who', obliging others to make their desires public, and the imputation of others' sexual desires from practices such as degree and frequency of proximity and certain forms of joking, teasing and play. On the surface, much of the talk and interactions surrounding sexuality appear rather mundane, even formulaic. For instance, the interactions between two kids that were 'going out' were mostly short and heavily scrutinized, with only a few words exchanged, or the odd note or gift. It was similarly so with talk about who was 'cute' or 'hot' or who made a good couple. The theoretical approach I adopt takes up the challenge of sorting through these everyday interactions, and centres them as the mediating and constitutive vehicle between subjectivity and ideology (Rampton, 2001). My primary interest is in the affective, semiotic and pedagogical nature of talk and interactions, where sexuality and race are entangled. In the next section, I discuss the conceptual framework for analysing the meanings and sentiments within this domain of experience.

The conceptual framework: The language and affect of race and sexuality

Building on the insights of sociocultural linguistics and Vološinov's (1973) mapping of the reciprocal relationship between social interactions and ideology, the most basic presupposition is that the processes explored here primarily occur through social interaction and are expressed in linguistic and extra-linguistic forms.[3] By focusing on language and sentiments – not only what kids say and how they say it, but the furtive glances, quickening pulses, nervous laughter, angst-filled legitimations and immense pleasures, I am contending that talk and sentiments reveal the various discourses that structure sexuality. This focus provides a window into the agentive practices of kids, struggling to make meanings as they construct their own racial and sexual subjectivities, practices that ultimately contribute to the reconstruction and transformation of larger meanings of sexuality, race and their interrelations.

Centring kids' practices and sentiments within everyday life is extraordinarily productive, for it enables access to those behaviours that are embodied, sensual, reflexive and holistic, and goes well beyond developmentalist conceits that privilege the cognitive or rational (Flyvbjerg, 2001). Social scientific perspectives that privilege cognitive understanding or that bifurcate emotion from knowledge construct children (and other marginalized groups) as immature, ignorant or innocent (cf. Walkerdine et al., 2001; McElhinny, 2010). A theoretical approach that views talk and sentiments as fully social and embedded in historical dynamics of change provides a nuanced challenge to this assumption of children and moves towards considering their unique contributions to the phenomena of study. Moreover, this perspective is particularly attuned to those creative ferments within the everyday, often found in kids' playful practices where they defamiliarize some of the most fully taken for granted aspects of daily life. In this way, children are represented as fully competent social beings, regardless of whether or not their talk and sentiments mirror those of adults (Kromidas, 2014). However differently or similarly children's sexualities are experienced, it is clear that sexuality is also a domain of pleasure, danger and risk; fraught as it is with the dangers of public rejection, humiliation, the anxieties of growing up and the future, and one where the body and all its embodied characteristics – language, ethnic origins, religion – come to be especially marked. The surveillance and control of children's sexuality only redouble the power of various discursive regimes. These in turn are inscribed on children's bodies and become expressed through language as well as forms of affect.

In the last decade, affect has received resurgent attention in anthropology and related disciplines, as analysts attempt to construct more socially and politically grounded accounts of personhood (Clough & Halley, 2007; Athanasiou et al., 2008; Ramos Zayas, 2011). Contemporary uses of affect focus on the everyday social manifestations of particular social circumstances, the emotional and bodily 'logic' of social relations (Mazzarella, 2009). For all the emphasis on social mediation, the affective lens can also be used to grasp indeterminancy and potentiality, those slippages, refusals and unruly agentive practices that challenge accounts of the unitary and omnipotent power of various discursive regimes (Blackman et al., 2008). As such, affect becomes exceptionally useful in the study of sexuality, particularly child sexuality.

On the one hand, sexuality and intimacy have historically been perceived to be not only presubjective but presocial, belonging to the realm of the instinctual and the 'natural' (Vance, 2005; Lyons & Lyons, 2011). The affective lens works to ground sexuality, allowing connections to be made with the totality of social and cultural facts (Herdt, 2004). On the other hand, theoretical engagement with affectivity can help map out slippages where sexualities violate the very cores of various institutions and ideologies that attempt to regulate it. While 'the education of desire' (Stoler, 2002) is part of the general constitution of subjects and subjectivity, ideologies can never wholly subsume the logic of sexuality. Perhaps this is why regulatory regimes become most frenzied when they surround child sexuality. For the proper regulation of children's sexuality would ensure not only the creation of proper gendered and (hetero)sexualized subjects, but proper racial subjects; that is, those who ascribe to conventional racial categories and meanings and reproduce them, figuratively through their own subjectivities, social relations, and literally through the actual bodies of their expected progeny.

The entanglement of race and sexuality: Present desires and reproductive futures

I examine sexualized talk in two vignettes in order to highlight the discourses that structure kids' experiences and expressions of sexuality, and how they negotiated within and sometimes beyond them. Sexuality was the context where the regimes of raciology and multiculturalism were most obligatory, amplifying the obstacles of social relations across difference as well as the urgency of interactional and interpretive work to mediate these obstacles. Much more so than friendships, individuals had to 'fit', 'make sense', 'be good for each other' or 'make a good couple' in the sense of being of the same group.[4] In the context of friendship, kids bridged or crossed differences in an almost spontaneous manner, and I never heard any mention of two friends not making sense because of their race/ethnic/cultural difference (Kromidas, 2011, 2012). Kids would be perplexed, however, if friendships crossed style boundaries. The dynamics within the sexual realm differed radically. Without exception, when kids expressed their own desires or discussed that of their peers, the issue of race was always already available and had to be taken into account, even when both parties were of the same socially defined race, ethnic or cultural group. Within the sexual realm, crossing boundaries was risky, and mediating difference became obligatory and characterized by angst. It is true that parents affected some of this angst, and not surprisingly, many parents had expectations and hopes that their kids would maintain some sort of continuity in terms of language, religion, culture and/or race. But to chalk up all the kids' creative mediations of difference concerning their sexual desires to some 'cultural thing', or to racist parents would too readily mystify the larger sociopolitical and historical force of racial ideologies in structuring everyday life, and especially our most intimate sentiments.

Interracial sexual relations in the US were historically hazardous affairs. Threatening the caste-like boundaries of race and white privilege, interracial relations were regulated by custom, law and often violence. Today, these relations are structured, that is discouraged, by ideologies that naturalize differences of race and culture. At their core, these ideologies of difference normalize the notion that there are indeed different 'types' or 'kinds' of people, that it is necessary to 'stick to your own kind' and that it is natural to feel discomfort, fear or repulsion towards Others. Conversely, these ideologies naturalize the notion that people just 'prefer their own' (Ahmed, 2004: 195). These powerful norms are reproduced and legitimated in a variety of discursive domains: by schools' sanctioning of multiculturalism, by parents' wishes for cultural, ethnic or racial continuity, by the everyday language of the neighbourhood, by the new science of genomics and the ancestry industry and by the racial common sense that suffuses the media, popular culture and the public sphere in the US. These intertwined levels of control work to construct a 'fit' between partners as a total social fact. While social facts are obligatory, this does not mean that they completely regulate desire. Which is to say that, just as often as not, the kids' desires exceeded the boundaries of their difference. Refusing these facts obliged kids to mitigate these obstacles through interpretive and interactional work. This work had to be performed even in seemingly straightforward cases where their desire was successfully regulated.

In his queer critique of the universalizing discourse of reproductive futurism, Edelman (2004) argues that the child is the emblem of futurity's unquestioned value and the figure through which the burdens of this discourse are represented. Always imagined as adults-in-the-making or in terms of their 'becoming' (Prout, 2005), it should be no surprise that kids incorporated this future orientation into their experiences of sexuality. Indeed, the entanglement of race and sexuality cannot be understood without the notion of reproductive futurism and kids' interpellation of themselves as proper heterosexualized subjects that will one day marry someone of the 'right type' and reproduce kids of their own. This often manifested in kids' talk and anxieties about future spouses. This is not to say that kids deferred their desires to the future. Rather, they creatively negotiated them in a way that made them speak to their experiences in the present and their making of themselves as racial, gendered and (hetero)sexualized subjects experiencing desire, pleasure, as well as anxiety and frustration in the here and now.

The following excerpt was recorded during an informal interview in the cafeteria with 11-year-old Carly (white, self-described as 'just American') and 11-year-old Izel, conventionally Mexican-American.[5] They were talking about their 'favourite subject', boys, as they watched boys walk across the cafeteria to throw out their trays. The excerpt shows how future concerns come into play with present desires, themselves both entangled with discourses of race and difference.

MK: So, who are the cutest [boys]?
Carly: [Jack! Not in our class, in Ms Z.'s. Oh my god! Oh my god! ((fanning her face))
Izel: [Andy! A little bit MJ, a little bit Blake, and a lot of bit Andy!
Carly: He's cute – for Izel.
Izel: The good thing is we're both Mexican. I saw him wearing one of these the other day ((shows MK her bracelet that reads 'I (heart) Mexico on it'))
MK: So Izel, you want to be with someone that's Mexican?
Izel: ((smiles widely and nods vigorously))
Carly: Isn't that your culture that you have to marry a Mexican?
Izel: I don't want to marry someone who's white, or who's American. Cause if I marry someone who was born here that would make me 100% American, because now I'm 50% Mexican and 50% American.
Carly: I can marry someone Bangladeshi. I don't have a culture. I'm just American. It's so boring.
Izel: Like what are you, English or something?
Carly: If I was English, I would talk like this [inaudible, in a British accent]. I'm like half Irish, half British, half German.

At first glance, this interaction seems to point to the reproduction of hegemonic norms surrounding race and sex. Izel, a Mexican-American, is properly attracted to a boy of the same 'type'. Her friend Carly approves and constructs this as a proper fit – 'He's cute – for Izel' – pointing to the suitability of the match in terms of what was understood to be the most important criterion. Izel immediately understood and agreed by explicitly elaborating the meaning to me, the outsider, 'the good thing is that we're both Mexican'. However, there are also counter-hegemonic claims and meaning-making involved in this interaction, as Izel's attraction to Andy was not just a direct adherence of having to 'stick with your own kind'. Rather, her comment ('I don't want to marry someone who's white...) suggests an undermining of multiculturalist ideology and its centring of whiteness, an assumption expressed by Carly's normalizing of herself as 'just American'. Her attraction to Andy has much to do with the making and crafting of her self and her future cultural orientation. Rather than static and essentialized, Izel viewed her Mexican and American cultural identity as fluid, open-ended and of her own making – a state of being and becoming. To understand Izel's excitement while looking and talking about Andy, we must understand it as both an aspect of her desire for Andy as well as excitement in the realization of her self-making and refusal to be made by others. In her own way, Izel understood the imbrication of sexual and racial subject-making but negotiated them in a way that disrupted her positioning as a future sexual subject in the making, and unsettled figurations of race and nation as static entities.

The way difference is always already embedded in kids' experiences of sexuality is also evident in the transcript below, recorded during an interview with Jacinta, a 10-year-old girl of Dominican descent, and one of her best friends, Sabrina, a 10-year-old girl of Albanian descent. The talk is emblematic of the informal pedagogical manner in which interactions concerning sex and race transpired, and how this talk became embodied in affective states. It also highlights how reproductive futurism only compounded the general anxieties surrounding sexual desire. At this point, Jacinta was telling me about her then current boyfriend.

MK: What's his name?
Jacinta: Raffi. He has a lot of things in common with me.
MK: Like?
Jacinta: Because um, well we're both not divorced child but uh, we're both from Dominican Republic, we both look great OK? ((laughs))
Sabrina: ((laughs))
Jacinta: Aaaand, I guess that's it.
Sabrina: Wow! ((sarcastic))
Jacinta: Wait wait and, he's not close to my age...
MK: How old is he? He's older?
Jacinta: Yeah, he's 11.

MK: Oh!

Jacinta: No, but/

Sabrina: So! He's supposed to be older!

Jacinta: Not that old!

Jacinta: He's not smart.

MK: How do you know that?

Jacinta: Cause every time I be telling him a problem, like just kidding you're stupid anyways, he's like 'no I'm not, tell me a problem, watch I could get it' and I would say something and he be like 'what?' and I'm like 'oh you got to be kidding me'.

MK: So intelligence isn't very important to you, looks are more important?

Jacinta: Well no/

Sabrina: Oh god! That's always what older people say/

Jacinta: Well not really because, because I don't know how like, it's not like I'm gonna spend the future with him, I'm not...

MK: Okay, so you just think he's cute.

Jacinta: Yeah.

MK: So you like him cause one, you're both from DR.

Jacinta: For some reason, um, I'm gonna tell you, all the boys from the Dominican Republic, um, they really don't, don't like working, and so they're lazy/

Sabrina: Your dad is lazy?

Jacinta: Well my dad is not lazy, some of them, most of them ((laughs)), they just like to hang out with friends, have girlfriends/

MK: Who told you this?

Jacinta: Well everyone I know that's Dominican, except me, ((laughs)) I'm not like that, I would like to work and get a nice future, cause then if I don't I'm just gonna end up outside without a house with like 500 kids and ((laughs))

MK: So you don't want to get pregnant at 15 and

Jacinta: NO! I don't like that.

Sabrina: No! I don't like that either.

Jacinta: I know my cousin that she, she had a baby when she was 16/

Sabrina: ((gasp))

Jacinta: [...] And the thing I didn't like is I could tell my cousin was going to get pregnant fast, cause she was always be hanging out with her boyfriend, she would always get piercing everywhere, every single day she would come with something new, let's say a tattoo here, a tattoo on the back/

Sabrina: Oh my god, I hate that.

Jacinta: Some things on her ears, and things like that whatever, and she likes gothic music and then one day...

MK: So the gothic music got her pregnant?

Jacinta: ((laughs)) Noooo.

Sabrina: Her boyfriend got her pregnant.

Jacinta: And also, you could tell that her boyfriend was trouble cause he would always like, he would always come in like he didn't care what anyone else thinks. You're not supposed to care what everyone else thinks but...

MK: A little bit.

Jacinta: Yeah, a little bit...

MK: So what kind of person do you see yourself with?

Jacinta: For some reason...I don't know.

Sabrina: I don't know.

Jacinta: No?

Sabrina: Because my cousin, my mom's cousin married someone that was Arabic but we're Albanian and I don't know now.

Jacinta: ((pause)) I don't know like, I don't, it's not like I really care cause it could be like any country that's good, cause I don't like being racist, like let's say it's Arabic, if he works if he's good and he treats my kids right...then it's good.

Sabrina: My mom's cousin which is my far far cousin, she got married and she got divorced because she like, her husband was bringing her [...] to her sister's house and the husband just left her like 30 blocks, like one mile away in the rain, with no cellphone, no umbrella, nothing. And she was just walking and she didn't have no money either, and he just keeps on like smacking her,/

Jacinta: What?

Sabrina: And screaming at her.

Jacinta: If a man hits me, it's over. OK?

Sabrina: They were only married for two months.

Jacinta: I'm not saying I would try to kill them, but I would just, it's like...Especially if you have a kid, cause if it's a boy he would think it's all right to do that to girls

Sabrina: I know.

MK: Exactly.

Jacinta: My dad doesn't think it's all right to hit girls and neither does my mom, cause if you hit girls you're a pussy.

MK: Well you know what happens, you know why some of these women stay/

Jacinta: Sometimes they think like 'Oh, how are my children gonna feel?' It's like ((exasperated)) 'How they gonna feel if they see you getting hurt and they have to hide somewhere?!'

While there are many rich meanings and agentive practices involved in this short talk, what concerns me here is how Jacinta's experience of sexuality, like Izel's, was negotiated through the discourse of reproductive futurism.

Both girls constructed their own sexualities not through simplistic adherence to someone of the 'right type' but in a way that connected their desires in the present with their future orientations. For Jacinta, this involved her upwardly mobile class aspirations. If anything, Raffi's Dominican-ness (and his perceived intelligence!) worked to quell her excitement and desire towards him as she imagined a future that looked different from many of the girls and women with which she was intimately familiar. Jacinta's classed subjectivity – as someone whose family was on public assistance – was more salient in the imbrication of sexuality, gender and race than it was for Izel, whose family was more or less middle-class. Jacinta's classed (and raced) subjectivity was also more salient in her performance of academic standing (just as 'smart' as her middle-class friends) and in the way she consumed pop culture. For instance, when I asked about her afterschool activities, Jacinta described her favourite website that let her design a house. She viewed this as training for a future career as an interior decorator and remarked, 'I know, I'm such a white girl, right?' Jacinta's making of herself as a classed and raced subject was incorporated into her experience of being a sexual subject, and her ambivalent feelings about her sexuality in the present and future cannot be understood without taking these dynamics into account.

Jacinta's ambivalence about her raced, classed and sexual future self stands in contrast to her unequivocal irreverence concerning the reproduction of racial/ethnic purity. It is clear that Sabrina disagreed with Jacinta's more counter-hegemonic pronouncements, as it was met by a cautionary tale about the dangers of crossing boundaries of difference within the sexual domain. Sabrina's position towards this type of boundary crossing was implicitly understood by her friends and until the final month of the school year, Sabrina only ever expressed desire for a boy 'back in my country', Albania. When her friends talked about their crushes and related the details of their flirting, Sabrina would talk longingly about how perfect the Albanian boy was for her, for no other reason really than the fact that he was Albanian. Jacinta interpreted Sabrina's tale much as I do – as a challenge to the moral lesson underlying Jacinta's preceding talk. Jacinta's response reiterated her previous sentiment, claiming 'any country' could work and that she doesn't like 'being a racist'. In the light of the presumed natural preference to desire one's own 'kind', Jacinta's challenge was indeed a formidable one. She emphasized this point by countering her friend's claim that the problem was one of crossing boundaries and continued to speak in more general terms about violence within intimate relations.

The two vignettes demonstrate the manner in which informal pedagogies of race circulated amongst the kids, and how sexuality was a site where different behavioural ideologies about race were made explicit. It is also important to note how, in both interactions, the counter-hegemonic pedagogies emerged from racially minoritized girls (Izel and Jacinta) in discussions with their white girlfriends (Carly and Sabrina). This demonstrates how race, class as well as gender are simultaneously operative in the kids experiences and expressions of sexuality, operating in divergent ways for different individuals at different times. This is precisely why sexuality is such an important domain for girls (as well as boys). For within sexuality, these often implicit racialized discourses are opened up and subjected to debate, thus becoming an important site where kids contributed to their transformation. While the entanglement of sexuality and race produced anxiety and obliged kids to creatively and laboriously mediate differences or legitimize their desires, this did not prevent them from experiencing the pleasures of sexuality as an important aspect of their embodied experiences. It is in these fleeting moments of pleasure and frustration that the core of racial ideologies was challenged.

Concluding thoughts

In *Racial Innocence*, Robin Bernstein (2011) persuasively demonstrates how childhood and, more specifically, dolls as scripted things were historically important sites of racial formation in the US, allowing white racial projects to appear natural and inevitable. Asking how the notion of 'childhood innocence' became a 'crucial element of contests over race and rights', Bernstein finds the root of these answers in the anti-miscegenation laws of the 19th century (2011: 2). Thus the seemingly unbreakable knot between childhood, race and innocence is in many ways crucially entangled with sex, a crucible that continues to shape large-scale racial projects and racial formation on the ground in a variety of ways. If part of the more exciting work in sexuality studies in the past 20 years has been to break down the separate spheres model and argue for the 'contradictory and conflictual ways' (McClintock, 1995: 5) in which sexuality, race, gender and class are related, then my work here is part of the project that insists that childhood is a critical aspect of this knot. In this chapter, I have demonstrated how discourses of childhood sexuality are inextricably interwoven with the first premise of all racial ideologies. Because my broader scholarly concerns revolve around how childhood is an important site in which the ontological certainty of race as natural type is reproduced (Kromidas, 2014), I focused on how sexuality is a crucial site for racial formation. While my emphasis on race is certainly part of the inherent bias of any researcher, I hope that my argument demonstrated that the compulsion of 'right types' is only second to the heterosexual matrix in the regulation of child sexuality.

If the fundamental part of learning race is understanding and embodying the fact that there are distinct types of people, and that these types must be protected and reproduced through heterosexual procreation, then it becomes clear that becoming a proper racial subjects is mutually constitutive with becoming a proper sexual subject. Violating these norms threatens the very existence of race, and the political order of Western nations where white supremacy provided the conditions for the emergence of modernity and the liberal individual (Eng, 2010: 8). The most dangerous terrains are those most likely to be governed by stringent rules, norms and rituals that function as a conservative force in society. These same terrains are also ripe with potential for social change. Child sexuality is one such charged domain. Although a site of intense surveillance and control, children's sexuality is also one of possibility, where alternative expressions of the kids' subjective experiences could emerge. Augursville kids' practices functioned as a critique of the racial order and provide us with hope and imagination for social change, however fragmentary. This vision contains more fluid and expanded conceptions of self and Other, one whose forms of being and belonging are much more convivial than those the children have inherited. Sexuality is thus an important site where kids refigure difference in inappropriate and unruly ways. Formal pedagogies can and should support the more counter-hegemonic impulses in these informal pedagogies, and must begin by taking the kids' experiences as the necessary and only valid starting point. Educators and academics working with them must understand how becoming racial, gendered, classed and sexual subjects are simultaneously operative processes. The question of how they intersect is an open-ended question that must be sorted out on the ground, much in the same ways that kids do, in the messy and unpredictable everyday practices of social interaction.

Notes

1. I use kids rather than children to refer to my participants as one aspect of an overall politics of representation. The term is doubly advantageous because it reflects how my participants referred to themselves, and because it avoids the condescending connotations of the term, which I reserve to refer to the social and discursive category of child.
2. I have altered the name of the school, neighbourhood and kids to ensure participants' confidentiality. The Institutional Review Board for the Protection of Human Subjects in Research at Teachers College, Columbia University approved the research on which this chapter is based, and I received consent from children and parents to use the data generated in reports and publications.
3. Following Bucholtz and Hall (2005), I use the term sociocultural linguistics as a general label for various interpretive perspectives that focus on naturalistic language in everyday life.
4. Of course, couples first had to make sense in terms of heteronormativity and the proper expression of gendered norms, and these discourses were imbricated with those discussed here.
5. A longer excerpt of this interaction is included in an earlier article exploring kids crossing into different language varieties (see Kromidas, 2011).

References

Ahmed, S. (2004) *The cultural politics of emotion*. Edinburgh: Edinburgh University Press.

Ali, S. (2003) *Mixed-race, post-race: Gender, new ethnicities, and cultural practices*. Oxford: Berg.

Allen, J. (2009) Blackness, sexuality, and transnational desire: Initial notes toward a new research agenda, in J. Battle, & S. L. Barnes (Eds.) *Black Sexualities: Probing Powers, Passions, Practices, and Policies*. New Brunswick, NJ: Rutgers University Press, pp. 82–96.

Allen, J. (2012) One way or another: Erotic subjectivity in Cuba. *American Ethnologist*, 39 (2), 325–338.

Allen, L. (2005) *Sexual subjects: Young people, sexuality and education*. London: Palgrave Macmillan.

Athanasiou, A., Hantzaroula, P., & Yannakopoulos, K. (2008) Towards a new epistemology: The 'affective turn.' *Historein*, 8, 5–16.

Bernstein, R. (2011) *Racial innocence: Performing American childhood from slavery to civil rights*. New York: New York University Press.

Bhana, D. (2007) Childhood sexuality and rights in the context of HIV/AIDS. *Culture, Health & Sexuality*, 9 (3), 309–324.

Biolsi, T. (2008) Race technologies, in D. Nugent, & J. Vincent (Eds.) *A Companion to the Anthropology of Politics*. Oxford: Blackwell Publishing, pp. 400–417.

Blackman, L., Cromby, J., Hook, D., Papadopoulos, D., & Walkerdine, V. (2008) Creating subjectivities. *Subjectivity*, 22, 1–27.

Bucholtz, M., & Hall, K. (2005) Identity and interaction: A sociocultural linguistic approach. *Discourse Studies*, 7 (405), 585–614.

Clough, P., & Halley, J. (Eds.) *The affective turn: Theorizing the social*. Durham, NC: Duke University Press.

Connolly, P. (2002) *Gender identities and young children: Social relations in a multi-ethnic inner city primary school*. New York & London: Routledge.

Donnan, H. (2010) *The anthropology of sex*. Oxford: Berg.

Edelman, L. (2004) *No future: Queer theory and the death drive*. Durham, NC: Duke University Press.

Egan, R. D. (2013) *Becoming sexual: A critical appraisal of the sexualization of girls*. Malden, MA: Polity Press.

Egan, R. D., & Hawkes, G. (2010) *Theorizing the sexual child in modernity*. New York: Palgrave Macmillan.

Eng, D. (2010) *The feeling of kinship: Queer liberalism and the racialization of intimacy*. Durham, NC: Duke University Press.

Epstein, D., Kehily, M. J., & Renold, E. (2012) Culture, policy and the un/marked child: Fragments of the sexualisation debates. *Gender and Education*, 24 (3), 249–254.

Epstein, D., O'Flynn, S., & Telford, D. (2003) *Silenced sexualities in schools and universities*. Stoke on Trent: Trentham Books.

Freedman, E., & D'Emilio, J. (2005) Problems encountered in writing the history of sexuality: Sources, theory and interpretation, in J. Robertson (Ed.) *Same-sex Cultures and Sexualities: An Anthropological Reader*. Malden, MA: Blackwell, pp. 162–174.

Herdt, G. (2004) Sexual development, social oppression, and local culture. *Sexuality Research & Social Policy*, 1 (1), 39–62.

Kromidas, M. (2010) Cyberculture, multiculture and the emergent morality of critical cosmopolitanism: Kids (trans)forming difference online, in D. Chappell (Ed.) *Children Under Construction: Critical Essays on Play as Curriculum*. New York: Peter Lang, pp. 233–258.

Kromidas, M. (2011) Elementary forms of cosmopolitanism: Beyond blood, birth and bodies in New York City. *Harvard Educational Review*, 81 (3), 581–605.

Kromidas, M. (2012) Affiliation or appropriation? Crossing and the politics of race in New York City. *Childhood*, 19 (3), 317–331.

Kromidas, M. (2014) The savage child and the nature of race: Lessons from the posthuman in NYC. *Anthropological Theory* 14 (4): 422–441.

Kucsera, J., & Orfield, G. (2014) *New York State's extreme school segregation: Inequality, inaction and a damaged future.* University of California, Los Angeles: The Civil Rights Project.

Lyons, A. P., & Lyons, H. D. (2004) *Irregular connections: A history of anthropology and sexuality.* Lincoln: University of Nebraska Press.

Lyons, A. P., & Lyons, H. D. (2011) Problems in writing about sex in anthropology, in A. P. Lyons, & H. D. Lyons (Eds.) *Sexualities in Anthropology: A Reader.* Sussex, UK: Wiley-Blackwell, pp. 1–6.

McClintock, A. (1995) *Imperial leather: Race, gender and sexuality in the colonial context.* New York: Routledge.

McElhinny, B. (2010) The audacity of affect: Gender, race, and history in linguistic accounts of legitimacy and belonging. *Annual Review of Anthropology*, 39, 309–328.

Mazzarella, W. (2009) Affect: What is it good for?, in S. Dube (Ed.) *Enchantments of Modernity: Empire, Nation, Globalization.* New York: Routledge, pp. 291–309.

Prout, A. (2005) *The future of childhood: Towards the interdisciplinary study of children.* London and New York: RoutledgeFalmer.

Ramos Zayas, A. Y. (2011) Learning affect, embodying race: Youth, Blackness, and neoliberal emotions in Latino Newark. *Transforming Anthropology*, 19 (2), 86–104.

Rampton, B. (1995) *Crossing: Language and ethnicity among adolescents.* London: Longman.

Rampton, B. (2001) Critique in interaction. *Critique of Anthropology*, 21 (1), 83–107.

Renold, E. (2000) Coming out: Gender, (hetero) sexuality and the primary school. *Gender and Education*, 12 (3), 309–326.

Renold, E. (2005) *Girls, boys and junior sexualities: Exploring children's gender and sexual relations in the primary school.* New York: RoutledgeFalmer.

Renold, E. (2013) *Boys and girls speak out: A qualitative study of children's gender and sexual cultures (age 10–12).* Cardiff: Cardiff University.

Renold, E., & Ringrose, J. (2013) Feminisms refiguring 'sexualisation', sexuality and 'the girl'. *Feminist Theory*, 14 (3), 247–254.

Stoler, A. (2001) Tense and tender ties: The politics of comparison in North American history and (post) colonial studies. *The Journal of American History*, 88 (3), 829–865.

Stoler, A. (2006) Intimations of empire, in A. Stoler (Ed.) *Haunted by Empire: Geographies of Intimacy in North American History.* Durham, NC: Duke University Press, pp. 23–70.

Vance, C. (2005) Anthropology rediscovers sexuality: A theoretical comment, in J. Robertson (Ed.) *Same-sex Cultures and Sexualities: An Anthropological Reader.* Malden, MA: Blackwell, pp. 15–32.

Walkerdine, V., Lucy, H., & Melody, J. (2001) *Growing up girl: Psychosocial exploration of gender and class.* Basingstoke: Palgrave.

Weston, K. (1998) *The long, slow burn: Sexuality and social science.* New York: Routledge.

Williams, R. (1977) *Marxism and literature.* Oxford and New York: Oxford University Press.

11
Children's Gendered and Sexual Cultures: Desiring and Regulating Recognition through Life Markers of Marriage, Love and Relationships

Kerry H. Robinson and Cristyn Davies

Introduction

Children's gendered and sexual cultures are dynamic and involve complex negotiations between various stakeholders, including children, families, educators, the media and the broader community. This chapter, based on qualitative research undertaken with children, parents/guardians and educators in Australia, examines how the discourse of marriage features predominantly in children's gendered and sexual cultures, significantly influencing their understandings of love, intimacy and relationships.[1] Employing a theoretical lens that encompasses feminist post-structuralism, queer theory and post-developmentalism, we explore how children constitute their own gendered and sexual subjectivities. Fundamental to this process is heteronormativity, which regulates many children's perceptions of the 'appropriate' girl and boy subject, ideals of romantic love and marriage. The ritual of marriage, which in Western cultures is linked to discourses of romantic love, family and having children, is central to children's enculturation within heteronormative values and morals. Children take up the discourse of marriage, mimetically incorporating its symbolic meaning into their imaginary worlds. The hegemony of the romantic, fairytale and carnivalesque nature of Western marriages further captures children's desire to be part of this sociocultural ritual.

We argue that an examination of children's sexual cultures and sexual subjectivities from the perspective of children is critical in understanding the complexities that are often absent from the sexualization debates that prevail in some Western cultures. These debates are characterized by arguments about the perceived erosion of sociocultural differences between adults and children and the alleged loss of childhood innocence, especially children's sexual innocence (e.g. Rush & La Nauze, 2006; Levin & Kilbourne,

2008). Central to many of these debates is the dismissal of children's knowledge and understandings, sexual subjectivities, desire and agency. Further, these debates reiterate gendered discourses that echo patriarchal, heteronormative, moralistic values and double standards associated with young girls' sexualities in particular (Renold & Ringrose, 2011; Egan, 2013). The children's comments in the research on which this chapter is based provide a counter-narrative to ways in which children are all too frequently constituted within these sexualization debates. Children demonstrated a critical engagement with gendered and sexual cultures and self-regulated their behaviours within the boundaries of what they viewed as possible. Learning about gendered and sexual cultures is a dynamic and fluid process, and within this context children actively interpret, negotiate and transform the discourses of love, marriage, relationships and sexuality that they take up as their own (Kontopodis et al., 2011).

The research approach

In this chapter, we discuss some of the findings about marriage and relationships from two separate but methodologically similar research projects. These projects examined the relationship between childhood and sexuality, with a focus on children's sexual cultures and knowledge of sexuality and relationships education. The first research project was a pilot study (see Robinson & Davies, 2008a; Davies & Robinson, 2010; Robinson, 2013) undertaken in the state of New South Wales,[2] and the second an Australian Research Council Discovery Grant (2011–2013)[3] conducted in New South Wales and the state of Victoria. Both projects investigated the sociocultural discourses operating around children's access to sexual knowledge; explored parents' approaches to speaking with their children about sexual knowledge; investigated children's understandings of intimate relationships; and adults' and children's perspectives of sexuality and relationships education. Unlike the pilot study which focused on children aged three to five, the larger study targeted primary school aged children aged five to 11 and investigated children's understandings of respect, how parents approached educating children about respect, as well as educators' perspectives of sexuality and relationships education in primary schools. Separate surveys targeting parents and educators of primary school aged children, which included short answer questions on all the areas identified above, were also an addition in the larger project.

Our discussion is based on focus groups and interviews with a total of 33 children across both projects. Children came from a range of family structures, sociocultural and economic backgrounds, recruited from long day care centres, primary schools, parent/family organizations, social networking sites, snowballing, and through a recruitment organization. Parents consented to their children's participation and relevant educational and governing bodies granted ethics approval. Discussions with children were initiated through the use of images found in magazines, postcards, newspapers and children's storybooks. This approach was used to begin conversations, similar to a storytelling activity that young children experience in their daily lives.

A Foucauldian discourse analysis was undertaken of the transcripts of interviews and focus groups. Discourse analysis provides a linguistic approach to an understanding of the relationship between language, knowledge, ideology and power (Lupton, 1992). Deborah Lupton states:

> Discourse analysis is composed of two main dimensions: the textual and contextual. Textual dimensions are those that account for the *structures* of discourses, while contextual dimensions relate these structural descriptions of various properties to the *social, political or cultural context* in which they take place.
>
> (1992: 145)

Discourses are historically and culturally formulated modes through which we understand knowledge, power and subjectivity. According to Michel Foucault (1974: 49) discourses are practices that systematically form the objects of which they speak; therefore discourses are key elements that constitute knowledge. Stephen Ball (1990: 2) defines Foucault's concept of discourse as:

> ...about what can be said and thought, but also about who can speak, when and with what authority. Discourses embody meaning and social relationships, they constitute both subjectivity and power.

Subjectivity (i.e. the self) is constituted within discourses that we draw upon in our communications with others and produce our conscious and unconscious thoughts and emotions, our sense of self and how we relate to the world, as well as the ways in which we are gendered, racialized, classed, sexualized, constituted as children and adults, and so on.

Similar to adolescents and adults, when undertaking a discourse analysis of children's interview and focus group transcripts, children's positioning in discourse/s becomes a focus of investigation. The various discourses (knowledge) that children take up constitute who they are and become the lens through which they view themselves, others and the world. These discourses are perpetuated through the language individuals utilize, through their daily interactions with others, through the texts they read, and visually through images they encounter, all of which portray very powerful ideas about people, objects and ideas. Each of the interview and focus group texts is analysed for the discourses each individual takes up as their own and for the sociocultural and political relations of power inherent in these discourses.

Children, like adolescents and adults, can have different belief systems, which can clash in focus groups. We are interested how differences in viewpoint and knowledge are negotiated amongst children. For example, in a focus group of three- and four-year-olds, being the older child can be used to establish power and authority in a conversation and can silence the ideas of others, or alternatively, persuade other children to support their position. Older children, often more aware of and experienced in relations of power in their environments, may choose to remain silent in focus groups and express their support or discomfort through body language – such embodied responses become part of the analytical process.

The discursive locations of individual subjects is dependent on negotiating relations of power, as well as the personal investments one perceives they have in taking up one discourse rather than another (Hollway, 1984; Robinson & Jones Diaz, 2006). Discourses officially sanctioned by social institutions (e.g. family, education, the law, medicine, government, media, religious groups), and supported by influential and authoritative individuals, groups and peers, wield greater power than other representations or perspectives. Often parents perceived that they had a greater influence over children's knowledge and the discourses through which this knowledge was articulated than was the case. Media and peers frequently had a greater influence.

Theorizing children's gendered and sexual cultures

Our understandings of children's sexual and gendered cultures are framed within feminist post-structuralism, queer theory and post-developmentalism. These theoretical frameworks provide a lens through which to critique the universalizing of childhood and to view the sociocultural historical discursive construction of childhood and children's relationships to sexuality and gender. Feminist post-structuralism offers a critical means through which to understand children's subjectivity; their shifting and contradictory position in discourse; agency (the power of individuals to actively participate in the construction of the self); and the macro relations of power that prevail in society, as well as the micro relations of power that children and others engage in their daily interactions (Davies, 1989; Weedon, 1997; St Pierre, 2000; Robinson & Jones Diaz, 2006; Davies & Robinson, 2010, 2013). Similar to feminist post-structuralism, queer theory views subjectivity as fluid, unstable, dynamic and constructed. Queer theorists argue that all identities are performative and challenge the heteronormativity inherent in gender and sexuality norms. (Butler, 1990; Jagose, 1996). Post-developmentalism takes a critical stance on the hegemony of mainstream Western developmental theory in constituting universalizing understandings of childhood (Blaise, 2011; Kontopodis et al., 2011).

Children are inextricably located within, negotiate, take up and resist dominant discourses that operate in the public sphere about children and sexuality. Children's sexual cultures are highly regulated by policies, law and practices that aim to protect children from harm. Within this context, children endeavour to construct themselves as agentic subjects, of which gender and sexuality play a critical component. In capitalist societies, sexuality is commodified to sell products and services. Children are not exempt as targeted consumers of clothing, music, magazines, leisure goods and services. Children are immersed in this world of advertising, in popular culture, family rituals and children's everyday play interactions with peers, and they actively take up components of these cultural practices as their own and modify and adapt these to their own cultural contexts. What is controversial in this process is when children take up sexual signifiers as their own from what is considered to be the sexual culture of adults.

Dominant discourses of childhood in Western societies are primarily founded on positivist theories of human development. Within this context, 'the child' is fixed and universalized in biological theories of child development that 'naturally' locate children on the spectrum of human development, in opposition to adults. However, some theorists of children's development, taking up a historical anthropological and sociocultural perspective, have challenged these positivist perspectives, arguing that the sociocultural environment in which children are located is central to children's learning and development. Christoph Wulf (2011) argues that in early childhood children experience the world through the process of mimesis. Through mimetic processes young children relate to others in their lives (parents, older siblings, other relatives, acquaintances and peers), taking part in cultural processes – participating in the performances of the practices and skills of their social group and appropriating its cultural knowledge (Wulf, 2011: 91). Young children have a mimetic desire to emulate not just adults, but older siblings and peers, and to become like them. A longing or an eagerness to be like an adult was certainly reflected in many young children's desire to engage in popular culture, relationships and the ritual of marriage. Children in particular viewed the latter as a rite of passage into adulthood. Young children frequently engaged in the ritual of marriage though mock wedding ceremonies and through the emulation of family relationships in their everyday play, both of which encompassed traditional gendered power relations.

Through mimetic processes children, as well as adolescents and adults, learn the values, attitudes and norms embedded in the institution of family, schooling and the workplace. As children learn, their knowledge, experiences and understandings of their environments increase, enabling them to encounter a broader range of discourses constituting the world in which they live. Within this process, often as a result of conflict and crises, children become more reflexive and aware of relations of power and the consequences of transgressing social norms, potentially leading to change in their position in discourse (Wulf, 2011).

Within positivist frameworks of childhood, the boundary between adults and children, and the ultimate signifier of the child, is childhood innocence, especially children's sexual innocence. Childhood innocence is a sociocultural historical construction and operates as a moral concept utilized as a powerful social control of both adults' and children's behaviours (Robinson, 2008, 2012, 2013; Davies, 2012, 2013). Childhood innocence has continued unabated to define the child and its place in the world today. In fact, any challenge to the sacrosanct concept of childhood innocence generally leads to a heightened level of concern in society (Renold, 2005; Blaise, 2010; Egan & Hawkes, 2010; Taylor, 2010).

Childhood innocence has been enshrined within traditional theories of human development, which have also constituted understandings of sexuality. Physiological sexual maturity is often perceived as a distinguishing point between adulthood and childhood (Gittins, 1998). Sigmund Freud's (1976 [1905]) theory of the proto-sexual polymorphous child provides a counter-discourse challenging this perspective that constitutes children's sexuality as absent or dormant. Freud argued that children had an active sexuality that needed to be expressed and considered childhood was centrally constructed around a flexible sexuality, a polymorphous perversity. Prior to children's understanding of social norms, Freud maintained that children found erotic pleasure and sexual gratification in any part of the body – behaviours considered perverse in adults. These behaviours were generally suppressed once social norms were learnt, resulting in the repression of sexual feelings. In the post-Freudian era of the 1970s and 1980s, however, sexuality has been largely represented as beginning at puberty and maturing in adulthood, correlating with developmentalist theories of the human, which reinforce biologically determined understandings of childhood and sexuality (Robinson, 2013). Thus, children's sexual immaturity is equated with 'innocence', which is considered naturally inherent in the child. Sexuality is viewed as the exclusive realm of adults, in which children are constructed as the asexual, naïve and innocent 'other' – a context in which children are perceived to be vulnerable and in need of protection. Within this discourse, sexuality is primarily perceived by the physical sexual act rather than as an integral part of one's identity, which is socially constructed, constantly reviewed and renegotiated by individuals as sexual agents, including children, throughout their lives (Jackson, 2006).

Sexuality is a site of difficult knowledge in many adults' perceptions and constructions of children's lives (Robinson, 2013). While the representative world of the child has expanded in the post-developmentalist era (Bruhm & Hurley, 2004; Robinson & Davies, 2008b), the proliferation of representations and the circulation of narratives about childhood have also generated new regimes for controlling and regulating the stories we tell about children, and the stories that children tell about themselves, as gendered and sexual beings.

Children often get mixed messages from competing discourses – those that constitute children as 'cute' when they are placed within the context of heteronormative romantic love; and those that constitute children as vulnerable to the affects of sexual imagery, potentially leading to children's early sexualization. However, children are always already sexualized through the heterosexualization of children as gendered subjects. The construction of children's gendered identities cannot be fully understood without acknowledging how the dominant discourses of femininity and masculinity are heteronormalized in children's everyday lives. That is, through the processes of gendering, children are constructed as heterosexual beings (Butler, 1990; Epstein, 1995; Robinson, 2005). Butler argues that 'gender is a kind of doing, an incessant activity performed, in part without one's knowing and without one's willing', and that 'it is not for that reason automatic or mechanical' but is instead 'a practice of improvisation within a scene of constraint' (2004: 1). Children's sexual cultures are constrained through the institutions of law, family and schooling, as well as through moral frameworks of the dominant cultures in the broader society. Children's gendered and sexual subjectivities are performative, and dominant heteronormative discourses that prevail in sociocultural, political, legal and educational institutions operate as sites of constraint on children's sexual cultures.

Overlapping the process of human development in Western societies are sociocultural scripts that operate as key life-markers and rites of passage, such as schooling, intimate relationships, starting work, voting, marriage, buying a house, reproduction, retirement, which all constitute successful citizenship. These markers operate to construct cultural boundaries between childhood, adolescence and adulthood. They ultimately become powerful markers of successful heteronormative citizenship (Halberstam, 2005). This research demonstrates that for many children, life-markers such as first 'special' relationships, marriage, kissing and having babies are integral to the narratives of their early lives and of their perceptions of their 'destinies'.

Children's enculturation into discourses of marriage

The discourse of marriage is central to the constitution of children's gendered and sexual subjectivities. In children's gendered and sexual cultures, many children desire and enthusiastically rehearse or play marriage, through mock weddings, and mother and father scenarios, which are legitimated by adults around them. Children are not passive in this process but are agentic beings actively constructing meanings around marriage and how it fits into their rights of passage. They are active agents in the constitution of their own subjectivity – they take up, resist, dispute or transform enculturating influences or normalizing discourses. Susie, aged eight, points out:

Researcher: How did you know about marriage? Who told you about it?
Susie: I don't know. It's just – I've been to two weddings so marriage is when you have a date with a lady and a man and then the man proposes to you and when he proposes to you, you plan a wedding that is for – so they can be together forever and they are like family.

Susie's comment highlights how knowledge is constituted through discourses that are generally invisible or not part of our everyday conscious awareness. She is aware that her experiences of attending weddings has provided her with insight into marriage, but is not conscious about the other ways she may have accrued knowledge about marriage.

Enacting fantasies of marriage, love and relationships is an integral part of children's everyday play and interactions. Confessions of love and prophecies of who one is going to marry are often secrets that children share with friends – quickly becoming the focus of teasing within children's peer groups when the secret is let out. Alex, a nine-year-old boy, commented on the way that his friends have feisty conversations about marriage:

Researcher: Do you talk about marriage with your friends?
Alex: Yes we do; sometimes we have fights saying who we're going to marry when we're older ... We have fights like the boys say I'm going to marry – like the boys say I'm going to marry this girl and then the girls say no I'm going to marry this boy and the boy is like no, no, I'm going to marry this girl.

Alex's comment suggests that popularity and power are key vectors through which children identify and select potential marriage partners. Power is a critical concept in understanding the process of subjectification, which is the way in which our subjectivity is made possible through the discourses that an individual has access to, throughout one's life. Both Alex's and Susie's comments reflect the way in which performativity is operational in subjectification, in this case of the construction of gender and sexual subjectivity. Butler (1994: 33) defines performativity as the 'aspect of discourse that has the capacity to produce what it names ... this production actually always happens through a certain kind of repetition and recitation'. The discourse of marriage, within a heteronormative framework, is repeatedly taken up by children as a normative and natural part of their lives and played out through their everyday interactions. This reflects Wulfs' (2011) understanding of mimesis as a crucial part of children's development, discussed previously.

Marriage: Framing children's perspectives of love, intimacy and kissing

The concept of marriage for many children operates as a moral regulatory framework, legitimizing sexual and romantic expressions of love and having children, intimacy, kissing, gendered and sexual relationships, and constructions of family. Marriage was not just the stepping stone to adult maturity for the children in these research projects but the context in which intimate sexual relations and 'having babies' were enacted and legitimized. Marriage was viewed as being different to relationships – having a boyfriend or girlfriend – in that it signified a greater commitment to a partner and the constitution of family.

Most of the children in this research viewed marriage as the key signifier of the pathway to intimate relationships, in particular the right to kiss another person. The language that children used to describe these relationships was to have a 'girlfriend' or 'boyfriend', whereas adults frequently used the euphemism 'special relationship', or 'special friend'. Adults' utilize this euphemistic language in an effort to reduce any sexual connotations that may be attached to children's relationships. Intimacy has been used both to describe types of interactions and types of relationships (Buhrmester, 1990). Features of intimacy can include: feeling understood, validated, cared for, engaging in mutual activities, self-disclosure and reciprocal feelings of satisfaction within a relationship or interaction. Some child developmentalists argue that 'friendships among preschool and elementary school aged children revolve primarily around playmate activities and group acceptance, whereas adolescent friendships become more intimate in nature' (Buhrmester, 1990: 1101). However, some young children in this research were engaging in interactions and relationships that reflected a level of intimacy with other children they professed to love and were proclaiming to marry when they were older. This intimacy was reflected in the comments of eight-year-old Melanie:

Researcher: Do you know what in love means?
Melanie: Yes.
Researcher: Can you tell me what it means?
Melanie: It means like you like the person very much and you just feel like it's – they're there for you and they feel the same way about you.
Researcher: When you say that you feel differently, can you explain what that feeling is? Does it make you feel a certain way?
Melanie: Yes, sometimes it just makes you feel a bit tingly and it just makes – and you know that you're in love when you are because you just feel it.

Researcher: Have you felt that?
Melanie: Yes.

Melanie's comments demonstrate an embodied understanding of what it means to be in love from a child's perspective.

As children progressed through the primary school years, their understandings of intimacy reflected that marriage was part of a process, which may begin with having one or more boyfriends or girlfriends, and results in the selection of one of these young persons to marry in the future when they are older. As we have argued elsewhere (Davies & Robinson, 2010), children's knowledge is frequently constructed through the framework of a 'procedure' where children follow set stages to reach their goal. Children's understandings of relationships, marriage and sexuality followed procedures that were located in moral and heteronormative discourses. Commenting on a picture of a boy and a girl in a mock wedding scenario, Rebecca, a four-year-old girl, made the following comments about marriage:

Researcher: What happens when you get married?
Rebecca: The girl dresses up pretty and the man dresses up too.
Researcher: Oh, right. And then what happens?
Rebecca: They kiss each other.

Not only is the wedding constituted as a spectacle where the bride and groom get to dress up, but it also provides, in the eyes of children, a legitimate and public space in which the couple can kiss. Children's perceptions of marriage in this research shifted from the early childhood educational space into the primary school context, which also reflects changing perspectives and understandings across the years. As part of engaging in the boyfriend or girlfriend culture, and cultures of play, kissing at school is more complicated than the concept of marriage, which signifies a more legitimate sociocultural practice in children's early years (Holford et al., 2013). A powerful discourse that emerged was the regulatory institutional environment of schooling in which children primarily understand the kiss as a taboo practice. This regulation and the 'no kissing policy' were often understood through the discourse of health, specifically 'because of germs'.

Children also learnt that normative intimate relationships did not involve marrying or kissing your parent, sibling or other extended family members such as cousins. Several mothers discussed how they had to regulate their young children's desire to kiss them on the mouth in the manner of adults' intimate kissing. These mothers were unsure if this was a normal practice for young children, or if their children were being overly sexual and they had somehow manifested this behaviour through their own practices.

The process of constructing families and responsibilities

Li, a five-year-old girl, shared her observations of an image of a girl and boy in a mock wedding scenario:

Li: They're gonna get married and go on a honeymoon.
Researcher: What else happens when you get married? What happens when you get back from the honeymoon?
Li: A baby starts to grow.

For many younger children, marriage was the initial point of the procedure of having a baby and constructing a family. For Li the 'honeymoon' was considered to be the discursive site in which the conception of a baby occurred; it was the second step after the wedding that was pivotal to the construction of family. Honeymoons are the traditional holiday taken by newly-weds in intimacy and seclusion.

Images of marriage in family photographs, children's witness to and involvement in the ceremonial spectacle of weddings, the focus on marriage in popular culture and in children's storybooks, constantly normalize the expectation of marriage in their future lives. Most children believed that they were going to marry in their adult lives, but often had strong opinions about what they considered was an appropriate age to marry. Eight-year-old Tom, who envisaged marriage as a romantic act, believed that it was important not to marry too early, that seeing the world should come first:

Tom: About 30-something... that's when I want to get married.
Researcher: Why 30?
Tom: Because I don't think you should get married at a young age. You should explore the world more.
Researcher: What do you think marriage is?
Tom: Marriage is when you bow down on one knee and say, would you like to marry me? If the girl says yes, you go – you will be really happy. I would celebrate but not go to a bar and really drink. I would just sit down and have a party and have soft drinks and water.

Tom's comments reflect discourses of traditional heteronormative romantic love in which a male is responsible for initiating a marriage proposal to a woman. He points out that a positive response warrants a celebration – in this context soft drinks and water, reflecting his age. In this research some parents, mainly mothers, were surprised that their sons were so invested in discourses of romantic love. Tom's desire to travel the world prior to marriage suggests that he has taken up adult advice in which becoming worldly and enjoying freedom, without family responsibilities or financial burden, is constituted through travel and experiencing different cultures before you settle down to marriage. While marriage is something to celebrate, the implications here are that it also restricts individual freedom, flexibility and mobility. Marriage is also constituted through socio-economic class in which freedom, flexibility and mobility are subject to and limited by financial success. Tom's concerns about marriage posing additional responsibilities were reiterated in relation to his concerns about his current girlfriend. Even though spending time with his girlfriend, Emma, made him feel 'really good', he was worried that getting too serious would lead to problems juggling his schooling, family and football responsibilities.

When Tom was asked why he thought people got married, his answer reflected on the role of marriage in building families, on gendered roles and on the complexities of his own family circumstances:

Researcher: Why do you think people get married?

Tom: Possibly to have a better life and possibly have some kids and help them learn and help them grow up.

Researcher: What do you think would be the good things about marriage?

Tom: Helping each other till the end and don't lay around while your husband or wife is cleaning.

Researcher: How do you know all this about marriage?

Tom: From my aunties and uncles because my mum and dad aren't married yet.

Researcher: Do you wish your mum and dad were married?

Tom: Yes.

Researcher: Why is it important for you for them to be married?

Tom: So we can be happier and dad doesn't have to – dad works, so mum has to stay home. My sister's in kindergarten – no, preschool, sorry. She's in preschool now and two years from now, she'll be in kindy. So I'm just hoping they can get married.

Researcher: Do you think it would make things better?

Tom: Yep.

For Tom, the potential of his parents' marriage is perceived to improve the family's quality of life. In this scenario it seems to be time sensitive in that he is concerned that his parents' marriage takes place before his little sister attends school. In schooling, family relationships are legitimated through the discourse of marriage. Tom is concerned that his little sister will fit into the normative discourses of schooling cultures, with which he currently struggles.

Heteronormativity, marriage and diverse family structures

Normative intimate relationships and marriage were constituted as heteronormative with children's wishes to marry their best friend of the same-sex, not just 'corrected' by parents/guardians and other adults but regulated by other children who were quick to exclaim that boys can't marry boys or girls can't marry girls (see Davies & Robinson, 2010). Proclamations of love and marriage proposals directed towards one's best friend of the same-sex diminished as children got older and more aware of what was considered a normative intimate relationship and began to understand the consequences of transgressing these norms. Younger children were more likely to see marriage as an expression of love that could be extended to include same-sex peers. However, for many younger children who participated in this research, being able to marry your same-sex peer as a young child was different from recognizing the possibility of two adult men marrying each other and having a family.

When considering an image of two dads with their baby, younger children were more likely to view the men either as brothers, cousins or friends, or a babysitter with a father and his child; the child's mother, who was viewed as temporarily absent, was often seen to be engaging in other traditional female activities, such as being in the kitchen cooking. Six-year-old Ella commented:

Researcher: Which one is the dad?
Ella: [points to picture].
Researcher: Who is the other guy in the picture then?
Ella: A babysitter that's helping him.
Researcher: A babysitter – so do you think that these could be – that this could be a family?
Ella: Um, no, friend and family.

Ella was adamant that one of the two men was a family member and the other a friend. Older children were generally more able to view the image as a representation of a gay relationship, reflecting an awareness of counter-discourses to heterosexuality, normative gendered family relationships, and gender roles and the power relations inherent in these. One nine-year-old girl, Lou, acknowledged the existence of same-sex relationships, while also sharing her understanding of traditional sex-gender roles and the labour associated with childcare and rearing:

Lou: Anyway, I wouldn't want to marry a girl.
Researcher: Sorry?
Lou: I wouldn't really want to be gay.
Researcher: Why is that?

Lou: I don't know. It would be – what if we both get born a baby, twice the job. That's why I just want to marry a man that – I just want to marry a man so I don't have two babies from two women.

Lou's main concern about being in a same-sex relationship was the perception that it would involve twice the amount of work, as it is assumed that both women would want to give birth to a child. Within this context, multiple discourses are in operation. While Lou's perception of gender roles and the women's desire to have children is framed through traditional and heteronormative discourses, the fact that Lou imagines that two women are able to have children together within a family context acknowledges an awareness of diverse family and sexualities.

Conclusion

In this chapter we have examined the ways in which children take up, adapt and resist dominant discourses of relationships, marriage, love and intimacy that are integral to their sexual cultures. Children's sexual cultures are framed through traditional heteronormative gendered relationships. For most children in this research, successful sexual citizenship is constituted through discourses of marriage. Children frequently understand marriage as part of a procedural formula that represents a critical life marker. Throughout early childhood and primary schooling years, this procedural formula changes according to the knowledge children accrue about intimate relationships, including boyfriend–girlfriend cultures.

Children's knowledge and practices are highly regulated by institutions, such as the family, school, the law, as well as by other sociocultural discourses. Children are self-regulating and operate in strong moralistic frameworks, stemming from these institutional policies, discourses and regulations that influence their understanding, awareness and practices as gendered and sexual subjects. Further, the discourses that constitute dominant meanings of childhood in Western cultures, such as childhood innocence, also influence adults' perceptions and regulatory practices around children. Children are agentic subjects who negotiate their own gendered and sexual subjectivities according to the knowledge and discourses they have available to them. In this process they adapt and reconstruct knowledge based on the fragments of information that they receive from family, peers, educators, children's literature and the media. Many children demonstrated an ability to be critical subjects and effectively negotiate the competing discourses that operate around gender and sexuality – children are, and can operate as, competent and informed sexual citizens in these areas often perceived as difficult by many adults. This point is critical to informing current debates about the sexualization of culture and its impact on children.

Notes

1. This publication is based on research supported by an Australian Research Council Discovery Project Grant (Grant number: DP110104431). The full research team included Kerry H. Robinson, Moira Carmody, Sue Dyson, and ethical permission was granted for Cristyn Davies to access the data. All participants' names have been changed.
2. This pilot research was conducted by Kerry Robinson and Cristyn Davies. It was funded by a University of Western Sydney grant.
3. The ARC Discovery project was conducted by Kerry Robinson and Moira Carmody from the University of Western Sydney, in New South Wales, and Sue Dyson from La Trobe University, in Victoria.

References

Blaise, M. (2010) Kiss and tell: Gendered narratives and childhood sexuality. *Australasian Journal of Early Childhood*, 35 (1), 1–9.

Bruhm, S., & Hurley, N. (Eds.) (2004) *Curiouser: On the queerness of children.* Minneapolis, MN: University of Minnesota Press.

Buhrmester, D. (1990) Intimacy of friendship, interpersonal competence, and adjustment during preadolescence and adolescence. *Child Development*, 61 (4), 1101–1111.

Butler, J. (1990) *Gender trouble: Feminism and the subversion of identity.* New York: Routledge.

Butler, J. (1994) Gender as performance: An interview with Judith Butler. *Radical Philosophy*, 67, 32–39.

Butler, J. (2004) *Undoing gender.* New York: Routledge.

Chapman, H. A., & Anderson, A. K. (2012) Understanding disgust. *Annals of the New York Academy of Sciences*, 1251, 62–76.

Davies, B. (1989) *Frogs and snails and feminist tales: Preschool children and gender.* Sydney: Allen and Unwin.

Davies, C. (2012) It's not at all chic to be denied your civil rights: Performing sexual citizenship in Holly Hughes' *Preaching to the Perverted. Sexualities*, 15 (3–4), 277–296.

Davies, C (2013) Constructing 'decency': Regulating government subsidised cultural production during the culture wars in. *NEA v. Finley, Cultural Studies*, 27 (1), 92–114.

Davies, C., & Robinson, K. H. (2010) Hatching babies and stork deliveries: Risk and regulation in the construction of children's sexual knowledge. *Contemporary Issues in Early Childhood*, 11 (3), 249–263.

Davies, C., & Robinson, K. H. (2013) Reconceptualising family: Negotiating sexuality in a governmental climate of neoliberalism. *Contemporary Issues in Early Childhood*, 14 (1), 39–53.

Egan, D. R. (2013) *Becoming sexual: A critical appraisal of the sexualization of girls.* Cambridge: Polity.

Egan, D. R., & Hawkes, G. (2010) *Theorising the sexual child in modernity.* London: Palgrave Macmillan.

Epstein, D. (1995) Girls don't do bricks': Gender and sexuality in the primary classroom, in I. Siraj-Blatchford & J. Siraj-Blatchford (Eds.) *Educating the Whole Child.* Buckingham: Open University Press, pp. 56–69.

Foucault, M. (1974) *The archeology of knowledge*. London: Tavistock.

Freud, S. (1976 [1905]) Infantile sexuality, in J. Strachey (Trans.) *Three Essays on the Theory of Sexuality*. New York: Basic Books.

Gittins, D. (1998) *The child in question*. London: Macmillan.

Holford, N., Renold, E., & Huuki, T. (2013) What (else) can a kiss do? Theorizing the power plays in young children's sexual cultures. *Sexualities*, 16 (5/6), 710–729.

Hollway, W. (1984) Gender difference and the production of subjectivity, in J. Henriques, W. Hollway, C. Urwin, C. Venn, & V. Walkerdine (Eds.) *Changing the Subject: Psychology, Social Regulation and Subjectivity*. London: Methuen, pp. 223–261.

Jackson, L. (2006) Childhood and youth, in H. D. Cocks & M. Houlbrook (Eds.) *The Modern History of Sexuality*. Basingstoke: Palgrave Macmillan, pp. 231–255.

Jagose, A. (1996) *Queer theory*. Victoria: Melbourne University Press.

Halberstam, J. (2005) *In a queer time and place: Transgendered bodies, subcultural lives*. New York: New York University Press.

Kontopodis, M., Wulf, C., & Fichtner, B. (2011) Introduction: Children, development and education – A dialogue between cultural psychological and historical anthropology, in M. Kontopodis, C. Wulf, & B. Fichtner (Eds.) *Children, Development and Education: Historical, Cultural and Anthropological Perspectives*. Dordrecht: Springer, pp. 1–24.

Levin, D. E., & Kilbourne, J. (2008) *So sexy so soon: The new sexualized childhood and what parents can do to protect their kids*. New York: Ballantine Books.

Lupton, D. (1992) Discourse analysis: A new methodology for understanding the ideologies of health and illness. *Australian Journal of Public Health*, 16 (2), 145–150.

Renold, E. (2005) *Girls, boys, and junior sexualities: Exploring children's gender and sexual relationships in the primary school*. London: RoutledgeFalmer.

Renold, E., & Ringrose, J. (2011) Schizoid subjectivities: Retheorising teen girls sexual cultures in an era of 'sexualisation'. *Journal of Sociology*, 37 (4), 389–409.

Robinson, K. H. (2005) 'Queerying' gender: Heteronormativity in early childhood education. *Australian Journal of Early Childhood*, 30 (2), 19–28.

Robinson, K. H. (2013) *Innocence, knowledge and the construction of childhood: The contradictory nature of sexuality and censorship in children's contemporary lives*. London: Routledge.

Robinson, K. H., & Davies, C. (2008a) Docile bodies and heteronormative moral subjects: Constructing the child and sexual knowledge in the schools. *Special Issue of Sexuality and Culture*, 12 (4), 221–239.

Robinson, K., & Davies, C. (2008b) She's kickin' ass, that's what she's doing: Deconstructing childhood innocence in media representations. *Australian Feminist Studies*, 23 (57), 343–358.

Robinson, K. H., & Jones Diaz, C. (2006) *Diversity and difference in early childhood education: Issues for theory and practice*. Maidenhead, Berkshire: Open University Press.

Rush, E., & La Nauze, A. (2006) *Corporate pedophilia: Sexualisation of children in Australia. The Australia institute*. Discussion Paper Number 90.

St Pierre, E. (2000) Poststructural feminism in education: An overview. *International Journal of Qualitative Studies in Education*, 13 (5), 477–515.

Taylor, A. (2010) Troubling childhood innocence: Reframing the debate over the media sexualisation of children. *Australasian Journal of Early Childhood*, 35 (1), 48–57.

Weedon, C. (1997) *Feminist practice and poststructuralist theory*, 2nd edn. Cambridge, MA: Blackwell Publishing.

Wulf, C. (2011) Mimesis in Early Childhood: enculturation, practical knowledge and performativity, in M. Kontopodis, C. Wulf, & B. Fichtner (Eds.) *Children, Development and Education: Historical, Cultural and Anthropological Perspectives*. Dordrecht: Springer, pp. 89–99.

Part III

Queering Young Sexualities: Gender, Place and History

12

'Istabane': South African Teenagers and the Regulation of Sexuality, Gender and Culture

Deevia Bhana

> Kanye (girl) It's simple, our culture and homosexuality don't go together, no matter what...
>
> Wenzi (boy) Being homosexual is good for other cultures, white people, but not for us as Africans....
>
> (Focus group discussions with African teenagers at Inanda High School, Durban)

In the eastern KwaZulu-Natal province of South Africa a group of young African teenagers, aged between 16 and 17 are contesting the association between culture and sexuality. Sixteen-year-old Kanye argues, 'culture and homosexuality don't go together'. These words draw from a study examining the ways in which young people at school mediate knowledge about, gender, sexuality and violence in and around schools. Such mediation, as the transcripts above illustrate, is situated against the backdrop of increasing tensions between the claim to sexual equality in the country and the heightening concerns about homophobic violence. The claim that homosexuality is incompatible with culture and 'un-African' has gained notoriety on the African continent where 38 out of 55 countries criminalize same-sex relationships (Altman et al., 2012; Sigamoney & Epprecht, 2013). Despite evidence showing the manifestation of homosexuality in pre-colonial Africa (Epprecht, 2008), a dominant view on the continent is that homosexuality is an alien import and a western invention. In contrast to the draconian policies of many countries in Africa, South Africa guarantees equality on the basis of sexual orientation. Yet as Roehr (2010) notes, South Africa's progressive sexual landscape has often been charged to be too white, too European and not truly African. Confirming this view, 17-year-old Wenzi above asserts that homosexuality is 'good for other cultures, white people, not for us as Africans'.

Contemporary moral panics around sexuality in the west often rotate around childhood sexuality and girls' sexualization as suggested by Renold and Ringrose (2013: 247). These authors argue that the moral panic concerning the premature heterosexuality of young girls is locked into class and race. In this conceptualization the moral panic operates to construct the racialization of white middle-class innocence versus the hypersexuality of working-class girls. This chapter complicates these hegemonic positions by focusing on young Africans in the context where homosexuality is supported by law, creating a cultural panic. The deployment of cultural arguments to regulate gender and sexuality are dangerous especially in the context of homophobic violence. Moreover, the cultural trope works to regulate and reinforce an idealized African identity, reproducing gender stereotypes and resulting in a witch-hunt for those who do not conform to the heterosexual ideal. In South Africa this witch-hunt has violent ramifications (Human Rights Watch, 2011). This is especially the case in the context of the 'curative rape' of African lesbians in township settings. 'Curative' rape is used to violently put masculinized women 'correctly' in their place within culturally normative understandings of gender and sexuality (Epprecht, 2008).

At this point in the chapter it is important to clarify the use of the term homosexuality, which differs from western usage of terms such as queer, LGBTQ, same-sex relations. Following Sigamoney and Epprecht (2013: 88):

> The term *homosexual* is part of the dominant sexuality discourse in present-day South Africa, including in human rights documents, messages campaigning against homophobia, scientific and other academic scholarship, and mass media, including a popular television show (*Generations*).

The use of the word 'homosexual' thus arises from the political and intellectual currency in the country. Elsewhere I have shown that the words gays and lesbians are far more entrenched within local school understandings of sexuality, with the word *istabane* (gay) foregrounded in rural and African township contexts (Bhana, 2014). In using homosexuality, this chapter is careful not to use concepts that might obscure local knowledge, a point corroborated by Sigamoney and Epprecht (2013) highlighting the politics of language in discussions about sexuality.

The thesis that homosexuality is un-African is impoverished. Yet such claims even from young teenagers as the transcripts have begun to show still remain strong. Scholars have illustrated how colonial forces and religious crusades have produced a version of sexuality that is considered hostile to and incompatible with homosexuality (Epprecht, 2008). Indeed research has indicated the ways in which African sexual and gendered cultures are fluid, dynamic, heterogeneous and adaptable (Arnfred, 2004; Hunter, 2010). The deployment of culture, it is argued, is a discursive strategy to claim an

African identity as exclusively heterosexual which reproduces gender hierarchies and inequalities. The cultural logic adopted by 16- and 17-year-old Kanye and Wenzi sets the scene for this chapter. This chapter builds on and contributes to the research that highlights the ways in which young Africans in a township context give meaning to homosexuality, and the social and cultural processes through which such meanings are produced within the backdrop of homophobic violence (Msibi, 2012).

Culture, gender and context

The teenagers in this study are living and growing up in a context of poverty. They give shape to their social positions and are shaped by the histories of apartheid, chronic unemployment and social deprivation. Within these communities, whilst modern values are rising, traditional Zulu cultural practices still hold sway. According to these practices, gender and age categories shape and influence how boys, girls and men and women relate to each other. Customary practices including *inhlonipha* (respect) and men's privileged status are recognized and valued. *Inhlonipha* for instance is premised on women's deferential posture and respect for men.

These values are deeply gendered and heterosexualized. Historically men's power was based on their ability to build a homestead, invested in the payment of *ilobolo* (bridewealth), marriage and to produce a lineage. Bridewealth, whilst based originally on transfer of cattle by the groom to the bride's parents, has been replaced in contemporary society by cash payments. Whilst this custom is complex, research illustrates that *ilobolo* functions as a marker of African identity (Rudwick & Posel, 2014). *Ilobolo* was deeply embedded in women's reproductive capacities, the growth of a homestead and children. Men who produced the most heirs were accorded respect and power. In contemporary KwaZulu-Natal, these practices have altered owing to changing economic and social circumstances. Migrant labour and a move to disposable income has altered family structures and led to changes in men's ability to marry and produce a lineage and thus men's ability to claim power.

Unable to pay bridewealth, men's ability to marry and build a home are diminished leading to notions of male weaknesses. Nonetheless, within gendered poverty, it is men who are able to provide and still sustain a better-off economic position than African women in township. Hunter (2010) conceptualizes 'provider masculinity' in this context, suggesting that whilst providing is key to masculine power, provider masculinity is heavily invested in heterosexual prowess and multiple partnering fostered through a hegemonic gift/money culture. In this context, whilst customary practices are changing, they do hold sway and remain powerful in shaping gender and heterosexual relations mobilized around male privilege.

At this point it is important to note that Zulu cultural practices are not homogeneous but fluid and open to modification. Structural inequalities, persistent unemployment, poverty and labour migrations have dented and altered Zulu cultural practices. The turbulent economic condition and the inability of men to demonstrate economic power has resulted in fragile and toxic forms of masculinities. The social and economic conditions often fuel the reinscription of cultural practices, and homosexuals are often targeted as scapegoats and threatening to cultural practices and community values. Homophobic violence and disparagement of gays and lesbians through naming such as '*istabane*' and '*inkonkoni*' (meaning hermaphrodite or freak of nature) must be seen against the broader cultural and largely collective nature of Zulu society. As Rudwick and Posel (2014) note, attempts to maintain, protect and preserve ideal cultural practices is key to claiming a Zulu identity.

The specific cultural practices amongst Africans in KwaZulu-Natal draws from an ethnic variable construct related to being 'Zulu'. Historical commentators such as Hunter (2010) and Rudwick and Posel (2014) suggest that Zulu cultural practices are heterogeneous and changing under changing social and economic circumstances in the province. However, the tendency to fix culture was still evident, as this chapter will show, as participants view culture as a key to Zulu identity and homosexuality as antithetical to it.

Background to the study

This chapter is based on an ongoing larger research project examining the ways in which children and young people conceptualize, experience and give meaning to gender, sexuality and the ways in which inequalities and violence manifest in these experiences and meanings. Concerns about gender violence in and around schools often ignore the manifestations of homophobic violence. Without much research about school-going learners' perspectives on these issues, this chapter sought to understand the contextual specificities in the mediation of such knowledge by focusing on a group of learners in a township context in KwaZulu-Natal. Townships are places created by apartheid for Africans working in urban areas of South Africa. It constitutes brick dwellings as well as makeshift homes, reflecting the stark social inequalities in the country. Combined with the history of apartheid and the continuing economic crises which has struck the poor, people in townships often face dire social distress and violence. Homophobic violence is particularly evident in townships (Human Rights Watch, 2011). The aim of this research is to build a contextually specific knowledge base about children and young people's meanings, experiences and mediations of gender/sexuality and violence in and around the school.

Unlike the West, where a rich body of educational research has revealed the ways in which teenagers are heavily invested in heterosexuality and the gendered processes through which homophobia manifests (Rasmussen, 2006; Marshall, 2013; Gowlett, 2014; Quinlivan et al., 2014), there remains a dearth of research on the African continent. Recently, though, an emerging body of studies in South Africa has begun to investigate how schooling processes privilege heteronormativity (Bhana, 2012; Msibi, 2012; Francis, 2012; Sigamoney & Epprecht, 2013; DePalma and Francis, 2014).

One way in which Southern African research has unravelled heterosexual domination and assumed fixity of meaning around African sexuality is to queer culture (Epprecht, 2008; Msibi, 2012). Influenced by the work of Butler (1990) and Warner (1993), queer theorizing unravels the assumed universalization of heterosexuality. Male power and privilege for instance occurs within a binary where sexual desires are expected to occur between men and women and other forms of sexuality are Othered. Whilst importing western versions of 'queer theories' without understanding the structural and cultural circumstances are problematic, interrogating heterosexual domination provides the leverage to reject the 'cultural' claim of an inherent African sexuality. The value of queering is the instability of meaning, as Butler (1990) posits, and opens up the possibility to illustrate the contradictions, fluidity and the dynamic nature of culture and sexualities. Without rehearsing the broad tenets of queer theorizing in this chapter, the value of queering culture is to uncover the ways in which heterosexual power and privilege within the sex/gender binary can be opened up.

Study details

The young people emerge from a school context that is very familiar to the researcher, who conducted previous research in the school (Bhana & Pattman, 2011). Access was negotiated, ethical approval was obtained and a female researcher conducted three focus groups.[1] These focus group discussions comprised one mixed sex (three male and three female) and two single-sex discussions comprising six male and six female learners aged 16–17 at the school, inviting them to discuss and to provide their perspectives on the issue of homosexuality. The research is premised upon a young person-centred approach to research which takes the views of, and the concerns raised by, young people as serious and worthy of attention (Frosh et al., 2002; Kehily, 2012; Ringrose, 2013). Like this body of work in the West, the young people in the township are seen as active subjects who can think, know and feel and as active agents are able to do so, with the ability to express their agency. Sexual agency, however, is normalized and heterosexualized as Butler (1990) suggests. In queering what young people say about homosexuality, the paper shows how heterosexual privilege is asserted, mediated and adjusted. Beyond the queering of sexuality, the analysis in this chapter pays attention to the local and cultural norms through which heterosexuality is given. The work of Mark Hunter (2010) and Rudwick and Posel (2014) illustrates the tension between agency and structure in the context where culture, whilst dynamic and changing, weaves through the mediation of gender and sexuality. Thus young people's agency is not conceptualized as free will but located in and influenced by a range of cultural and gendered norms, which affects how meanings of sexuality are conceptualized.

'A man is a man ... nothing in-between': Culture, sexuality and the regulation of masculinities

Dominant cultural norms associated with masculine power were accommodated by teenage Africans, leading to the castigation of homosexuality as an illegitimate expression of African identity. By invoking cultural arrangements that placed emphasis on male heterosexual power, Sandile (b²) notes during the focus group discussions that 'culturally it's [homosexuality's] wrong and it questions *inhlonipha*, the respect and dignity of men ... it humiliates us as boys'. Whilst scholars writing about masculinities in South Africa have pointed out that cultural configurations of gender are patriarchal, there is widespread evidence of alternative masculinities which defy a homogeneous understanding of monolithic heterosexual African male power (Ratele, 2008). Whilst these alternative masculinities have not challenged the hegemonic masculinity, a prominent view constructed by teenage men and women was the unfailing, unchanging African male leader embedded within an unchanging cultural context:

> Kanye (g) ... According to our culture boys are expected to behave in a certain way ... like showing leadership ... being tough ... they are prepared to be heads of households ... Gay people's behaviour is totally against what is expected by our culture.

Culture is used to hold heterosexuality in its place whilst simultaneously defining and regulating acceptable versions of masculinity. Zulu cultural practices, as Hunter (2010) confirms, are hierarchically differentiated and governed by notions of respect and male power whilst simultaneously according women and children a subordinated position within gender and cultural relations. South African research describes the significance of cultural dynamics in upholding male power (Hunter, 2010). Integral to male power, as Kanye elucidates, is the expectation to behave in a 'certain way' that is indicative of strength and provider status. In accommodating culture, Kanye rejects the behaviour of gays when he says that boys have to behave like heads of household, and in doing so also accommodates the expression of male power which has been criticized for involvement in substantial gender power inequalities in the country that are complicit in high incidences of gender and sexual violence.

Derived from *inhlonipha*, the respect and social position of men is reproduced within normative constructions of heterosexuality. Being a real man
requires association with hegemonic forms of conduct including leadership
and toughness. In contrast, Kanye argues, gay behaviour is outside cultural
expectations and insulted through names like *'istabane'*. *Istabane* is a common isiZulu term for men who engage in same-sex relations, although it can
also mean an effeminate man (Hunter, 2010):

> Mfeka (b)...a man must be strong...be able to protect himself and his
> family...gay men are...not man enough...

Cultural scripts in the interviews were used to reproduce versions of masculinity that emphasized strength and the men's gendered role as protector –
a role that gay men were 'not man enough' to perform. Understanding
inhlonipha and how it relates to gender and sexuality is crucial as it demar-
cates an acceptable form of masculinity and femininity, as Wenzi argues
below:

> Wenzi (b) A man is a man, there is nothing in between. In our culture
> only men and women are allowed to be in a sexual relationship...they
> will get married and bear children...

The regulation of sexuality is produced through the intersecting threads
of culture, masculinity and sexuality. In doing so, masculine heterosexual power is asserted, 'a man is a man...nothing in between'. It is argued
here that culture is invoked to provide the logic of heterosexual coherence
through which men (and women's) role is regulated. The repeated patterns
of claims to cultural constancy are key to the making of Zulu identity.
As Hunter (2010: 58) has argued, cultural practices are often used to project
the 'very essence of being Zulu'. In defending Zuluness and thus patriarchal cultural values, Lula in the quote below suggests that homophobic
violence must be understood within this context where the disruptive force
of homosexuality is addressed through violence:

> Lula (b) All that violence...things are done to gays so that they'll change
> back to be real men. They were born as men and if they can change back,
> we [men] will have our respect back.

Lula above refers to the backdrop of homophobic violence against gays and
lesbians and suggests how violence operates within normative understandings of gender and culture which repudiates homosexuality. Of particular
concern here are the ways in which culturally normative processes naturalize violent consequences, 'All that violence...things are done to gays so that
they'll change back to be real men.' Homosexuality is considered to be an

affront to culture. What is at stake here is not simply heterosexual power but significantly how an attack on male power is deemed as an assaulting cultural notion underlined by respect/*inhlonipha*. In Rudwick and Posel's (2014) study in KwaZulu-Natal, they found that when people did not show respect (meaning subservience to a gender and generational hierarchy) they were severely frowned upon by family and the community. Conversely respect was seen as an important means to claim an identity and become someone within contemporary culture. The fallacy of the fixity of culture, male power and heterosexual compulsion is evident when Lula suggests that sexualities are changeable. There is nothing fixed about men's role and men's power, and this contrasts sharply with the position taken to privilege a distinct and coherent system of African culture where a man is a man: 'nothing in-between'. Changing back provides an important counter-argument to the overly deterministic way in which culture has been constructed by the participants in this study and the assumed hegemony of heterosexual patriarchy. As Foucault (1979) suggests, no discourse is closed to contestation. Sexuality is changeable and provides a space in which to contest the prevailing cultural constancy through which young people create and reproduce heterosexual compulsion.

'If a boy in a family is gay, that family is as good as dead': Culture and the building of families

In Zulu society heavy emphasis is placed on reproductive capacity of women and lineage. In Hunter's (2010) historical study of Zulu men and women in South Africa at the turn of the 20th century, marriage was valued and deeply embedded in notions of male power and producing a lineage. The cultural practice of bridewealth (*ilobolo*) was an important means through which building homesteads were forged. The building of families and the cultural value in reproduction still has currency today, as teenagers placed emphasis on children in the interviews. The impossibility of building families is highlighted here as a significant reason why young people repudiated homosexuality, claiming its incompatibility with African culture. There was vehement opposition to homosexuality on the basis that it stopped the 'bloodline' and the growth of families:

> Spha (b) Most parents don't understand it. Parents grew their kids up so they can build their own families. It becomes difficult for them when they come across a situation where a boy is sexually attracted to another boy ... there is this perception in our communities that there is something wrong with a person who is gay ....

> Wenzi (b) For me I just want the family to grow, and the family name to multiply.

Sandile (b) If a boy in a family is gay that family is as good as dead. It won't grow, their bloodline will just end there...Gay boys will not have children which is totally against our culture.

Reproduction and male investment in the lineage was strongly associated with culture. Building families was positively correlated with culture and heterosexual norms, and conversely families with gays were viewed as 'as good as dead' and a violation of culture. The analyses of young teenagers are tightly constrained and serve as custodians of cultural traditions, suggesting a seamless understanding of gender, culture and sexuality. Exclusionary mechanisms were deployed and, as Spha notes, there was a consistency in meaning within families and communities that 'there was something wrong with a person who is gay...'.

The incompatibility of homosexuality with building families led many of the participants to link homosexuality with evil spirits. Indeed, in many parts of KwaZulu-Natal province, traditional world views have been retained and include invocations to ancestral spirits (*amadlozi*) (Hunter, 2010). One view that remains relevant here is that it is important to appease ancestral spirits by complying with cultural practices and in so doing avoiding sorcerers with evil intentions (Cock & Moller, 2002). Respecting *amadlozi* is regarded as being part of appropriate Zulu etiquette (Rudwick & Posel, 2014). A gay child is thus interpreted to be an evil spirit, as Wenzi suggests below:

Wenzi (b)...A gay child, it's a disgrace in the family with no children... and when things don't go well in the community they just blame this one homosexual person, the evil spirit.

Cock and Moller (2002) maintain that the blame for misfortune in the community (whatever form it might take) is often attributed to a breach of customs and traditions or to evil spirits who are instructed to do harm by sorcerers. The regulation of and the maintenance of cultural explanations to fix heterosexuality as African is clear in Wenzi's statement above. However, Christian religious values overlapped with cultural views rendering homosexuality as evil and punishable, as Lungi makes clear below:

Lungi (g)...in the Bible homosexuality is a sin...there is this story in the Bible about Sodom and Gomorrah. Homosexuals were destroyed...

Cultural practices combined with Christian religious principles produced an environment, where homosexuality was regarded as spiritually dangerous and unacceptable in the building of families.

Participants also deployed *ilobolo* to exclude homosexuality:

Manca (b) If I have a daughter, as a parent I am waiting for *ilobolo*.

Manca anticipates that in the future, as a father of a daughter, the traditional customary practice requiring a male to pay bridewealth to the family of the bride should be upheld. *Ilobolo* is constructed as a fixed tradition of Zulu identity. Not subscribing to *ilobolo* may be regarded as disrespectful to culture. Whilst marriage rates in South Africa have declined because of men's inability to pay *ilobolo*, the emphasis placed on *ilobolo* serves as an important discursive strategy to reproduce the power of culture and denounce homosexuality. However, the material realities are such that the expectation of *ilobolo* must also be seen under harsh economic conditions where cash payments attached to the practice are appealing. At a symbolic level, *ilobolo* has important currency in carving out an 'authentic' African identity.

Gays and lesbians: 'Show-offs' and 'not in your face'

This section explores how cultural norms regulate and create a sexual pecking order in relation to what constitutes an 'authentic' African identity within a broader community context. The ways in which gays and lesbians in the community were constructed and contrasted by participants had direct relevance to gender and sexual hierarchies. Gay men in particular were admonished as being non-compliant and defiant of cultural norms, bringing masculinities into the spotlight:

> Spha (b)…What is mainly a problem about homosexuals is that they like to show off their behaviour, bad behaviour in the community. Everywhere they are, they want to draw more attention to people. The way they talk, walk and interact with other people change altogether? Sometimes it makes me feel uncomfortable. Even here at school they do it.

Against the dominant community environment which sanctions heterosexual norms, the presence of gays in particular was seen as a violation of gender and cultural norms. Sigamoney and Epprecht (2013) note that claiming an African identity is hinged upon the public display of certain culturally sanctioned practices. For instance, even the president of the country often dresses in animal skins for Zulu ceremonies, demonstrating publicly the traditional cultural values espousing male domination. In contrast, the public show of gay sexuality as evident in Spha's notion of sexual stylization of walk, talk and daily interactions was viewed as discomforting both within and outside the school. Gays were admonished for bringing attention to their nonconforming behaviour and were derided (Ansell, 2001). A common word used by participants to describe the nonconforming behaviour was 'show-offs'. Gay conduct was seen as a violation of cultural norms and blamed for the negativity surrounding them. In the discussion below Londi et al. refer to the nonconforming behaviour which draws negative attention to homosexuals. As Butler (1990) has argued, heterosexuality is assumed to be the only normal way of being. Non-normative behaviour is exposed, shamed, ridiculed and regulated and controlled by a range of discursive strategies including violence. Rigid norms including cultural expectations about the proper way to be a 'real' man, including how to behave, are regulated, monitored and policed. A real man is given further content by cultural idioms and expectations within the local context. As Butler (1990: 194) notes, these values are shaped by 'the grid of cultural intelligibility through which bodies, genders and desires are naturalized'. The force of the heterosexual intelligibility means that the transgressions of these norms are expelled and excluded. Thus heterosexuality, whilst unstable, relies on the enforcement of normative behaviour, dress and stylization based on expected and assumed understandings of gender in order to maintain domination (Bhana, 2014). The discussion must be seen not only as reflecting the heteronormative order but also reproducing it:

> Londi (g)... these people in this country are harassed or killed like in other countries, which shows that we not have accepted them. But they are the ones who attract negativity to themselves, that is why they need to be taught how to behave.

> Nonsi (g) For me I don't have a problem with them, but it's their behaviour that's a problem. They always like to compete and they also like to draw attention... they don't respect other people....

> Manca (b) I don't know really, but what I know is that through money they attract lots of friends especially boys. They buy booze for them and lots of other things, so in that way they continue to show off and to get some form of respect from their peers.

When Nonsi says that gays like to compete, drawing attention to themselves, she claims that the public display of homosexuality is disrespectful to the heterosexual majority where cultural systems based on respect are heavily invested in the heterosexual norm. There is qualified acceptance if by implication their behaviour is not visible (thus silenced and marginal), thus giving a semblance of continuity, heterosexual coherence and respectfulness of the cultural norms. Sigamoney and Epprecht (2013) note that the contests around homosexuality are not only about the transgressions of sexual norms but also about how to make the homosexual subject acceptable.

Whilst concerns have been raised about the constricted versions of meaning, within the depressed social and economic environment, Manca positions gays as men with money. Unlike the majority of people who remain poor and economically unstable, gay men (from his perspective) are able to 'buy booze', earn respect (through money) and wield power. Materiality, sexuality and power are complexly intertwined and significantly point to changes in cultural and gender relations. Such possibilities are also evident in the statement below, derived from South African law. In the transcript below Thobi, like Nonsi before her, suggests qualified acceptance, showing both fluidity and constraint:

> Thobi (g) Gays need to be accepted. But we cannot change our culture because of them. Our culture was adopted by our grandparents a long time ago and we cannot change it now just to accommodate them ... even the law of the country has allowed them a right to marry each other ... but they use their freedom in a very wrong way. They like to show off. It's like they advertise who they are, they overdo things. I believe they deserve to be treated properly but they also need to manage their behaviour.

Thobi opens up the constricted views of homosexuality discussed thus far, suggesting that gays must be accepted as indicated by the law but that their freedoms are used 'wrongly' and in defiance of culture. In reproducing cultural logic, she argues that gays advertise, and 'overdo', their behaviour like 'show-offs'. Being a show-off is suggestive of inciting the heterosexual majority and violating culture. Negotiating homosexuality within the broader cultural norms requires the management of discreet behaviour without exhibition of sexuality. Being a show-off defies the cultural norm and makes homosexuality too obvious within the broader cultural climate that repudiates it.

Whilst gay men and masculinities were brought under the spotlight for the violation of gender and cultural norms by Thobi above, lesbians on the other hand were 'respectful' of norms: their sexuality was 'not written in the face'. In the discussion below the different ways in which gays and lesbians were positioned within the broader gender dynamic becomes evident. Whereas gays were castigated for publicly inciting the heterosexual majority and violating masculine norms, lesbians were regarded as respectful girls who did not 'show off'.

> Nona (g): The only difference is that girls are more respectful in their behaviour then boys. They do whatever they want to do privately, unlike boys who always like to show off.
>
> Kanye (g): There is one gay boy here at school who behaves like girls and some other boys do not treat him well. They say it's because of his behaviour ... they don't treat him like other boys ... you'll find that he is just walking in the veranda ... they'll just laugh at him ... but with lesbians it's not common because they behave like other girls ... they wear skirts like other girls.
>
> Wenzi (b): No one takes note of her, it's only the gay boys who are noticed.
>
> Scelo (b): The thing is, lesbian girls are very private and they behave very well. Even if they have sexual relationship with other girls no one notices.

Wenzi (b): It's not written in the face that they're lesbians whereas gays like to be seen.

A pecking order of gender and sexualities are premised upon cultural norms and expectations regarding appropriate behaviour. Gay sexuality is called into question here and attacks the powerful cultural expectation around masculinity. This was seen in the public display of nonconforming behaviour violating gender norms and bringing gay masculinity under public siege. Lesbians are framed as private, not demonstrative or displaying their sexuality. They 'wear skirts' like other girls and do not violate gender patterns of 'feminine' conduct, and in doing so on the surface position even if contradictorily into *inhlonipha* (respect). As Sigamoney and Epprecht (2013: 101) state:

> In general, harsh opinions against homosexuality could be assuaged by the exercise of discretion on the part of same-sex attracted individuals their maintaining the appearance of heteronormativity.

In this section, there is a level of qualified acceptance of the homosexual subject within the overall domination of heterosexual cultural norms. Young people are not simply castigating gays and lesbians, but their acceptance is dependent on the extent to which they can conduct themselves in discreet ways that do not break the dominant gendered norms around respect whilst maintaining a heterosexual look. The construction of lesbian behaviour as private versus gay behaviour as exhibitionist prompted a reaction that made lesbians more acceptable. In other words, homosexuality is actively negotiated not as un-African, but if gays and lesbians fashion their sexuality in discreet ways, giving the semblance of heterosexuality, their sexuality becomes acceptable.

Conclusion

The claim that homosexuality is un-African is still common. A central argument made in this chapter is that young teenage Africans' conceptualization of culture and homosexuality is not approached simply as victims of culture, but in order to access their claim to an African identity they both reproduce and challenge cultural practices. Within the impoverished contexts, with little access to power and resources, the claim to an identity remains a significant force.

Gendered constructions of sexuality provide an important basis in their pursuit of an African identity. Masculinities are also central, and these must be seen as being constructed through social, political and cultural processes and practices rather than some kind of innate African sexuality. When teenage Africans construct sexuality, they did so by invoking normative understandings of masculinity, family and gendered patterns of conduct. The cultural conceptualizations of sexuality cannot be abstracted from social and gender relations. Whilst the dominant views were restrictive and reproduced stained versions of culture and sexuality, young people in this study actively sew themselves into the very fabric of culture through their own agency, challenging and reproducing sexual and gender inequalities.

Queering culture and the constancy through which heterosexuality is viewed is key to revisioning teenage conceptualizations of sexuality. The chapter began with strong foundational associations being made between homosexuality and culture as problematic and as un-African. However, it is clear that nothing is closed to contestation and young people position not only within dominant cultural and sexual norms but their testimonies are illustrative of disruptions and ruptures to dominant identity categories (Sears 2005; Talburt & Rasmussen, 2010). In queering culture the possibility exists to work with teenage South Africans in ways that could expand alternate options in rethinking homosexuality. There is ample evidence in this paper of qualified acceptance and of the rights values that have dented hegemonic notions of African culture.

So far there is little evidence of interventions to promote sexual equality that target young people. Schools have yet to implement programmes that translate the equality clause into programmes that address sexual orientation. Interventions that deal with teenage conceptualizations of homosexuality must address the social and cultural context through which meanings are located. Programmes aiming to promote sexual equality and diversity must challenge teenagers' interpretation of culture that reproduces exclusionary practices. The ability to claim a gay and lesbian identity and to publicly display sexual freedoms is severely circumscribed when the context in which it is situated is based on hegemonic cultural assumptions and where violence is naturalized to force change.

The flexibility in meanings and the potential to work with young people is both necessary and possible. Contradictions in meanings and the scope provided by constitutional equality contests fixed understandings of culture. Whilst the equality clause resolves the tensions between freedom and culture, the chapter has shown how freedoms are tenuous. To be effective, any programme must challenge the dominant notion of culture as static and unchanging and the association with an 'authentic' African identity.

Notes

1. This publication is based on research funded by the National Research Foundation (NRF), South Africa Reference: CPRR13082831328. All place names and participants' names have been changed.
2. Throughout the paper, b refers to boys and g to girls.

References

Altman, D. et al. (2012) Men who have sex with men: Stigma and discrimination. *Lancet*, 380 (9839), 439–445.

Ansell, N. (2001) 'Because it is our culture!' (re)negotiating the meaning of 'Lobola' in Southern African secondary schools. *Journal of Southern African Studies*, 27 (4), 697–716.

Arnfred, S. (2004) *Re-thinking sexualities in Africa*. Uppsala, Sweden: The Nordic Africa Institute.

Bhana, D. (2014) *Under pressure: The regulation of sexualities in South African secondary schools*. Braamfontein: Mathoko's Books.

Bhana, D. (2012) Understanding and addressing homophobia in schools: Views from teachers. *South African Journal of Education*, 32, 307–318.

Bhana, D., & Pattman. R. (2011) Girls want money, boys want virgins: The materiality of love amongst South African township youth in the context of HIV and AIDS. *Culture, Health & Sexuality*, 13 (8), 961–972.

Butler, J. (1990) *Gender trouble*. New York: Routledge.

Cocks, M., & Moller, V. (2002) Use of indigenous and indigenised medicines to enhance personal well-being: A South African case study. *Social Science & Medicine*, 54 (3), 387–397.

DePalma, R., & Francis, D. A. (2014) The gendered nature of South African teachers' discourse on sex education. *Health Education Research*. doi: 10.1093/her/cyt117.

Epprecht, M. (2008) *Heterosexual Africa? The history of an idea from the age of exploration to the age of AIDS*. Athens: Ohio University Press.

Foucault, M. (1979) *Discipline and punish: The birth of the prison*. A. Sheridan (Trans.) London: Penguin.

Francis, D. A. (2012) Teacher positioning on the teaching of sexual diversity in South African schools. *Culture, Health & Sexuality*, 14, 597–611.

Frosh, S., Phoenix, A., & Pattman, R. (2002) *Young masculinities*. New York: Palgrave.

Gowlett, C. (2014) Queer(y)ing and recrafting agency: Moving away from a model of coercion versus escape. *Discourse: Studies in the Cultural Politics of Education*, 35 (3), 405–418.

Human Rights Watch (2011) We'll show you you're a women: Violence and discrimination against black lesbians and transgender men. Retrieved 18 March 2014 from http://www.hrw.org/reports/2011/12/05/we-ll-show-youyou-re-woman.

Hunter, M. (2010) *Love in the time of AIDS: Inequality, gender and rights in South Africa*. Pietermaritzburg: University of KwaZulu-Natal Press.

Kehily, M. J. (2012) Contextualising the sexualisation of girls debate: Innocence, experience and young female sexuality. *Gender and Education*, 24 (3), 255–268.

Marshall, D. (2013) Queer breeding: Historicising popular culture, homosexuality and informal sex education. *Sex Education*, 13 (5), 597–610. doi: 10.1080/14681811.2013.811577.

Msibi, T. (2012) 'I'm used to it now': Experiences of homophobia among queer youth in South African township schools. *Gender and Education*, 24 (5), 515–533.

Quinlivan, K., Rasmussen, M., Aspin, C., Allen, L., & Sanjakdar, F. (2014) Crafting the normative subject: Queerying the politics of race in the New Zealand health education classroom. *Discourse: Studies in the Cultural Politics of Education*, 35 (3), 393–404.

Rasmussen, M. (2006) *Becoming subjects: Sexualities and secondary schooling*. New York: Routledge.

Ratele, K. (2008) Analyzing males in Africa: Certain useful elements in considering masculinities. *African and Asian Studies*, 7, 515–536.

Renold, E., & Ringrose, J. (2013) Feminisms re-figuring 'sexualisation', sexuality and 'the girl'. *Feminist Theory*, 14(3), 247–254.

Ringrose, J. (2013) *Postfeminist education? Girls and the sexual politics of schooling* London: Routledge.

Roehr, B. (2010) How homophobia is fueling Africa's HIV epidemic. *British Medical Journal (BMJ)*, 11 (340), c2245.

Rudwick, S., & Posel, D. (2014) Contemporary functions of ilobolo (bridewealth) in urban South African Zulu society. *Journal of Contemporary African Studies*, 32 (1) 118–136.

Sears, J. T. (2005) *Gay, lesbian, and transgender issues in education: Programs, policies, and practices.* Philadelphia, PA: Harrington Park Press.

Sigamoney, V., & Epprecht, M. (2013) Meanings of homosexuality and Africanness in two South African townships: An evidence based approach for rethinking same sex prejudice. *African Studies Review*, 56 (2), 83–107.

Talburt, S., & Rasmussen, M. L. (2010) After-queer: Tendencies in queer research *International Journal of Qualitative Studies in Education*, 23 (1), 1–14.

Warner, M. (1993) *Fear of a queer planet: Queer politics and social theory.* Minneapolis University of Minnesota Press.

13
'Flaming Gays' and 'One of the Boys'? White Middle-class Boys, Queer Sexualities and Gender in Icelandic High Schools

Jón Ingvar Kjaran

Icelandic masculinities

Being a small island society close to the Arctic Circle, Iceland has depended on its agricultural and fishing industries since its settlement in the late 9th century. Thus, historically, Icelandic society has valued stoic characters, independence, strength and resourcefulness for both men and women; a blend which has been referred to as 'Viking masculinity' (Björnsson, 2002). In the 19th and 20th centuries, the construction of Icelandic masculinity was connected to nation-building (see Matthíasdóttir, 2004; Hálfdanarson & Rastrick, 2006). Indeed, Björnsson (2002) notes a gradual shift from a 'Viking masculinity' during that time to a more bourgeois masculinity, epitomized in the nationalist leader Jón Sigurðsson. Men were still supposed to be strong and good providers for their family, but at the same time they were supposed to be rational and nurture self-discipline (Björnsson, 2002). Thus, during the main part of the 20th century, for most young men, a combination of bourgeois and 'Viking masculinity', being independent, strong, rational, self-disciplined and hard-working, was perceived as a manifestation of hegemonic masculinity.

Following the advent of the feminist movement and more progressive legislation with respect to gender equality, as well as a three-month non-transferable paternity leave (Einarsdóttir & Pétursdóttir, 2004; Gíslason, 2006, 2007, 2010) at the end of the 20th century, bourgeois/Viking masculinity yielded to a more inclusive notion of what constituted masculinity. Thus, young men growing up in the 1980s and 1990s developed changed attitudes towards household activities, fatherhood and child caring (Gíslason, 1997, 2010). Nevertheless, 'Viking masculinity' remained an enduring and residual part of the image of 'real' masculinity, gaining renewed capital during the economic boom at the end of the millennium and culminating with the economic crash in 2008. During that time, the discourse of the 'Viking' repeatedly surfaced in representations of masculinity both in the media and among politicians who valorized the qualities of initiative, rationality, expansionism and the general superiority of the male Viking culture (Pétursdóttir, 2011). Executives, stockbrokers and bankers were the 'heroes' of the new economy of the 21st century. In the media, they were referred to as 'Viking raiders' or 'young entrepreneurial Vikings' (Pétursdóttir, 2011). Thus, many young boys looked up to these new heroes and wanted to be lawyers, bankers or executives, as evidenced by increased enrolment in business subjects at the University of Iceland before the economic crash in 2008.[1]

After the economic crash in 2008, the discourse of the Viking was rarely cited. Bankers and executives are no longer held up as male role models and heroes. Neither are nurses nor kindergarten teachers. The image of the 'real' man is still connected to stoic character, self-reliance, risk-taking and being active, referring here indirectly to the discourse of the Viking. However, some boys are expressing a more inclusive notion of masculinity, manifested in hugging and even kissing their male friends, embodied expressions that no longer signify non-heterosexuality, but are rather regarded as tokens of care and friendship (see Anderson, 2009, 2011; Kjaran & Jóhannesson, 2013; Anderson & McCormack, 2014). Indeed, these more inclusive notions of masculinity are expressed within a highly privileged space of white middle-class boys, who are often physically strong and incorporate the image of hegemonic masculinity (see Anderson & McCormack, 2014). Still, the dominant discourse about a 'real' man centres around physical control and being popular among women. Thus, in order to offset any features of femininity and draw a line between themselves and other less masculine boys, they often cite homophobic or sexist discourse under the rubric of the joke (Nayak & Kehily, 1997; Pascoe, 2007; McRobbie, 2009; Jóhannsdóttir & Hjálmarsdóttir, 2011).

In Iceland, as in all societies, multiple manifestations of masculinity are operating. As discussed in this section, these performances of masculinity draw on the discourse of 'Viking masculinity', but at the same time cite an inclusive notion of masculinity. Queer boys are well aware of these multiple discourses of masculinity, and for many white middle-class gay and bisexual boys there is a dialectic notion of how to embody available discourses of masculinity and understand themselves as both queer (non-heterosexual) and 'real' men. Thus, the objectives of this chapter are twofold: first, to describe and analyse the various strategies white middle-class gay and bisexual boys use to negotiate their sexuality and gender performances (Martino, 1999, 2012; Pascoe, 2007) and second, how young male sexual and gendered identities are mediated through discourses of heteronormativity (Butler, 1993; Epstein, 1997; Nardi, 2000; Nayak & Kehily, 2006; Gilbert, 2014).

Background: Method and data

The data drawn on in this chapter include seven semi-structured interviews from a larger dataset, a total of 20 interviews with LGBTs aged 18–25 and visual data collected during fieldwork at one high school in Reykjavík, given the pseudonym *Circle*. After reading all interviews with the male participants, who had attended six different high schools (age 17–21), these seven interviews were considered to represent different strategies they used to negotiate sexuality and gender: One strategy was to internalize the discourse of (hetero)masculinity and what I referred to in the previous section as Viking/bourgeoisie masculinity. Another strategy was to adopt more inclusive performances of masculinity, thereby giving the possibility of queering or disturbing hegemonic masculinity. All the boys belonged to white middle-class families of non-immigrant background and were accessed through local LGBT youth support groups or by snowballing. Each interview took approximately 90 minutes and some interviewees were reinterviewed. The interviews were conducted in Icelandic and transcribed verbatim. Selected quotes presented in this chapter have been translated into English.

When analysing the interviews the focus was on the retrospective aspect of their high school experience, particularly during their formative years with respect to negotiating school-based gender and sexual cultures. Thematic analysis formed the analytical framework of the study (Flick, 2006) and themes were mainly identified on the basis of repetition (Ryan & Bernard, 2003). Furthermore, concepts such as the heterosexual matrix, heteromasculinity and queer masculinities were useful heuristic devices to understand how the participants came to terms with their performances of masculinity vis-à-vis sexuality.

The term heteromasculinity demonstrates the intersection of heterosexuality and masculinity in the formation of a male subject in Western societies. Accordingly, the 'authentic' man should ideally be straight whereas being gay or bisexual is seen as a deviation from hegemonic performances of masculinity (Pronger, 1990). Moreover, Butler's concept of the heterosexual matrix is also useful in analysing the processes involved in the construction of (hetero)masculinity. Accordingly, a male (sex) is generally read to be masculine (gender) and as heterosexual (sexuality). Thus, according to the 'logic' of the heterosexual matrix, the lesbian or gay subjectivity is a deviation from the 'correct' performances of either femininity or masculinity (Butler, 1990, 1993). As will be explored further and my data has revealed, some of my participants had internalized the 'logic' of the heterosexual matrix vis-à-vis sexuality and gender, while others had adopted queer masculinities: 'ways of being masculine outside heteronormative constructions of masculinity that disrupt, or have the potential to disrupt, traditional images of the hegemonic heterosexual masculine' (Heasley,

2005: 310). Thus, I find Butler's heterosexual matrix a useful analytical tool to explore how the dominant discourse sustains normative gender performances. At the same time, it opens up the possibilities of queering those same performances of gender and sexuality, by rendering them unintelligible, which some of my participants did in relation to their social and cultural environment.

Negotiating and performing queer identity and (hetero)masculinity

Three boys, Benedikt, Hrafn and Tom, negotiated their queer identity by performing (hetero)masculinity. Indeed, Hrafn's narrative offered an in-depth examination of the local hegemonic practices regulating boys' peer cultures in school, particularly during PE lessons, which revolved around football, and which he viewed as a rite of passage in performing and consolidating a heteromasculinity. Hrafn, who tried hard to conform to local hegemonic performances of masculinity, discussed how the game of football sustained heteromasculinity. He had practised football until he was 18 years old and gradually found it difficult to be gay and practise the game, because he somehow felt that his teammates did not feel too comfortable about his non-heterosexuality. He was able to clearly articulate that boys who identify as gay have very few or almost no role models when it comes to football. In fact, there are very few openly gay professional football players. It took Hrafn three years after quitting high school football to come out. Furthermore, attitudes and 'language' in the game of football are both heterosexist and homophobic (Kimmel, 1996, 2005; Skelton, 2000; Price & Parker, 2003). Consequently, it is unsurprising that many gay and bisexual males have, like Hrafn, quit the sport after they have publicly come out to their peers as gay. However, Hrafn was able to take up the game again when he joined *Styrmir* (The Storm), the Icelandic LGBT football club, founded to create a social space for LGBTs within sports (Stasi & Evans, 2013).

Benedikt, in contrast to Hrafn, had dated girls and played the heterosexual script expected of him before he 'came out'. After his second year in high school, he revealed his non-heterosexuality, by adopting first bisexual identity and then gradually self-identifying as gay. To his surprise, he soon gained a high position within the students' council at his school, 'being even elected as its president' during his last year in high school. Furthermore, he competed for his school in various competitions, such as rhetoric and quizzes.

In comparison to Hrafn and Benedikt, Tom was subject to sexual bullying (being called 'fag' and 'sissy') at his primary school and during the first year at high school. Reflecting on his 'coming out' experience, Tom spoke of 'not wanting to be gay because it was from the start the difficult way of life'. However, after changing high schools, he gradually accepted his gay-identity and eventually gained the support of his sister (who self-identified as lesbian) and her friends. However, Tom, often referred to his past stigmatization and was acutely aware of the 'panoptic' view of his social environment and how it regulated his gender and sexual identity. He often talked about acting 'straight' and normatively 'masculine', so as not to draw too much attention to his non-heterosexuality. In fact, all three boys emphasized the importance of distinguishing themselves from 'gay stereotypes' and the pressure to perform hegemonic (hetero)masculinity, as Benedikt's morning ritual illustrates below:

> I am not *so* gay. For example, I neither blow-dried my hair every morning before I went to school nor used make-up. I have never had any joy of wearing women's clothes and in fact, I have always disliked these things. This seems to be the image many people have when they think about gays, and for me and others we have a bit of a dislike against such gays as they somehow are defining gayness and same sex desires because they are the most prominent ones, in television, shows and films.

From an early age, Benedikt had internalized a negative image of the 'feminine gay', from which he felt the urge to dissociate. He also has some understanding of how 'femininity' can 'spoil' the image of 'authentic' masculinity (see Connell, 1995; Martino, 1999, 2006; Martino & Pallotta-Chiarolli, 2003; Jóhannesson, 2004). According to the discourse of Viking masculinity referred to before, men should be strong and not overly concerned with beautification practices such as 'blow-drying', using cosmetics or wearing women's clothes. Furthermore, by dissociating himself from the gay stereotype, Benedikt is also perhaps protecting the self by Othering those who do not fit the gendered 'norm', particularly when he says that 'we [referring to those gays that have the same opinion as he does] have a bit of a dislike against such gays'. In fact, he rejects discourses or 'games of truth' that link gayness to effeminacy (see Nardi, 2000; Martino, 2006; Landreau & Rodriguez, 2012).

Tom and Hrafn also expressed their concern over the pressure to conform to gender normativities in order to be recognized as 'authentic' Icelandic young men. Hrafn talked about how his peers only accepted him being gay as long as he behaved in socially acceptable 'manly' ways. For example, Hrafn mentioned that he refrained from being too 'camp or feminine so they [his male friends] did not feel uncomfortable being around me'. He talked about the different ways in which he tried to be 'able to be gay without being a threat to others' by fitting in, and not drawing attention to himself. Tom also discussed the pressure of performing socially recognizable and legitimate ways of 'being a boy' in his high school. He said that he was often conscious about his behaviour and appearance, not wanting to be too gay, or, as he described below, a 'flaming gay':

> For example, [once] my classmates told me to calm down because they thought that I was going over the top. They were criticizing my behaviour and said to me that you do not want to be labelled as flaming gay. Therefore, I am trying to lie low, calm down a bit, and I want to be told if I am doing something wrong because I do not realize when I am too hyper or flamboyant, making a fool of myself. I just want to be one of the boys.

Here, Tom vividly describes how his schoolmates in the context of the high school environment regulated the ways in which he expressed himself. He is aware that he must not be too 'hyper' (i.e. excessively emotional or extrovert) or 'go over the top', in order to defend himself against the insult of 'flaming gay' (e.g. by flaunting and/or having effeminate traits), a well-known cultural gay stereotype. In many ways, for Tom to 'be one of the boys' and 'avoid making a fool' of himself he looks to his peers to police when he is 'doing something wrong': that is, when he deviates from socially appropriate boundaries of acceptable hegemonic masculinity (Connell, 1995; Foucault, 1995; Martino, 2006).

Tom's desire to be 'one of the boys' and not draw attention to his non-heterosexuality was in many ways predominantly about conforming to the hegemonic performances of masculinity. It was also a strategy to repudiate the discourse of the 'fag' (see Pascoe, 2002), a routine insult from his schoolmates after he kissed a boy when at primary school:

> I had so many friends that were boys but after I kissed a boy, all of them stopped talking to me and called me fag. It was before I came out and still today, I am sometimes afraid, you know, kissing the wrong boy and then everybody will stop talking to me.

Thus, all three boys seemed only to be accepted as gay by their male peers as long as they conformed to local masculinizing practices, which, as outlined earlier, have their roots in a hybrid of Viking/bourgeoisie masculinity. They all dissociated themselves from the image of the 'flaming gay' in a bid to be accepted by their male peers. However, it is important to note that although Hrafn, Tom and Benedikt invested their discourse with local hegemonic masculinity, they were nevertheless critical of how heteronormativity and heterosexist views disciplined and set limits both for gay and straight students. Hrafn, for example, discussed how difficult it was to kiss a boy or express intimate emotions with boys. Indeed, they each had to tread a tightrope of socially acceptable gendered and sexual performances so as neither to be perceived as a 'threat' to the heterosexuality of their male peers nor experience past stigmatization of being called 'fag' or 'girl'. This, however, was not the case for all boys, as illustrated by the four participants discussed in the next section.

Queering masculinity – Queer masculinities

In the introduction to their edited collection of 'Queer Masculinities', Landreau and Rodriguez (2012), argue that within masculinities studies there has so far been little space for discussion of queer masculinities and of their possibilities of 'queering' hegemonic gender performances. Focusing on 'queer masculinities' opens up the potential, they argue, of 'a more comprehensive and nuanced understanding and study of the category of masculinity itself' (Landreau & Rodriguez, 2012: 2). Working with 'queer in terms of its capacity to make visible and critique heteronormativity' (Landreau & Rodriguez, 2012: 3), in this section I emphasize the disruptive notion of queer masculinities by drawing attention to the reality and experiences of queer boys who are coming to terms with their feelings and sexuality, fighting for their being in the world and their legitimacy, whilst running the risk of exclusion and marginality. While these feelings were articulated by all the participants introduced in this chapter, some boys talked about actively adopting and performing 'heteromasculinity' (as discussed in the previous section), while others sought to accommodate their non heterosexualities (as gay or bisexual) with alternative non-normative notions of what an Icelandic masculinity could look and be like. This section focuses on the narratives of Gísli, Gunnar, Jónas and Rafn.

Gísli and Gunnar self-identified as gay when they were in high school, Jónas and Rafn as bisexual. All of them 'came out' during their time in high school. However, in contrast to Hrafn, Benedikt and Tom, who actively attempted to invest in local and historical Icelandic masculinities, which privileged toughness and emotional constraint (Jóhannesson, 2004), these boys were more able to express non-normative gender and sexual identities and sought direct support from the gay community in Iceland. For example, each of them had made contact with Organization '78 (The Icelandic LGBT association) during their high school days. Some of them spoke of going there with their parents to see a social worker, while others regularly participated in the youth group of Organization '78. Indeed, they did not feel the urge to dissociate themselves from femininity in their performances of 'doing boy', nor did they speak negatively about gay men who expressed their sexuality or gender in non-normative ways, or were considered by the other boys as being too 'flaming'. They were also critical towards the hegemonic discourse of masculinity that regulated their experiences of growing up as boys, and were accepting of their difference as non-heterosexual, as Gísli discusses below in his love of Barbie dolls and dresses:

> When I was younger, I sometimes played with Barbie dolls and wore dresses. It was great fun. Today, I of course do not wear women's clothes although I liked to do it in the past. I don't think that I am different from the 'normal' boy. I am just like the other guys. I just don't like girls, I mean sexually. That's the only difference I suppose.

In contrast to Benedikt, Gísli talked about sometimes applying cosmetics such as make-up and lipstick, especially when he was at home, when nobody saw him doing it. Thus, Gísli seems to have created a private space, a queer space, through which he could challenge the hegemony of masculinity. He did not feel the need in interviews to express prejudice towards the 'feminine' gay stereotype and wearing dresses or using make-up did not, in his eyes, make him less of a 'man'. However, it is important to note that it was only in the private and domestic space of the home or in the organized marches of gay pride, supported by the youth group Organization '78, that he could express and celebrate his sexuality publicly. Local peer cultures were much more difficult to navigate.

Gunnar talked at length about how local peer cultures policed boys' masculinity through the discourses of homophobia (Kimmel, 1999; Martino, 1999, 2006; Pascoe, 2002). Indeed, he was critical of the dominant discourse that constructed effeminate boys as gay:

> My classmate was skinny and has soft movements and voice. At our school, he was assumed to be gay, although he has had many girlfriends and identified as straight. However, because he did not fit 100% the image of masculinity and had a rather 'feminine' appearance, he was assumed to be gay. I find this rather stupid because you cannot tell from the appearance of a person whether s/he is gay or not. The massive and athletic guy in your class can, for example, be gay.

Gunnar experienced the powerful presence of a heteronormative peer culture that regulated both his gender and sexual identity. In the example above, he emphasizes the importance at his high school to perform gender in the 'right' way; that is, adopting a socially acceptable, hegemonic masculinity. Those boys who deviated from the script 'assigned' to their gender, even if they performed heterosexuality by having 'many girlfriends', were assumed to be gay. Thus, performing masculinity in non-hegemonic ways incurred the risk of being marginalized, even excluded by male peers, of which, for example, Benedikt and Hrafn who attended *Circle*, the same high school as Gunnar, were well aware.

The ways in which discourses of heteronormative gender permeated school-based cultures could also be seen in the visual representations of young people's organized leisure activities. Figure 13.1 is a poster advertising the *Busaball* – young people's first high school dance, aged 16. It portrays six students attired in suit jackets and bow ties (men) or dresses (women), with the female students (unlike the young men) stroking their hair or with their hands on their hips. The poster stresses gender binaries as well and indirectly indicates the heterosexual space of the dance, by portraying presumably heterosexual pairs in their best clothes going to the ball together. This was also the underlying understanding of the students themselves, particularly the males, who told me that going to the *Busaball* was all about 'getting lucky', meaning a successful date and possible sexual interaction with a girl. Thus, this poster and other similar ones (e.g. Figure 13.2) I noticed during my fieldwork had the purpose of strengthening and visually representing the heteronormativity and the dominant gender performances at *Circle* (see Pascoe, 2002; Best, 2005) (Figures 13.1 and 13.2).

Rafn and Jónas were, like Gunnar, critical towards the heteronormative social environment of their high school and made some efforts to disturb and challenge the ubiquitous heterosexual matrix. Jónas, for example, dyed his hair pink after he came out when he was sixteen years old. He revealed that he did this in order to provoke and unsettle his peers, particularly at his high school, which he found to be conservative and restrictive in terms of sexual and gender diversity. Rafn also tried to disturb his social environment when at high school: 'I used nail polish to break down this wall between men and women. Some people commented that I was just drawing attention to my sexuality or myself.' Martino has discussed the pedagogic significance of embodying masculinity as 'a site for interrupting heteronormativity' (Martino, 2012: 22). Accordingly, the body can be viewed as 'a text, information, knowledge and politics' (Martino, 2012: 22). Therefore, the body can be used constructively in order to gain some political means. Rafn and Jónas seem to have realized this and used their bodies informatively, pedagogically and politically, both to enlighten their classmates and friends about the instability of the gender system, but also to destabilize and disturb the performances of hegemonic masculinity. Both of them mentioned during our talk that their behaviour and appearances had sometimes initiated discussions about different performances of masculinity and caused both positive and negative reactions from their environment, as Jónas reveals in the following quote:

> I did not want to be the flamboyant gay, when I decided to come out. However, I wanted everybody to know about my feelings. This was one reason I dyed my hair pink. Actually, I got a positive response from some classmates, signified by their saying to me that I should take my own decisions and that they were proud of me. So, the feeling I got was, you know, was rather liberating. You are out and free and you feel that you can do everything.

Figure 13.1   Busaball Poster A (anonymised)

Jónas discussed the emancipatory aspect of his coming out experience in school, particularly how he used his body to give out messages in order to queer his local social and cultural environment. This was his strategy to create a queer space for himself. This could also be interpreted from Rafn's narrative, as he revealed in our talks that he gained increased confidence

Figure 13.2   Busaball Poster B (anonymised)

after he came out and was more willing to confront his local social and cultural environment.

Indeed, Jónas and Rafn's nonconformity to dominant gender-sexuality scripts troubled the inherent logic of the heterosexual matrix, which enabled them to queer their local social and cultural environment even further and draw attention to the instability of the gender system. Furthermore, all of them spoke of the oppressive nature of hegemonic masculinity, for straight and queer boys alike. All of them, therefore, overtly embraced queer masculinities, performing their masculinity outside the hegemonic 'norm'.

'One of the boys'? Conclusions

Notably absent in any of the 'sexualization' media and governmental moral panics are the ways in which heteronormativity features in and pervades children's and young people's peer cultures, from football to *Busaball*. This chapter has offered a series of young men's narratives to render visible the ways in which hegemonic heterosexuality is both implicitly assumed and explicitly privileged (Butler, 1990; Pascoe, 2007). Thus, boys who trouble the coherence of the hegemonic heterosexual matrix, because they perform their gender or sexuality outside the 'norm', risk being questioned on or asked to prove their masculinity and (hetero)sexuality, with some boys being subject to verbal sexual abuse as 'fags' and 'sissies' (Martino, 1999; Martino, 2006; Pascoe, 2007). Some of the boys who experienced the extreme policing often attempted to defeminize their gender performance in an attempt to expand the parameters of 'Viking' masculinity to include their non-heterosexuality. Positioning themselves as self-disciplined and strong, the young men attempted to reinscribe the loss of social capital that comes from having a culturally 'deviant' sexuality. They strove to be 'one of the boys' and wanted to be accepted by their peers, not being a 'threat' to them by acting too 'feminine' or flamboyantly. Thus, for them, being gay was 'tolerated' or even 'accepted' by their peers, as long as they stuck to the rules of hegemonic Viking masculinity. This shows the sacrifice of their strategy: passing the social test at the cost of having to endorse performances of hegemonic Viking masculinity, without being able to embody alternative performances of masculinity. This the other group of boys did, embodying queer masculinities, thus trying to challenge the logic of the heterosexual matrix. They strove to disturb the manifestations of hegemonic masculinity in order to carve out a queer space.

Why these boys were able to perform their gender and sexuality differently than the others needs to be explored more fully and was not addressed specifically in this chapter, as many factors were at play. However, their narratives and embodied experiences draw attention to the complexities of how boys are navigating the heterosexual matrix in different cultures and contexts and of how they are coming to terms with their sexual identity vis-à-vis masculinity in different ways. In order to better understand these processes, one needs to focus more on the intersection of gender (performances of masculinity) and sexuality and of how homophobia and the discourse of the feminine 'fag' is still used to police the behaviour of young men and boys, whether straight or queer. In contrast to the research of Anderson and McCormack (Anderson, 2009; Anderson & McCormack,

2014), my participants felt, even within their privileged space, being middle-class white of non-immigrant background, that it was sometimes necessary to repudiate the stigma of the 'fag' in order to be perceived as a 'real' man. Thus, some of them felt the pressure of adhering to hegemonic gender norms, any deviation from which runs the risk of losing social capital and not being accepted as 'one of the boys'.

Note

1. http://www.hi.is/adalvefur/heildarskraning_nemenda_i_haskola_islands_fra_upphafi_0

References

Anderson, E. (2009) *Inclusive masculinity: The changing nature of masculinities*. London: Routledge.

Anderson, E. (2011) The rise and fall of western homohysteria. *Journal of Feminist Scholarship*, 1, 80–94.

Anderson, E., & McCormack, M. (2014) Cuddling and spooning: Heteromasculinity and homosocial tactility among student-athletes. *Men and Masculinities*, 1–17. doi: 10.1177/1097184X14523433.

Best, A. (2005) The production of heterosexuality at the high school prom, in C. Ingraham (Ed.) *Thinking Straight: The Power, the Promise, and the Paradox of Heterosexuality*. New York: Routledge, pp. 193–215.

Björnsson, P. (2002) Að búa til íslenska karlmenn: Kynjaímyndir Jóns forseta [Constructing Icelandic men...]. 2. *Íslenska söguþingið, ráðstefnurit*. Reykjavík: Sagnfræðistofnun Háskóla Íslands.

Butler, J. (1990) *Gender trouble: Feminism and the subversion of identity*. New York: Routledge.

Butler, J. (1993) *Bodies that matter. On the discursive limits of 'sex'*. New York: Routledge.

Connell, R. (1995) *Masculinities*. Cambridge: Polity.

Einarsdóttir, Þ., & Pétursdóttir, G. M. (2004) *Culture, custom and caring: Men's and women's possibilities to parental leave*. Akureyri: Centre for Gender Equality.

Epstein, D. (1997) Boyz' own stories: Masculinities and sexualities in schools. *Gender & Education*, 9 (1), 105–116.

Flick, U. (2006) *An introduction to qualitative research*. London: Sage Publications.

Foucault, M. (1995) *Discipline and punish. The birth of the prison*. New York: Vintage Books.

Gilbert, J. (2014) *Sexuality in school: The limits of education*. Minneapolis, MN: University of Minnesota Press.

Gíslason, I. V. (1997) *'Karlmenn eru bara karlmenn.' Viðhorf og væntingar íslenskra karla ['Men are only men.' Expectations and views of Icelandic men]*. Reykjavík: Skrifstofa jafnréttismála.

Gíslason, I. V. (2006) *Fostering caring masculinities. Icelandic national report*. Akureyri: Jafnréttisstofa.

Gíslason, I. V. (2007) *Fæðingar- og foreldraorlof á Íslandi- Þróun eftir lagasetninguna árið 2000 [Paternal leave in Iceland]*. Akureyri: Jafnréttisstofa.

Gíslason, I. V. (2010) Gender changes in Iceland: From rigid roles to negotiations. *Arctic and Antarctic*, 3, 121–149.

Hálfdanarson, G., & Rastrick, Ó. (2006) Culture and the construction of the Icelander in the 20th century, in A. Cimdina, & J. Osmond (Eds.) *Power and Culture: Hegemony, Interaction and Dissent.* Pisa: Edizioni Plus – Pisa University Press, pp. 101–117.

Heasley, R. (2005) Queer masculinities of straight men: A typology. *Men and Masculinities*, 7 (3), 310–320.

Jóhannesson, I. Á. (2004) *Karlmennska og jafnréttisuppeldi* [Masculinity and Equality Upbringing]. Reykjavík: Rannsóknarstofa í kvenna- og kynjafræðum við Háskóla Íslands.

Jóhannsdóttir, Á., & Hjálmarsdóttir, K. A. (2011) Skaðleg karlmennska? Greining á bókinni *Mannasiðir Gillz. Netla – Veftímarit um uppeldi og menntun* [Harmful Masculinity: Discourse Analyses of the book Mannasiðir Gillz]. Retrieved from http://netla.hi.is/greinar/2011/alm/005/005.pdf

Kehily, M. J., & Nayak, A. (1997) 'Lads and laughter': Humor and the production of heterosexual hierarchies. *Gender and Education*, 9 (1), 69–88.

Kehily, M. J., & Nayak, A. (2006) Gender undone: Subversion, regulation and embodiment in the work of Judith Butler. *British Journal of Sociology of Education*, 27 (4), 459–472.

Kimmel, M. (1996) *Manhood in America: A cultural history.* New York: Free Press.

Kimmel, M. (1999) Masculinity as homophobia: Fear, shame and silence in the construction of gender identity, in J. A. Kuypers (Ed.) *Men and Power.* New York: Prometheus, pp. 105–128.

Kimmel, M. (2005) *The gender of desire. Essays on male sexuality.* Albany: State University of New York Press.

Kjaran, J. I., & Jóhannesson, I. Á. (2013) Manifestations of heterosexism in Icelandic upper secondary schools and the responses of LGBT students. *Journal of LGBT Youth*, 10 (4), 351–372.

Landreau, J. C., & Rodriguez, N. M. (2012) *Queer masculinities: A critical reader in education.* Dordrecht: Springer Netherlands.

McRobbie, A. (2009) *The aftermath of feminism: Gender, culture and social change.* London: Sage.

Martino, W. (1999) Cool boys', 'party animals', 'squids' and 'poofters': Interrogating the dynamics and politics of adolescent masculinities in school. *The British Journal of the Sociology of Education*, 20 (2), 239–263.

Martino, W. (2006) Straight-acting masculinities: Normalization and gender hierarchies in gay men's lives, in C. Kendall, & W. Martino (Eds.) *Gendered Outcasts and Sexual Outlaws.* New York: Routledge, pp. 35–60.

Martino, W. (2012) Queering masculinities in male teachers' lives, in J. C. Landreau, & N. M. Rodriguez (Eds.) *Queer Masculinities: A Critical Reader in Education.* Dordrecht: Springer Netherlands, pp. 21–33.

Martino, W., & Pallotta-Chiarolli, M. (2003) *So what's a boy? Addressing issues of masculinity and schooling.* Maidenhead & Philadelphia: Open University Press.

Matthíasdóttir, S. (2004) *Hinn sanni Íslendingur. Þjóðerni, kyngervi og vald á Íslandi 1900–1930* [The True Icelander. Nation, Gender and Power in Iceland 1900–1930]. Reykjavík: Háskólaútgáfan.

Nardi, P. (2000) *Gay masculinities.* Thousand Oaks, CA: Sage.

Pascoe, J. (2007) *Dude you're a fag. Masculinity and sexuality in high school.* Berkeley: University of California Press.

Pétursdóttir, G. M. (2011) Sköpun alþjóðlegrar viðskiptakarlmennsku: Íslenskt tilvik [The creation of international business masculinity: An Icelandic case], in S. B. Ómarsdóttir (Ed.) *Rannsóknir í félagsvísindum XII. Stjórnmálafræðideild. Erindi flutt á ráðstefnu í október 2011* [Research in the Social Sciences. Conference Proceedings]. Reykjavík: Félagsvísindastofnun Háskóla Íslands, pp. 60–68.

Price, M., & Parker, M. (2003) Sport, sexuality, and the gender order: Amateur rugby union, gay men, and social exclusion. *Sociology of Sport Journal*, 20 (2), 108–126.

Pronger, B. (1990) *The arena of masculinity: Sports, homosexuality, and the meaning of sex.* New York: St Martin's Press.

Ryan, G. W., & Bernard, H. R. (2003) Techniques to identify themes. *Field Methods*, 15 (1), 85–109.

Skelton, C. (2000) 'A passion for football': Dominant masculinities and primary schooling. *Sport, Education and Society*, 5 (1), 5–18.

Stasi, M., & Evans, A. (2013) Glitter (foot)ball tactics. Negotiating mainstream gender equality in Iceland. *Men and Masculinities*, 16 (5), 560–578.

14

Resisting the Taint, Marking the Slut: Middle-class Lesbian Girls and Claims to Sexual Propriety

Elizabethe Payne

Introduction

The good girl/slut or virgin/whore binary is a central characteristic of heterofemininity (Tolman, 2006; Bryant & Schofield, 2007; Charles, 2010) and has a long history of disciplining bodies and desires of Western women and girls, regardless of sexual orientation and identity (Payne, 2010). This binary positions women's 'sexuality dichotomously as morally good or bad' with the former requiring 'sexual passivity' and the latter attached to sex involving 'women's initiation and/or active participation' (Bryant & Schofield, 2007: 324). To be a woman of value means to be a 'good girl' in compliance with Western and local culture's moral expectations based upon sex, gender and presumed future heterosexuality – expectations which are inherently raced and classed. Good girls express no sexual agency, deny desire, postpone sexual exploration or confine it to committed heterosexual relationships (within which they subjugate their own needs to those of male partners) and participate in judging themselves and other young women through the patriarchal lens of the virgin/whore binary (Tolman, 2006). Compliance with expectations for hegemonic femininity is linked to cultural rewards for 'correctly' aligning sex and gender, and to a moral discourse surrounding the standards for being both 'good' and a female-bodied person (Payne, 2013). That compliance includes adherences to 'age-appropriate' sexuality (McClelland & Hunter, 2013).

Cultural norms for 'proper girl behavior' create resources for divisions between 'self' and 'other'/ed women (Charles, 2010: 37). Most often, middle-class identities such as 'good girl' establish moral standards against which working- and lower-class identities are measured (Jackson, 2011). Sexual behaviour and its marking is then 'used as the currency through which other differences are articulated' (Charles, 2010: 37) and evaluated. Current

'sexualization panics' draw on classed and raced expectations for sexual propriety, heteronormative patriarchal assertions that female sexuality must be
contained and that 'sexual liberation' has been damaging to girls (Ringrose,
2013: 42). Today's girls are seen as even more 'at risk' as increased 'bad influences' in modern life threaten to transform 'middle-class white girlhood into
something monstrous and pathological' (Egan, 2013: 7).

These moral discourses reaffirm a cultural history that negates girls' sexual
autonomy and the validity of their desires while reasserting links between
chastity and the goodness of girls. Such heteronormative standards for
girl 'goodness' can create conflict for lesbian-identifying girls who wrestle
with tensions between the sexualized and marginalized identity of 'lesbian',
the cultural imperative to 'be good' and their efforts to see themselves as
valuable individuals (Payne, 2013).

This chapter will explore the ways Southern, White, middle-class lesbian
young women stake their claims to lesbian moral goodness by making
repeated value-laden distinctions between those – straight and lesbian –
who keep their sexual desire in check and those who do not (Payne, 2010).
While actively resisting their own sexualization, they both 'other' sexually experienced young women and reassert their middle-class privilege as
tools to distance themselves from the raw sexuality associated with working-
and lower-class female sexualities, masculinized sexualities and the taint of
lesbian desire.

Good girls, sexuality and social class

In recent decades, 'lesbian' as a sexual identity has been framed as one of
potential liberation from the confines of heterofemininity, from the suppression of sexual desire (Rich, 1980) and from the limitations of social class
(Heapy, 2012). It has been argued that by the late 20th century, lesbian and
gay identities had become 'post-class', shaped by a move towards individualized identities and away from collective, materialist ones (Heapy, 2013).
While possibilities for living lives of sexual and gender diversity are indeed
increasing, that increase is not experienced in monolithic ways. Lived experience of gender and sexual diversity is shaped by sociocultural contexts
and positionalities, including gender, race, social class, age and geography
(McDermott, 2011). Sexual 'morality' has long been 'class specific' (Jackson,
2011: 17). 'Idealized American girlhood privileges the traditional', middle-
class values of monogamy and abstinence – 'values which are historically
linked and inextricably tied to whiteness, heterosexuality, and normative
femininity.' 'The good girl', by adhering to these standards, becomes a
'beacon of morality' (Brown, 2012: 162) for those around her.

'Class is part of the micropolitics of people's lives. It is lived in and through
people's bodies and permeates their thinking' (Reay, 1998: 265). Middle-class
girls' acceptance of the imperative to deny sexual desires and delay sexual

activity reflects belief in a classed future where adult success and stability is achieved through self-control and determination in the present. Sex is therefore not age-appropriate for girls who have yet to secure education, independence and a stable heterosexual relationship. In contrast, the 'excessive heterosexuality' of young working-class women is culturally positioned as a 'backwardness', attached to their sexualized appearances and inferred lack of character, self-control and good decision making which could lead to a healthy future (Taylor, 2011: 7). It is against the foil of excessive, sexualized, working- or lower-class bad girls that the sound choices and morality of the middle-class good girl are reaffirmed.

Slut shaming is a deeply classed discourse (Ringrose & Renold, 2012). Marking differences in sexual behaviour and body can be tools for a distancing of self from 'lower class status' and 'sexual promiscuity' (Charles, 2010: 37). Through 'associating "sluts" with "prostitutes" and "whores"' (Ringrose & Renold, 2012: 336), heteronormative and classed discourses are employed to diminish a woman's 'value'. The personification of the working-class 'slut' reinforces 'the middle class figure of respectability' (Hubbs, 2011: 63). 'Lesbian' is not a position released from cultural binds, and the marked deviance of that identity is created and reproduced through expectations for female bodies that lie in the intersections of race, class and gender.

Sluts and sexed-up lesbians

Sexualized distinctions between 'good' and 'bad' girls begin as early as elementary school. Young girls may be marked as 'sluts', 'bitches' and 'whores' for demonstrating assertive behaviour, wearing make-up,certain kinds of clothing, or pursuing boys – actual sexual engagement not required (Eder, 1995). Such labelling 'becomes part of a continual attempt to limit [girls'] sense of sexual autonomy and identity' (p. 153). As girls get older, pursuing sexual gratification, engaging in sex outside of committed (hetero) relationship, having more than one sexual or romantic partner, admitting to embodied desire or sexual knowledge, and bisexuality are among the short list of things that can mark a young woman as a 'slut' with serious long-term social consequences. Girls are expected to demonstrate heterosexuality, prove their ability to be desired by boys and maintain good reputations (Tolman, 2006). Girls who begin to 'develop their own autonomy regarding sexual behaviors' – particularly girls who are othered by class and 'other middle class norms' – are silenced and punished, reminding all girls to mind their gendered role (Rahimi & Liston, 2009: 514). Young women marked by peers as 'oversexed' are socially 'annihilated' (White, 2002: 65) through continual assaults on their value as human beings (Payne, 2010).

These tensions are difficult for all girls to navigate, but even more so for lesbian girls. 'Heterosexual attraction' is culturally 'presumed to be the only "natural" form of sexuality' (Elley, 2011). 'Hegemonic scripts still position woman's desire as a response to man, "sex" as heterosexual intercourse, and practices that deviate from this narrow norm as problematic or perverse' (Ussher, 2005: 27). Additionally, to be named 'lesbian' is to have one's core sense of self tied to sex, sexual desire, and sex acts culturally deemed 'deviant' (Ussher & Mooney-Somers, 2000: 183). Young lesbian and queer women are 'caught materially and discursively in ways that are most oppressive. Held responsible for bodies considered disobedient and problematic, they are punished for sexual desire and excess at every turn' (McClelland & Fine, 2008: 91).

Moral goodness in the Southern US

There are significant national and regional variations in attitudes towards girls' desire and sexual experience within the White middle class (Schalet, 2010). Texas is an important context for understanding the stories of the young women in this study. Southern adolescent girls gain popularity and prestige through 'moral behaviors', 'having a good reputation' and 'being a virgin' (Suitor & Carter, 1999: 96–98). 'Highly prescribed notions of femininity' are 'often more confining in the south than in other parts of the country' (Berbary, 2012: 619). 'Discourses of Christianity and expectations peculiar to Southern femininity' (Liston & Moore-Rahimi, 2005: 214) 'tighten' (p. 225) the ways young Southern women evaluate their own sexual behaviour and that of other women – regardless of personal religious beliefs. Though none of the young women in this study identified as 'religious' or regularly attended church at the time of the interviews, larger discourses of Christianity swirl around them, potentially shaping their understandings of what is valued in young women.

In many states, 'fundamental religious ideologies have influenced schools', seeking to 'extinguish or punish young women's desire in classrooms' (McClelland & Fine, 2008: 84). Sex education in Texas has been 'abstinence only', which 'lodges sexuality education in fear and shame, firmly burying discussions of desire and pleasure' (McClelland & Fine, 2006: 306). Research on public school teachers in the Southern US has shown a range of attitudes and practices that reproduce White middle-class expectations for 'lady-like' (Rahimi & Liston, 2009: 521) behaviour and suppression of girls' sexual desires. Rahimi and Liston (2009) found that teachers in the South 'may let harassment of so-called bad girls be perpetuated in their classrooms to attempt a kind of moral policing of the sexuality of young women' and that teachers' classroom practices supported the idea that 'good girls do not have sexual desires' (p. 529).

We know little, however, about how lesbian youth navigate tensions between their same-sex attractions and cultural expectations to be good and valued girls (Payne, 2013). Existing research points towards experiences of adolescent lesbian desire framed through the cultural contexts of heterofemininity, resisted, reappropriated but always present (Dempsey et al., 2001; Payne, 2010, 2013). 'Lesbian' and 'good girl' are discursively produced as identities in opposition to each other, and girls must do 'identity work' to resolve these tensions (Payne, 2013). This chapter draws on a critical life history study which explores the identity stories Southern, middle-class, White American lesbian adolescents tell about who is 'good' and who is 'bad' – stories through which they make themselves 'imaginable' as 'the normal girl' through 'the presence of the not "normal" girl' (Charania, 2010: 309) who is marked by her desire, her sexual behaviours and her failure to conform to middle-class standards of propriety.

Participants: Demographics and recruiting

The data presented here are from a larger study on the experiences of adolescent, lesbian-identifying young women, ages 18–21, in a major metropolitan area in Texas, in the southern US. Two participants were in high school, one had graduated high school the month prior to the interviews and six were in college. Seven of the young women attended, or had attended, large public high schools in the area. Two of the young women had attended private religious high schools. None of the young women attended the same high school. The two high school students and one recent high school graduate were accessed through the local LGBT youth support group. The college students were located through postings on area campuses.

The initial Institutional Review Board (IRB) application for this research proposed participants ages 15–19, but IRB set the lower age limit at 18. 'Adolescence' is not a stable category; it can begin 'before age 10 and the upper age boundary may be defined as 21 or even 25, or at the time of economic independence' (APA, 2002: 2). There are also class distinctions, with middle class extending the period of some dependence through the undergraduate years. Therefore, the young women in this study were understood to still be adolescents (ages 18–21) at the time of the interviews and within the life period they were being asked to recall. All were enrolled students, sharing stories not yet reconstructed through adult experiences.

All participants self-identified as 'lesbian' and used female pronouns. Only one described herself as 'kinda more masculine than some other girls'. She identified with 'tomboy' but not 'butch'. Self-labelling as lesbian while in high school and age were the only criteria for research participation. All identified by their sophomore year. It is not assumed that all the young women who participated in this study attached the same meaning to the label 'lesbian', or that 'lesbian' is a stable category.

Participants were all White and middle class, though race and class were not criteria for participation. The girls were not asked about their class status and none directly discussed it. Middle-class status was determined for each girl by assessing the following information: schools attended, area of residence, parent occupation and expectations for or enrolment in higher education. This information emerged within each interview.

Self-identifying as lesbian in the same geographic area within the same socio-historic time frame and from shared demographic positions, the young women in this study encountered similar resistances and had similar resources available to them to address these as they developed their lesbian identities. The similarities in their stories are best understood through exploring the systemic pressures they encountered as young, White, middle-class, Southern girls moving into the marginalized and stigmatized space of 'lesbian' (Payne, 2010).

Interview method and analysis

This study utilized a new method of life history interviewing – critical life story (Payne, 2009). Integrating anthropological approaches to life history with the life story method of Linde (1993) (which focuses on the identity act of life-storying) and with the critical methodology of Phil Carspecken (1996) provides theoretical and practical support for conducting life history research within a critical framework. Life story is understood as a social act through which the narrator creates a 'comfortable sense' of self as 'a good, socially proper, and stable person' in order to engage with and be thought valuable by others. Stories told are rooted in culture, 'claim or negotiate group membership and demonstrate that we are in fact worthy members of those groups, understanding and properly following their moral standards' (Linde, 1993: 3). Stories are fluid and change with experience, re-memory, audience and culture shifts. They also serve to establish a 'private sense of self' (p. 98).

The critical life story interview is fully open ended. Questions specifically about sexuality were asked only as probes after the participant introduced the topic as central to an area of her story. No questions about sexuality, sexual identity, sexual behaviour, dating or self-labelling moments were introduced by the researcher. The goal was to allow participants to include sexuality in the areas of their story where they felt it central and not to craft stories where sexuality was privileged for the sake of the interviews. Interviews averaged 3.25 hours in length, were audiotaped, and transcribed verbatim with field notes added in. Two participants were interviewed twice.

Mapping of identity and normative-evaluative claims within participants' stories utilized Carspecken's critical ethnographic method (1996). A claim to identity only has meaning when understood in relation to other possible identities constituted within a system of value (Carspecken, 1996). The themes of 'slut' and 'good girl' emerged from the data and were not predetermined categories of analysis.

Sluts are 'sooo much worse' than nice lesbians

When Lindsey was a freshman in high school, she was traumatically 'outed' by the first girl to whom she expressed romantic feelings. This young woman publicly humiliated Lindsey, calling her names and announcing her same-sex desires to the entire school. Lindsey was crushed and ostracized. In telling this story, Lindsey includes what happened to the young woman who humiliated her:

> Well, actually, what happened was she fell in love with someone who was, like, 40 years old and had a baby with him and then when she came back to school her junior year, she had to, like, eat humble pie and wasn't so snotty any more.... You know, everyone knew she was a slut and she was, like, I was so bad for being gay and, like, asking her out and then she's doing things like that...and I thought 'Oh, yeah, that is sooo much worse'.

Lindsey draws on classed images of the 'white trash' girl – a teen having sex with an older man and losing her reputation through high school pregnancy. The cultural norms violated are laid out one by one: high school girlsare not supposed to have sex with 40-year-old men; smart girls are supposed to be sexually responsible and not get pregnant; girls with a future do not have babies in high school. This young woman loses her social standing and had to 'eat humble pie' once her slut status was revealed. Lindsey then compares the social sins committed that led to the marking of each girl – her own lesbian identity to behaviour of the school slut – and asserts that she, the lesbian, is morally superior. Lindsey relies on middle-class norms to reclaim her own personal worth and reposition herself as a good girl.

Narrated contrasts: Slut versus chaste lesbian

The 'acceptable face' of youthful womanhood is the 'nice girl'; the 'unacceptable face(s) are the lesbian and the slag' (Griffin, 2005: 2). The 'nice girl' is heterosexual. The young lesbian participants challenge the required heterosexuality of nice girls by comparing their own restrained sexual behaviour to the excessiveness of others. The articulation of the 'slut' – or excessively desiring/sexually experienced bad girl – served several purposes in the narratives of the participants: 1) the bad girl was a contrast to and validation of their own claims to 'good girl' status; 2) naming the bad girl reflects the taint of sex away from the sexualized identity of 'lesbian'; 3) it positioned these young lesbians as a moral authority; 4) it allowed them to assert their privilege and highlight the part of their identities that carried cultural value; 5) naming the bad girl provided a justification for them to 'be mean' and still think of themselves as 'good' girls; finally, 6) using the good girl/bad girl binary to evaluate themselves gave them some sense of control over their own 'goodness' – they were not doomed to worthlessness by their same-sex attractions. All of these purposes are deeply rooted in White middle-class values. I have explored both slut marking (Payne, 2010) and their claims to lesbian good girl status (Payne, 2013) in greater depth and with additional data in previous papers. This chapter focuses on the othering based upon social class present in those stories.

Identity claims are often made through articulating contrasts between possible identity positions. The good girl is understood in contrast to the bad girl, the slut to the chaste girl, the nice girl to the mean girl. Each of these claims asserts class privilege. The ideal middle-class girl is understood as superior in juxtaposition with the sexualized working- or lower-class girl. In these stories, 'lesbian good girl' is positioned against the socially derogated 'white trash' woman, marked for her sexual behaviour. Identity claims made by participants acknowledge the cultural association between lesbian and sex, and between sex and 'bad woman', and they provide a classed framework for contesting sexual as a primary component of a lesbian identity. They do not, however, challenge the pre-understanding of female sexuality as bad, nor the middle-class value system that imagines the idealized virginal girl. Their challenge is limited to the ways sexual behaviour and its negative valuation are necessarily attached to 'lesbian' (Payne, 2010), and they rescue 'lesbian' from sexual deviance by drawing on middle-class values. The following sections provide examples of this pattern.

The wrong 'kind of' woman

Identifying as lesbian is to be defined by sexuality and sexual acts in ways that are not true for heterosexual young women (Ussher & Mooney-Somers, 2000). Young women in this study mark the position of desiring woman, regardless of sexual orientation. It is the uncivilized, uncontrolled, sexually desiring, sexually experienced female body that is 'bad' – not 'being' lesbian. Through their stories of women who had sex too young, had multiple partners, actively pursued women or men, cheated on them, pressured them for sex or liked to have sex, the young lesbian participants pull from the discourses of sexualization to paint a portrait of class distinction between themselves and the wrong kind of woman. The white trash of cultural imagination is characterized by aggression, promiscuity and predatory sexual behaviour – including inappropriate age differences between partners, alcoholism and drug use, poor decision-making, selfishness, laziness, unregulated emotion, illegal behaviours, both hyper-heterosexualized and masculinized women, a lack of morality, an inability to envision future consequences of behaviours, and lower levels of intelligence, education and employment (Wray, 2006; Hubbs, 2011; others). Through their contrast claims, the young women in this study were 'able to deploy other

forms of visible identity as resources, such as middle-class cultural dispositions, to offset this marginalization and make their claims [to validity]
known' (Skeggs, 2005: 294). The women in this study narratively move
the boundaries between good girl and bad girl and offset their own lesbian
marginalization by narrating the white trash girl.

The titty-bar working drug user

Linda focused much of her interviews on her first relationship with LuLu
during the Eighth Grade. Linda described LuLu as 'the root of all evil'.
In speculating about what might have happened after high school to LuLu,
who continued to date guys during her romantic friendship with Linda, she
said, 'Probably working at a titty bar. I don't know. She has a drug problem.
She had no sense of self, you know. All those guys'. Linda had a two-year
tumultuous romantic friendship with LuLu – often wanting more in terms of
time and emotional energy than LuLu was willing to give her. Linda believed
that it was the ever-present 'guys' that distracted LuLu from giving her attention. She finally ended the relationship and now marks LuLu as someone of
low moral character and low social class – working at a 'titty bar' and doing
drugs (Payne, 2010).

In her larger discussion of this relationship, Linda positions herself as
'giver', willing to do anything for the relationship even at great personal
cost. This provides a clear contrast to the behaviours of LuLu who is represented as not only 'slutty', but selfish – taking and offering nothing in
return, a trait historically forgiven in men but not in women.

> She treated me like shit all the time. And, like, when we fought, what
> would happen is no matter whose fault it was, I would call her up or go
> to her house crying, saying I was sorry, asking her to come back.... But
> she, like, she had a ton of boyfriends and she felt incredibly used, which
> I don't blame her, but she was just, she just started taking it out on me,
> like, for them using her ... but I didn't [use her.] If anything, she used me

Linda paints LuLu as both victim and agent. LuLu's expression of her sexual
agency with a 'ton of boyfriends' had gendered emotional consequences for
her. She felt 'used', and Linda's acknowledging this feeling as appropriate
removes LuLu's sexual agency, returning her from masculinized subject to
heterofeminine object. Linda suffers for the boys 'using' LuLu when LuLu
'takes it out' on Linda. Lulu is then remasculinized, positioned as the 'user'
of Linda. Linda relies on this narrative of the suffering and dedicated partner to further highlight the differences between herself and LuLu, placing
LuLu as the slutty 'bad girl' and reiterating her own claim to 'good girl'
status (Payne, 2010). Using white trash signifiers to mark a woman who
hurt her and to reinforce her own good girl position, Linda links LuLu's

'bad girl', status with bad choices leading to a decimated life of drugs and stripping.

The older, pot-smoking, college drop-out

Lissa considers her second lesbian relationship during her junior year of high school a mistake. The story she tells is of an older woman – an adult – pressuring a young lesbian into more sex than she wanted. She says:

> When I started talking to Sarah, I thought she was really cute. So, I started dating her and it was ridiculous. She was older, like way older. I was 17 and she was 22 – so five years difference. She, like, wanted the relationship to be way more sexual than my relationship had been with Laura and so I learned a lot but it was not a great way to learn, I don't think. We fought about it way too much. And, of course, she, like, smoked pot and hadn't finished college and wanted to be a musician but wasn't playing music and she just wasn't the kind of person I should've been dating and it was a huge drama.

Lissa begins her presentation of this 'ridiculous' relationship naming the inappropriate age difference followed immediately by stating the difference in desire. The much older girlfriend wanted the relationship to be 'way more' sexual than Lissa had experienced previously. Lissa was forced to learn 'a lot' about sex – measuring the difference in sexual experience between herself and Sarah. Lissa makes clear her resistance to this sexual element, but her reluctance was not respected. The implied pressure for sex and the age difference masculinizes Sarah's desire and marks her as predatory. Positioning Sarah as the bad girl and herself as the less-desiring and inexperienced youth, Lissa deflects the taint of 'slut' associated with dating an older partner (Stewart, 1999) away from herself and repositions herself as 'good'.

After she has established Sarah as 'a lot' more sexually experienced and 'way' too sexually desiring, she lists other character faults and implies that these should not be surprising. Given her sexual experience – 'of course' Sarah did other bad things too. Sarah's lack of concern for her future, failure in higher education, inability to reach goals (college and music), self-indulgence in the present (sex and drugs), and lack of employment put her far outside middle-class expectations for deferred gratification and achieving a productive future. Life with Sarah was 'a huge drama' – a descriptor also associated with white trash – and not the place for a future-oriented good girl. References to white trash sensibilities in American culture mark lower-class Whites as 'a breed apart, a dysgenic race unto themselves' (Wray & Newitz, 1997). Sarah wasn't the 'kind of person' for Lissa – marked both through her sexual desire and through her class position; she was 'a breed apart'.

The older, lying, drinking, drug-using cheater

Sexuality is a dividing line between childhood and adulthood. Older partners can be seen as high-risk, bringing age-inappropriate sexual information to younger, vulnerable and inexperienced youths (McClelland & Hunter, 2013). Eighteenand in high school at the time of the interviews, Amy preferred to only date 'virgins'. She had made two exceptions and believed those relationships were mistakes. She describes one of her experiences dating a non-virgin, an older woman:

> She was older and she wasn't a virgin and she pressured me and once sort of instigated having sex but I turned her down and that's how that went.... Things started happening where I found out she lied to me and she had an alcohol problem. So, I broke up with her soon afterwards and realized that she did a lot more, like, she cheated on me and she started using drugs, so that relationship wasn't too good.... I just feel weird that that was a person that I liked and that person could be a person like that, would get into so much trouble like that. That bothered me.

As in Lissa's story, the dating partner here is masculinized and made predatory through the age difference and sexual pressure. Her non-virgin status implicates her as suspect. Amy discovers the girlfriend lied, had an alcohol problem, cheated, and used drugs. Amy has trouble believing that she 'liked' 'a person like that' – a bad girl who 'would get into so much trouble'. It made her feel 'weird' and 'bothered' that she had been attracted to someone 'like that'. Again like Lissa, Amy's critique of this girlfriend utilizes 'abject white working class', – the designated white trash position – 'to mark the limits of proper personhood' in ways that specifically draw on normative expectations for gender and sexuality (Skeggs, 2005: 295).

After two relationships with 'non-virgins', Amy decided to not date anyone who was not a 'virgin'. She said: 'I am still a virgin and I went with two other girlfriends and they weren't virgins and I thought I was fine with it but now.... I have a problem with it'. Amy links the non-virgin status of her former partners to the difficulties in those relationships and to their other behaviours associated with 'bad girls' (Payne, 2010). Women's sexual experience is 'bad' and women with that experience are bad. A woman with sexual experience is a different sort of person and one to be avoided.

Not wanting to be defined by their sexuality can lead young lesbian women to distance themselves from sex (Ussher & Mooney-Somers, 2000) and to take a moralistic position on women's sexual behaviour, both straight and lesbian. The girls in this study contrast their own good girl behaviour with the behaviour of other young women who exhibit sexual desire and acquire sexual experience. In deflecting the taint of sexual desire away from themselves, they pull from the discursive representation of the lesbian as perverse and predatory (Ussher & Mooney-Somers, 2000) and reify that representation through their contrast claims. 'I'm not THAT KIND of lesbian' acknowledges the sexually predatory lesbian but raises the possibility for a different construction of lesbian – the 'lesbian good girl' (Payne, 2010, 2013). The sexually predatory lesbian is a position that is historically and culturally both masculinized and working classed (Kennedy & Davis, 1993). Distancing themselves from the image of the sexually assertive lesbian is also a distancing from the 'bogey of female masculinity' and the 'moral deviance' associated with pursuit of sexual pleasure for pleasure's sake (Detloff, 2006: 90).

Strategies of resistance to the oppression of lesbian sexuality differ by social position and are deeply classed (Kennedy & Davis, 1993). Lesbian girls – even if they are White and privileged – are 'assumed to be bad' and feel the pressure 'to be thought of as good, moral, and normal' (Tolman & Higgins, 1996: 208). Through their stories, the girls reference the cultural imagery of southern white trash – sexually promiscuous and predatory, drug- and alcohol-using, without morals, without education, lying, cheating, selfish and pleasure-seeking at the expense of others. Excessive women – straight or lesbian – are the bad girls. White trash signifiers are used to mark 'those bodies that exceed the class and racial etiquettes required of whites if they are to preserve the powers and privileges that accrue to them' (Hartigan, 1997: 320). Participants argue that they have not exceeded those etiquettes. They have limited their sexual experiences to long-term committed relationships and kept their desires in check (Payne, 2010, 2013), so they are entitled to the power, privilege and respectability of the middle-class girl.

Conclusion

'[S]ocially sustained discourses about who it is appropriate and valuable to be inevitably shape the way we look at and constitute ourselves' and others (Reay, 1998: 264). Lesbian desire is culturally constructed as highly sexual, perverse, predatory and masculine. It is at odds with society's conceptions of moral worth and the classed expectations for the idealized American girl. 'Classed and gendered heterosexual norms and discourses ... continually shape young people's experiences' and possibilities (Elley, 2011) and are central in the ways the young lesbian participants mark sexual desire and assert their own 'good girl' identity claims.

These young women expand the 'good girl' category to include lesbians conforming to the middle-class 'rules' governing female sexuality, while they continue to rely on the good girl/bad girl binary as their primary tool for evaluating others (Payne, 2010, 2013). The discourses available to young lesbian women to understand themselves as sexual beings and as 'good' people are limited. Social identities draw from cultural themes that rely on beliefs about the differences between categories of people and also reconfigure those categories (Carspecken, 1996). 'Good girl', for these young women, is not tethered to sexual identity but rather to sexual behaviour, sexual agency and resistance to desire (Payne, 2010). Through narrating a culturally recognizable 'bad girl', they made themselves intelligible as moral subjects through the good girl/slut binary by deflecting the taint of sex associated with the lesbian label away from themselves.

Understanding how young lesbians navigate the social world requires an understanding of more than their romantic attractions and sexual identities – it requires an understanding of the ways in which they position themselves in the world given the loss of social capital that comes from having a culturally deviant sexuality and deviant gender. 'Class shapes lifestyles, opportunities and choices, which are still materially as well as morally bounded, circumscribed by constructions of "appropriate" femininity' (Taylor, 2011: 7). What it means to be middle class, White, young, female and lesbian in the southern United States 'shifts and changes, not only from one historical era to another, but for individuals over time as they negotiate the social world' (Reay, 1998: 266). Boundaries between groups have a 'distinctly moral dimension', are normative and 'routinely establish basic distinctions between good and bad people' (Wray, 2006: 16). Here, the good people are the middle-class, sexually contained lesbians.

References

Berbary, L. (2012) Don't be a whore, that's not ladylike: Discursive discipline and sorority women's gendered subjectivity. *Qualitative Inquiry*, 18 (7), 606–625.

Brown, A. (2012) She isn't whoring herself out like a lot of other girls we see: Identification and 'authentic' American girlhood on Taylor Swift fan forums. *Networking Knowledge*, 5 (1), 161–180.

Bryant, J., & Schofield, T. (2007) Feminine sexual subjectivities: Bodies, agency and life history. *Sexualities*, 10 (3), 321–340.

Carspecken, P. F. (1996) *Critical ethnography in educational research: A theoretical and practical guide.* New York: Routledge.

Charania, M. M. (2010) Reading the body: The rhetoric of sex, identity and discipline in girls' education. *International Journal of Qualitative Studies in Education*, 23 (3), 305–330.

Charles, E. C. (2010) Complicating hetero-femininities: Young women, sexualities and 'girl power' at school. *International Journal of Qualitative Studies in Education*, 23 (1), 33–47.

Dempsey, D., Hillier, L., & Harrison, L. (2001) Gendered (s)explorations among same-sex attracted young people in Australia. *Journal of Adolescence*, 24, 67–81.

Detloff, M. (2006) Gender please, without the gender police: Rethinking pain in archetypal narratives of butch, transgender and FTM masculinity. *Journal of Lesbian Studies*, 10 (1/2), 87–105

Eder, D. (1995) *School talk: Gender and adolescent culture.* New Burnswick: Rutgers University Press.

Egan, R. D. (2013) *Becoming sexual: A critical appraisal of the sexualization of girls.* New York: John Wiley & Sons.

Elley, S. (2011) Young women, class, gendered heterosexuality: The implications of educational aspirations and social networks for sex education messages. *Sociology*, 45 (3), 413–429.

Griffin, C. (2005) *Impossible spaces: Femininity as an empty category*. ESRC Research Seminar Series: New Femininities.

Hartigan, J. (1997) Unpopular culture: The case of 'white trash'. *Cultural Studies*, 11 (2), 316–343.

Heapy, B. (2012) Situating lesbian and gay cultures of class identification. *Cultural Sociology*, 7 (3), 303–319.

Hubbs, N. (2011) 'Redneck Woman' and the gendered poetics of class rebellion. *Southern Cultures*, 17 (4), 44–70.

Jackson, S. (2011) Heterosexual hierarchies: A commentary on class and sexuality. *Sexualities*, 14 (1), 12–20.

Kennedy, E. L., & Davis, M. D. (1993) *Boots of leather, slippers of gold: The history of a lesbian community*. London: Routledge.

Linde, C. (1993) *Life stories: The creation of coherence*. New York: Oxford University Press.

Liston, D., & Moore-Rahimi, R. (2005) Disputation of a bad reputation: Adverse sexual labels in the lives of 12 Southern women, in P. J. Bettis & N. G. Adams (Eds.) *Geographies of Girlhood: Identities In-between*. New York: Lawrence Erlbaum Associates, pp. 211–230.

McClelland, S. I., & Fine, M. (2006) Sexuality education and desire: Still missing after all these years. *Harvard Educational Review*, Fall 2006, 76 (3), 297–337.

McClelland, S. I., & Fine, M. (2008) Rescuing a theory of adolescent sexual excess: Young women and wanting, in A. Harris (Ed.) *Next Wave Cultures: Feminism, Subcultures, Activism*. London: Routledge, pp. 83–102.

McClelland, S. I., & Hunter, L. E. (2013) Bodies that are always out of line: A closer look at 'age appropriate sexuality', in B. Fahf, M. L. Dudy & S. Stage (Eds.) *The Moral Panics of Sexuality*, pp. 59–76.

McDermott, E. (2011) The world some have won: Sexuality, class and inequality. *Sexualities*, 14 (1), 63–78.

Payne, E. (2009) Lesbian youth and the 'Not Girl' gender: Explorations of adolescent lesbian lives through critical life story research, in R. Winkle-Wagner, C. Lawrence, and A. Hunter (Eds.) *Methods on the Margins: Doing the Subversive in Educational Research*. Palgrave MacMillan.

Payne, E. (2010) Sluts: Heteronormative policing in the stories of lesbian youth. *Educational Studies*, 46 (3), 317–336.

Payne, E. (2013) Lesbian goodgirls: The absence of embodied desire in the stories of lesbian youth. Revised 2011 AESA conference paper. (submitted for review)

Rahimi, R., & Liston, D. (2009) What does she expect dressed like that? Teacher interpretation of emerging adolescent female sexuality. *Educational Studies*, 45, 512–533.

Reay, D. (1998) Rethinking social class: Qualitative perspectives on class and gender. *Sociology*, 32 (2), 259–275.

Rich, A. (1980) Compulsory heterosexuality and lesbian existence. *Signs*, 631–660.

Ringrose, J. (2013) *Postfeminist education? Girls and the sexual politics of schooling*. London: Routledge.

Ringrose, J., & Renold, E. (2012) Slut-shaming, girl power and 'sexualisation': Thinking through the politics of the international slut walks with teen girls. *Gender and Education*, 24 (3), 333–343.

Schalet, A. (2010) Sexual subjectivity revisited: The significance of relationships in Dutch and American girl's experiences of sexuality. *Gender and Society*, 24 (3), 304–329.

Skeggs, B. (2005) The making of class and gender through visualizing moral subject formation. *Sociology*, 39 (5), 965–982.

Stewart, F. (1999) *Once you get a reputation, your life's like ... 'wrecked': The implications of reputation for young women's health and wellbeing.* Faculty Presentation, Deakin University, AU.

Suitor, J., & Carter, R. (1999) Jocks, nerds, babes and thugs: A research note on regional differences in adolescent gender norms. *Gender Issues.* Summer, 17 (3), 87–101.

Taylor, Y. (2011) Sexualities and class. *Sexualities*, 14 (1), 3–11.

The American Psychological Association (2002) Developing Adolescents: A Reference for Professionals. *APA.* http://www.apa.org/pi/families/resources/develop.pdf.

Tolman, D. (1994) Doing desire: Adolescent girls' struggles for/with sexuality. *Gender and Society*, 8, 324–342.

Tolman, D. (2006) In a different position: Conceptualizing female adolescent sexuality within compulsory heterosexuality. *New Directions for Child and Adolescent Development*, 112, 71–89.

Ussher, J. (2005) The meaning of sexual desire: Heterosexual and lesbian girls. *Feminism and Psychology*, 15 (1), 27–32.

Ussher, J., & Mooney-Somers, J. (2000) Negotiating desire and sexual subjectivity: Narratives of the young lesbian avengers. *Sexualities*, 3, 183–200.

White, E. (2002) *Fast girls: Teenage tribes and the myth of the slut.* New York: Berkley Publishing Group.

Wray, M. (2006) *Not quite white: White trash and the boundaries of whiteness.* Durham, NC: Duke University Press.

Wray, M., & Newitz, A. (1997) White trash. *Race and Class in America.* New York: Routledge.

15
Mud, Mermaids and Burnt Wedding Dresses: Mapping Queer Becomings in Teen Girls' Talk on Living with Gender and Sexual Violence

Emma Renold and Gabrielle Ivinson

Introduction: Locating the violence of heteronormative belongings

In her chapter on 'geographies of desire', Deborah Tolman (2002: 172) argues how the significance of where girls live and the histories of sexualities in place is a key mediating feature of how girls come to embody and experience their sexed bodies and sexuality. This was certainly true of our longitudinal ethnographic research with young people (aged 12–14) living and growing up in an ex-mining semi-rural community in the South Wales valleys (UK). Here, 'growing up girl' (Walkerdine et al., 2001) and the subject position of girlfriend and mother loomed large (Ivinson & Renold, 2013a). Girls' talk was infused with tensions that seemed to bear the signs of industrial legacies of what girls and women were expected to do and be. This was most noticeable in their talk of sexual safety and danger. Often, sexual violence was never far away from talk about coupledom and being 'in relationship', as the following two examples go some way to illustrate:

> *Kayleigh (age 13): Dafydd...he pushed me on the track before, he did, coz I wouldn't go out with him...and then he chucked a glass bottle at me.*
> *ER: Because you wouldn't go out with him?*
> *Kayleigh: Yeah...and I just chased after him...*
> *ER: Did you? Do you fight back if someone does something like that?*
> *Kayleigh: Yeah...when somebody gets the bad side of me, I tell you what, I hit the roof*

(Individual photo-elicitation interview
transcript, school classroom, Cwm Dyffryn)

We are at the youth centre, sitting on the sofa chatting to the girls about clothes and nights out. There is a pause in our conversation and Beth (age 15) rolls up her sleeves to uncover a number of red marks on her arm 'Look, Liz (youth worker), look at my bruises'. She goes on to describe an encounter with her boyfriend in her bedroom. She was lying down he crossed her arms behind her back and didn't stop when she told him 'that hurts'. She 'got angry' with him, fought back and it 'got violent then'. Liz immediately interjects with the following advice: 'when this happens, what you need to do is, make your body go limp...go limp and then withdraw, back away...if you carry on winding him up he'll hurt you...he's a boy'.

(Fieldnotes, ER, Youth Centre, Cwm Dyffrn)

The landscape of south Wales has many villages backing onto open mountainous scapes that afford the possibility for a rich and physical engagement with the wild. While many young teen boys talked animatedly about the adventures they had and continued to have with the wild and their local outdoors, girls, in contrast, spoke about how they had given up the physical activities they used to do, such as den-building, biking, skateboarding hiking and climbing. Some girls made direct links with how their everyday practices of 'girling' (e.g. hair, make-up, not 'getting dirty' or 'sweaty') compromised and disrupted continuing with these outdoor pursuits. Their narratives inducted us into the many different ways they felt their adolescent bodies to be under surveillance. We felt their ubiquitous fear in their talk of being 'constantly watched', needing to 'know where you could run to', where you 'could hide' and how 'to avoid' places and people who might 'take you', 'attack you' and 'rape you'. Other girls, like Kayleigh above, disclosed specific details of online and offline heterosexual violence, including the physical violence incurred on rejecting heterosexual advances and her refusal to couple up with a boy. Not far from the surface talk of 'wanting a boyfriend' to create and enhance a normative heterofemininity, was talk of 'needing a boyfriend' to protect them from physical violence in their community (see Renold, 2013, see also Lombard, 2013, 2015). This coupling up had very little to do with the 'premature' or 'accelerated' sexualization of white middle-class moral panics (Renold & Ringrose, 2011; Egan, 2013) Rather, this push for hetero-togetherness demands to be understood as a historically situated set of more-than-human relations which we theorize via the notion of 'sexuality assemblage' (see Fox & Alldred, 2013) that afforded girls physical and ontological security.

Indeed, we have written elsewhere how community messages steeped in a history where generations of strong women have kept families afloat demand girls stay close and couple up with boyfriends to keep boys safe and out of trouble (Ivinson & Renold, 2013b). Our ethnographic research at the local youth centre was where we saw this dynamic surface in the most extreme ways. Girls were implicitly and explicitly encouraged to be 'in a relationship', not just to keep boys safe, but in view, where youth workers could reach them. Indeed, the interaction between Liz and Beth above is fundamentally one of male protection. Beth is called upon to produce a limp body to keep an essentialized and uncontrollable violent masculinity in check. Moreover, she is encouraged by the youth worker to control her own rage, and not fight back so as not to get hurt. However, rather than individualize the scene as a universal depiction of patriarchal gender relations we need to understand them in their socio-historical moment (Lombard, 2013). Serving the institution of heterosexuality as girlfriend, wife and mother operated historically as a way of saving and securing a socio-historical hegemonic masculinity that in many ways operated as community survival in this specific socio-historical context (see also Walkerdine & Jimenez, 2012). To violate this code, to resist and refuse heterofamilial bonds for girls and women was and is risky, dangerous and ultimately, we argue, a queer endeavour in their rupturing of heternormative belongings and future imaginaries.

In dialogue with recent queer and post-queer theorizing of young sexualities research (see for example Ruffalo, 2009; Gowlett & Rasmussen, 2014), we are not working with a notion of queerness as a sexual 'identity', and thus in terms of recognition or representation. Neither are we drawing on queer to expose the cracks in heteronormative regimes or setting up binaries that ascribe practices as either normative or non-normative. Rather, we are thinking of queer becomings more as 'alternative modalities of belonging, connectivity and intimacy' (Puar, 2007: 208, Berlant & Edelman, 2013) that trouble and extend sexuality beyond identitarian frames, and, as we outline below, entangle with the more-than-human. Queer becomings can thus include girls, like Kayleigh above, who fight their abusive boyfriends in local-historical cultures which expect couples to stay together, through to girls' passionate attachments to places, spaces, movements and nature that free and liberate (Renold & Ivinson, 2014).

Queer assemblages, becomings and how the more-than-human matters

Our aim in this chapter is to work creatively with discursive data to trace a range of queer becomings across human and non-human sexuality assemblages (Fox & Alldred, 2013, 2014). We draw upon a feminist posthuman perspective, which demands an exploration of how living beings and matter mesh and 'become more and other than their histories through their engagement with dynamic environments' (Grosz, 2011: 2). Feminist and queer scholarship on new-materialism is useful here in encouraging social scientists to think with new ontologies of the decentred and posthuman subject (Probyn, 1996; Braidotti, 2002/2005, 2006, 2012, 2013; Barad, 2007;

Alaimo & Hekman, 2008; Grosz, 2011). This is a subject that is formed through, 'shared worlds' via 'a series of encounters which it does not author or control' (Moore, 2011: 184). This scholarship pushes us to think critically about post-anthropocentric relations and the intra-action (Barad, 2007) of more than human worlds (e.g. animal worlds, environmental worlds, material worlds).

Entanglements of intra-acting phenomena are always located in time, history and place. So, when we consider the everyday practices that girls are part of and undertake in the valleys, we come to see these as practices that carry affective traces of the past that leap between any number of what Deleuze and Guatarri call 'existential territories'; that is, those 'transversal flashes' (Guatarri, 1995: 93) of affective space, created by experience in assemblages. As Henrietta Moore, on discussing how we cannot work with affect as disembedded and free-flowing in boundless spaces, argues: 'Affective responses have deeply sedimented personal and social histories, and while they can surprise us, they are rarely random' (2011: 199).

If we focus on the mud-girl assemblage (as we do later), we can recognize the specifically emplaced (i.e. south valleys coalfields) and historical (patriarchal and capitalist) bonds between girls, dirt and valleys life, where generations of woman would spend a significant part of their routine keeping the coal dust at bay – the affective practices of which endure in ex-mining communities. Thus, 'assemblages' can be made up of all manner of matter, corporeal, technological, mechanical, virtual, discursive and imaginary, that carry affective charges. As Bennett (2010: 23) argues, bodies can enhance their power, their agency or what we would theorize as 'becomings' 'in or as a heterogeneous assemblage' and 'agency becomes distributed across an ontological heterogeneous field'. We see their capacity to affect and be affected, to create change, emerge in the intra-action of elements in assemblages.

Towards a diffractive methodology for researching young sexualities

The chapter draws on the data generated across two different but connected research projects. Project 1, The *Young People and Place* project, was methodologically funded research, designed specifically to experiment with different ways of creating research encounters that could capture the more multi-sensory and affective relations of space and place (see Walkerdine, 2010, 2013; Lury & Wakeford, 2012; Hughes & Lury, 2013).[1] The research has become a multi-phased ethnography, organically evolving as opportunities and new connections and possibilities arise. The second project, 'Girls and Boys Speak Out: A qualitative research study of children's gender and sexual cultures' (Renold, 2013), was an interview-based study that used a range of creative methods, from drawing to photo-elicitation with friendship groups of pre-teen children (age 10–12, n = 125) across rural and urban south Wales, including the south Wales valleys. Friendship group interviews were followed up with narrative individual interviews with a smaller sample of children (n = 25).

In this paper we draw on Karen Barad's (2007) diffractive methodology (see also Taylor and Ivinson, 2013) to explore how talk in seated interviews intra-act with historical data (e.g. on myths and legends or domestic practices of coal miners' wives) and feminist materialist theory in order to trace how the gendered and queer legacies of the valley's mining past surfaces affectively in girls' talk about their everyday lives. Working this way allow us to map the affective 'ontological intensities' (Deleuze & Guatarri, 1987) of those often imperceptible micro-moments of teen girls' becomings (see also Coleman, 2009; Renold & Ringrose, 2011; Juelskjaer, 2013; Ringrose, 2013; Gonick & Gannon, 2014) and the focus of this paper is mapping those becomings, 'where something new is created out of something given' (Ruffalo, 2009: 304) in lives where gender and sexual violence is commonplace.

Through the narrative interviews of valleys' girls Sharman (Project 1) and Mo (Project 2) we try to locate moments when queer becomings enable girls to connect to assemblages which enable them to survive their everyday lives, and when more expansive becomings come into view that connect to assemblages that, even if not fully realized, 'throw us forward into other relations of becoming and belonging' (Probyn, 1996: 59). Working creatively with the data we get a glimpse of 'the real as energies, events, [and] impacts that pre-exist and function both before and beyond, as well as within, representation' (Grosz, 2011: 85). This involves us making what Barad (2007) would call 'agential cuts' in our data, where we might pause to connect to historical affects and vital materialities (Bennett, 2010). In these moments, we glimpse at how live and dead matter, affect, memory and history entangle to 'enrich, and complicate our understanding of the subject, its interior, and what the subject can know' (Grosz, 2011: 86).

Queer becomings as survival

'My life has been really weird and not normal. It's just not safe for me' (Sharman, age 13).

Sharman describes her life as 'weird', 'not normal', explaining how 'many things have happened to me'. She talks about how she and her mum had to move away from her violent father when she was little and stay off the Internet so he couldn't 'track her down'; when her mother's friend got injured by a train; and when she was physically attacked by nine boys from her primary school, who 'came onto' her in a car park, leaving her badly shaken, with scars on her shoulder and elbow. Mo's interview is also replete with stories of not 'fitting in' and of broken bodies, bodies in pain and bodies that hurt.

She talks about her battle with long-term bullying for a physical disability that becomes visible to others when she runs; her uncle who crashed his car and died in his early 20s; her mum's ex-boyfriend who suffered from severe depression, and after multiple suicide attempts, died from an overdose of pills and alcohol.

In sum, both Sharman and Mo shared experiences of being directly or indirectly confronted with having to manage and negotiate physical violence in hetero-relationship cultures in the home (Sharman), in their extended families (Mo), in their peer cultures and in their encounters with local known and unknown boys and men in public space.[2] Where other girls in their year group who were enduring similar forms of violence, and would talk about having to 'watch yourself...you've got to worry all the time' and/or were 'not eating', 'cutting' themselves or 'getting off their heads' to manage and cope with the often unbearable and overwhelming feelings of being trapped and feeling unsafe, Mo and Sharman were connecting to and creating Other attachments.

We were struck with how the girls' stories were interlaced and enlivened with creative affective practices which afforded girls a different way of being and belonging.Sharman tells us that while she has close friends who are girls *and* boys, her 'three best friends are boys':

> My best friends are Josh, Andrew and Daniel. We are just really close. Josh sort of stuck up for me when I got beaten up and it was, I just know um, we are really friendly and close.

While Josh offers closeness through a protection-safety assemblage Sharman connects with other assemblages, in which she traverses gendered territories, captured below in her descriptions of sartorial experimentation with her best friend Andrew. Prompted by the photo we used to represent bedroom cultures, she states:

> Sharman: *The wardrobe is a good one because me and my friends always try on clothes from each others' wardrobes and borrow each other's clothes.*
> INT: *Is that with the boys as well?*
> Sharman: *Yeah...well I had a sleep over and I invited some of the boys. My mother didn't mind because she knew we were just friends, and my best friend Andrew, he tried on one of my dresses, and we put my mother's wig on him. It was fun [...] we dressed Andrew up in my glittery dress, he tried on some eyeliner as well.*
> KM: *Sounds really good fun.*
> *[...]*
> Sharman: *I go to their house and they put their tracksuit bottoms on me.*

Sharman seems to demonstrate not only an ability to switch back and forth between groups of girls and boys, but also in ways that playfully ruptured the normalized boundaries of binary gendered social worlds. She was one of the few girls in both research projects who managed to forge and sustain close relationships with boys that were not so swiftly heterosexualized in boyfriend-girlfriend assemblages (Renold, 2013).

Her story is one of capture and release, where for every violent assemblage she becomes entangled in, there is another assemblage just around the corner that she connects with and which we see as affectively holding, protecting and nurturing Sharman in ways that perhaps enable her to survive and manage a series of tragedies. Indeed, on being asked at the end of the interview if there is anything else she would like to talk about concerning living in Cwm Dyffryn, she chooses an incredibly powerful visual image of a wedding dress on fire:

> *Sharman: There was a woman who burnt her wedding dress for some reason*
> *INT: Did she burn it where you could all see?*
> *Sharman: [nods] Mmm. Where I live is a bull-ring, a big patch of green ... she*
> *got paper, her wedding album and lit it on fire and she chucked her dress in.*
> *It was weird!*

Sharman could have picked on any number of events, but it was the burning of the wedding dress and wedding album that came forward at this moment. For us, this image not only viscerally captures the affective force of compulsory hetero-relationships that we have been mapping, but simultaneously operates as a spectacular moment of rupture and survival, a leitmotif throughout Sharman's interview. Indeed the luminous 'fire – wedding dress – album – bullring' assemblage when seen in the context of the often violent forces through which compulsory coupledom is experienced in valleys life (and a regular refrain in Sharman's interview) may be reflected on by Sharman as a 'weird' witnessing. But, in that moment, in the intra-active space of the interview, perhaps it operates as and opens up a moment of queer becoming, promoting what Amit Rai (cited in Puar, 2007: 208) calls 'affective confusion' – a confusion that 'allows for new affects, and thus new politics to emerge' – and helping Sharman navigate her own 'not normal' life.

Mo lives with her dad, her six-month-old baby sister, her 20-year-old stepsister, whom she shares a bedroom with, and a large collection of reptiles. Mo spends most of her time and every weekend with her best friend Alys and her family: 'I basically live there ... she's got a better lifestyle than me'. She tells us that Alys has never met her family and she likes to keep it that way: 'I don't really want her to meet them. I mean if I had a choice, I wouldn't either'. Mo's closest relationships are with girls and she forges close dyadic girl friendships. Towards the end of the individual interview, she brings out a journal that she keeps in her school bag and that she says she takes with her 'everywhere'. It contains thought bubbles and scribbles, poems she has written, song lyrics she has copied or made up, all of which are illustrated with decorative and elaborate swirls. I read them out and Mo turns the pages:

> *'Don't look at a couple or boy and girl and think that is what I want too'.*
>
> *'For all you know they could be in the middle of a break up or even a divorce'.*
>
> *'If love seems so happy why does it always end in tears'.*
>
> *'Some people say that you can't live without love. I think that Oxygen is more important'.*
>
> *'Friends are like balloons. Once you let them go you can't get them back, so I am going to tie you to my heart so I never lose you'.*

Each quote puts a question mark around the assumptions that others make on the meanings, practices and affects of love, romance and coupledom. Mo troubles the appearance of the 'happy couple', the desire for hetero-relationships, and problematizes love as a panacea or as the elixir of life. The most positive of romantic attachments is Mo's quote about her best friend Alys. While love-in-relationship is hauled over the coals, cross-examined and critiqued, love-in-friendship, while fragile, is worth investing in, and draws in those affective 'ties that bind'.

Mo's queer becomings seem to connect not to aspirations of social mobility for a better life that other girls articulated (see Ivinson & Renold, 2013a), but for life itself. Love in hetero-relationships is entangled with divorce and death. She replaces oxygen with love, and relocates the attachment of love in (hetero)romance to love in friendship, maybe not because she is trying to stay clear from compulsory coupledom to secure a better future, but (or and) because hetero-relationships bring physical and economic collateral damage and trauma. What we find most compelling is how these queer becomings materialize in her journal, which she carries with her wherever she goes, and which perhaps help her to survive everyday life – to breathe a little. This is a queerness which not only departs from identitarian politics, by depriveleging binary oppositions between queer and non-queer subjects, it also moves away from a knowable-in-advance queerness as dissenting, resistant or alternative. Our attention is on what queer becomings in assemblages 'do', and for us this involves paying attention as much to the textual quotes in Mo's journal as it does to the affective resonance of how it feels to carry a journal, in a bag, every day, that touches your body, that you can bring out, flick through, play with, scribble on, be scribbled on, share and keep private, to your friends, to a researcher.

Indeed, it is in mapping the affective practices of how the vitality of matter (Bennett, 2010) entangles in the making of queer becomings that we turn our attention to next. This, as Puar (2007: 204) argues, necessitates a creative and 'affective analyses that approaches queernesses that are unknown or not cogently knowable, that are in the midst of becoming, that do not immediately and visibly signal themselves as insurgent, oppositional or transcendent'. This approach to queerness is a departure from the more visible becomings in the data above, such as the burnt wedding dress, cross-dressing and naming and shaming the pain and violence of compulsory heterosexuality. Let us dive further into the material becomings of water-filled dreams and muddy encounters.

Queer becomings as lines of flight

We continue with the stories from Sharman and Mo to consider, in their talk of mud (Sharman) and mermaids and water (Mo), what Berlant and Edelman (2013: 49), drawing on Bollas, refer to as a 'stretching out to figure things out'. This extending out is a meeting of Other attachments via an entanglement of matter, movement and becoming otherwise, but always where 'new orientations and modes of attention and extension exist alongside their old formulas' (p. 25). In our analysis below we attend to how bodies and their becomings congeal with mud and flow in water, and consider these as agency assemblages which bring forth what Bennett (2010, 118) writes about as 'active becomings' whose fusions birth 'a creative not-quite-human force capable of producing the new'. We begin with Sharman and the joy of rolling in mud.

Joy-ful dirt and mud-dling through

> The girl, Maggie, blossomed in a mud puddle ... playing and fighting with gamins in the street, dirt disguised her. Attired in tatters and grime, she went unseen.
>
> (Crane, Maggie: A girl of the streets, 1893)

Sharman's interview was animated with vivid and visceral descriptions of seeking out, and playing in mud. Being with boys, moving the way they do, at speed, always at the threshold of risk, and most of all, getting dirty were expressed with pure delight:

Yeah. Get my hoodie on, get my tracksuit, old trainers, not my new ones and go out in the mud. Don't bother about my hair and makeup ... we go up the country park, or anywhere where it's muddy [...] we go like, 'I feel like rolling in mud', and then we go rolling! [...] We make mud slides and slide down them, get mud all down our backs and we sort of throw mud at each other, it's FUN! We are like, 'where can I find MUD'.

[...]

KM: (starts raining outside) *Look at that rain. You're just looking at the mud aren't you? I can see the glint in your eye. Everyone else is going 'oh no it's raining', and you're going 'oh yes, lots of mud'.*

[…]

Sharman: Me and the boys try and go down there [skatepark] at least once a week. It's fun … when it's wet it's the BEST. You slip … you slip and slide down the bottom into the puddles.

[…]

KM: Does your mum mind you coming back covered in mud?

Sharman: No, as long as I sort of, because we got a curtain in the front door, because the front door is glass, because my dressing gown is over the coat hanger, I take off my clothes and put my dressing gown on, then I will put them in the wash. As long as I do that, I'm all right.

Iris Marion Young (2005: 44) writes about how girls struggle to live as mere bodies, and how they 'must take a distance from and exist in discontinuity with her body'. She adds that for a girl to 'open her body in free, active, open extension' is to 'invite objectification' and this 'objectifying regard' is 'what keeps her in her place' (Young, 2005: 44). This hesitancy and objectification, mingled with the threat of capture and attack were assemblages which seemed to still girls' movements (see Ivinson & Renold, 2013a, 2014). However, throwing off the materiality of girl ('don't bother about hair and make-up'), being-boy and becoming-mud, affords Sharman (like Maggie) with a 'disguise' that wards off heterosexual attack and sexual sub/objectification, and the very real danger of being-girl. She throws, rolls, slides around in and thoroughly congeals with all things muddy without hesitancy, living with the full force of what (else) her body and what (else) mud can do. Moreover, the environment intra-acts. Tapping rain on the windows sonically penetrates the space, and perhaps propels more talk about how 'wet is best' for 'sliding into muddy puddles'. A further assemblage is recalled conjuring skatepark-bowl-rain-mud-sliding bodies. Like Maggie, Sharman blossoms, and Kate (researcher) picks up on the joy-ful intensity in the telling.

The topological and spatial dimension of material (muddy) becomings are brought into being when Kate asks about whether Sharman's mum manages her mud-play and we become attuned to the flow of dirt into the (non-muddy) domestic space of the home. It is here where we want to pause and make an 'agential cut' (Barad, 2007) in our analysis about the affective historical traces that perhaps surface in the vitality of matter. Mary Douglas (1966/2002) theorizes dirt as 'matter out of place'. For the ex-mining community coal dust above ground had its place, on the clothes, hair and skin of the coal miners. On and engrained in men's bodies, dirt signified precarious labour, productivity, masculinity and hardship. In contrast, and more ambivalently, for girls and women, coal dust/dirt on bodies was only *matter in place* when girls and women were working in the mines. However, once they were prevented from doing so by Acts that drew upon discourses of sexual purity and modesty to create a binary division of women's (above ground) and men's labour (below ground), coal dust on women's bodies became *matter out of place* (see Renold & Ivinson, 2014).

The affective traces of matter out of place (e.g. mud on the girl body) and the rhythm of miners stripping at the threshold of the domestic space resonate for us in Sharman's talk about changing into her dressing gown and putting her clothes into the wash. This contemporary assemblage connects us to historical assemblages of how dirt on women's bodies enabled them to disguise themselves as men to work in the pits, and simultaneously trapped them in domestic drudgery in the endless cleaning and scrubbing. For Sharman, we see her connecting to the vitality of dirt on her body, in assemblage after assemblage, that affords protection and a line of flight that connects to the specific affective history of miners' bodies – which when dirty, were productive bodies, enabling communities to survive (and sometimes prosper). As we have argued elsewhere (Ivinson & Renold, 2013a), habitual practices associated with the history of places carry affects that are often experienced unconsciously through bodily rhythms. We thus see Sharman traversing not *any* hetero-gendered binary, but a specific classed heterogendered binary rooted in place and time. This is not Sharman becoming boy or Sharman as phallic girl (Renold & Ringrose, 2011), rather a series of historically situated queer becomings in the dynamic interplay of assemblages that propel her forward, to both confront and reorient away from adversity. We feel similar reroutings in becomings in Mo's mermaid dreams and water talk.

Mermaid dreams and the vitality of 'being in water'

The landscape of Wales is rich in lakes, rivers and wells and the south Wales valleys are no exception. Indeed, they are well known for their wild-swimming opportunities, with many new pools and lakes constructed on or around pits that have closed down. Our interviews with young people include many stories of jumping in rivers (night and day), splashing and swimming en masse, sometimes up to 40 young people at a time, in the many lakes in and around Cwm Dyfryn. Other young people enjoyed solitary swimming in local isolated remote pools, connecting to the pastime of grandparents and great-grandparents who bathed and, importantly, washed their bodies and clothes in the very same pools. We return to the affective traces of the historical practices and legends of lakes and the magical tales of mythical water-bodies below. First, we begin with Mo's connection to water and her mermaid dreams.

Early on in the interview, Mo describes inhabiting a 'lighthouse crib' in one of her favourite video games, 'Saints Row'.[3] She talks about how she was 'swimming for hours' because she 'didn't have a boat to get into it'. Swimming and water-body talk enters the interview space next after vivid descriptions of literally struggling to keep afloat as she relates how she has navigated her way through a series of tragedies, of death, poverty and loss. It enters in relation to the activities that she would like to do more of, but is economically constrained to realize:

> Mo: *I have always wanted to swim with dolphins, always yeah, I always used to dream that I was a mermaid as well, I still do actually, that I am a mermaid*
> ER: *Do you? How wonderful!*

Mo continues to talk about a mermaid in the computer game 'Dead or Alive 4' where at each level the player can unlock a short video. She describes one of the videos:

> Mo: *There is this girl on it and she, she is, for starters you are on a beach and she is a mermaid and she is swimming with her fish, her pet fish and she gets caught in a net and then she wakes up and she is in her dream.*
> ER: *And you dream of being a mermaid?*
> Mo: *I used to yeah but I am like, oh no it is not going to happen is it (listen).*
> [...]
> ER: *What is it about mermaids that you love?*
> Mo: *I don't know, I just like water.*
> ER: *Yeah, OK.*
> Mo: *Swimming in water.*
> ER: *So you like swimming as well?*
> Mo: *Yeah.*
> ER: *What is it that you enjoy about swimming?*
> Mo: *I don't know. I just like being in water.*
> [...]
> Mo: *Being in water is probably the best really.*

Digital mermaids trapped in their own dreams seem to connect us to Mo's own unrealizable post-human mermaid becomings ('Oh no, it's not going to happen'), which enliven swimming talk, and the simple and pure pleasure of 'being in water'. To assist us with this water-body assemblage, we draw on Probyn's (1996: 41) analysis of Carol Anshaw's novel about swimming and desire:

> 'Swimming works only when the swimmer and the water become other than their separate functions. The body translates matter into energy that becomes velocity...legs pumping, arms pulling, back straining, muscles melding' (ibid). The body becomes a fully functioning part of the machinery of movement and through physical activity the swimmer 'leaves herself behind'.

Could it be that the corporeality of swimming, of 'being in water', enables at that moment a transcendence or 'singularity' (Deleuze & Guattari, 1987) when Mo, the swimmer, becomes 'what she can do'? We glimpse the intensity in the simple repetition of being a body in water, a becoming that 'materializes desire as that productive force which compels a theory of belonging' (Probyn, 1996: 41). And while part of this belonging is an entanglement with a digital assemblage of mermaids and lighthouse cribs full of life-affirming and life-destroying affects (enhanced by the game's title, 'Alive and Dead'), it is also a belonging entangled with affective traces surfacing from the past. We pause one final time to make a further agential cut, and locate what else mermaids and water can do in local myth and legend.

Wales has a rich Celtic history of lake legends. Gathering over 40 different legends, Fernandez's (2012) thesis on lake mythology opens up a world of water-maidens, magic and ghostly happenings that connect directly to local disasters (e.g. floods and fires). Of particular interest for Mo's mermaid and water-body becomings are the fairy marriages and the healing properties of water. Fernandez describes how Welsh lakes are replete with myths of encounters with lake-bound fairies, and the most common and regular narrative is of broken water-maiden marriages with man mortals who break their promises and trap the water-maidens in the lakes forever, such as Lyn-y-forwyn, the 'Maiden's Lake' in Ferndale (Rhondda Cynon Taff), home of the 'enchantress Nelferch'.[4] Mo's trapped mermaid, and her journal of the trauma and loss of broken hetero-relationships, connects with these legends. However, the vitality of her own body-in-water, connects to other powerful Welsh lake legends of the magical healing properties of water and water worship. As Fernandez argues, 'lakes and water bodies were much more than a place to live or fish...water had a magic component...a mysterious power and attributes...that could cure diseases' (7). We connect these 'magical' aquatic forces to the freedom that perhaps Mo feels in her body, restoring movement and speed to legs that are dis-abled on land (like a mermaid), and where her water-body can move and flow like the swirls in her journal, a vitality that enables her to breathe.

The final group of water assemblage legends are the pre-industrial catastrophe legends which link to real floods and natural disasters, where lakes hide sunken or lost lands and settlements and villages, the majority of which are to be found in south Wales (Fernandez, 2012: 17). With lakes and pools in the valleys often created from the unproductive open pits that were dewatered during mining (aka 'pit lakes[5]'), swimming in lakes connect to historical legacies below ground, and of the grinding instabilities and historically sedimented poverty of post-industrial Wales. These catastrophe legends perhaps connect to and entangle with Mo's shame of poverty, of not sharing her peer's 'lifestyle' and threatening always to reterritorialize and trap her becomings and any sustained line of flight which being-in water might temporarily lighten.

Conclusion: Undoing queer and the promise of diffractive methodologies for young sexualities research

'We need to understand in more explicit terms how newness, change, the unpredictable, are generated, and what mechanisms are available, perhaps below the level of the social, to explain the very unpredictability of social and political change' (Grosz, 2011: 86).

This chapter develops our previous attempts to radicalize sexuality by exploring what a girl body can do, become and bear in communities where sedimented heterogender roles inherited from the industrial past surface, invade and grate painfully alongside the stifling and often simultaneous emergence of becoming otherwise. Our aim has not been to categorize sexuality as an identity or an act. Rather, our approach refutes the trappings of a unifying identity-based and anthropomorphic understanding of sexuality that dominates policy, practice and research in the fields of education and childhood/youth studies. In research which does foreground a pre-known and measurable sexuality, less emphasis is given to interrogating the potentiality that emerges in the dynamic relational web of bodies and things where Other attachments to the more-than-human are tried on and forged, albeit momentarily (Berlant & Edelman, 2013).

Indeed, we began the chapter by describing teen girls' entanglement in patriarchal assemblages of gender and sexual violence in local peer cultures, family life and wider community practices. Here, we illustrated how valleys girls who act out of step with local practices of heteronormative femininity (e.g. refusing to couple up) are always in danger of upsetting the very fabric of life in the community, and, moreover, that being out of step could be theorized as a queer endeavour. However, this is not a queerness that promises 'consistency, stability and normalization' through discourses of inclusion and tolerance, but a practice of undoing, that dislodges sex/uality from its 'normative function as the mechanism of emotional cohesion that sustains aggressive heteronormativity' (Berlant & Edelman, 2013: 13). The moments we map with our diffractive approach in Mo and Sharman's interviews are more akin to a life force that is pulsating and vibrating, and which we saw as enabling girls to survive valleys life. It is also perhaps no surprise that these moments foreground non-human matter and materiality, given the overwhelming and often violent force of the social.

Indeed, it is the micro moments and experiments made by young people that sometimes provide glimpses of freedom – proto possibilities that emerge as becomings. By glimpsing these often unrecognized potentialities we can begin 'to understand in more explicit terms how newness, change, [and] the unpredictable, are generated' (Grosz, 2011: 86) so that we are not only able to map the sexual discriminations and violences in young people's lives, but also the inventiveness through which they survive and momentarily transcend.

Notes

1. This publication is based on research supported by the Wales Institute of Social and Economic Research, Data and Methods (WISERD) funded by the UK Economic and Social Research Council (Grant number: RES-576-25-0021) and the Higher Education Funding Council for Wales. The main research team included: Gabrielle Ivinson, Emma Renold, Kate Moles and Mariann Martsin. All place names and participants' names are pseudonyms.
2. The pseudonym Mo is short for Morforwyn (Welsh translation: mermaid).
3. 'Saints Row' is an action adventure video game series based around the storylines of a gang called the 'Third Three Saints'. It contains high levels of violence, black comedy, parody and fantasy. See http://en.wikipedia.org/wiki/Saints_Row_ (series).
4. RCT website on 'myths and legends': 'When he broke a vow not to ask her about her past she left him penniless and aged far more than the years of their marriage. Her spirit haunts the lake to this day, palpable in the gloom where steep cliffs shut out the sun from the shore'.
5. Pit lakes form when the dewatering pumps are removed and where ground water and surface water seeps into the pit, creating lakes.

References

Alaimo, S., & Hekman, S. (Eds.) (2008) *Material feminisms*. Bloomington: Indiana University Press.

Barad, K. (2007) *Meeting the universe halfway: Quantum physics and the entanglement of matter and meaning*. Durham, NC and London: Duke University Press.

Bennett, J. (2010) *Vibrant matter: A political ecology of things*. Durham, NC and London: Duke University Press.

Berlant, L., & Edelman, L. (2013) *Sex, or the unbearable*. Durham, NC and London: Duke University Press.

Braidotti, R. (2002/2005) *Metamorphoses: Towards a material theory of becoming*. Cambridge: Polity Press.

Braidotti, R. (2006) *Transpositions: On nomadic ethics*. Cambridge: Polity Press.

Braidotti, R. (2012) *Nomadic theory: The portable Rosi Braidotti*. New York, Chichester, West Sussex: Columbia University Press.

Braidotti, R. (2013) *The posthuman*. Polity Press: Cambridge.

Coleman, R. (2008) *The becoming of bodies: Girls, image, experience*. Manchester: Manchester University Press.

Crane, S. (1893) *Maggie: A girl of the streets*. Retrieved from http://classiclit.about.com/ library/bl-etexts/scrane/bl-scrane-mag-5.html

Deleuze, G., & Guattari, F. (1987) *A thousand plateaus: Capitalism and schizophrenia* B. Massumi (trans.). Minneapolis: University of Minnesota Press.

Douglas, M. (1966/2002) *Purity and danger: An analysis of concepts of pollution and taboo*. London: Routledge and Kegan Paul.

Egan, D. (2013) *Becoming sexual: A critical appraisal of the sexualisation of girls*. Oxford, UK and Boston MA: Polity Press.

Fernandez, C. (2012) *Legends of the lakes of Wales: Thematic classification and analysis*. MSc Thesis. Trinity St. Davids, University of Wales. http://dspace.tsd.ac.uk/dspace/bitstream/10412/252/1/CARLES%20FERNANDEZ.pdf, Accessed 6 June 2015.

Fox, N., & Alldred, P. (2013) The sexuality-assemblage: Desire, affect, anti-humanism. *Sociological Review*, 61 (4), 769–789.

Gonick, M., & Gannon, S. (2014) (Eds.) *Becoming girl: Collective biography and the production of girlhood*. Toronto: Women's Press.

Gowlett, C., & Rasmussen, M. L. (2014) The cultural politics of queer theory in education research. *Discourse: Studies in the Cultural Politics of Education*, 35 (3), 331–334.

Grosz, E. (2011) *Becoming undone: Darwinian reflections on life, politics and art*. Durham, NC: Duke University Press.

Guatarri, F. (1995) *Chaosmosis: An ethico-aesthetic paradigm* Paul Baines (Trans.). Sydney: Power Publications.

Hughes, C., & Lury, C. (2013) Re-turning feminist methodologies: From a social to an ecological epistemology. *Gender and Education*, 25 (6), 786–799.

Ivinson, G., & Renold, E. (2013a) Valleys' girls: Re-theorising bodies and agency in a semi-rural, post-industrial locale. *Gender and Education*, 25 (6), Special issue: Feminist Materialisms and Education, 704–721.

Ivinson, G., & Renold, E. (2013b) Subjectivity, affect and place: Thinking with Deleuze and Guattari's body without organs to explore a young teen girl's becomings in a post-industrial locale. *Subjectivity*, 6 (4), 369–390.

Juelskjaer, M. (2013) Gendered subjectivities of spacetimematter. *Gender and Education*, 25 (6), 754–768.

Lombard, N. (2013) Young people's temporal and spatial accounts of gendered violence. *Sociology*, 47 (6), 1136–1151.

Lombard, N. (2015) *Young people's understandings of men's violence towards women*. Surrey: Ashgate.

Lury, C., & Wakeford, N. (2012) *Inventive methods: The happening of the social*. London: Routledge.

Moore, H. L. (2011) *Still life: Hopes, desires and satisfactions*. Cambridge: Polity Press.

Puar, J. (2007) *Terrorist assemblages: Homonationalism in queer times*. Durham, NC: Duke University Press.

Probyn, E. (1996) *Outside belongings*. London: Routledge.

Renold, E. (2013) *Boys and girls speak out: A qualitative study of children's gender and sexual cultures* (age 10–12). Cardiff: Cardiff University.

Renold, E., & Ringrose, J. (2011) Schizoid subjectivities: Re-theorising teen-girls' sexual cultures in an era of sexualisation. *Journal of Sociology*, 47 (4), 389–409.

Renold, E., & Ivinson, G. (2014) Horse-girl assemblages: Towards a post-human cartography of girls' desire in an ex-mining valleys community, *Discourse: Studies in the Cultural Politics of Education*, 35 (3), 361–376

Ringrose, J. (2013) *Postfeminist education?: Girls and the sexual politics of schooling*. London: Routledge.

Ruffalo, D. (2009) *Post queer politics*. Surrey UK: Ashgate.

Taylor, C., & Ivinson, G. (2013) Material feminisms: New directions for education. *Gender and Education*, 25 (6), 665–670.

Tolman, D. (2002) *Dilemmas of desire: Teenage girls talk about sexuality*. Cambridge, Massachusetts, New York: Harvard University Press.

Walkerdine, V. (2010) Communal beingness and affect: An exploration of trauma in an ex industrial community. *Body & Society*, 16 (1), 91–116.

Walkerdine, V. (2013 iFirst) Using the work of Felix Guattari to understand space, place, social justice, and education. *Qualitative Inquiry.* doi:
10.1177/1077800413502934.

Walkerdine, V., & Jimenez, J. (2012) *Gender, work and community after deindustrialization: A psychosocial approach to affect.* Basingstoke: Palgrave Macmillan.

Walkerdine, V., Lucey, H., & Melody, J. (2001) *Growing up girl: Psychosocial explorations
of gender and class.* Buckingham: Palgrave MacMillan.

Young, M. I. (2005) *On female body experience: 'Throwing like a girl' and other essays.*
Oxford: Oxford University Press.

Part IV

Young Sexualities and the Cultural Imaginary

16
A Doll Has No Holes: On the Queerness of Brazilian Children in Xuxa

Diego Costa

A pink spaceship descends into a Brazilian television studio. A 5-foot 10-inch blonde woman is inside the spacecraft. She is wearing knee-high boots, a short, tight-fitting ensemble and pigtails. The landing of the shuttle is prolonged so as to maximize the euphoria of the awaiting children below it, non-paid non-actors who chant, scream and cry as they look up at the giant woman inside the pink blob of a shuttle, which is accented by enormous red lips (surely the spacecraft's windows).

Xuxa [Shoo-sha] is too tall to be ordinarily female, too white to be ordinarily Brazilian. Her teeth couldn't be whiter, her skin couldn't be paler, and her hair couldn't be blonder, or finer. As reported by the press, the children are often shocked to find out that Xuxa, the Aryan alien stepping out of the pink spaceship, actually pees.

The children on the set don colourful pompoms and handmade banners expressing their unwavering devotion. They burst into tears in anticipation of Xuxa's extended exiting. The excitement is so manic you would think Xuxa's landing were a rather rare affair akin to a Virgin Mary appearance, or the apparition of a comet. Yet, this scene, and its continuation, repeated itself every single morning, from Monday to Saturday, for five consecutive hours on Brazilian television from 1986 until 1992.

Gilberto Felisberto Vasconcellos describes Xuxa as an *anti-housewife whore* ('rapariga ante-dona de casa'), the perfect embodiment of the family's fantasies: the one who will do to father all the sexual things the housewife won't (in *child drag*, nonetheless), a role model for daughter's heterosexual dreams of replacement and incestuous seduction, and something for the heterosexual son-in-training to look forward to, as his turn will come sooner than later. This leaves the queer child, or the child's queerness, without recognition, but certainly not without a place – albeit not a readymade one.

259

The sartorial in/of Xuxa is a multivalent currency, able to *prop up* a variety of identificatory and sexual investments from children and adults, and needs to be analysed in its potential modularity and resignification. I here, then, fall back into the place of the queer child watching Xuxa in my native Brazil in the 1980s in order to flesh out such an analysis.

If the father can fondle Xuxa with his very eyes in the present, in her massive entirety made visible by the television screen (we first see her from below, towering over the hysteric children, as though we could peek at her underwear), the children's investment seem linked to a deferral (I can have her later, I can look like her later), until they are able to purchase Xuxa's products (her line of clothes, sandals and knee-high boots for kids) and experience her erotic promises in the present, in the flesh, justified by the ludic that makes up Xuxa's world. But if the father's perception can function as a type of fondling in the present, the queer child can also touch Xuxa, the child *tout court* can also get in touch with queerness through Xuxa.

Xuxa's toys are geared towards little girls who can make the deferred whitening eroticness of the Xuxa experience a (mock-up) reality not only for themselves, but for the adults (the fathers) looking at them – through consumption of her products. The heterosexual boys-in-training are left to consume Xuxa through the father's visual investments (as in Freud's theory of perception, in which the eyes are basically tentacles), as well as through a sublimation of, and strategized re-encounter with, the pleasures of looking at her not as a reminder of the ideal bodies that might soon be available for their sexual feasting, but for the clothes themselves. It turns out Xuxa isn't just apt material for the pleasures of femininity by proxy of queer boys, but for soon-to-be heterosexual boys' falling backward onto/into/through queerness as well: the queerness of Xuxa's clothes, whose gaze is largely permitted as she is *the only thing to look at* (in morning television). Looking at Xuxa, as though forced to give in to her feminine excesses, the boy is able to take in the pleasures of the sartorial without compromising his masculine position – in the eyes of the adult or the nation.

A doll without orifices and the sexual logic of (colonial) intercourse

Freud describes Leonardo da Vinci's drawings as 'props' for his anatomical investigations, an alibi-practice that enables other kinds of practices and discoveries (Freud, 1957). Jean Laplanche describes sublimation, which appears as a doing 'something else' with sexual energy, sometimes in opposition, sometimes working together with sexuality, as an instinct of 'excessive strength [that] triggers the earliest childhood sexual theories,' the first of which revolves around 'Where do babies come from?' Not from Xuxa's pink spaceship, nor from her very body without cavities (Laplanche, 1984: 20). Laplanche gives the example of the mother's pregnancy with another child as igniting that puzzling question. It provokes an investigation linked to a fantasy of construction faced with the parents' refusal to come up with an adequate answer, establishing a connection between sublimation in the form of having-to-know and 'turning back' (Laplanche, 1984: 17).

Xuxa's erotic anxiety-soothing powers, her holelessness – her myth takes away from her the possibility of pores and orifices (though she comes out of a pink one every morning on TV), may soothe similarly primal fantasies of origin for Brazilians. As Vasconcellos argues, the first Brazilian was mix-raced, the child of a European father and an *Ameraba* (Native Brazilian) mother; perhaps not unlike the child Xuxa would have had with legendary soccer player Pelé, 'the black millionaire celebrity' she dated before rising to stardom (Simpson, 1993: 32).[1] A central part of the genesis of Xuxa's myth (of holelessness) is that she was a virgin, at age 17, when she started going out with Pelé, who was 40, and allegedly refused to deflower her, leading Xuxa, whose real name is Maria da Graça, to lose her virginity with someone else first, and then go back to Pelé. For Amelia Simpson, their relationship offers a 'proof of immunity to racism, which then functions as a license to exploit the appetite for the blond and blue-eyed ideal in a country with the largest black population outside Africa' (Simpson, 1993: 32).

Although the primal question that both produced and terrorized the first Brazilian child, *Who is my father?* cannot be claimed to be exclusively Brazilian, such a child's question was sustained by a very specific narrative. From the beginning, this child's question was not just triggered by a genealogical-ontological curiosity, but brought forth by a colonial act of rape. A series of questions torment the first Brazilian child as he wonders about the mother–father coitus in that April of the year 1500, visualizing, or rather constructing with his very eyes-cum-hands the *mise en scène* of the nation's primal scene.

Was it love at first sight? Or did they leave it for the morning after? Was there no love, only sex? If my father spoke a language that my mother did not understand, how did their communication take place? Or was there copulation without linguistic communication? Voices, gestures, moans, whispers, yet no dialogue to speak of? Was there only a transmission of the signifier, but not of the signified: each one's words addressed to their own selves, or to the sky of Bahia's coastline? (Simpson, 1993: 45)[2]

This child is thus not only a 'ballet dancer' owing to the 'ludic disposition' such not-knowing (yet knowing) must have inaugurated, as Vasconcellos has it, but an *accident* (Simpson, 1993: 45).[3] An accident which perhaps Xuxa would have avoided, either because a doll without orifices would never get pregnant, the child wouldn't have been produced (he is dead from the beginning), or because in the event that she did get pregnant, her biological aesthetics would have matched the European father's, at which point the child could signify an effect of mutual parental Desire, not a colonializing rape.

A fantasy of Xuxa as the original mother (nature) would certainly work to abate anxieties around what Christopher Bollas calls 'the sexual logic of intercourse'. Xuxa's dollish impenetrability, akin to the not-yet-deflowered young girls watching her show, would have meant the child no longer has to deal with the problematic (racial) mismatch of the parents' intercourse. Despite the history of violence inherent to this set of symbolic parents (the original Brazilian non-family), 'intercourse' appears as a disruptive key figure in 'any' three-year-old child's sexual epiphany that, 'apart from Jesus (or "the Holy Family"), the child did not enter existence through maternal immaculate conception' (Bollas, 2000: 169).

In this epistemological crisis the child realizes that instead of being the centre of the universe, she may actually just be 'an after-effect of parental sexual passion sought after for its own sake'. The crux of such narcissistic crisis represented by the notion of the 'intercourse', as opposed to some kind of divine alignment of the stars to produce a child God, is the idea that the self may be mere fallout from an act that actually wasn't meant to be *productive*, but merely *conducive*. This disruption takes the child away from his status of an effect of Desire and closer to a barebacking accident.

Reclaiming woman's skin

It wasn't until the 18th century that the investment in bodily exhibition became woman's business, reserving for men the labour of looking. The naturalization of ornate dress as a domain of woman guaranteed by the l/Law – juridical and symbolic – is, then, a relatively new process, and one filled with anxiety particularly for boys who must give up on the objects that have served as signs and substitutes for Mother, whereas girls (and a certain type of queer boy) don't. When Xuxa comes out, some of mother's properties that had to be given up as objects of desire fall back into the frame of possibilities for visual, tactile and erotic pleasure for any boy, no matter how conscious their fascination with femininity in the sartorial may be.

Of course, while boys may not be allowed to wear the clothing or speak about it, they do, in many ways, control it in their manifested resignation (but latent omnipresence). In this sense, Xuxa serves as the Mother who goes along with the child's *ludic disposition*, willing to *put on* and *model* the sartorial for him (Xuxa began her career as a fashion model, after all). This dynamic in Xuxa echoes one of the gender system's most basic naturalized fictions: the appearance of woman collapses the *look* with the (her)self as an unquestionable given. What is put on is read as skin – as if the costuming that renders her visible as woman were as natural and inevitable an effect of nature as an epidermis.

In the formation of man's self- display as unsheddable realness (while accoutrements make the woman, the non-detachability of the penis itself makes the man), there is nothing, really, to *take off* if there is nothing to *put on*; it is woman whose visible artifice renders her susceptible to loss. Xuxa fosters a reclaiming of what has been renounced by boys, the pleasures of the sartorial (coded as feminine), as, despite the specificities of one's Desire, the child is radically confronted with the clothing that (un)settles, while assuaging it. Xuxa's well documented relationship to nature – she repetitively claims that only children and animals ('*bichos*', a word dangerous close to '*bichas*', one of many Portuguese terms for 'faggots') understand her; that she has, like Michael Jackson, a zoo at home – helps seal the deal. When boys 'usurp' Xuxa's iconography, to use Winnicott's term, are they not usurping 'the mother's position and her seat or garments' (Winnicott, 1990: 85)?[4]

The queer boy is granted access to Xuxa through an imaginary usurping (rendered possible by the secretive extensions, and aims, of his *ludic disposition*) or through the literal stealing of the Xuxa products, or *props*, including a doll that is at least three times Barbie's size, that might belong to his sister(s). Without a symbolic system that accounts for his presence in the world, this is the queer boy's dynamic for life: usurping the Other's object through fantasy. The heterosexual(izing) Brazilian boy is here, then, able to enjoy Xuxa's/Woman's feminine *props* without getting blood on his hands owing to Xuxa's televisual omnipresence as electronic babysitter on the most watched network in Brazil, *Rede Globo*.

Under the aegis of omniscience

Xuxa's goodbye, five hours after her spectacular surfacing, is just as dramatic, extensive and ritualized as her arrival. The children's desperation in face of her departure is akin to a child's reading of a parent's going away as abandonment. Xuxa's farewell is an unbearable interruption like that of a dream, like that of intercourse. When her show is over, real life begins. The children bawl, they scream, they beg her to stay. They profess their love for her with gifts, pleading that the banners they hold with loving messages for Xuxa be read.

At this moment, Xuxa acts as though she has been put in a situation, in her own show, that is out of her control. She reads some of the banners with loving messages, often begging the director (of the show, and of Xuxa's career and finances), Marlene Mattos, rumoured to be Xuxa's lesbian lover – Xuxa is the body, Marlene is the head, the saying goes – to allow her to read more banners before she is forced to hop back into her pink spaceship. She asks, 'Marlene, one more banner, please.' And begs, 'Zoom in on that one, too, please, please.'

It is significant that while the children's pleading for this towering alien (m)Other to stay is directed at her very apparition, Xuxa's plea for the camera to show more banners is addressed to the disembodied authority of 'Marlene', whom no one gets to see. Without ever having seen Marlene, we know, from press accounts and gossip, what she looks like, and it's enough to scare us into accepting, and understanding, her controlling role: she is mannish, she is dark-skinned, she comes from the poor north-eastern part of Brazil; she is the anti-Xuxa.

If the children seem to be begging Xuxa-cum-Mummy to stay, Mummy's *coup de théâtre* involves her own pleading to Marlene-cum-Daddy's authoritative omnipresent-absence. The fact that Marlene is mannish, yet not a man, suggests another kind of queer usurpation here, of the masculine position, at the heart of Xuxa's worlding. Contrary to Winnicott's childrearing advice that the father be present 'at breakfast', for Colette Soler the father is much more present when he isn't actually there – and thus remains invulnerable to the eventual contradictions that grant him his status as father, risking an unmasking. If the father surrendered his clothes in the name of an irrevocable naturalization of his standing in the great masculine renunciation of the 18th century, as Silverman argues, by now his body can (must?) be safely taken out of view to guarantee and guard his position. Xuxa's world, then, dramatizes the heterosexual gender dynamic at its most basic as she parades around the stage bearing man's rejected skin, resignified as feminine skin, while Marlene, the man-like creator running the show, ventriloquizes the action without granting the audience her/his very materiality. Xuxa is probed; Marlene is safe (Soler, 2013).

A child is cumming

Very little has been said about Xuxa's bacchanal, and virtually nothing from the point of view of the child such bacchanal has helped to produce. For if stars are fabricated by a complex and contradictory network of signifiers – from the hypercontrolled concoction of her idealized image (her image *in theory*, we could say) to the non-diegetic images that befall alongside it (the image *in practice*), so are the children, the *baixinhos* ('small ones'), as Xuxa calls them (Dyer, 2003: 7.). Yet, since the position of the child qua child keeps her/him from speaking, or, rather, keeps us from listening, to talk about children is often to talk down to them, reiterating the very infantilizing fantasies (of inherent purity and innocence, for example) that have manufactured the figure of the child as we know it.

Xuxa's relationship to children has always been based on the refusal to treat them as *children*. Her refusal to use 'baby talk', addressing them as though they were adults, just physically smaller, was often read as a violence she performed against them.[5] Amelia Simpson's 1993 book *Xuxa: The Mega-Marketing of Gender, Race, and Modernity* remains the only lengthy academic text devoted to the Xuxa phenomenon. Simpson thoroughly contextualizes the glorious Xuxa years right before her decline (in the late 1990s, when she has a child of her own, demystifying her holelessness, and cuts her hair short), locating the star as the materialization of a perfect storm onto which Brazilians could project their fantasies of escape from that country's descent from a series of *coups d'état* into a hopeless socio-economic reality in the 1980s and 1990s.

But Simpson offers little nuance in her reading of Xuxa, which is mostly based on popular press accounts and interviews with the star. She often demonizes Xuxa as an emblematic cog in the machinery of Brazilian self-delusional fantasies of racial, gender and economic harmony, democracy and progress towards a First World-like modernity that promises happiness through consumption.

Simpson ignores not only the possibility for imaginary usurpation from the child producing and being produced by Xuxa, downplaying the child's own (queer) agency and overestimating Xuxa's, but also the ways her performance actually lends itself to such (queer) usurpations. The star is an agent of transcendence, but what of the (queer) child who doesn't coincide so hermetically with the heterocapitalist Brazilian project driven by Anglo-Saxon mimicry? What of the child who falls short, or behind, and is left to grow sideways, or in whatever other ways?

Serge Lebovici reminds us that *identification* is a way of resolving an infantile conflict. Identification in Oedipus, for example, involves 'being like' (Daddy) in order to have (Mummy, or someone like her). Given that a queer Oedipus would leave a child left out of a clear lining up of that being-and-having scheme, Xuxa's alienness could function as a signpost for *something else altogether*: a non-mummy, even an anti-mummy without orifices, *still* able to seduce Daddy – without leaving traces (which the child identifies as). Xuxa can appear, then, against her own project of post-colonial magnetism, as an assuaging figure for the violent schisms of childhood's queerness.

In reading Xuxa as a symptom for Brazil's post-colonial proclivities, Simpson never turns to the Brazilian child whose queer growth coincides with his/her country's own miraculous emergence from a *baixinho* in the 1980s and 1990s to a major global economic player in the 2000s, at which point Xuxa's star and virtual babysitting services are dismissed as grotesquely passé. Simpson follows the familiar way in which work that directly involves children fails to actually hear them, or make room for their presence as children, not as an adult fantasy of them.

Simpson, for instance, highlights the status quo-supporting contradictions that Xuxa symbolizes, and reiterates en masse, but doesn't pay attention to the way such child-effacing readings may also help produce retrograde ideas about the inherent purity of the child who arrives into the world only to get spoiled by a horrible system ailing with post-colonial inferiority complexes. In this logic, Xuxa would represent little new in the landscape of Brazil's fascination with a 'civilized' and 'modern' ideal of a nation based on hygienic fantasies of North American and European 'progress'; besides the primal anxieties around the origins of the first Brazilian owing to the unbearable ontological distance between his parents: the civilized European who raped the Native Brazilian woman to produce the un-Desired child that is *I*.

Brazil's eugenic ideal was packaged from mass consumption since the early days of cinema. The history of film in Brazil is often described as yet another kind of rape, with the invasion of 'the offices of large yankee companies' (Bicalho, 1993: 22) which monopolized movie distribution and exhibition after the First World War, and gave rise to several publications that specialized in the dissemination of feminine images produced abroad. It also helped create a national cinematographic industry that aimed to display a kind of Brazil that did away with undesirable elements that were incompatible with the images of modernity imported from the cinema of the 'civilized world'. This promotion of a whitewashed national image involved an assimilation of:

> the eugenic ideals accompanying the aesthetic standards of cinema of the United States and Europe, especially in regards to the 'Aryan' model of screen personalities (. . .) The nation should be represented on screen by the image of the pure, white woman, symbol of moral integrity as well as racial eugenics.
>
> (Bicalho, 1993: 24)

The child as the one who (already) knows

Part of Xuxa's stock defence against criticisms that she isn't pedagogical has always been that she has never intended to teach children, but to conduct the fun in their break from school. Interestingly, years after Xuxa's heyday, she is relegated to the role of the pedagogical master of ceremonies in a series of DVDs named *Xuxa Só Para Baixinhos* ('Xuxa Only for Little Ones', a play on the warning message printed across female nude magazines in Brazil, *Só Para Maiores*, or 'Only for Those 18 and Over'). By the time Xuxa turns to a baby talk aesthetic, in 2000 (eight years after *Xou da Xuxa* goes off the air), talking to children like babies, covering her now chubbier body and singing innocent songs that teach little kids how to count, she is largely regarded as a gauche clown living off a dead hysteria that has turned into a lukewarm niche market.

One of the greatest critical responses against Xuxa at her peak is that she spoiled an entire generation of kids by sexualizing them too early. The assumption here is that kids aren't inherently sexual when we know the opposite is true. We know this from looking and listening to children as children, both from a science-centric approach (even foetuses have erections and masturbate in the womb) and from the body of knowledge, theoretical and clinical, borne out of children's psychoanalysis. We can say that this logic (the sexual in the child) functions as one of psychoanalysis' main pillars. From Freud we can also surmise that the construction of a child's sexuality begins way before conception, through the symbolic inheritance (the history of the child's family and nation, for example) that predates the child's birth and will certainly serve as raw material for the constitution of his or her subjectivity.

Freud recognized not only babies' and children's ability to self-inflict pleasure, but their incredible investment in it as masturbatory, whether or not the corporal area of choice was genital. 'Thus the quality of the stimulus has more to do with producing the pleasurable feeling than has the nature of the part of the body concerned.' Here we clearly see the queerness of psychoanalysis as a mode of looking at children that recognizes not only their relationship to (sexual) pleasure as always there, but renders the entirety of the human body (and beyond) as potential sources, and objects, for such pleasure (Freud, 2000: 52, 49).[6]

We also know that not only are children sexual (they have, perform and are driven by a sexuality, even if they aren't having sex – although some are), but adults can take a roundabout paedophilic pleasure in looking at children, a pleasure that is put in motion by, for example, the very discussions about whether Xuxa, Mary Kay Letourneau or the latest Calvin Klein ads are doing the unthinkable and mixing childhood with sex.[7] Panic over the possibility of a sexual child, contradicted by the avid production of the *sexy child*, emblematizes a culture bent on presuming that sexuality comes from outside the child, imposing on him/her, always as an unspeakable violence, as though 'we' weren't all inextricable to a child-loving culture that projects the link between sexuality and the infantile into a perverse Other (the homosexual, the sexual predator, or Xuxa, for instance) so that it can 'save' the children from a sexual threat that could never come from ourselves, that would never be the founding condition for our own subjectivity.

We can think of Joon Oluchi Lee's 'The Joy of The Castrated Boy' as one intervention in the way the child's purity is guaranteed by his/her muteness. Lee structures his reading of Toni Morrison's novel *Sula* around and through the child (s)he once was. His selfcentric reparation attempt involves a rereading of his gender-assigned-at-birth, and policed thereafter at penalty of getting his 'pee-pee' cut off if he didn't 'stop acting like a girl and start being a boy', and whose favourite objects could only become part of his ludic disposition through usurpation. They included his little sister's beige coat ('which I wore once with a sash'), lipstick ('addicted from the moment I slathered my mother's on in bathroom secrecy') and 'books for girls, filled with love stories starring medusa-curled girls with huge galaxy for eyes, filled with stars and rainbows and tears, of happiness and depression'. (Lee, 2005).[8]

Lee's falling back into queer-childness for the purpose of critical analyses (among others) illustrates what Heather Love describes as 'feeling backward', a non-hagiographic scavenging of the (queerness of the) past (Love, 2009). It is also predicated on Kathryn Bond Stockton's concept of the *ghostliness* of the (always already) queer child: a child can only speak, or be heard, in remembrance (*re-member-ance*), in the precarious act of reappearance, *après coup* (Stockton, 2009).

Lee's deployment of the child's voice and sensorial experiences ('castration grew on me' [Lee, 2005: 36]) are evidently a redramatization of what was once inescapably lived in the flesh without the luxury of *becoming-adult* retrospect. While such inevitable strategy of producing knowledge is obvious in Lee, it becomes a different device, albeit triggered by a similar *disposition*, in G. Winston James's *Uncle* (James, 2009), a short story about a boy fascinated by his uncle's physical presence, experienced with the anxiety-giving precariousness of the apparition we see so dramatically performed in Xuxa's arrival and exit.

James's story is completely told in the first person. A child speaks. Now. We hear a child. His sexuality is not yet to come. The child is cumming. This is certainly not the child whose innocence must be saved from the predatorial Other. This is a child invested in the thickness of his uncle's eyebrows ('so thick I can't even tell if there's skin underneath'), the smooth darkness of his skin and the way his eyes go from light brown to blue when exposed to the sunlight ('It's kinda scary, but kinda nice.') (James, 2009: 2).

James's child is in touch with what touches him, and what he would like to touch (the uncle's body). This child's ludic usurpation is a form of paranoid telekinesis. The child's burden, and his blessing, is the urgent need to outsmart the readymade paths for horizontal growth that have been paved and signposted as devoid of alternatives. His is a haptically aware child ('His fingers and his lips kinda tickle my ear when they brush it'), a sexually aware child who is articulated into being, *as child*, through James's literary device, revealing to the reader the ways in which, in some register, a child *is* like a small adult, a *baixinho*, negotiating the tension between sexual desire and ability to have the (supposedly satisfying) object (of desire).

While we may think of *sexual* and *innocent* as antithetical terms, the child's so-called innocence itself appears as particularly sexual in James, as it does in Xuxa, and in the queer boys we can imagine to have mimicked her in the bathroom for their own uncles (never) to see.

The child in theory, the child in practice

Xuxa's rise as non-Brazilian Brazilian royalty in the 1980s and 1990s coincides with Brazil's trajectory of emergence, from a global *baixinho* to the world's sixth largest economy, 'expected to move up to 4th place ahead of Japan' by 2050.[9] Brazilians' emergence, from childhood into the presumed adulthood of capitalist-style progress, involves socio-economic growth and a symbolic unsettling that amounts to what we could call a positive crisis. Like Stockton's (ghostly) queer child, these changes are also achieved through *sideways* growth, as when one is unable to grow according to the dicta provided by the normative moulds/modes of growing – upwards.

Taking the emerging country-child analogy further, we can say that the price for Brazil's emergence (upward emergence, sideways emergence, re-emergence of the repressed) has been the death of the child – of its child(ren) and itself as child, particularly if we take television programming as an emblematic symptom for a country 'of illiterate folk' where, according to Gilberto Felisberto Vasconcellos, 'what isn't television has no cultural value' (Vasconcellos, 1991: 118).

The string of events that illustrates Brazil's multipronged emergence (vertical, horizontal, diagonal, jagged and in ways we can't yet map) largely involve an investment, financial and symbolic, of properties (of aesthetics, class, race) that do not line up with what Xuxa represented. If Xuxa's zenith was built on a stoking of post-colonial inferiority complexes and anxieties about ambiguous lines between the Brazilian class system, the post-Xuxa years have been characterized by an embracing of what counts as Brazilian, or a fantasy of what constitutes the lower class for the higher classes, which are still the producers of television content, having ceded some of the place within the television frame to representatives of the (previous) lower classes.

What used to fall under the category of bad taste, that is, poor folks' taste, and thus deemed *un-televisable* now occupies centre stage in television shows dominated by Brazilian country music artists, a much larger number of brown and black actors in soap operas, and, for the first time, set in the poor slum-like suburbs of Rio de Janeiro, instead of mansions and modelling agencies.

We can follow the traces that lead to this shift in taste, and thus, in the specificity of objects deemed *televisable*, in various events that have produced Brazilian history in the 21st century – from the 40 million people pulled out of poverty in the Lula years (2002–2010) to the ruling by the Brazilian Supreme court that same-sex couples are legally entitled to civil unions in 2011. These signal not the fostering of ghostly apparitions from abroad that land in Brazilian territory to fill its lack, but to a literal changing of positions and meanings, with an unexpected investment of what was previously seen as shamefully Brazilian into the poster children (and here the children are precisely not literal, for they are absent) of the new Brazil.

Of course, the raw material sustaining this new country had already been 'used' in a very different way, and for very different purposes, in the aesthetics of hunger of Glauber Rocha's cinema of the 1960s, which portrayed Brazilian misery as misery, not as happiness *despite conditions*, in the hopes of ringing a revolutionary alarm. For Giberto Felisberto Vasconcellos, Rocha's death in 1981 was felt to be a relief by the cultural industry, largely controlled by Xuxa's network, Rede Globo – the same network which would appropriate the hunger of the new middle class (the 40 million Brazilians who went from *miserables* to consumers) into soap opera material: 'now we don't have to hear that old crap about hunger, porno-chanchada, the Third World anymore. Now everything is possible' (Vasconcellos, 1991: 98).[10]

For Vasconcellos, Rocha's death marks the end of the dictatorship years, and the engaged critical responses ('that old crap about hunger') they had triggered, as well as the beginning of an opening at the end of the 1970s, when the Brazilian intellectual was invested in doing whatever it took not to seem like a moralist. 'It thus follows that Xuxa would come about as the epitome of such de-sublimating *in*-video tendencies', whose performance wasn't seen through the framework of repressive/obscene, but under the rubric of *modernization* (Vasconcellos, 1991: 101). This propensity was able to sustain Xuxa's phenomenon despite the criticisms hurled at her.

This modernization, at the time, was only a dream, exactly the *stuff* Xuxa was made of on daily television, and as purchasable goods – a dream that wouldn't catch up with Brazil for at least two more decades after Xuxa's first apparition. In the meantime, Vasconcellos claims Xuxa was entrusted with the chore of making childhood 'as brief as possible'. He refers to her as a 'comedian' (Vasconcellos, 1991: 113) – for Freud, the comic is an awakening of the infantile[11] – doing Hollywood's colonizing work, and her show as a televised brothel whose mission was the production of adults through the killing of the children 'and the compulsory elimination of kids' qualities' (Vasconcellos, 1991: 107).

Whether we call Brazil's new phase modernization, progress or emergence, this encounter of (a version of) *the actual* nation with *the imagined* nation, the moment and aftershock when Brazil begins to embody aspects of living that could only have been thought of as a life beyond its borders, is not only (unevenly distributed) new class mobility, but it fosters the desire for more, and it demands the unsettling of positions that had been naturalized as static. Brazil's surprising and massive wave of protests that began in June 2013 is also a (re-)emergence of a new/old 'crap about hunger'. They also make evident the unpredictable ways in which Desire arranges itself, always volatile to changes of form, scarcity and tending towards an excess that is bound to leak, drown, wash up and wash away.

Notes

1. 'Pelé and Xuxa represent the extremes on the scale of black and white. Pelé's features, hair, and complexion are what Brazilians consider truly black, while Xuxa, whose grandparents come from Austria, Poland, Italy, and Germany, is even whiter than the white of Portuguese origin' (Simpson, 1993: 32).
2. My translation.
3. The Portuguese term is '*disponibilidade lúdica*', which Vasconcellos borrows from Brazilian historian and anthropologist Luís da Câmara Cascudo (Vasconcellos, 1991: 49).
4. Freud links sight to touch, viewing perception as the 'sending out of feelers, of sensitive tentacles, at rhythmic intervals' (Laplanche, 1984: 15).
5. On reproductionist futurism and the notion of the child as the embodiment of an innocence that must be saved as heterosexuality's fundamental, and fundamentally harmful, and anti-oppositional device, see Lee Edelman (2004).
6. Beatriz Preciado takes Freud's point on the latency of any body part, 'real' or phantom, as an erotic zone further in *Manifeste Contra-Sexuel* (Preciado, 2000).

For Preciado, any body part can also be/work as a penis, which makes the penis itself not the phallus, but a dildo.

7. On anxiety over children's exposure to paedophiles, see Adler (2011). Also see Egan and Hawkes (2010), Angelides (2004) and Kincaid (1998).
8. Also see Lee's ghostly intervention/reparation take shape in his blog, lipstickeater.blogspot.com.
9. PwC report, 'World in 2050. The BRICs and Beyond: Prospects, Challenges and Opportunities,' January 2013. http://www.pwc.com/en_GX/gx/world-2050/assets/pwc-world-in-2050-report-january-2013.pdf (accessed 12 June 2013).
10. Rocha was, for Vasconcellos, the number one enemy of Rede Globo's cultural monopoly, established with the help of military officers in power during the dictatorship years. (Vasconcellos, 1991: 114).
11. Freud traces the relationship between that which is funny with a difference that is recognized, or projected, in the way *I* does something and the way *the Other* does it: 'he does it as I used to do it as a child' (Freud, 1990: 279, 280).

References

Adler, A. (2001) The perverse law of child pornography. *Columbia Law Review*, 101, 209–273.

Angelides, S. (2004) Feminism, child sexual abuse, and the erasure of child sexuality. *GLQ*, 10 (2), 141–177.

Bicalho, M. F. B. (1993) The art of seduction: Representation of women in Brazilian silent cinema. *Luso-Brazilian Review*, XXX, 21–33.

Bollas, C. (2000) *Hysteria*. London and New York: Routledge.

Dyer, R. (2003) *Heavenly bodies: Film stars and society*. London: Routledge.

Edelman, L. (2004) *No future: Queer theory and the death drive*. Durham, NC: Duke University Press Books.

Egan, R. D., & Hawkes, G. (2010) *Theorizing the sexual child in modernity*. London: Palgrave Macmillan.

Freud, S. (1957) *Leonardo da Vinci and a memory of his childhood*. J. Strachey (Ed. and Trans.). London: The Hogarth Press.

Freud, S. (1990) *Jokes and their relation to the unconscious*. New York: W. W. Norton & Company.

Freud, S. (2000) *The three essays on the theory of sexuality*. New York: Basic Books.

Halper, K. (20 June 2013) Yes, Fetuses masturbate. *Salon*. Retrieved from http://www.salon.com/2013/06/20/the_science_of_masturbating_fetuses/>.

James, G. W. (2009) Uncle. *Shaming the devil: Collected short stories*. Hollywood, FL: Top Pen Press.

Kincaid, J. (1998) *Erotic innocence: The culture of child molesting*. Durham, NC: Duke University Press.

Laplanche, J. (1984, Spring) To situate sublimation. 28 October.

Lee, J. O. (2005, Fall–Winter) The joy of the castrated boy. *Social Text*, 23 (3–4), 84–85.

Love, H. (2009) *Feeling backward: Loss and the politics of queer history*. Cambridge, MA: Harvard University Press.

Simpson, A. (1993) *Xuxa: The mega-marketing of gender, race, and modernity*. Philadelphia, PA: Temple University Press.

Soler, C. (6 July 2013) Presentation at the research group of clinical formations of the Lacanian field seminar. *The Names of the Father and Fathers*. Paris.

Stockton, K. B. (2009) *The queer child, or growing sideways in the twentieth century*. Durham, NC: Duke University Press.

Vasconcellos, G. F. (1991) *Eu & a Xuxa: Sociologia do Cabaré Infantil*. São Paulo: Editora Leia Mais.

Winnicott, D. W. (1990) *Playing and reality*. London: Routledge.

17

Boys' Love Manga for Girls: Paedophilic, Satirical, Queer Readings and English Law

Anna Madill

Suzuhara's collection of yonkoma (four-panel) comic strips 'Here in Magic Land' are published in 'J-BOY by Biblos' (2006). This is an English-language anthology of original Japanese manga (comics) of the genre known as Boys' Love (BL).[1] The cast of characters and the scenarios they imply indicate some of the motifs around which BL revolves:

Magic Land Friends

Shiro: A boy from the cat family became Al's apprentice in hopes of becoming a wizard.
Al: A great wizard...but not a responsible adult. Always lusting after Shiro.
Kett: The butler at Al's estate. There's a person under the bunny costume.
Tora: Shiro's older brother. Visits Al's estate often out of worry for Shiro and desire to see Kett.

The *sine qua non* of BL is the portrayal of romantic and sexual relationships between young, often adolescent, males. It is sometimes very explicit and can contain themes of intra-familial attraction, BDSM[2] and seeming inter-species eroticism (e.g. between human(oids) and cat-boy hybrids such as the character Shiro).

Manga has developed in a commercial context in which products are designed to appeal to markets segmented by age and gender, and BL is a subgenre of Shōjo manga targeted at females from early adolescence to early adulthood. The visually cute characterization, embellished drawing style and creative panelling typical of Shōjo is found in BL and it is known that most BL mangaka (artist-authors) are female, as are most of the consumers (Mizoguchi, 2003). Not only are the majority of BL readers female, they tend also to be teenagers or young adults (Pagliassotti, 2008b). Most female BL readers in Japan may identify as heterosexual (Pagliassotti, 2008b), but there is growing evidence that a larger proportion of female readers in the West do *not*: that is, 54% of Pagliassotti's female participants did not identify as heterosexual and, with an interim of 2012 responses, this figure is even higher at 59% in my own ongoing survey of anglophone BL Fandom (https://leeds.onlinesurveys.ac.uk/blfandomsurvey). Moreover, the queer nature of the BL phenomenon itself presents a challenge to, and may parody, reified sexual orientation and gender categories (Wood, 2006).[3]

BL is massively popular across East and South-East Asia (e.g., Noh, 1998; Abraham, 2008; Li, 2009; Zhou, 2009), and has a growing international audience, and increasing availability of commercially translated manga across the world has contributed to the wave of influence known as the 'Japanification' of youth culture (West, 2008). With this has come concern that manga contain an inordinate amount of sexual violence and other noxious sexual material, particularly the paedophilic, and this has spurred contemporary sexualization debates (e.g. Allison, 2000; Perper & Cornog, 2002). The manga genres Lolicon and Shotacon contain erotic material portraying young, often pre-pubescent, girls and boys respectively. Male-male Shotacon is sometimes considered a BL subgenre but 'Almost Crying' (Takahashi, 2006) is probably the only original Japanese Shotacon commercially available in English. However, other manga marketed in English as BL have strong Shotacon resonances, such as 'Here in Magic Land', in which, in terms of both context and presentation, some characters seem designed to be understood as pubescent or younger.

Sexualization debates are, therefore, very relevant to BL as a site within which teenage girls and young women are negotiating global, sexualized cultures and the controversially young characters that are sometimes portrayed in this erotica. Moreover, BL is particularly interesting because it appears to challenge assumptions about the nature of young women's erotic interests, their engagement with what might be considered transgressive pornography, and turn on its head stereotypes regarding whom is creating and consuming such material. And all this is happening within the context of increasing legislative regulation.

English legal context relevant to BL

... out of worry for Shiro ...

Several interrelated areas of law are potentially relevant to BL manga, including those on obscenity, child pornography and copyright. The following discussion refers to legislation covering England, some of which applies also to other parts of the United Kingdom. For simplicity, I will often use the term 'English' but provide the detailed jurisdiction for specific legislation in endnotes.[4]

The Obscene Publications Acts[5] 1959 and 1964 concern the dealing of obscene material, or possession with intent to deal. The test of obscenity in relation to these acts has come to be understood as the powerful and corrosive tendency to deprave and corrupt a significant proportion of the likely audience. This is a relatively stringent test and books and magazines have the additional defence of 'merit' in terms of science, literature, art or learning, as do other media and art forms, though to a lesser extent, and there is a requirement to consider the material as a whole. More recently, Section 63[6] of the Criminal Justice and Immigration Act 2008 has extended criminal liability to the possession of extreme pornographic images deemed to be obscene, graphic and realistic, citing specifically necrophilia, bestiality and violence which is life-threatening or which might result in serious injury. Importantly, 'obscene' here has the less demanding meaning of grossly offensive or disgusting when considered in context. There have been relatively few successful convictions for obscenity under these acts, making it difficult to conceive what (non-paedophilic) material might be considered incontrovertibly noxious, and it is unlikely that BL falls foul of these legislations. BL may include Act-defined extreme elements such as (seeming) bestiality but, as drawings, could not be mistaken for the real thing and, as artwork with a well-documented stylistic pedigree, could probably claim some artistic merit.

Of growing relevance to manga, and to genres such as BL in particular, are the laws relating to child pornography. In England, this legislation has built up in stages and it is worthwhile considering several significant steps. The Protection of Children Act 1978[7] made it illegal to take, make and distribute indecent photographs of children, or to possess such material with intent to distribute. Possession, itself, of such material was made illegal in the Criminal Justice Act 1988,[8] and the Criminal Justice and Public Order Act 1994[9] extended this to include photographic derivatives such as tracings and pseudo-photographs, for example photograph-like material made by computer graphics. The Sexual Offences Act 2003[10] then redefined a 'child' from being a person under 16 years old to a person under 18 years old. Even more stringently, the Coroners and Justice Act 2009[11] created a new offence of possessing a prohibited image of a child, extending this to include images of adults where the predominant impression given is that it is a child. This latter legislation also clarified, for the first time, that a non-photographic prohibited image of a child includes computer-generated images (CGIs), cartoons, manga images and drawings.

As this short summary illustrates, the English child pornography laws have become increasingly stringent. Legislation was first against production and dealing and then extended also to possession; moved from a narrow, actual-age-based definition of 'child' to a wider, impression-of-age-based one; and expanded the type of prohibited image from the photographic to include also freehand drawings of fantasy encounters which might involve imaginary beings. Moreover, specific use of the word 'manga' in recent legislation demonstrates how it has attracted particular concern in England.

Most BL in commercial English translation contain a disclaimer on the credits page to the effect that 'all characters depicted in sexually explicit scenes in this publication are at least the age of consent or older'. Such statements may be problematic on the global stage. Age of consent for specific kinds of sexual acts (e.g. depending on partners' sex or age) varies according to jurisdiction. In Japan, the national age of consent for heterosexual relations is 13 years, but is as high as 18 years in some prefectures, and legislation is mute on same-sex activity. However, significantly, in England, as explained, it is not age of consent, or even age of participants per se, which is definitional of child pornography, but predominant impression of a personage being under 18 years old (see Clough, 2012).

Manga's relationship to the impression of protagonist age is particularly complex. As a cartoon form, manga illustrations usually do not attempt to portray characters realistically (Cohn, 2013). In fact, caricature is almost an inherent feature of comics, as is the incorporation of fantasy beings such as super-heroes, cyborgs and anthropomorphized non-human animals. Shōjo manga, in particular, has evolved a visual style which exaggerates youthfulness, including large eyes, domed foreheads and small chins as a convention of kawaii (cute) culture for which Japan is famous. Large eyes can codify age, but also female gender and relative innocence which have no necessary link to age (Grigsby, 1999). Moreover, the visual age of a character can vary across the narrative because rendering style, such as extreme deformation, is used to portray effects such as fleeting inner states and may infantilize character appearance. Character portrayal, including apparent age, may also be inconsistent over the course of a narrative owing to time constraints and the use of assistants. These kinds of stylization, codification and practical issues mean that protagonist age cannot be read from manga images in terms of realism,[12] and sexually explicit stories may appear populated by characters who look, at times, very young but who are in contexts that make it clear they are to be understood to be adults (e.g. in college, university and the workplace). This is not to say, however, that age ambiguity is always inadvertent.

The Coroners and Justice Act 2009 specifies that Prohibited Images of Children (from here on PIC) can include cartoons, manga and drawings. However, for non-photographic images of children to reach prohibited status they must fulfil all of three specified criteria: they must be (1) pornographic (with reference both to the image itself and to the context in which it appears); (2) grossly offensive, disgusting or otherwise of an obscene character (according to the ordinary dictionary definition of 'obscene'); and (3) focused on the child's genitals or anal region or portray any of a given list of acts (including sex acts in the presence of a child and/or involving a child).[13] If a prosecution is brought, fulfilment of these criteria is for the magistrates, district judge or jury to determine. Even though BL may include characters in sexual contexts who are interpretable as 'children' under English law (i.e. predominant impression of being under 18 years old), it is by no means certain that such texts would meet the required criteria of being also porno-graphic and obscene. As a literature, BL is diverse and spans tender love stories and dramas through to more transgressively themed erotica but, even when exploring socially deviant sexuality, tends to emphasize relationships, subjective experience and feelings such as embarrassment, which is not typ-ical of pornography and provides a context in which to understand sexual explicitness as not obscene.

Probably in response to copyright laws, many manga include on the cred-its page a disclaimer that 'any likeness of characters, places, and situations featured in this publication to actual persons (living or deceased), events, places, and situations is purely coincidental'. In relation to English legisla-tion, the accuracy of this statement is vital with regard to sexualized images of characters appearing to be under 18 years old, and at least one BL mangaka has been accused of using photographs of adult men from gay pornography as source material without permission. Hence, there is a risk that some BL may contravene the Criminal Justice and Public Order Act 1994 because its creation involved the tracing or copying of photographs of actual children in sexualized contexts. Innocent possession of such images, that is having no reason to believe that they are anything other than imaginary and hand-drawn, is a defence under the Criminal Justice Act 1988, presumably as long as the images do not also contravene the Coroners and Justice Act 2009 (i.e. that they are not also pornographic and obscene). Finally, even if copyright permission is obtained to include manga images in other material, such as research reports, drawings presented out of context could meet the criteria of a prohibited image of a child under English law, even if they do not do so within the original work taken as a whole.

Having provided an overview of relevant English law, I will now explore how BL problematizes key assumptions of the recent PIC legislation, and raises concerns about its ramifications, including, but extending beyond, the profound definitional ambiguities of the terms 'pornography', 'obscene' and 'child'. Specifically, I argue that the legislation invites a literal, and privileges a singular, reading of fantasy, erotic, visual texts – such as BL. The legisla-tion invites a *literal* reading through implying that given criteria coherent for the assessment of representational texts (e.g. photographs of children[14]) can be applied also to non-representational texts (i.e. fantasy drawings) and awarded moral status similar to that of the real (e.g. that protagonist age in manga can, within the ordinary everyday parameters of impression, be determined has been critiqued above). Perhaps even more problematic, the legislation invites a *singular* reading of texts through priming a search for the reified elements by a defined audience (magistrates, district judge or jury) under the remit that a certain constellation may warrant prohibition. Specif-ically, it alerts hegemonically empowered or hegemonically representational groups to a *paedophilic reading*, and disavows other possible readings as irrelevant if *these* groups can find *that* reading.

Figure 17.1   Yonkoma 'Imagination Blizzard', Here in Magic Land by Suzuhara (2006)

Critiquing the legislative invitation to a single, literal, paedophilic reading

A boy from the cat family . . .

I prefaced this chapter with the character list of Suzuhara's humorous collection of 28 BL yonkoma 'Here in Magic Land' and will use this non-explicit manga to ground my critique of PIC because this example allows me to raise important issues of wider applicability. I comment on this manga in general, but select for particular consideration the yonkoma 'Imagination Blizzard!' (Figure 17.1) because it facilitates in condensed form three important readings: paedophilic, satirical and queer, each engaging a distinct affective register: titillation, ridicule and anguish. Each is a reading from within a different frame of reference but they are not mutually exclusive and can be appreciated in different ways at a different – but also at the same – time. None of these is the correct reading and others are also possible. My argument is, however, that the paedophilic reading is privileged in PIC.

Paedophilic reading: Stop corrupting Shiro!

Shotacon often draw on childhood themes in their titles (e.g. 'Jack in the Box' by Kirico Higashizato or 'Toy Player' by Negi Yokoyama). Similarly, 'Here in Magic Land' invites association with nursery rhymes, fairy tales and, particularly, the children's literature *Peter Pan* (Neverland) and *Alice in Wonderland*. The paedophilic resonances of both books have infiltrated popular culture and are explored, for example, in Alan Moore and Melinda Gebbie's (2006) graphic novel *Lost Girls*. The title panel of 'Here in Magic Land' shows Al – the wizard – sitting on a crescent moon reaching towards the reader with a small star cupped in his hand and the caption: 'Twinkle, twinkle little star. Become a wonderful dream and reach out to everyone!' Shiro is pictured to the side, clinging precariously to a large star, in ambiguous spatial relationship to Al. He could be merely next to Al or his predicament could be a close-up of the star in Al's hand. The latter implies that Shiro's safety is 'in Al's hands' but also, maybe, that he is being 'taken in hand' – particularly since the manga is presented as Shiro's 'training diary' – evoking the connotation that he is being sexually groomed. This interpretation is amplified in the first yonkoma. Following the introduction that 'Shiro just keeps on learning so many odd things', Shiro proudly demonstrates the 'neat trick' Master Al has taught him, pulling his cat tail between his legs and announcing to Kett's horror: 'it's a cock'.

Although no age is specified in the text, Shiro wears the short trousers associated with elementary school-age boys in Japan, is small relative to other characters, is presented as childlike (e.g. holding a doll in the image of Al, easily moved to tears, chirpy and physically affectionate), and is identified as being the wizard's apprentice. This context suggests that he is to be considered pre-adolescent and that Al's desire for, and sexualization of, Shiro indexes Al's wish for – and possibly development of – a pederastic relationship.

In 'Imagination Blizzard!' Shiro is shown cross-dressed sequentially in three outfits: a strapless basque-like dress and long gloves; an air-hostess uniform; and a short nightdress. As Shiro walks past, seemingly unperturbed by this clothing, he is watched in silent shock by his visiting older brother. By the third panel Tora can take no more. He assumes that Al is 'ordering' Shiro to wear these inappropriately sexualizing costumes and demands that he stop complying: 'Take that off'. However, in the fourth and final punchline panel Shiro is transformed into wearing a girl's nightdress right in front of Tora's eyes, and this reveals that what Tora is actually witnessing is 'imagination magic' in which Al the Wizard is making manifest his sexual fantasies.

'Here in Magic Land' is readable as a titillating portrayal of Al the paedophile's exploitation of power over his charge in order to realize his sexual desires, the yonkoma 'Imagination Blizzard!' showing how he does so right under the nose of his victim's family and is unabashed by the moral outrage his behaviour inspires. The dark humour in this reading is produced by the daring and succinct capture of the paedophilic imagination.

Satirical reading: Is he naked under that?!

Satirical humour ridicules its subject matter and can offer insightful social critique. Cartoons are a traditional medium for social and political satire (Tower, 1982), with, for example, cultural anxieties over paedophilia parodied in series such as 'Family Guy' in which elderly neighbour John Herbert's predilections and inappropriately sexualizing innuendos are missed by Peter and Lois who employ him to babysit their children. One technique of satire is exaggeration, and a source of humour throughout 'Here in Magic Land' is that Shiro is flirtatious yet obtuse to Al's salacious intentions to an outlandish extent. Specifically, in 'Imagination Blizzard!' he appears to be amazingly unaware of how he is dressed or, at least, of the titillating effect it may have. A satirical reading raises the possibility that Shiro has more agency and is more knowing that he seems – and Shiro's ownership of an 'Al doll' with which he can 'play' hints at his possible power. This, then, alludes to the socially taboo ramification that Shiro may, to some extent, be deliberately inciting attention – Al's lust but also Tora's shock – and playing the two men off against each other.

Al's behaviour throughout the manga is also exaggeratedly outrageous and so can be read as satirising the social demonization of the paedophile: a figure who, by implication, is imbued with extraordinary power – like that of a wizard. Mirroring this cultural preoccupation, legislation has become increasingly stringent and focused on inspecting texts for their propensity to incite paedophilic desire. Paradoxically, this requires individuals to partake in the 'paedophilic gaze': to look at texts as they imagine a paedophile would look (Adler, 2001; Stapleton, 2010). And in 'Imagination Blizzard!' this is what Tora does. Although shocked, he can 'see' Al's fantasy and understands that Shiro may be sexually arousing in these costumes. More than this, however, Tora seeks out sexualizing detail beyond what might be deemed necessary, asking 'Is he naked under that?!' This raises for critical inspection the possible prurience of extensive social and legislative interest in, and prioritization of, paedophilic readings of texts. Moreover, given that Tora's concern over Shiro's possible lack of underwear makes sense only within the diegesis of the manga (there is, of course, no 'under' a drawing), a satirical reading ridicules the point of view that affords non-representational drawings moral status akin to that of actual children and which, by implication, risks demeaning the seriousness of real harm done to them.[15]

Queer reading: Imagination blizzard!

Queer theory in its deconstructive iteration (e.g. Sullivan, 2003) draws attention to, and celebrates, slippage between dichotomously conceived categorization and in so doing challenges a hegemonic world view that disavows that which is betwixt and between. Where categories are placed in opposition, one is usually associated with greater hegemonic value and the second Othered. Hence, queer theory is also a critique of dominant status and power hierarchies. As outlined in the introduction, BL can be understood to parody bifurcated social categories, particularly those associated with sexuality and gender, and 'Imagination Blizzard!' facilitates a profoundly condensed and extensive exploration of the queer. Unrecognized in majority culture, that disavowed is abjected and so a queer reading of the yonkoma evokes the anguish of non-identity, or at the very least, of devalued identity: a preoccupation also associated with the liminal stage of adolescence (Erikson, 1968), which is when the majority of readers start engaging with BL (Pagliassotti, 2008b; Li, 2009).

I identify eight ways in which 'Imagination Blizzard!' offers a queer critique of opposed categories – and likely there are more. I articulate the identified relevant categories with what is arguably the higher status pole, with respect to the UK context, placed first.

1. Male/female: Owing to the cross-dressing, isolated from context, Shiro's gender is held in suspense until the final panel where it is captured in pronoun: 'Is *he* naked under that?!' Within the wider context of the manga, it is clear that Shiro is to be considered male, but the ease with which he appears to wear women's clothing and could pass for female in the yonkoma raises for critical inspection the restricting social conventions of attire and associated reification and dichotomization of gender.
2. Heterosexual/homosexual: Given that Al's fantasy in this yonkoma is Shiro dressed as a female, the nature of Al's sexual attraction is not clearly either homosexual or heterosexual.
3. Human/animal: Shiro and Tora are drawn as humanoid-feline hybrid. This mixes and confounds the strongly enforced and emotive boundary between human and animal, particularly with regard to sexuality (Fudge, 2002). Al, himself, is portrayed as a human(oid) and hence his desire for Shiro could be both paedophilic and bestial, but in a way possible only in fantasy since the personages could not exist in reality.
4. Reality/fantasy: The yonkoma portrays Al's sexual imagination made real and hence plays with and explores the relationship between fantasy and reality. However, Al is able to realize his fantasy only as an aesthetic fabrication and within the diegetic premise that he is a wizard. A queer reading therefore engages a critique that concern over non-representational, erotic visual texts is a conflation of categories in paradoxical bolstering of the literal.
5. Animate/inanimate: In the first panel of the yonkoma Shiro carries a broom, which is a recognizable prop of wizardry. Earlier in the series, Shiro is taught how to make his broom speak through 'conversation magic' and hence merges the boundary between animate and inanimate. This is a specific example of a wider exploration of the boundary between reality and fantasy but one which is very pertinent given the critique that PIC risks conflating the moral status of real, 'animate' children with fantasy, 'inanimate' drawings.
6. Public/private: That Al's fantasy is made visible to Tora plays with and explores the permeability of the boundary between public and private. Within context, this raises wider issues around public scrutiny and

assessment of the private sphere, particularly in terms of the policing of non-hegemonic sexualities. More than this, the yonkoma raises critique of legislative reach into the sexual *imagination* as manifested in non-representational visual texts (McLelland, 2012).

7. Caucasian/Oriental: 'Here in Magic Land' is an original Japanese manga and yet the characterization, as is typical of much manga, is racially odourless (Iwabuchi, 2002). Protagonists are interpretable as Oriental, Caucasian, Asian, Eurasian – amongst others – and, hence, conceives 'race' as a queer concept.

8. West/East: Al is dressed in Western attire and Tora in a Japanese kimono, each with a respective culturally compatible name, and throughout the manga no clear 'real-world' setting is implied. The cultural situatedness of 'Here in Magic Land' is therefore made pertinent but also made queer through ambiguation. Interestingly, it is Al (the 'West') who is presented as perverse and Tora (the 'East') as upholding sexual morality. This suggests the critique that international concern over aspects of Japanification is a manifestation of the West's own sexual preoccupations.

The sheer number of dichotomous categories played with and ambiguated in this yonkoma allows an interpretation of its title – 'Imagination Blizzard!' – as indexing the creatively disorienting potential of queer readings to unsettle taken-for-granted hegemonic value hierarchies and meanings.

Is the intended audience unimportant?

> ... not a responsible adult ...

PIC is clear in its position on authorial intent and interpretation in relation to the works with which it is concerned. Intent and interpretation are heavily theorized in scholarly consideration of texts and provides a context for understanding the position set out in the law. In deciding whether or not an image is pornographic it is stated in PIC that '(i)t is not a question of the intentions of those who produced the image'. This disinterest in authorial intent is consistent with the poststructuralist displacement of origin as arbiter of meaning (Barthes, 1967). However, whereas poststructuralism conceives texts to be malleable cultural products open to a range of legitimate interpretations, PIC specifies the groups whose reading practices will decide the pornographic, and ultimately the prohibitive, status of relevant texts: '(w)hether this threshold has been met will be an issue for the magistrates, District Judge or jury to determine'.

Clearly, then, 'audience' is important within PIC but only to the extent that the reading practices of proscribed groups are privileged. These groups inhabit positions of social authority (magistrates, district judge) and/or deliberately represent majority culture (juries). Importantly, these groups do not represent the intended or actual BL audience which is young, female and often highly informed with regard to contemporary Japanese popular culture. Extending the queer reading above, the English legislation reproduces a hegemonic hierarchy of power (male, heterosexual, human, reality [literal], public, Caucasian, West, animate) and is in fundamental tension with BL which provides a space for that which is Othered (female, homosexual, animal,[16] fantasy, private, Oriental, inanimate). The BL readership is therefore relatively disenfranchized culturally and, I argue, represents a specific, non-hegemonic *interpretative community* as identified in Jenkins's (1992) research on fandom (which, pertinently, was developed from his work on Western, female, amateur erotica writers of male–male slash fiction).

Fandoms as interpretive communities are defined by their ardent interest in, and active sense-making in relation to, the popular culture texts of shared focus. Of particular importance in fandom is the ability to understand both the canonical oeuvre and non-canonical versions and the terms of reference within which disputes around interpretation can be based. There is little research on the frames within which fans read BL but a common theme is that it is considered primarily entertainment (e.g. Li, 2009). Scholarly research suggests that entertainment value may arise from BL understood as *Bildungsroman* (coming-of-age narratives), romantic comedies, or even as a new subgenre of male–male-romance-for-girls (Pagliassotti, 2008a). As I have shown, sometimes at least, more critical readings such as satire or queer are also possible. However, more commonly, I suggest that BL with sexual content partakes of a distinct imaginary space that might be termed *explicit romance* (i.e. not pornographic or obscene) or *sensitive pornography* (i.e. possibly pornographic but not obscene).[17]

English legislation becomes most problematic for Lolicon and Shotacon. There appears to be little research on Shotacon in Japanese and only passing comments on the genre in English language sources (e.g. McLelland, 2000; Zanghellini, 2009) and, unlike BL in general, Saitō (2007) suggests that Shotacon is produced and consumed by males and females in about equal proportions. In relation to PIC, the age and gender of producers, or of the majority or target audience, is irrelevant. These factors may, however, impact the nature of the material, and a distinction is made in the manga community between male-oriented and female-oriented Shotacon, with the latter considered by Saitō (2007) to be very similar in theme and style to BL. The implication is that female-oriented Shotacon, although explicitly sexualizing male children and youths and incorporating male–male eroticism, are essentially romantic and dramatic narratives. Most importantly, what evidence there is suggests that female readers are not interpreting erotic manga with visually young characters as paedophilia (Tribunella, 2008), reading it out of lascivious paedophilic interest (McLelland, 2000), or being catalysed by it into paedophilic activity – given the low rates of female sexual offending, in general, and the complex and disturbed life contexts in which female sexual abuse of children tends to occur, specifically (Cortoni, 2011).

Conclusion

There's a person under the bunny costume.

A central principle underlying child pornography prohibition is that its production, distribution and viewing does actual harm to children. Although this invites scrutiny in relation to the definition of 'child', 'pornography' and 'harm', I do not wish to pursue critique of this principle with regard to the potential exploitation of young people. A related, but distinct, principle is that child pornography does moral harm to society through condoning and promoting the sexualization of children, even when no children are harmed in its production. Globalization, particularly through the Internet, has increased the market for, and hence production of, child pornography, and there is a case that the sexualization of 'children' in any form should not be tolerated. However, paradoxically, the attempt to ban sexualizing images of children has had the, arguably destructive and distracting, effect of privileging paedophilic interpretations of commonplace and culturally innovative texts from family photographs to artwork (Kalha, 2011; White, 2011), likely incites boundary pushing in advertising (Vanska, 2011) and may divert attention and resources away from the prevention of real harm to real children.

Drawings might be used to groom children into sexual activity through provoking curiosity and implying that such behaviour is normal. However, legislating against imaginary, non-realistic media such as manga must be of concern since it places overly paternalistic restriction on the expression and sharing of pure fantasy (McLelland, 2012) without evidence that such products are, in themselves, harmful and, seemingly, without adequate understanding of genre conventions (narrative and visual) which *are* understood by the intended audience. With specific reference to PIC, Professor Suzanne Ost has gone as far as stating that we now have 'an offence with expansive, ill-defined descriptors which may well violate human rights and that could lead to the inclusion of a wide range of material in the ambit of criminalisation' (2010: 254). Similar legislation in the United States[18] was struck down by the Supreme Court in 2002 (Fischel, 2013) only to be resurrected in slightly amended form in the PROTECT Act of 2003 (Wood, 2013).[19]

The young female readers of BL problematize the legislative invitation to a single, literal, paedophilic reading of suspicious texts and the position that the intended audience of these texts is unimportant. What within majority culture may seem to be pornography of the most noxious kind may actually be relatively safe for young women because it avoids sexualized images of females (which are difficult to disentangle from misogynist conno-tations), innovatively subverting and sidestepping gender inequalities and, in so doing, offering some women a palatable erotica with regard to which they are extremely underserved in comparison to men. This is not to argue that BL is unproblematic, and I am deeply intrigued by the way these texts can be read as innocuous contra their apparently transgressive subject mat-ter. It is important to understand the content of these works and – a major Western cultural challenge – how intelligible, meaningful, non-paedophilic frames are available for reading non-realistic, erotic texts involving visu-ally young characters. However, currently, well-meaning efforts to protect children will potentially criminalize a sexually benign youth demographic, most of whom are teenage girls and young women, literate with the conven-tions of explicit romance in which the protagonists are, to many of them, age-appropriate boys and youths.

Notes

1. Variously called, with subtle differentiation, Boys' Love (BL), yaoi, or Shōnen-ai.
2. Bondage, Discipline, Domination, Submission, Masochism.
3. It is also likely that the gender binary female and male are problematic for some BL readers.
4. Main sources of information are the Crown Prosecution Service website http://www.cps.gov.uk/ and http://www.legislation.gov.uk/
5. England and Wales.
6. England, Wales, and Northern Ireland.
7. England and Wales with some provisions extending to Scotland and Northern Ireland.
8. England, Wales, Scotland and Northern Ireland.
9. England, Wales, Scotland and Northern Ireland.
10. England and Wales with some provisions extending to Scotland and Northern Ireland.
11. England and Wales with some provisions extending to Scotland and Northern Ireland.
12. Similarly, characters' race or ethnicity is often visually problematized.
13. That the image focuses solely or principally on a child's genitals or anal region, or portrays any of the following acts: the performance by a person of an act of intercourse or oral sex with or in the presence of a child; an act of mastur-bation by, of, involving or in the presence of a child; an act which involves penetration of the vagina or anus of a child with a part of a person's body or with anything else; an act of penetration, in the presence of a child, of the vagina or anus of a person with a part of a person's body or with anything else; the performance by a child of an act of intercourse or oral sex with an animal (whether dead or alive or imaginary); the performance by a person of an act of intercourse or oral sex with an animal (whether dead or alive or imaginary) in the presence of a child.
    (Accessed 17 October 2013, http://www.cps.gov.uk/legal/p_to_r/ prohibited_images_of_children/index.html#an04)

14. I acknowledge, but do not wish to engage with, critique of photographs as representational here and mean merely that, unlike BL manga, photographic media in this context can be considered to be images of real children.
15. Here, it seems perverse that a passage articulating a duty not to possess photographic child pornography, which allegedly appeared in an earlier draft, was removed from recent legislation restricting the sale of erotic manga and anime in Tokyo prefecture (see Anime Network [2010]. *Tokyo ban on sex in anime, manga, games*. Accessed 15 October 2013. https://www.theanimenetwork.com/component/option,com_kunena/Itemid,183/catid,7/func,view/id,70350/).
16. Interestingly see Azuma's (2009) theory of otaku (young, usually male, extreme manga, anime, and gaming fans) as 'database animals' and that a Chinese term for female BL fans is 'danmeilang' 耽美狼 which translates literally as 'indulge-in-the-beautiful wolves' (Liu, 2009).
17. Following 'Sensitive Pornograph' (2007) by Ashika Sakura, 801 Media.
18. Child Pornography Prevention Act 1996.
19. Prosecutional Remedies and Other Tools to end the Exploitation of Children Today.

References

Abraham, Y. (2008) Boys' love thrives in conservative Indonesia, in A. Levi. M. McHarry, & D. Pagliassotti (Eds.) *Boys' Love Manga: Essays on the Sexual Ambiguity and Cross-Cultural Fandom of the Genre*. North Carolina: McFarland & Co., Inc, pp. 44–55.

Adler, A. (2001) The perverse law of child pornography. *Columbia Law Review*, 101, 209–273.

Allison, A. (2000) *Permitted and prohibited desires: Mothers, comics, and censorship in Japan*. CA: University of California Press.

Azuma, H. (2009). *Japan's database animals*. J. E. Abel, & S. Kono (Trans.). Minneapolis: University of Minnesota Press.

Barthes, R. (1967/1977) The death of the author, in S. Heath (Trans.) *Image/Music/Text*. New York: Hill and Wang, pp. 142–147.

Clough, J. (2012) Lawful acts, unlawful images: The problematic definition of 'child' pornography. *Monash University Law Review*, 38, 213–245.

Cohn, N. (2013) *The visual language of comics: Introduction to the structure and cognition of sequential images*. London: Continuum Publishing Corporation.

Cortoni, F. (February 2011) Female sexual offenders: A special sub-group. Dealing with high-risk sex offenders in the community: Risk management, treatment and social responsibilities. Annual Conference on the Management of Adults and Juveniles with Sexual Behavior Problems, Austin, TX, 27 February 2011.

Erikson, E. H. (1968) *Identity, youth and crisis*. New York: W. W. Norton Company.

Fischel, J. J. (2013) *Pornographic protections? Itineraries of childhood innocence. Commentary essay prepared for WPSA discourses on LGBT politics*. New Haven, CT: Yale University.

Fudge, E. (2002) *Animal*. London: Reaktion.

Grigsby, M. (1999) The social production of gender as reflected in two Japanese culture industry products: Sailormoon and Crayon Shin-Chan, in J. A. Lent (Ed.) *Themes and Issues in Asian Cartooning: Cute, Cheap, Mad, and Sexy*. Bowling Green, OH: Bowling Green State University Popular Press, pp. 183–210.

wabuchi, K. (2002) *Recentering globalisation: Popular culture and Japanese transcultural-ism.* Durham, NC: Duke University Press.

enkins, H. (1992) *Textual poachers: Television fans and participatory culture.* London: Routledge.

Kalha, H. (2011) What the hell is the figure of the child? Figuring out figurality in, around, and beyond Lee Edelman. *Lambda Nordica,* 16 (2–3), 17–4.

Li, Y. (2009) *Japanese Boy-Love manga and the global fandom: A case study of Chinese female readers.* MA: Thesis, Department of Communication Studies, Indiana University, USA.

Liu, T. (2009) Conflicting discourses on boys' love and subcultural tactics in mainland China and Hong Kong. *Intersections: Gender and Sexuality in Asia and the Pacific, Issue 20, April 2009.* Retrieved 12 April 2014, http://intersections.anu.edu.au/issue20/liu.html.

McLelland, M. (2000) No climax, no point, no meaning? Japanese women's boy-love sites on the internet. *Journal of Communication Inquiry,* 24, 274–291.

McLelland, M. (2012) Australia's 'child-abuse material' legislation, internet regulation and the juridification of the imagination. *International Journal of Cultural Studies,* 15, 467–483.

Mizoguchi, A (2003) Male-male romance by and for women in Japan: A history and the subgenres of yaoi fictions. *U.S.-Japan Women's Journal. English Supplement,* 25, 49–75.

Moore, A., & Gebbie, M. (2006) *Lost Girls.* Marietta, Georgia: Top Shelf.

Noh, S. (1998, Fall). Reading yaoi comics: An analysis of Korean girls' fandom. *Paper Presented at Korean Society for Journalism and Communication Studies Annual Meeting, Fall 1998.* Retrieved 28 June 2012, http://astro.temple.edu/~moongsil//study/yaoi_eng.pdf

Ost, S. (2010) Criminalising fabricated images of child pornography: A matter of harm or morality? *Legal Studies,* 30, 230–256.

Pagliassotti, D. (2008a) Better than romance? Japanese BL manga and the subgenre of male/male romantic fiction, in A. Levi, M. McHarry, & D. Pagliassotti (Eds.) *Boys' Love Manga: Essays on the Sexual Ambiguity and Cross-Cultural Fandom of the Genre.* London: McFarland and Co, pp. 59–83.

Pagliassotti, D. (2008b) Reading boys' love in the west. *Particip@tions,* 5. Retrieved 19 July 2010 from http://www.participations.org/Volume%205/Issue%202/5_02_pagliassotti.html

Perper, T., & Cornog, M. (2002) Eroticism for the masses: Japanese manga and their assimilation into the U.S. *Sexuality and Culture,* 6, 3–101.

Saitō, T. (2007) 'Otaku sexuality', *Robot Ghosts and Wired Dreams.* Minneapolis: University of Minnesota Press, pp. 222–249.

Sakura, A. (2007) Sensitive pornograph. 801 Media Inc.

Stapleton, A. (2010) Knowing it when you (don't) see it: Mapping the pornographic child in order to diffuse the paedophilic gaze. *Global Media Journal – Australia Edition,* 4 (2), 1–21.

Sullivan, N. (2003) *A critical introduction to queer theory.* New York: New York University Press.

Suzuhara, H. (2006) Here in Magic Land, in *J-BOY by Biblos.* CA: Digital Manga, pp. 305–312; 337–344.

Takahashi, M. (2006). *Almost crying.* CA: Digital Manga Publishing.

Tower, S. A. (1982) *Cartoons and lampoons: The art of political satire.* New York: Messner.

Tribunella, E. L. (2008) From kiddie lit to kiddie porn: The sexualisation of children's literature. *Children's Literature Association Quarterly*, 33, 135–155.

Vanska, A. (2011) Seducing children? *Lambda Nordica*, 16 (2–3), 69–101.

West, M. I. (Ed.) (2008) *The Japanification of children's popular culture: From Godzilla to Miyazaki*. Blue Ridge Summit, PA: Scarecrow Press.

White, J. N. (2011) Kiddie porn in the gallery: Defending the artist's corpus or invading the corporal integrity of the subject. *Jeffrey S. Moorad Sports Law Journal*, 18 (2) Article 10.

Wood, A. (2006) 'Straight' women, queer texts: Boy-love manga and the rise of a global counterpublic. *Women's Studies Quarterly*, 34, 394–414.

Wood, A. (2013) Boys' love anime and queer desire in convergence culture, transnational fandom, censorship and resistance. *Journal of Graphic Novels and Comics*, 4, 44–63.

Zanghellini, A. (2009) Underage sex and romance in Japanese homoerotic manga and anime. *Social & Legal Studies*, 18, 159–177.

Zhou, N. F. (2009) Yaoi phenomenon in Taiwan from interviews with female readers. *Journal of Gender Studies Japan*, 12, 41–55. Translated for Anna Madill by Mayumi Shinya 2012.

18
Documentaries on the Sexualization of Girls: Examining Slut-shaming, Victim-blaming and What's Being Left Off-screen

Lindsay Herriot and Lara E. Hiseler

Introduction

There is a robust public debate about the effects of a sex-saturated culture on youth. Experts appear in books, magazines, newspapers, blogs and documentaries to warn of the potential negative impact of an increasingly sexualized environment on young girls in particular. The pervasiveness of sexual content available through the Internet, combined with the marketing of sexual products to younger and younger audiences, have resulted in a public outcry for something official to be done. Within the academy, for instance, the American Psychological Association formed a Task Force on the Sexualization of Girls in response to these expressions of public concern (APA, 2010).

Other professionals have also taken up this subject. Intending to educate the lay public on girls and sexualization, film-makers have created documentaries to foster awareness and identify proactive strategies to address the impact of sexualization on girls (*Sexy Inc.*, 2007). While the history of such documentaries dates back nearly 70 years (see *Are You Popular*, 1947; *Going Steady*, 1951; *Girls Beware*, 1961; and so on) current 21st-century releases purport that the sexualization of girls is a new phenomenon requiring urgent intervention.

Since the late 2000s, a number of such documentaries have been released. While similar in substance to the films of earlier generations, these modern films emphasize the ubiquitous role of technology in facilitating what they identify as 'sexualization.' Based on their widespread popularity, similarity of subject matter, and being released within a five-year span, four contemporary North American documentaries have been selected as the subjects of our research:

- Canadian Broadcasting Company (2012) *Sext Up Kids: How children are becoming hypersexualized* – Canada
- Virgil Films (2012) *Miss Representation* – United States
- National Film Board of Canada (2007) *Sexy Inc.: Nos enfants sous influence* – Canada
- Media Education Foundation (2011) *The Purity Myth* – United States

These retell the same narratives that earlier films in the genre portrayed, morality tales of foolish young girls who are preyed on, yet should know better. The films of the early 21st century also present subject matter in an ahistorical vacuum, wherein girls' sexuality is both a problem to be solved, and a vulnerability in need of protection. By analysing how the films perpetuate dominant conceptions of gender, age, and sexuality, we are able to identify some of the contours of popular childhood theorizing. Suggestions are offered as to how such films can be shaped to more thoroughly and accurately document this complex phenomenon.

Theorising sexualization

We understand these films from the intersection of several theories on childhood and particular discourses around 'sexualization.' With regard to theorizing on the social and sexual locations of childhood, we draw primarily from three theoretical perspectives. The first refutes the concept of a naturally and universally (hetero)asexual child, and instead positions children as possessing sexuality and a sexual orientation (see Bruhm & Hurley, 2004; Stockton, 2009; Egan, 2013). Tied to this, we are informed by literature challenging the construct of an overvalued and perpetually surveilled child (see Faulkner, 2010, 2011), which situates children's alleged (hetero)asexuality as foundational to notions of children's 'innocence.' Last, we draw upon the notion of *childism*, an umbrella concept that 'highlight[s] the fact that prejudice is built into the very way children are imagined' (Young-Bruehl, 2012: 5), wherein young people are blamed for negative or undesired traits in adults. Similar to Egan's (2013) commentary on how adults have 'displac[ed] our impotence onto something more manageable and potent – the cultural and sexual corruption of the girl child' (p. 9), we see the films positioning girls as a vehicle through which anxieties about adult sexual identities and practices can be voiced and 'fixed.'

Theories of sexualization are a distinct subsection of childhood theorizing and they provide crucial context for analysing the films. Discourses of sexualization typically rest on four assumptions: (1) sexualization is universal, monolithic and inherently harmful; (2) sexualization targets passive, agent-less children; (3) sexualization is the instigating force behind all girls' sexual expressions; and (4) sexualization is about the deviant sexuality of girls (Egan & Hawkes, 2008). While all the films studied reinforced these discourses to varying degrees, we broaden our approach to sexualization, seeing it as 'encompass[ing] not simply children's self-concept and range of comportments and behaviours, but more precisely, how *adults view* children' (original emphasis, Faulkner, 2010: 106). We found that three of the four films place such heavy emphasis on expounding adult anxieties about girls' sexuality that they omit or distort the lived realities of youth sexuality, focusing instead on perceived threats to adult fantasies of children's constructed sexual innocence.

Emerging themes and data analysis

Braun and Clark's (2006) thematic analysis was used to explore representations of childhood, sexuality and shame in the films. We utilized an inductive approach, which allowed for construction of theories grounded in the data. Implicit and explicit ideas are identified and then grouped into higher themes to capture the meanings that are present. Researchers then compared/contrasted these themes with those established in popular and academic childhood theorizing. Reflective practice included serial memoranda, which provided an audit trail of the research process and an account of thoughts and emotions throughout the analysis.

Four distinct themes emerged from the data: (a) historical revisionism and children's presumed (hetero)asexuality; (b) the commodification of youth sexuality; (c) victim-blaming part 1: slut shaming as gendered and aged; and (d) victim blaming part 2: 'protecting' girls from violent young masculinity. We analyse each theme in relation to three of the films: *Sexy Inc.*, *Sext Up Kids* and *Miss Representation*, and then shift our attention to how *The Purity Myth* marks a departure in documentary films about the sexualization of girls. We conclude with a discussion of how this research contributes not only to current understandings and constructions of childhood, but also how it can shape the necessary conversations about the sexualization of young girls in the media.

Historical revisionism and children's presumed (hetero)asexuality

Sexy Inc., *Sext Up Kids* and *Miss Representation* distort the reality of sexual norms by implying that all sexual activity prior to 1990 took place between happy, married, consenting, heterosexual adults. Only *The Purity Myth*, in quoting Anderson Cooper, acknowledges that 'Nine out of ten Americans, both men and women, have had premarital sex, and it's been that way since the 1950s' (*Purity Myth*, 2011). A girl in *Sexy Inc.*, by contrast, disdainfully remarks that, 'These days, it's like let's have sex, let's go. No need to love the person.' Sex negativity, the position that sexual acts are generally bad and should be repressed, hangs in this comment. The film-makers do not further explore the topic, such as by asking the youth why she thinks that (a) more love-based sexual acts were performed in previous generations; (b) what precipitated the change to 'these days;' (c) is it better/best for a consenting agent to be 'in love' with a sexual partner; or (d) what does it mean to be 'in love?' Instead, there are sweeping generalizations with vague references to the widespread availability of contraception and technology as culprits of this apparently new trend. The comment further implies that when today's adults were themselves youth, they 'loved' their sexual partners, which is wiser than today's youth, who apparently do not. Adults are positioned as not only 'knowing better' than today's youth, but are also portrayed as having better sexual mores when they were younger.

Sexy Inc., *Sext Up Kids* and *Miss Representation* appear to exist in a larger historical vacuum; they make no reference to the sexual health products and policies that inform today's decision-making. No reference is made to the history of women's sexuality, which demonstrates how women participants in the overwhelming majority of sexual encounters across human time and space did/do not have the legal or normative ability to consent nor did/do they have legal or bodily autonomy to make decisions about pregnancies (French, 2008). Omitting this important history decontextualizes girls' sexualities so that viewers may be misled into thinking that girls' lack of sexual autonomy or engagement in sexual activity are recent phenomena, either causally or corollary to Internet technologies.[1] By choosing to rely on pop-psychology, instead of well-developed social science research on centuries of feminist struggle and activism around these issues, the videos are instead able to rely on normative myths, half-truths and generalizations about families. For example, that all Western anglophone families in the recent and distant past were white, heterosexual, nuclear families, centred around a male breadwinner (Coontz, 2000). Without full, multi-perspective, historical accounts of sexual health norms and policies, we find the film-makers and participants are disingenuous in speaking to the 'newness' of the sexualization of girls.

Despite dominance in Western constructions of childhood, the films perpetuate anxieties that childhood (hetero)asexuality is under a new form of attack (Egan & Hawkes, 2008; Faulkner, 2010; Robinson, 2013). They perpetuate 150 years of panic around children's sexuality, from concerns about risky novels in the 1890s, comic books in the 1940s, television in the 1980s and the Internet today (Egan & Hawkes, 2010; Egan, 2013). Access to new technologies is consistently understood as having a direct causal effect on the sexual activities of young people (Egan & Hawkes, 2010; Bragg & Buckingham, 2012), which are then universally condemned. For instance, in *Miss Representation*, a sensationalist journalist reports that 'more than

20% of girls under the age of 14 are having sex.' In *Sext Up Kids* a horrified paediatrician exclaims, 'anal is becoming the new oral!' Here, (bad) anal sex is highlighted for shock value. These claims are never supported by any research; we do not know who these girls are, who they are having the purported sex with, or how sex is being defined. Nor are the possibilities that these sexual experiences could be consensual and pleasurable are ever acknowledged. The notion that these sex acts could have taken place without being facilitated by Internet technology, or that they could represent consistency rather than aberration in youth sexuality, is similarly unexplored.

None of the three films acknowledges the fact that youth have consistently engaged in and experimented with sexual acts across time and space, or that engaging in healthy consensual sex acts, either alone or with a partner, is a normal part of human development (American Academy of Pediatrics, 2005). Healthy, consensual sexual activity is any sexual activity that fosters intimacy, bonding, shared pleasure and mutual respect between consenting partners (Sexual Information and Education Council of the United States, 2004). Youth's legal ability to consent to sexual activities with other youth of a similar age (Government of Canada, 1985) recognizes that youth sexual activity is developmentally appropriate. In the words of Coleman and Charles (2001), 'young people do not wake up on their 13th birthday, somehow transformed into a sexual being overnight. Even young children are sexual in some form.'

Despite evidence from medicine, sexology, psychology, education and history that sexuality is present in very young children (see Egan & Hawkes, 2010), the films nonetheless present sexuality as antithetical to the essence of childhood. An educator in *Sext Up Kids* positions sexuality and girlhood as dichotomous, saying that girls should 'Resist the pressure to sexualise themselves and focus on what matters most – their childhood.' There is no space within this binary for healthy, consensual sexuality to be part of the childhood life phase. Rather than subverting the dominant patriarchal and heterosexist values responsible for the false dichotomy of children and sexuality, these messages reinforce the myth that children are naturally and universally asexual.

Instead of being about the sexual activities of youth per se, these statements seem indicative of a greater narrative; adults are increasingly anxious about how their fantasies of the natural, universal, (hetero)asexual child are not matching with young people's realities. This frustration-fuelled panic with youth's sexual behaviours is reminiscent of the 'masturbation phobia' of the 19th century, where physicians, quacks and self-help gurus sadistically and often violently sought to mould 'deviant' children who masturbated into more acceptably asexual youth (Egan & Hawkes, 2010). Just as the subject of these films – the sexualization of girls – is not new, the accompanying adult anxieties around this phenomenon have existed for generations.

Commodification of youth sexuality

Faceless advertisers and media conglomerates are positioned as the clear villains in what's described as an epidemic of girls' sexualization. Three of the films take issue with how 'three-years olds are being marketed to as thirteen year olds' (*Sext Up Kids*, 2012), and then draw a causal relationship between that marketing and preschoolers' ownership of items such as padded bras (called 'bralets'), thong underwear, Bratz dolls, and T-shirts with slogans such as 'I Heart Dickies.'

In their discussion of sexualized products for young girls, the films make the claim that 'now more than ever, kids do have their own money' (*Sexy Inc.*, 2007), implying that children are purchasing these items for themselves. And indeed, depending on the class and age of particular youth, some girls are likely going to stores and buying these items on their own. Missing from the analysis, however, is acknowledgement of one of the constants of early childhood: young children do not make their own money. If they are in possession of currency, it is because an adult has given it to them. Similarly, young children do not generally go to stores and buy toys or clothing independently. A thread of childism is woven through the moral panic around sexualized consumer products for girls. The filmmakers divorce girls' purchasing or otherwise obtaining these goods from the relationships they have with the adults who either supply them with the goods themselves, or with the funds to obtain them. Since adults design, produce, market and buy these goods, the creation and maintenance of a 'girl market' is largely distinct from girls themselves.

The relationship between sexualized consumer goods and boys is also absent from the conversation, as none of the films mention this phenomenon. In focus groups with Scottish parents on sexualized goods, Bragg and Buckingham (2012) found that, when the parents mentioned sexualized consumer goods, 'boys' potentially "sexualised" consumption practices were generally viewed with amusement rather than alarm ... ' (p. 650). Viewing boys' sexualized goods as humorous shows how it is girls' bodies and behaviour that is under scrutiny, and the film-makers generally eschew discussion of boyhood masculinity altogether. This gendered application of childism reiterates the shaming of girls/invisibility of boys that is imbued throughout the films.

Victim blaming part 1: Slut-shaming as gendered and aged

There is a long and complex history between shame and sexual desire/activity, particularly with regard to girls and women. Rebuking Freud's (1933) claim that sexual shame is the 'female characteristic par excellence' (132), feminist theorists instead locate the origins of women's sexual shame in unequal relationships between men and women, particularly with regard to gendered divisions of labour (Benjamin, 1988). Sexual shame is therefore displayed as gendered behaviour, with men turning passivity into action and dominance, while women are expected to demonstrate submissiveness and accept sexual shame (Elise, 2008). Research consistently demonstrates that girls and women, more so than boys and men, are socialized during childhood to not only be ashamed of their bodies and sexuality, but also not understand the workings of their own bodies, be uncomfortable touching parts of their bodies and be given inaccurate information about their reproductive systems (Dio Bleichmar, 1995; Schooler et al., 2005; Elise, 2008).

Owing to its relationship with shame, womens' sexuality has been subject to intense, often forceful, regulation. One means of regulating girls' sexuality through shame is slut-shaming. As a form of victim blaming survivors of attempted or completed sexual assault, slut-shaming rhetorically regulates the clothing, grooming and behavioural choices of females who are thought to enjoy sexual activities (Ringrose & Renold, 2012). Slut-shaming is supported by fantasies of an evolutionarily uncontrollable male sexual desire, dominance and violence, and the alleged power that the female body has over these otherwise responsible men (Garner, 2012). A distinctly gendered and aged phenomenon, slut-shaming is rarely applied to boys and men, or to older/elderly women; slut-shaming is instead one of the many devices used to regulate younger women and girls.

With varying degrees of sophistication, girls' engagement in sexual activity is (nearly) universally presented in *Sexy, Inc.*, *Sext Up Kids* and *Miss Representation* as a bad thing; a shameful aberrant from an imagined norm that requires urgent adult intervention. None of the films' statistics or reports on girls' scandalized sexual activities mention who (else) is involved in these activities. As quoted earlier from *Miss Representation* (2012), 'more than 20% of girls under the age of 14 are having sex' was used as a foundation-less shaming device. The audience is not invited to question if these girls are acting alone, with a partner, or multiple partners. How do the partners involved identify their gender(s)? Is there consent and/or pleasure in these activities? Purposefully not including this information, or not bothering to ask these questions, conforms to the normative trope whereby girls' engagement in sexual activity is inherently bad (Connell, 2005).

Meanwhile, the presumed males with whom these girls are engaging in sex acts are rendered invisible and therefore beyond judgement. The films present no parallel statistics or examples of boys engaging in sexual acts other than some quantified, largely decontextualized, data on boys' consumption of Internet pornography, which presumably consists of sexual performances by girls or women. By not interpreting the data on boys' pornography consumption (e.g. what is being watched, why is it being watched, how do boys understand their use of pornography?), viewers are led to conclude that boys' consumption of Internet pornography is a normative, unchangeable phenomenon.

Attaching differing gendered labels to sexual activities is a common feature of slut-shaming. When girls engage in sexual activity, labels such as 'slut,' 'whore,' and 'dirty' give social cues that sexual activity is shameful for girls. This was demonstrated in an interview in *Sexy, Inc.*, when, upon learning that the word 'promiscuous' meant 'slut,' a grimacing middle school aged girl says 'yuck.' *Sext Up Kids* similarly denigrates and shames sex work by exclaiming, 'The Bratz dolls are like Sesame Street walkers!' Conversely, boys engaging in sexual activity are given positive socially successful labels such as 'player' and 'pimp,' insinuating that this is a social position of power and control (*Sexy, Inc.*, 2007). Socializing messages predominate that girls should hide and feel shame for sexual acts, whereas boys are praised and given high fives.

Stemming in part from the slut-shaming of girls' real or perceived sexual activities is a thread of finger-wagging at girls for engaging in sexual activity 'like adults.' A physician in *Sexy, Inc.* uses an anecdote about how 14-year-olds have a difficult time setting clear boundaries with their partners to illustrate how teen sex is out of control (*Sexy, Inc.*, 2007). Similarly, a commentator in *Sext Up Kids* asks, 'Are young people really understanding what constitutes positive, comfortable, healthy sex?' (*Sext Up Kids*, 2012). Yet decades of research on sexual assault demonstrates that many *adults* experience difficulties in setting clear sexual boundaries and enjoying positive, healthy sex (Stitt & Lentz, 1996; Beres, 2007; Statistics Canada, 2013). Identifying difficulties with sexual boundary setting as an exclusively youth problem, misses the fact that defining and respecting consent is a global human problem.

Zeroing in on youth's transgressions of more universal issues around sexual boundaries, consent and technologies indicates how the childist ways in which youth are being used a vehicle through which adult anxieties about *adult* sexual identity are being (re)defined (Faulkner, 2010). Similar to Taylor's (2010) conclusions about the Australian media's sexualization of children, the film's shaming of children appears to be a safe way for the adults who produce and consume these films to address their own shame around sexual identity and activity. In doing so, adults are able to project sexual deviance on to someone else. In Taylor's research, this was demonstrated by a shadowy, ever-lurking paedophile; in these films, it is youth who are assumed to be unable to set sexual boundaries. By focusing on the sexual shame of the other, adults are able to talk about sexual shame without feeling shamed themselves.

Shaming, which includes slut shaming, can have perverse long-term effects. Prolonged unaddressed shame can have destructive emotional and behavioural impact on a person, such as anxiety (Gilbert, 2003), depression (Kim et al., 2011), anger (Tagney et al., 1992) and post-traumatic stress (Lee et al., 2001). The films do not distinguish whether the negative effects of sexualization on girls reported by the APA (2010) is due to sexualization itself, or resultant of slut-shaming imbued in conversations of sexualization.

Victim blaming part 2: 'Protecting' girls from normatively violent young masculinity

Perhaps the most unsettling and counterproductive theme is the film's implicit endorsement of victim-blaming as a means of correcting young girls 'bad' behaviours, with the goal of making them safer from boys and men. This blame is especially apparent around 'sexting,' which is defined as 'the creating, sharing and forwarding of sexually suggestive nude or nearly nude images' (Lenhart, 2009: 3). In a *Sext Up Kids* vignette, a shame-faced 13-year-old girl is interviewed in a confessional setting where she talks of the 'deep regret and . . . embarrassment' she felt when she consensually sexted a photo to her boyfriend, who then distributed the photo over school listserves without her consent. The advice given by film-makers and the girls themselves was to be 'very careful' about female sexting, as images can be quickly spread through the Internet (*Sext Up Kids*, 2012).

This advice is simply an application of patriarchal offline behaviours to cyberspaces. The girl in the story was portrayed as a 'fallen woman' who had learned her lesson. She has repented by sharing her shamed actions with others in hopes of preventing similar scenarios for other girls. The boyfriend, who allegedly distributed private photos without her permission, is neither interviewed nor taken up as a central character. He is not shamed, nor is it reported that he is encouraged or required, by school policy or the law, to take any responsibility for his actions.

This highlighted scenario is, unfortunately, a common vignette. For example, *Megan's Story*, an Australian public service announcement, follows the same narrative arc with the same admonishment that girls 'think again' before sexting (Albury & Crawford, 2012: 463). The UK-based short film *Exposed* carries a similar message (Ringrose et al., 2013). The victim-blame around sexting is in many ways the same victim-blame that holds women responsible for the sexual violence against their bodies; however, it is now applied to a new technology. It is the same message that Eve Ensler's (1996) 'My Short Skirt' monologue challenged a generation ago. Why then is the repetition of this morality so culturally palatable?

The film-makers' editorial decision to recycle the trope of female self-protection is understandable only when a powerful absent referent, unquestioned normative masculinity is recognized. Under the 'boys will be boys' mentality, male harassment, violence and criminality are excused as a 'natural' part of masculinity (Garner, 2012; Renold & Ringrose, 2012; Stoltenberg, 1989). Nowhere is the films' endorsement of this dangerous masculinity as obvious than in *Miss Representation*, when normative objectification of young girls' bodies is explained away with 'We are a nation of teenage boys!' (*Miss Representation*, 2012). This comment, besides being awfully degrading to teenage boys, begs the question, what does it mean to be a teenage boy? *Sext Up Kids* characterizes young men as unable or unwilling to understand consent or boundaries, much less be considerate, respectful decision-makers in their interactions with others. Both subtle and obvious, young masculinity is presented and accepted here in the demeaning and limiting ways, and as a fixed constant in political, social, and sexual life. A young woman states emphatically, 'it's impossible to get someone to stop sexting you'. As in many of the topics addressed so far, the films do not engage with research on boyhood and young masculinity, which in fact interrogates and dismantles the stable, deterministic and potentially violent masculinity presented in the films (see Hyde et al., 2009; Korobov & Thorne, 2006; Martino et al., 2003).

These normative, violent and misogynistic masculinities are ironically enough protected from change by well-meaning programmes designed to 'empower' girls, such as iGirl in *Sext Up Kids*, or the *Miss Representation* curriculum, which are posited as antidotes to the moral panic addressed by the films. While it appears from the filming of such programmes that they create lovely safe(r) spaces for young girls to be in, we are dubious of their effect on the stated problem of media hypersexualization of girls, or the un(der)stated problem of male-perpetuated sexual violence. The most apparent absent referent is acknowledgement that because men and boys create, perpetuate and are excused for sexualized violence against women and girls, it is perhaps men and boys who need to be 'empowered' to not rape, harass or assault.

The empowering girls programmes endorsed by the films are not only as functionally useless as the rape whistles provided in college dorms, but also communicate the far more dangerous message that male sexualization of their bodies is inevitable and unchanging. No amount of 'empowering' girls is likely to stop the troubling sexualization and fetishization of women and girls by men and boys. Indeed, recent research from Wales indicates that children identify sexual harassment from their peers, not sexualization, as a more distressing and salient issue in their lives (Renold, 2013). Rather than trying to give voice to the voiceless, it is time to give 'ears to the earless' (Currie et al., 2009), perhaps by producing documentaries that address dominant conceptions of performative masculinity – which are incidentally the same conceptions of masculinity that undergird sexual harassment – that also underpin sexualization.

The Purity Myth

Based on a book by Jessica Valenti (2009) of the same name, *The Purity Myth* offers substantially different arguments from those of the three films discussed thus far. Although the stated subject matter of *The Purity Myth* is the sexualization of the abstinence movement and is therefore somewhat different than that of the previous films, it nonetheless adds a significantly different perspective to ongoing conversations about girls, sexuality and sexualization. For instance, *The Purity Myth* alone draws attention to how moral warriors fetishize childhood innocence:

> The bottom line is that while proponents of things like purity balls argue that they're aiming to protect girls from sexualization, they're actually doing exactly the opposite. By focusing on girls' virginity, they're positioning girls as sexual objects before they even hit puberty. And in this way, they're actually enforcing the very problem they claim to want to fix.
>
> (*The Purity Myth*, 2011)

Further distinguishing itself from the canon of moral panic around the sexualization of girls, *The Purity Myth* recognizes how purity discourses ignore the multiple intersectional subjectivities of girlhood.

> The very word virginity conjures images of white dresses and unspoiled femininity. But the perfect virgin is not just any woman.... She's always young, white, and skinny.... She's never a woman of color – who are too hypersexualized in our culture to ever be considered virginal. She's never a low-income girl. She's never fat or transgender. She's never disabled.
>
> (*The Purity Myth*, 2011)

Here, *The Purity Myth* brings to a popular audience the arguments that the panic over the sexualization of girls is inextricably bound up in anxieties about race and class (see Egan, 2013). Virginity and indeed girlhood are not universally under attack, but contextually so; only *some* girls and *some* virginity are worth panicking about. This represents a radically different approach than *Sexy, Inc.*, *Sext Up Kids* and *Miss Representation*, which have a narrow focus on white, middle-class, presumably heterosexual girls. Where *Sexy, Inc.*, *Sext Up Kids* and *Miss Representation* seem to miss not only how other subjectivities are interwoven with sexualization, *The Purity Myth* addresses these intersections head on, and in so doing, includes a larger proportion of actual girls as the films' subjects.

The Purity Myth's differences from the other films could stem largely from the subjectivities and politics of its creator. Jessica Valenti is the founder of Feministing.com, a website that is explicitly by and for *young* women. Feministing began out of then-25-year-old Valenti's frustration with the 'profound unfair[ness] that an elite few in the feminist movement had their voices listened to, and that the work of so many younger women went misrepresented or ignored altogether' (Cobble, Gordon, & Henry, 2014: 2). The film continues her work on the intersections of youthfulness and gender by creating spaces within the feminist movement in which young women's subjectivities can be spoken and heard. Coupled with her own relative youth (she was 30 years old when she wrote the film), Valenti's commitment to youth voice and feminist politics allow her film to avoid the childism, historical revisionism, and slut-shaming of the other three documentaries.

Conclusion

Documentaries have tremendous pedagogical potential to inform public and popular conversational about important phenomena. While *Sexy, Inc.*, *Sext Up Kids* and *Miss Representation* indicate that the contours of popular theorizing about children and sexuality in documentary films have not changed substantially since the 1940s, *The Purity Myth* demonstrates how younger voices are nonetheless creating spaces to subvert, resist and add to ongoing dialogues around sexualization and girls.

While these films were well received by the public, we feel that important questions remain unaddressed. We propose a radical and subversive new approach when using film to meaningfully educate about the sexualization of girls. Three main recommendations are proposed. Without turning away from women and girls, our analysis of the films calls for a dramatic re-teaching and redefining of masculinities, from boyhood through manhood. Building on the growing body of work pertaining to pro-feminist masculinity in general, and young masculinity in particular (Kimmel, 2008; Martino & Pallotta-Chiarolli, 2003; Murphy, 2009; Stoltenberg, 1989), the unquestioned acceptance of normative masculinity in the films illustrates an urgent need for this field to not only grow, but to move outside the academy and into popular theorizing. Here, we echo Garner's (2012) call for 'the missing link' – masculinity – to be more comprehensively integrated into conversations about sexualization and sexual citizenship for young people (see Robinson, 2013).

Our findings also indicate that rather than piggybacking on concern for youth, *adult* (sexual) anxieties and subjectivities need to be addressed with transparency. With regard to healthy sexual boundary-setting, it is clear that narrowing the discussion to focus on how girls are negotiating sexual activities distorts what is in fact a global human problem. The same can be said for the role of Internet communication in human life. Documentaries that address this subject free from childist insinuations about how youth are using virtual communications immaturely, implying that adults do much better, will likely have more to contribute to both the subject matter and to theory-building on childhood besides recycled panic.

Finally, we advocate for the meaningful and substantial inclusion of children's views, which are typically 'absent, sidelined, ignored or simplified in the "sexualisation" debates' (Renold, 2013: 5) within conversations on sexualization, including documentary films on this subject. Rather than contributing occasional interviews to a narrative that is otherwise constructed by adults, youth can be involved at all levels of production, such as conducting interviews, writing, filming and editing. In so doing, the documentaries on children, sexuality and sexualization might produce more varied and complex storylines. For instance, recent scholarship indicates that sexuality and sexual learning is a part of childrens' everyday lives, and is experienced as 'a mixture of fun, power, powerlessness, anxiety, danger and risk' and that children 'were more worried about scary images than "sexually explicit" images' (Renold, 2013: 9). Coupled with the inclusion of youth, we suggest better integration of research from the humanities and social sciences as a means of contextualizing and grounding documentaries on these important subjects.

There are broader implications of such documentaries that can inform pedagogy in the social sciences. While the films all accurately demonstrate how the expansion of communicative technologies has influenced youth and sexuality, they do not contribute any other new insights to popular childhood theorizing beyond this point. The films readily show the shaming and policing that occurs at the intersection of femaleness with childhood in the form of the sexualized girl, who must be controlled not only because of her youth, but also her gender. With the exception of *The Purity Myth*, the films largely reiterate and reinforce the same troubling, reductive and ultimately violent theories about gender, youth and sexualities that were promoted in films from the 1940s onwards. Addressing these absent referents will not only enhance the pedagogical potential of the films, but also facilitate better understandings of the complex nuanced nature of this phenomenon in order to enact more efficacious change.

Note

1. See Eberwein (1999) for comprehensive history of how these anxieties manifested in North American sexual health education films throughout the 20th century.

References

Albury, K., & Crawford, K. (2012) Sexting, consent and young people's ethics: Beyond Megan's story. *Continuum: Journal of Media & Cultural Studies*, 26 (3), 463–473.

American Academy of Pediatrics (2005) *Preventing sexual violence: An educational toolkit for health care professionals web version*. Retrieved from http://www2.aap.org/pubserv/PSVpreview/pages/behaviorchart.html

American Psychological Association (2010) *Report of the APA task force on the sexualization of girls*. Retrieved from http://www.apa.org/pi/women/programs/girls/report-full.pdf

Benjamin, J. (1988) *The bonds of love: Psychoanalysis, feminism, and the problem of domination*. New York: Pantheon.

Beres, M. A. (2007) Spontaneous' sexual consent: An analysis of sexual consent literature. *Feminism and Psychology*, 17 (1), 93–108.

Bissonnette, S., & National Film Board of Canada (2007) *Sexy Inc: Nos enfants sous influence*. Canada: ONF/NFB.

Bragg, S., & Buckingham, D. (2012) Global concerns, local negotiations and moral selves. *Feminist Media Studies*, 13 (4), 643–659.

Braun, V., & Clarke, V. (2006) Using thematic analysis in psychology. *Qualitative Research in Psychology*, 3, 77–101.

Bruhm, S., & Hurley, N. (2004) Curiouser: On the queerness of children, in S. Bruhm, & N. Hurley (Eds.) *Curiouser: On the Queerness of Children*. Minneapolis: University of Minneapolis Press, pp. 1–12.

Canadian Broadcasting Corporation Media Education Foundation (2012) *Sext up kids: How children are becoming hypersexualized*. Northampton: Media Education Foundation.

Cobble, D. S., Gordon, L., & Henry, A. (2014, August 31). From riot grrrls to 'Girls': Tina Fey, Kathleen Hanna, Lena Dunham and the birth of an inspiring new feminism. *Salon*. Retrieved from http://www.salon.com/2014/08/31/from_riot_grrrls_to_girls_tina_fey_kathleen_hanna_lena_dunham_and_the_birth_of_an_inspiring_new_feminism/

Coleman, H., & Charles, G. (2001) Adolescent sexuality: A matter of condom sense. *Journal of Child and Youth Care*, 14 (4), 17–18.

Connell, R. (2005) Desire as interruption: Young women and sexuality education in Ontario, Canada. *Sex Education*, 5 (3), 253–268.

Coontz, S. (2000) *The way we never were: American families and the nostalgia trap*. New York: Basic Books.

Coronet Instructional Films (1947) *Are You Popular?* Retrieved from https://www.youtube.com/watch?v=l92Mu4-Dheo

Currie, D. H., Kelly, D. M., & Pomerantz, S. (2009) *'Girl power': Girls reinventing girlhood*. New York: Peter Lang.

Dio Bleichmar, E. (1995) The secret in the constitution of female sexuality: The effects of the adult's sexual look upon the subjectivity of the girl. *Journal of Clinical Psychoanalysis*, 4 (3), 331–342.

Eberwein, R. (1999) *Sex ed: Film, video, and the framework of desire*. New Brunswick, NJ: Rutgers University Press.

Egan, R. D. (2013) *Becoming sexual: A critical appraisal of the sexualisation of girls*. Cambridge: Polity Press.

Egan, R. D., & Hawkes, G. (2008) Endangered girls and incendiary objects: Unpacking the discourse on sexualisation. *Sexuality & Culture*, 12 (4), 291–311.

Egan, R. D., & Hawkes, G. (2010) *Theorizing the sexual child in modernity*. New York: Palgrave Macmillan.

Elise, D. (2008) Sex and shame: The inhibition of female desires. *Journal of American Psychoanalytic Association*, 56 (1), 73–98.

Ensler, E. (1996) *The vagina monologues*. New York: Villard.

Faulkner, J. (2010) The innocence fetish: The commodification and sexualisation of children in the media and popular culture. *Media International Australia*, 135, 106–117.

Faulkner, J. (2011) *The importance of being innocent: Why we worry about children*. Melbourne: Cambridge University Press.

French, M. (2008) *From eve to dawn: A history of women*. New York: Feminist Press City University of New York.

Freud, S. (1933) *Three essays on the theory of sexuality*. New York: Basic Books.

Garner, M. (2012) The missing link: The sexualisation of culture and men. *Gender and Education*, 24 (3), 325–331.

Gilbert, P. (2003) *The compassionate mind: A new approach to life's challenges*. Oakland, CA: New Harbinger Publications.

Government of Canada (1985) *The criminal code of Canada*. Retrieved from http://laws-lois.justice.gc.ca/PDF/C-46.pdf

Hyde, A., Drennan, J., Howlett, E., & Brady, D. (2009) Young men's vulnerability in constituting hegemonic masculinity in sexual relations. *American Journal of Men's Health*, 3 (3), 238–251.

Thally, S., Earp, J., Valenti, J., Morris, S., Young, J., & Media Education Foundation (2011) *The Purity Myth*. Northampton: Media Education Foundation.

Kim, S., Thibodeau, R., & Jorgensen, R. S. (2011) Shame, guilt, and depressive symptoms: A meta-analytic review. *Psychological Bulletin*, 137 (1), 68–96.

Kimmel, M. (2008) *Guyland: The perilous world where boys become men*. New York: Harper.

Korobov, N., & Thorne, A. (2006) Intimacy and distancing: Young men's conversations about romantic relationships. *Journal of Adolescent Research*, 21 (1), 27–55.

Landis, J. T., & Coronet Instructional Films (1951) *Going Steady?* Retrieved from https://www.youtube.com/watch?v=RAKSX7oHBVE.

Lee, D. A., Scragg, P., & Turner, S. (2001) The role of shame and guilt in traumatic events: A clinical model of shame-based and guilt-based PTSD. *British Journal of Medical Psychology*, 74 (4), 451–466.

Lenhart, A., & Pew Internet and American Life Project (2009) *Teens and sexting: How and why minor teens are sending sexually suggestive nude or nearly nude images via text messaging*. Washington: Pew Internet & American Life Project.

Martino, W., & Pallotta-Chiarolli, M. (2003) *So what's a boy?* Maidenhead: Open University Press.

Murphy, P. F. (2009) *Feminism and masculinities*. Oxford: Oxford University Press.

Newsom, J. S., Scully, R. K., Winfrey, O., O'Donnell, R., Rice, C., Ling, L., Pelosi, N., & Virgil Film (2012) *Miss representation*. New York: Virgil Films.

Renold, E. (2013) Boys and girls speak out: A qualitative study of children's gender and sexual cultures (age 10–12). *National Society for the Prevention of Cruelty to Children*. Retrieved from http://www.nspcc.org.uk/Inform/research/findings/boys-and-girls-speak-out_wda100425.html

Ringrose, J., & Renold, E. (2012). Slut-shaming, girl power and 'sexualisation': Thinking through the politics of the international SlutWalks with teen girls. *Gender and Education*, 24, (3), 333–343.

Ringrose, J., Harvey, L., Gill, R., & Livingstone, S. (2013) Teen girls, sexual double standards, and 'sexting': Gendered value in digital image exchange. *Feminist Theory*, 14 (3), 305–323.

Ringrose, J., & Renold, E. (2012) Slut-shaming, girl power and 'Sexualization': Thinking through the politics of the International Slutwalks with teen girls. *Gender and Education*, 24 (3), 333–343.

Robinson, K. H. (2013) *Innocence, knowledge, and the construction of childhood: The contradictory nature of sexuality and censorship in children's contemporary lives*. London: Routledge.

Schooler, D., Ward, L. M., Merriwether, A., & Caruthers, A. S. (2005) Cycles of shame: Menstrual shame, body shame, and sexual decision-making. *Journal of Sex Research*, 42 (4), 324–334.

Sexuality Information and Education Council of the United States (2004) *Guidelines fo. comprehensive sexuality education: Kindergarten – 12th grade*, 3rd edn. Retrieved from http://www.siecus.org/_data/global/images/guidelines.pdf.

Sid Davis Productions (1961) *Girls, Beware!* https://www.youtube.com/watch?v= TV7IdCPs_FY

Statistics Canada (2013) *Measuring violence against women: Statistical trends*, http:/. www.statcan.gc.ca/pub/85-002-x/2013001/article/11766-eng.pdf

Stitt, B. G., & Lentz, S. A. (1996) Consent and its meaning to the sexual victimizatior of women. *American Journal of Criminal Justice*, 20 (2), 237–257.

Stockton, K. B. (2009) *The queer child, or growing sideways in the twentieth century* Durham, NC: Duke University Press.

Stoltenberg, J. (1989) *Refusing to be a man: Essays on sex and justice*. Portland, OR Breitenbush Books.

Tagney, J. P., Wager, P., Fletcher, C., & Gramzow, R. (1992) Shamed into anger. The relation of shame and guilt to anger and self-reported aggression. *Journal o Personality and Social Psychology*, 62 (4), 669–675.

Taylor, A. (2010) Troubling childhood innocence: Reframing the debate over the media sexualization of children. *Australian Journal of Early Childhood*, 35 (1), 48–57

Valenti, J. (2009). *The purity myth: How America's obsession with virginity is hurting youn, women*. Berkeley, CA: Seal Press.

Young-Bruehl, E. (2012) *Childism: Confronting prejudice against children*. New Haven CT: Yale University Press.

Part V

New Media, Digital Technology and Young Sexual Cultures

19

New Visibilities? 'Using Video Diaries to Explore Girls' Experiences of Sexualized Culture

Sue Jackson and Tina Vares

In spring 2006 an anniversary issue of the New Zealand youth culture magazine *Pavement* featured 'Lost Youth', a collection of photographic portraits of young people, mostly aged 15–19, accompanied by each young person's narrative. In some of the images, young women were posed in explicitly sexual postures and 'dressed' in ways typically seen in *Playboy* magazine. But it was an image of 10-year-old Jessica Thompson in the collection that met with a hostile public reaction. The head and shoulders image of Jessica depicted her gazing directly at the camera, her lips parted and coated with bright red lipstick. This image drew claims of inappropriate sexualization, most vociferously from a child advocacy group which laid a complaint with the Broadcasting Standards Authority. In her narrative, Jessica described herself as 'just an average' girl who liked sleepovers and raising chickens, loved her teddy bear and enjoyed doing modelling work. Countering claims of her daughter's sexualization, Jessica's mother told news media her daughter had liked to play with make-up from an early age. Around the same time as Jessica's appearance in *Pavement* magazine, the Australia Institute *Corporate paedophilia* report was released, generating its own set of alarming concerns about the sexualization of children in, through and by media. Both of these media-highlighted events raised important questions for us, as researchers, about the meanings of 'child sexualization' and the substance to claims that girls were being sexualized by 'sexualizing' media images. These questions were the impetus for undertaking the research project discussed in this chapter.

Crucially absent in the *Corporate paedophilia* report, and the sexualization of girls literature that has followed in its wake (e.g. Hamilton, 2007; Levin & Kilbourne, 2008; Oppliger, 2008), is empirically derived knowledge about the ways girls are responding to, managing and making sense of the sexually saturated media that they are growing up with. Undertaking such research

307

faces the challenges of any sexually related empirical work with girls, particularly pre-teen girls. For example, how can researchers enable girls to speak about sexual media in cultural conditions that construct sexuality as taboo for pre-teen girls or that represent them as being at great risk through sexuality and sexualization? Addressing the research challenges of 'sexualization' research, this chapter adopts a methodological focus in which we discuss the use of media video diaries to investigate girls' negotiation of hypersexy representations in 'tween' popular culture. Our intention is to reflect on the ways in which this visual methodology contributed different and sometimes unique perspectives of girls' experiences of consuming 'sexualized' popular culture. More specifically, we show how video cameras contextualized girls' engagement with sexualized media in the everyday of their bedrooms and social lives and expanded possibilities for girls' self-expression in relation to sexualized popular culture. In taking a methodological approach, we hope to both build upon and expand the toolkit of methods engaged by researchers in their endeavours to meet the challenges of researching girls' negotiation of sexually saturated media.

Girls and sexualization: Methodological challenges

Undertaking research with girls in a context of 'sexualization' shares some of the challenges of broader sexuality research with girls, the more so where those girls are children. Historically much of the research about children and sexuality excluded the child perspective, instead drawing on adult interpretations of children's behaviour (Myers & Raymond, 2010). This adultcentric dominance may reflect, at least to some extent, a normative construction of children as sexually unaware, naive and devoid of sexual subjectivity (Renold, 2006, 2013; Egan, 2013). Renold (2006) also observes a tendency in some ethnographic studies towards positioning children's sexuality as 'play' or 'trying out' adult sexuality which fails to bring to light the complications and contradictions children must deal with in terms of being and becoming sexual. Yet it is also the case that adopting a perspective of children as active, meaning making sexual subjects in qualitative research, casts its own research shadows. From a 'sense of obligation to provide data', perhaps through a position of vulnerability or desire to please (Holland et al., 2010), to a privileging of responses that resonate with researchers' ideologies of child participants as autonomous, sexually aware and reflexive (Gill, 2012), qualitative studies present various ethical challenges around questions of agency and power. These questions infiltrate researchers' expectations on children to speak of sexual matters, ways that children/girls perspectives are represented/analysed and how the research is conducted. Holland et al. critique the view that participatory research is somehow more 'empowering' for children since even where it seems children are given 'control' over method (e.g. taking photographs) they are directed as to content. Issues of agency and vulnerability in the research process are magnified within the discursive blanket that envelops meanings of girlhood sexuality, impacting on what stories are told (or not) in the research context, and we turn to considerations of this cultural context next.

Researching girlhood sexuality in a culture that has so profoundly problematized girls' sexuality (e.g. around risks and danger) and sidelined, if not silenced, sexual pleasure and desire (Fine, 1988; Tolman, 2002) has implications for what girls may feel able to share with researchers. Morality discourses of the 'good girl' (Walkerdine, 1990) or the 'child innocent' (Egan, 2013), for example, constitute girls as asexual and work against disclosures that may align them with participation or even interest in sexual practices or sexual material. Fine's (1988) well-known work in the 1980s on the missing discourse of desire amply illustrated ways that discourses of girlhood sexuality exerted constraining effects on girls' communications about sexuality. Fine's investigation revealed that in the US public school system discourses of risk, danger and victimization allowed only a 'whisper' of desire to be voiced. In a contemporary 'sexualization' social context, these discourses operate through constructions of the 'sexualized' girl as the object and potential victim of a paedophilic, dangerous gaze; simultaneously, a sexualization discourse fixes the pre-teen girl as a sexual innocent (Egan & Hawkes, 2008). In part, these discourses of risk and innocence are at odds with the post-feminist discourses of girls' sexuality that circulate widely in girls' popular culture; here, the girl-subject is predominantly constructed as heterosexually desiring and desirable, compelled to constitute herself as knowledgeable and technically skilled in matters of sexuality and sexual attractiveness (Griffin, 2004; Gill, 2007). As a number of feminist researchers have observed (e.g. Renold & Ringrose, 2011; Jackson & Vares 2013; Renold, 2013), such contradictory discursive contexts greatly complicate girls' participation in a popular culture territory that is awash with 'pornified' heterosexy representations, a recent example being Miley Cyrus's 'twerking' performance at the 2013 MTV Music Video Awards.

Attuned to this complex and contradictory discursive territory within which girls engage with a sex-saturated culture, researchers need to consider how the methodologies they choose can work with (and perhaps against) the 'schizoid' conditions that typify the contemporary social moment (Renold & Ringrose, 2011). Building on their earlier work on 'thick desire' (Fine & McClelland, 2006), and addressing the methodological challenges of working with the discursive and sociopolitical constraints in and through which young women must speak, McClelland and Fine (2008) conceptualize the researcher's task (and challenge) as finding ways to 'peel back' the layers of 'collective discursive cellophane' that 'weigh down' young women's tongues, limiting what can and cannot be spoken. They propose expanding the methodological imagination through the use of 'release methods' that enable researchers to 'acknowledge, engage and queer' the role of 'cellophane'. Amongst the examples they discuss are theoretical frameworks that connect experiences or narratives to dominant discourses and sociopolitical contexts ('thickening' research data), participatory action research and performative methods. Within the small but increasing body of feminist research exploring girls and young women's experiences of sexualized culture there is strong evidence of a methodological imagination at work. Renold and Ringrose (2011), for example, explored girls' negotiations of sexuality and sexualization through self-productions on Bebo sites and home video recordings within a Deleuzian framework that attended both to the 'macro' (e.g. regulatory discourses) and 'micro' (girls' negotiations, 'lines of flight') worlds of girls. Duits and van Zoonen (2011) directly asked girls to 'reflect on' sexualization in their own words and frames of reference, simultaneously recognizing girls' perspectives as 'discursively and socially situated' (p.495). Focused on an older age group (18–21), Dobson (2011) has explored young women's 'heterosexy' self-representations on MySpace within a performative theoretical framework. In our own work we have found a feminist post-structuralist framework (Gavey, 1989) useful in terms of working with the contradiction, complexity, plurality and social regulation that characterises the 'sexualization' field (Jackson & Vares, 2011; Vares et al., 2011). In the study we discuss here, we selected video diaries as our 'release method', recognizing the potential of video cameras to not only enable diverse ways of responding but also to ground the project in the everyday lived worlds of the girls. In the next section we flesh out more detail about the use of visual methodologies and document our specific approach to conducting the media video diary arm of the project (this method combined with focus groups; see Jackson & Vares, 2011) to explore girls' sense-making of 'sexualized' popular culture.

Visual methodologies

In contemporary popular culture the visual plays a key role in constituting femininities through an unprecedented attention to bodies (Aapola et al., 2005; Gill, 2007), on the one hand refixing them as objects of the gaze while simultaneously constructing them as modes of subjective empowerment. This emphasis on the visual body as integral to contemporary female identity lends a certain 'common sense' quality to working with visual methodologies. Moreover, the concerns with the sexualization of girls organize most intently around the 'pornified' visual, captured in the book covers of popular culture texts which uniformly present girls' sexualization through the looked-at body: for example, images of girls in very short skirts (Levin & Kilbourne, 2008) and midriff-baring tops (Hamilton, 2007), applying make-up (Durham, 2008), wearing zipped down jeans with crop top (Oppliger, 2008). Giving girls video cameras holds the potential for them to use the lens to gaze at this highly visual popular culture and 'talk back' to it

(Driver, 2007). Driver argues that video enables 'queering the gaze', allowing the 'constantly viewed young person' to become the viewer. As Pini (2001) cautions, however, using video cameras does not straightforwardly confer agency since participants remain aware that they are producing video diaries for a research gaze and interpretation. Nonetheless, video cameras provide scope for participants to use multiple modalities of expression – talk, gesture, movement, performance and so on – and they may also access knowledge about the ways in which participants 'live feelings and experiences through [our]their bodies' (Reavey & Johnson, 2011). Documenting their use of video diaries and cameras, Bloustien and Baker (2003) highlight girls' use of cameras as 'ways of interpreting and redefining their world, ways which frequently expressed far more than what the girls were saying' (p.69). Moreover, liberated from the use of words alone, participants may find alternative means to critique, subvert or transgress normative age, gender and class requirements of them (Frith et al., 2005; Driver, 2007). Performance methods, for example, allow for creative, dramatized expressions that may be conducive to experimentation outside norms (Rasmussen & Wright, 2001; cited McClelland & Fine, 2008).

In designing our project *Girls 'tween' popular culture and everyday life* we were encouraged by this potential of video cameras to broaden possibilities around what and how girls may narrate their views and experiences of sex-saturated media, and accordingly adopted media video diaries to complement the use of focus groups. In the interests of space, we are unable to document full details about the method, which included focus groups and a second year follow-up. Elsewhere (e.g. Vares et al., 2011) we have provided information about girls' backgrounds, ethics and our research process and feminist post-structuralist theoretical framework. To briefly capture our video diary research process here, however, we worked with 71 girls aged 11–13 in the first year of the project located in one North Island and one South Island metropolitan area of New Zealand. Girls were primarily middle class and came from diverse, mixed ethnic backgrounds. We worked initially with girls in their schools in focus groups of 7–10 following which they were instructed on video camera use and guidelines about filming, incorporating broad ideas on content. Thus at any time one North Island and one South Island group would have video cameras for one month to record a regular video media diary (i.e. talking about, showing media they engaged with). At the end of the month, girls gathered for a final group meeting to reflect on the media video diaries and to talk about their experiences of being in the project. The project required careful consideration of ethics around who could be filmed and where and also regarding girls' safety and confidentiality, for example possible pressures from others to show video diaries or to use the camera. Camera use was limited to girls' homes, the filming of family members only with consent given on camera, and filming of friends only if they were also in the project.

In the next section we address the question of what using media video diaries informed us about the ways in which girls are responding to/understanding 'sexualized' representations in media. We also contemplate, where suggested, those aspects that may have been uniquely captured through the use of a production method. Our discussion focuses on three spaces opened up by video cameras that illustrate different dimensions of girls' engagement (or not) with the hypersexy representations strongly associated with sexualization claims: bedroom spaces, consumption spaces and creative spaces. It is not our intention here to analyse girls' data as we have done elsewhere (Jackson & Vares, 2011, 2012, 2013) but to provide girls' material as examples of the kinds of data the methodology produced.

Bedroom spaces

In their study of girls and subcultures during the 1970s, McRobbie and Garber (1976) ventured that girls' bedrooms, unlike participation in male subcultures, provided a cultural space of their own. The authors suggested that in this 'bedroom culture' girls consumed media and experimented with make-up and fashion in constructing a sense of self. In the late1980s to early 1990s, Steele and Brown (1995) also focused on bedrooms as a media-rich environment in their research with young people. These earlier bedroom culture studies primarily involved researchers interviewing young women/people in their bedrooms. In a modern technological context, equipping girls with cameras or video cameras enables the bedroom to become a more ongoing research site, and grants researchers privileged access to this highly personal space without requiring a physical presence. Arguably, the absence of researchers allows girls to direct their own content within the parameters of producing a video diary about the popular culture they engage with in everyday life. Although we did not specify the bedroom as a place to film in our project (and indeed girls did occasionally film in the lounges of their homes and sometimes in the garden), girls uniformly filmed their media video diaries in their bedrooms. So how did girls' filming in their bedrooms inform questions about how they are engaging with sexualized media? One of the suggestions we gave girls was that they might like to conduct a 'bedroom tour' to show us the kinds of popular culture they used and perhaps also include a 'wardrobe tour' to show us the clothes they liked to buy and wear. Through showing us their bedrooms and talking to us about the objects that they filmed, the material conditions of girls' lives were strongly present. Socio-economic privilege revealed itself in bedrooms that were richly populated with media technologies such as a TV, iPod or MP3 player, computer, book-filled shelves and mobile phone. At the other, less common, end of the spectrum were rooms with none or few of these things. Girls' tours of their bedrooms similarly revealed the diversity of popular culture they engaged with; for example, music CDs/iPods were widely filmed and at least one popstar poster was generally present on the wall, but for some girls the books they showed us were a passion while for other girls it was their magazine collection. Importantly, however, popular culture was just one aspect of material life viewed through the lens, and girls also filmed photographs of friends, self, pets and family, awards from school or sporting successes or things they had made. This visual kaleidoscope, alongside girls' narratives about family, pets, out of school activities and interests, suggested that popular culture was simply a part of their lives and not the all-absorbing activity implicated in the girls' sexualization literature.

Girls interested in clothes and shopping responded to the invitation to show us their wardrobes, and often extended this to showing us the clothes they bought when they had been shopping. In the girls' sexualization literature, the 'hypersexy', porno-chic-styled clothes depicted in post-feminist media culture are presented as commonplace amongst girls and also as 'evidence' of their sexualization by media. The video cameras granted research access to the clothes girls wear and buy in their everyday lives, and we would argue that this 'real world' view is a unique contribution that complements what interview and focus group studies with girls have found. Uniformly, girls' clothing 'reveals' indicated an absence of the 'hypersexy' styles associated with sexualization, and where there was the possibility of 'sexy' readings girls provided explanations with their clothing display. For example, dresses with spaghetti straps or shoes with a low heel were for special occasions, short skirts required leggings and a sheer top needed to be worn with something underneath it (see Jackson & Vares, 2012, 2013). We are mindful of the possibility that girls had items of 'hypersexy' clothing elsewhere that they did not show us. On the other hand, its apparent absence is consistent with girls' talk about their avoidance and/or careful negotiations of 'sexy' clothing in order to avoid being labelled as 'skanky' or 'slutty' (e.g. Rysst, 2010; Duits & van Zoonen, 2011; Renold, 2013).

Consumption spaces

As suggested in studies of 'bedroom culture', the bedroom is a key site for girls' consumption (and production) of media (Kearney, 2007). Filming their consumption of media in 'real time' as they viewed it was a well-used approach amongst the girls in the project, allowing girls to simultaneously show us media and talk about their responses to it. Magazines, music videos, social networking and Internet sites were all forms of media popularly presented in this 'real time' (re)viewing. In the case of magazines, for example, girls typically conducted a magazine 'tour' flicking the pages and stopping to make comment on particular images. From behind the camera lens, girls showed and commented on a range of images that might be considered sexualized. Eryn (12), for example, talked for 19 minutes about *Girlfriend* in one of her diaries, responding to a photo feature about Miley Cyrus with an animated 'yuk, yuk, yuk.', a reaction later contextualized in her account of Miley's highly publicized semi-nude photo shoot for *Vanity Fair* as being 'so gross'. In another example, Heather also produced a detailed page by page review of *Girlfriend* magazine and drew attention to one particular page filled with small advertisements about which she commented, 'sometimes you can buy porno for your phone and it's in here – it's a bit gross. We don't like that stuff.' As well as operating as a conduit for critiques and spontaneous reactions to sexualized media, the cameras also functioned to convey girls' actively emerging subjectivities as they related media representations to self. This could be seen in Daria's distancing from an image of Rihanna in *Girlfriend* magazine dressed in a 'see through', porno-chic-styled black net bodysuit: 'This clothing right here that Rihanna is wearing is see through and the poses she is doing in this photo is just really, just ew, I never do anything like that'. In the same magazine she reacted to a girls' underwear fashion shoot with the comment that the girl was 'only 14 years of age and already posing half naked in a magazine that any old dirty man could pick up and get quite excited over, I would never do that.' (See Jackson & Vares, 2013 for analysis of girls' use of distancing as a tool to locate themselves inside moral and age-appropriate discourses.) Sometimes this emerging subjectivity in 'real time' responses was imbued with affective registers such as frustration, sadness or feeling bad about themselves. During her magazine flick Ilsa, for example, spoke of how hard it was for girls to see all the images of people with perfect skin and told us how this made her feel:

> most of the girls that I know have a skin problem called eczema and that is just like me I have eczema and it is really bad because seeing ads with people with perfect skin compared to mine makes me feel kinda sad, makes me feel like I wish that I had a better life.

On some occasions, the process of filming provided opportune material about girls' negotiations of sexualized content only because the camera was turned on during a 'media consumption' session. This aspect of the video cameras was particularly well illustrated in the video diaries of Jessica and Lily. In one of her diary entries Jessica filmed the Lady GaGa music video *Paparazzi* as she and her friend watched. Partway through the video Jessica's father entered the room. The video scene playing at this moment switches between GaGa dressed in a gold metallic Madonna-like bodysuit raising herself on crutches from a wheelchair to GaGa clad in a BDSM-styled black outfit performing sexually evocative movements on a sofa. Jessica's father's comment cannot be heard but Jessica responds to him with: 'It's **not** slutty, this one's not **slutty**. *(Dad leaves)* Did you see his face?' Not only does Jessica's comment suggest a previous conversation with her father may have taken place about what 'slutty' is, but the discursive work needed around being 'caught out' watching sexually laden content by a parent is also uniquely captured on film. So too does this example illustrate how the video cameras were able to contextualize girls' popular culture within the social; what is viewed and how it is made sense of may depend on who is involved in the viewing. In Lily's video diary the camera recorded the interactions between her and her cousin as they viewed a collage of Avril Lavigne images on YouTube. Prior to this video diary entry Lily had expressed her admiration of Avril Lavigne as a popstar whose videos were 'not about the kind of **dodgy**, sexy kind of, um, kind of **video**, like, where they have to wear like all, next to **nothing** and, you know, act all, touch themselves *(shudders)'*. As she and her cousin, Rosa, view the Lavigne collage a photo of Lavigne in a 'sexy' pose wearing short shorts appears on screen to which Rosa responds 'Whoa, look at that butt!' Perhaps aware of the inconsistency of the image with her accounts of Lavigne elsewhere, Lily counters with an admonishment of her cousin 'Rosa!' followed by, 'Well, as I said, we <u>don't</u> watch it for the music video!' As in Jessica's video diary, the video camera has again uniquely enabled a capture of a 'real-time' social situation requiring negotiation of a 'slutty' performance *as it unfolded*. While the video camera is not unique in allowing us to see girls' negotiation of sexualized media, we suggest it is able to locate that negotiation in girls' everyday use of media, be it alone, with friends or with family.

We suggest that the girls' technique of allowing us to share a magazine, or watch a music video (or explore a website with them) logged us into not only the popular culture sites they used but also to a 'live', real-time sense-making process as (often) unpredictable or unanticipated content came into view. We also suggest that the camera may have played a facilitating role in girls being able to share 'sexualized' content with us. More specifically, there is an argument to be made that the process of directing the camera at media and narrating from behind the lens provided distance that facilitated talking about sexualized content in ways that may be difficult for some girls in the face-to-face situation of focus groups. On the other hand, claims cannot be made that narratives from behind the lens peel back any more of the 'discursive cellophane' than is possible with creative approaches to focus groups (McClelland & Fine, 2008) since age, morality and sexualization discourses may inform girls' responses to hypersexual images. Such peeling back appears to be far more promising in the creative performance potential of video cameras, which we turn to next.

Creative spaces

Although all of the girls' media video diaries can be described as a performance of self (Pini, 2001), the focus in this section is on creative performance. Such performances included girls' creation of their own versions of pop songs. None of these creative performances adopted the 'sexy' appearances or moves depicted in sexualized music videos in contrast to studies where girls have deployed sexy moves in performances of pop songs found elsewhere (e.g., Baker, 2004; Renold & Ringrose, 2011). Although this absence could be read perhaps as reflecting girls' mindfulness of the adult researchers who would view the videos, it might also reflect the use of creative forms to explicitly critique media representations. Two additional forms of performance in girls' video diaries were a multi-episode TV show critiquing media (*Iris Rocks the Bedroom*) and several parodies of modelling shows. Here, we present the latter as an example of performance methods as 'experiential and experimental processes where forms of cultural signs and representations are deconstructed and reconstructed' (Rasmussen & Wright, 2001, cited McClelland & Fine, 2008, p. 247). Three groups of girls, not connected through friendship or school classes, used the video camera to film their own productions of television modelling shows, each of which can be described as a parody not only of the original form (modelling show) but also of the hyperfeminine, hypersexual subject that characterizes celebrity media. Elements that define parody are its humour, its obviousness of imitation, its spectacle and its exposure of the taken for granted (Kenny, 1999). Parody can be a powerful means of destabilizing gender although, as Butler (1990) argues, it is not of and in itself subversive and some forms are more gender-troubling than others. Butler focused on drag as a destabilization of femininity through rendering it as performance but, as Ferreday (2008) points out, this focus obscures women's parodies of femininity. Ferreday suggests that new burlesque troubles practices of femininity in much the same way as the excesses of femininity displayed through drag expose gender as performance. In the girls' modelling show parodies, this exposure could be seen in performances of overdone, hyperfeminine girliness.

One of the ways in which girls' modelling shows undermined girlie femininity was through voice and gesture. In a parody of Paris Hilton, for example, Lisa adopted a high-pitched, exaggerated girlie American accent accompanied by affected, flamboyant hand movements associated with comedy renditions of 'camp'. Similarly, Isla, Emily and Lana opened their modelling show (produced as a movie) with a high-pitched, girlie chorus of a prolonged 'Hey' executed in an American accent and voiced through fixed wide smiles ensued by girlie giggles and small, affected, handwaving gestures. These girls described the movie that they had made (of which they filmed parts and narrated for the video diary) as a 'take-off' of *America's Next Top Model*, clearly locating it as parody. Another way in which the hyperfemininity and hypersexuality of the modelling world were threatened in girls' performances was through the exaggerated use of red lipstick. Ferreday (2008), in her lengthy account of red lipstick in relation to new burlesque as parody, observes its troubling effects through its obvious visibility and its 'flaunting of artifice' that contrasts with expectations that women make invisible the work of beautification practices. Isla and Lisa's use of red lipstick overstated the obviousness or the visibility of their painted mouths through purposively extending the lipstick beyond the lipline. In Lisa's parody this ridiculed sign of excess femininity played a key part. For example, at one point she told the 'audience' in her affected voice, 'I have so much wrong with my make-up this morning' (raising her hand affectedly to indicate her mouth), and the red smudged mouth later drew comment from show compère Hannah, 'Uh your lips are a little bit- mm', to which Lisa replied, 'Uh, I did make myself look really beautiful this morning.'

In addition to parodies of appearance in modelling shows, girls also incorporated parodies of the 'sexy' poses and moves of catwalk models. This was particularly so in Carla and Jessica's show, which also undermined (hyper)sexy fashion. In the opening of the show, for example, Carla 'models' an enormous pair of red hands (souvenirs from a netball game where the audience used them to cheer the national Silver Ferns netball team), wiggling her hips a little then strutting across the room, her hips swinging from side to side before she stops to pose with one oversized hand held behind her head, the other on her hip, finally blowing a kiss to the audience. As the compère, Jessica encourages her to 'Shake that!', and Carla exaggerates a wiggle then collapses to the floor on her bottom as her finale. Effects of parody are carried by the perversity of two gigantic hands being constructed as 'fashion' and being modelled in a 'sexy' way and the 'undoing' of sexiness in the finale of the sequence. Jessica continues the theme in her modelling of an oversized dowelling star which she models with twirls, hand on hip poses and a hair flick finale. Throughout their show, the girls appropriate the post-feminist language of hypersexiness as they compère one another's catwalks; for example 'Wooh! Oh that is hot, hot, hot!', 'Uh-shake that thing', 'Oh shake that ass, Jessica, shake it!' These references to sexy moves repeatedly juxtapose the ridiculous 'unsexy' (clothes, props), exposing the fragility of the 'sexy' femininity.

Through commonalities with drag (the overdone make-up, the flamboyant movements) and new burlesque (the painted mouth), together with the exaggerated girliness and the undermining of hypersexiness through fashion and movement, the girls' practices may be read as deconstructing and destabilizing femininity. We suggest that these forms of subversion largely rely on the visual to accomplish their effects and, as such, are uniquely enabled by the video camera. Importantly, in the context of 'peeling back the discursive cellophane' (McClelland & Fine, 2008), the creative processes enabled by the cameras provided a way for girls to critique the hypersexy forms of post-feminist media in a way that circumvented reliance on regulatory discourses of sexuality (e.g. discourse of the 'slut', see Ringrose & Renold, 2012) that are most widely available to them. We argue this to be a major strength of using our video diary methodology.

Concluding commentary

Our intention in this chapter has been to offer insights into the ways in which a visual methodology enables different possibilities for exploring girls' sense-making and responses to sexualized media. Importantly, we do not wish to overstate the case for the use of visual methods as a method for researching sexualization but rather see it as complementary to other methods in sexuality research with girls. Nor do we accord greater 'authenticity' or 'truth' to girls' material because of our physical absence or the 'real world' filming. As in all research, the girls' material is socially and contextually situated, embedded in the discursive resources available to them. We would argue, however, that there is much to be gained in gathering girls' perspectives of sexualized media via a video camera. Locating the bedroom as a research site, for example, identified the kinds of popular culture girls surrounded themselves with in everyday life and the breadth of girls' lives beyond their media consumption. Viewed through the camera lens, girls' bedrooms were also a site that troubled ideas about their consumption of sexualized goods and clothing. From another perspective, girls' ability to use the camera as an 'eye' on sexualized media, showing media to the researchers as they respond in 'real-time' moments of viewing, would seem to be another valuable aspect of the method. As Driver (2007) suggests, this represents a subversion of the gaze wherein the media becomes the critical object of the girls' gaze in an 'undoing' of the media's scrutiny of female bodies. We offer the suggestion that narrating from behind the lens provides a safe, distancing place from which to speak. We also venture that the 'real-time' feature of the camera enabled a capture of in-the-moment negotiations of sexualized media which occurred opportunely as girls filmed. However, as we noted above, the creative opportunities enabled by the use of video cameras are arguably the greatest strength and the unique aspect of the methodology in enabling girls to 'gaze back' critically at popular culture. It would be highly misleading to suggest that putting video cameras in the hands of girls somehow liberates them from the 'discursive cellophane' that constrains their self-expression but, on the other hand, cameras allow for the possibility of providing a 'release point' towards enabling different visibilities about how girls are using and making sense of sexualized media.

References

Aapola, S., Gonick, M., & Harris, A. (2005) *Young femininity.* Houndmills, Basingstoke: Palgrave Macmillan.

Baker, S. (2004) 'It's not about candy': Music, sexiness and girls' serious play in after school care. *International Journal of Cultural Studies,* 7, 197–212.

Bloustien, G., & Baker, S. (2003) 'On not talking to strangers'. Researching the micro-worlds of girls through visual auto-ethnographic practices. *Social Analysis,* 47, 64–79.

Butler, J. (1990) *Gender trouble: Feminism and the subversion of identity*. London: Routledge.

Dobson, A. (2011) Heterosexy representations by young women on MySpace: The politics of performing an 'objectified' self. *Outskirts Online Journal*, 25 November, 1–14.

Driver, S. (2007) *Queer girls and popular culture*. New York: Peter Lang.

Duits, L., & van Zoonen, L. (2011) Coming to terms with sexualisation. *European Journal of Cultural Studies*, 14, 491–506.

Durham, M. G. (2008) *The Lolita effect*. Woodstock, New York: The Overlook Press.

Egan, D. (2013) *Becoming Sexual*. Cambridge, UK: Polity.

Egan, R. D., & Hawkes, G. (2008) Girls, sexuality and the strange carnalities of advertisements: Deconstructing the discourse of corporate paedophilia. *Australian Feminist Studies*, 23 (57), 307–322.

Ferreday, D. (2008) 'Showing the Girl', the New Burlesque. *Feminist Theory*, 9 (1), 47–65.

Fine, M. (1988) Sexuality, schooling, and adolescent females: The missing discourse of desire. *Harvard Educational Review*, 58, 29–53.

Fine, M. & McClelland, S. (2006) Sexuality and desire: Still missing after all these years. *Harvard Educational Review*, 76 (3), 297–338.

Frith, H., Riley, S., Archer, L., & Gleeson, K. (2005) Editorial. Imag(in)ing visual methodologies. *Qualitative Research in Psychology*, 2, 187–198.

Gavey, N. (1989) Feminist poststructuralism and discourse analysis. Contributions to feminist psychology. *Psychology of Women Quarterly*, 13, 459–475.

Gill, R. (2007) Postfeminist media culture: Elements of a sensibility. *European Journal of Cultural Studies*, 10 (2), 147–166.

Gill, R. (2012) The sexualisation of culture? *Social and Personality Psychology Compass*, 6/7, 483–498.

Griffin, C. (2004) Good girls, bad girls: Anglocentrism and diversity in the constitution of contemporary girlhood, in A. Harris (Ed.) *All About the Girl. Culture, Power and Identity*. London: Routledge, pp. 29–43.

Hamilton, M. (2007) *What's happening to our girls*, Camberwell, VIC: Penguin.

Holland, S., Renold, E., Ross, N., & Hillman, A. (2010) Power, agency and participatory agendas: A critical exploration of young people's engagement in participative qualitative research. *Childhood*, 17 (3), 360–375.

Jackson, S., & Vares, T. (2011) Media sluts': Girls' negotiation of sexual subjectivities in 'Tween' popular culture, in C. Scharff, & R. Gill (Eds.) *New Femininities: Postfeminism, Neoliberalism and Identity*. London: Palgrave.

Jackson, S., & Vares, T. (2012) Fashioning girls, in A. Sparrman, B. Sandin, & J. Sjoberg (Eds.) *Situated Consumption or Moral Panic? A Critical Approach to Childhood Consumption in the 21st Century*. Lund, Sweden: Nordic Academic Press, pp. 195–212.

Jackson, S., & Vares, T. (2013) 'The whole playboy mansion image': Girls fashioning and fashioned selves within a postfeminist culture. *Feminism & Psychology*, 23 (2), 143–162.

Kearney, M. (2007) Productive spaces: Girls' bedrooms as sites of cultural production. *Journal of Children and Media*, 1 (2), 126–141.

Kenny, K. (1999) 'The performative surprise': Parody, documentary and critique. *Culture and Organisation*, 15 (2), 221–235.

Levin, D., & Kilbourne, J. (2008) *So sexy so soon. The new sexualised childhood and what parents can do to protect their kids*. New York: Random House.

McClelland, S., & Fine, M. (2008) Writing on cellophane, in K. Gallagher (Ed.) *Creative Critical and Collaborative Approaches to Qualitative Research.* New York: Routledge pp. 232–261.

McRobbie, A., & Garber, J. (1976) Girls and subcultures, in S. Hall & T. Jefferson (Eds. *Resistance through Rituals: Youth Subcultures in Post War Britain.* London: Hutchinson pp. 209–222.

Myers, K., & Raymond, L. (2010) Elementary school girls and heteronormativity. The girl project. *Gender & Society,* 24 (2), 167–188.

Oppliger, P. (2008) *Girls gone skank: The sexualization of girls in American culture* Jefferson, NC: McFarland & Company Inc.

Pini, M. (2001) Video diaries: Questions of authenticity and fabrication. *Screening the Past,* 13. Retrieved from http://www.latrobe.edu.au/screeningthepast/firstrelease. fr1201/mpfr13a.html

Rasmussen, B., & Wright, P. (2001) The theatre workshop as educational space: How imagined reality is voiced and conceived. *International Journal of Education and the Arts,* 2 (2). Retrieved from http://www. ijea.org/v2n2/index.html

Reavey, P., & Johnson, K. (2011) Visual approaches: Using and interpreting images, ir P. Reavey (Ed.) *Visual Methods in Psychology,* Hove: Taylor and Francis, pp. 296–314.

Renold, E. (2006) They won't let us play. Unless you're going out with them: Girls boys and butler's heterosexual matrix in the primary years. *British Journal of Sociology of Education,* 27 (4), 489–509.

Renold, E. (2013) *Girls and boys speak out: A qualitative study of children's gender and sexual cultures (age 10–12).* Cardiff: Cardiff University.

Renold, E., & Ringrose, J. (2011) Schizoid subjectivities?: Re-theorising teen-girls sexual cultures in an era of 'sexualisation'. *Journal of Sociology,* 47 (4), 389–409.

Ringrose, J., & Renold, E. (2012) Slut-shaming, girl power and 'sexualisation': Think ing through the politics of the international slutwalks with teen girls. *Gender and Education,* 24 (3), 333–343.

Rush, E., & La Nauze, A. (2006) *Corporate paedophilia. Sexualisation of children in Australia.* Discussion Paper No. 90. www.tai.org.au/documents/downloads/DP90 pdf

Rysst, M. (2010) I am only 10 years old: Femininities, clothing-fashion codes and the intergenerational gap of interpretation of young girls' clothes. *Childhood,* 17, 76–93

Steele, J., & Brown, J. (1995) Adolescent room culture: Studying media in the context of everyday life. *Journal of Youth and Adolescence,* 24 (5), 551–576.

Tolman, D. (2002). *Dilemmas of desire.* Cambridge, MA: Harvard University Press.

Vares, T., Jackson, S., & Gill, R. (2011) Pre-teen girls read popular culture: Diversity complexity and contradiction. *International Journal for Media and Cultural Politics,* 7 139–154.

Walkerdine, V. (1990) *Schoolgirl fictions.* London: Verso.

20
Is There a New Normal? Young People Negotiate Pornification

Monique Mulholland

The emergence of a pornified aesthetic across popular, media and consumer cultures – a trend commonly termed 'pornification' – has generated virulent public panics, chiefly focused on harm, danger and children (Tankard-Reist, 2008; Dines, 2010). These concerns have translated into focused public policy initiatives in Western nations, generating a series of government reports (Egan & Hawkes, 2008). In response to such panic-fuelled public and policy discourses, some interesting questions arise about the mainstreamed presence of porn in public spaces. Have representations of explicit sex really become such a 'normalized', commonplace feature of young people's cultural worlds? What happens when the illicit attains a publicness? Does this publicness translate into an 'anything goes' ethos for young people?

This chapter suggests that cultural anxieties generated by pornification rest on historically persistent fears about young people's sexuality and the corruptible power of explicit sexual representations. Constructions of 'good' sex in Western modernity are firmly attached to the 'private' and the 'adult' (Rubin, 1984), along with a sustained disavowal of young people's sexual agency. Central to this disavowal has been a deep-seated urgency since the 18th century to keep illicit materials out of the hands of children, especially the hands of middle-class girls (Kendrick, [1987]1996; Egan & Hawkes, 2010; Egan, 2013). In view of this, the saturation of popular media cultures by images deemed to be 'pornographic' presents a significant challenge to this long-held relationship. In profound ways, the historical function of the illicit to be secreted away is experiencing a serious revision.

Despite the panics about children, there is a notable absence of extensive qualitative studies exploring young people's negotiation of pornification discourses. In response to public panics which have the effect of silencing young people's voices, a set of groundbreaking empirical studies have sought to address this gap (Buckingham & Bragg, 2004; Jackson Vares & Gill, 2011; Ringrose, 2011; Mulholland, 2013; Renold, 2014). This chapter builds on this work, and asks the following questions: What is 'normal' sexuality for young people? Are the panics that swirl around young people's access to pornified culture justified? Here I present the findings of a large-scale four-year project undertaken with 12–16 year olds in South Australian schools,[1] offering some insights from the Australian context. Contra to popular panics – which claim porn has become a normal part of life and 'so mainstream – it's barely edgy' (Paul, 2005: 6) – the young people in this study tell us something quite different. On the one hand the illicit is described as entirely public and familiar. However, countering the claims of pornification discourses, porn and the illicit are not being normalized by young people in the ways generally suggested. Within this new terrain, anything does not go: the distancing strategies employed by young people keep porn and the mainstreamed pornified aesthetic at arm's length through parody and humour. In addition, publicly explicit representations are deemed respectable or otherwise in ways that suggest historically persistent signifiers of gendered and classed respectability.

In the first section, I explore what is meant by normative sexuality, and how it has been constructed in modern Western contexts, based on a set of culturally and historically specific discourses (Foucault, [1976]1990). Constructions of 'good' sexuality rely on notions of respectability, adulthood, heteronormativity and the private, and establish the normal as respectable, restrained and moral, based on a series of raced, classed and gendered assumptions. As the other to 'good' sex, I map out the historical construction of the perverse and the illicit and its relationship to children, a relationship based on an imperative to keep the perverse secret and private. I then move to describe the 'pornification' trend, along with the dominating set of discourses circulating across policy, media and popular texts, discourses which have the effect of oversimplifying the issues and silencing the voices of young people. Such fears, it will be argued, rest on an urgent desire to shore up the historical function of the illicit to be secret, private and 'adult'. Countering such fears, the remaining chapter describes the study, exploring the complex and fascinating ways young people negotiate pornified cultures. As will be seen, such negotiations fly in the face of popularized panics.

Children and pornography: A dangerous relationship

As sexuality studies and queer theory have long argued, discourses of sexuality rested on the binary of 'good' and 'bad' sex (Foucault, [1976]1990; Weeks, 1986; Butler, 1990). The mapping out of 'good sex' in relationship to its perverse Other centred monogamous, heterosexual, reproductive, private and 'adult' as the only legitimate model of sexuality (Rubin, 1984). These categories set up a series of judgements around which individuals came to discipline their sexual identities, standards of 'normal' that rest 'on the successful propagation of the belief that "normal" sexuality and desire are not only possible, but imaginable, natural, and right' (Berlant, 2012: 44). In addition, these characteristics were connected to emergent class structures of 18th-century industrialized modernity, whereby the notion of respectability marked bourgeois sexuality as civilized in relation to classed and raced 'Others' (Strathern, 1992; Stoler, 1995; Skeggs, 1997). In contrast to bourgeois subjectivities, viewed as moral, restrained, civilized, decent, legitimate, worthy, self-controlled and self-determined, the 'massified' working classes (and racialized Others of the colonies) were deemed pathological, deviant and potentially dangerous.

Central to constructions of normative sex was the virulent regulation of children's sexuality. Indeed, as argued by Lindsey (2005) and Egan and Hawkes (2010), a volatile and dangerous set of relationships has always existed between 'childhood', 'sex' and 'risk' in Anglo-European culture. Aries' classic study (1962) elucidates this in detail, arguing that in contrast to pre-18th-century models, the role of family took on a moral dimension, wherein it was the duty of parents to civilize, educate and regulate childhood. The 18th-century forms of regulation were based on the idea that children were 'preliminary sexual beings' and as such required the interventions of parents, experts, doctors and psychologists to hold this sexual potential in check. During the 19th century, the focus shifted to construe children as 'innocent' and asexual, in need of protection from 'adult only' practices (Egan & Hawkes, 2010; Jackson & Scott, 2010). Whether children are seen to be dangerously sexual or innocently asexual, both views work to regulate the sexuality of children (Egan, 2013). As such, the ability to enact a sexual citizenship, and express an agency in relation to it, becomes something firmly positioned in the terrain of the adult.

Constructions of normative sexuality, firmly based on the disavowal of children's sexuality, also worked through an urgency to keep the illicit secret and private. Indeed, two fascinating studies – Kendrick's *Secret museum* ([1987] 1996) and Lyn Hunt's *The invention of pornography* (1996) – explore how the invention of pornography in the 18th century was linked to emerging discourses of sexuality and constructions of normative 'adult' sex. While they argue there had always been explicit sexual representations, the categorization of pornography *as distinct* became an important element in newly emerging discourses of sexuality in order that it signified the 'out of control', the uncivilized, disrespectable and unrestrained. As I explore in more detail elsewhere (Mulholland, 2013), as the Other to good sex, the perverse was banished to private, secret places, most especially because its frank and open explicitness challenged the normative.

The obsession with secreting away pornographic material was due to fears about obscenity 'getting into the wrong hands'. The 'wrong hands' were those belonging to children, as well as women and 'the great unwashed'. This occurred along raced, classed and gendered lines. This material was seen to reflect the innate degeneracy of raced and classed Others, and thus feared for its potential to exacerbate this degeneracy. For bourgeois women and children (especially girls), it was secreted away to secure their innate respectability. In short, it was not the case that pornography per se was banished, but rather that it was banished from particular bodies (Kendrick, [1987] 1996). Children – particularly girls of the newly emerging bourgeoisie – became one such 'body' from which the illicit and perverse was urgently disallowed.

Pornification: 'Will somebody think of the children!!' *(Boy, aged 16, School 1)*

A contemporary trend – summed up by the word *pornification* – presents a significant challenge to this long-held relationship between children and the illicit. As noted by prominent researchers in the field of sexuality and pornography studies, pornification refers to a phenomenon whereby a pornographic aesthetic increasingly characterises the bulwark of sexualized representations in the West (Attwood, 2006/2009; McNair, 2002; Paasonen et al., 2007). The mainstreaming of porn (McNair, 2002) points to an escalating and pervasive presence of pornographic iconography across a wide range of media and popular representations Such instances range from Playboy products in tween and teen marketing, pole-dancing classes, porno styling on music videos, sexting and ease of access to porn on the Internet (Smith, 2010).

This trend has engendered a powerful and persistent set of public panics circulating policy, media and popular texts. These public anxieties represent a continuation of the historical desire to construe children as innocent, in need of protection from sexually explicit cultures. As argued by Egan and Hawkes (2008) in relation to sexualization discourses, the ways in which the panics are constructed have the effect of disallowing young people's agency (especially girls) who form the focus of the fears (Smith, 2010; Egan & Hawkes, 2012), and on the whole oversimplify and generalize the issues in view of this. Sexualization is viewed in universalizing and monolithic terms, while childhood is similarly viewed as 'mechanistic and passive' (Egan & Hawkes, 2008: 293).

As I argue elsewhere (2013), and at the risk of oversimplifying a diverse set of debates and texts which are beyond the scope of this chapter to explore,[2] pornification discourses make similar claims with similar discursive effects (see Mulholland, 2013). Firstly, pornification discourses similarly decontextualize the trend. Porn is construed as normalized across public life, whereby porn has become so normalized as to lose all meaning. This sentiment is perfectly reflected in Tankard-Reist's claim that 'it is often said that young people have to go "searching" for porn. More often now, it seems that porn is searching for them, so ubiquitous and commonplace has it become' (Tankard-Reist, 2008: 12). The set of products and instances drawn on to epitomize 'pornification' are not contextualized, nor are the multiple and complex ways such products might be read and interpreted by young people (Smith, 2010). Secondly, young people are similarly generalized, decontextualized and psycho-medicalized, based on linear notions of child development and sexual development. Children are cast as victims of this harmful and dangerous set of products in very generalized terms (Mulholland, 2013). More specifically, and similar to sexualization discourses, the focus remains on girls as 'passive, endangered and overly susceptible to the influence of corrupt images' (Egan & Hawkes, 2008: 304).

One of the most powerful effects of these discourses is to marginalize the voices of young people. In the Australian context, the inclusion of young people in policy, media and popular debates remains a glaring omission, despite some notable exceptions (see Mulholland, 2013). It is to these voices the chapter now turns. As Egan and Hawkes (2008: 308) suggest,

> Moving away from universalizing arguments can help us gain a better understanding of the various ways both girls and boys make sense of the media in their everyday lives. Offering children voice in both the research process and outcome would promote agency and collaboration as opposed to only protection. This would also help promote a broader understanding of the context and variability of the term 'sexualization.'

As will be seen, the ways in which young people negotiate pornified culture complicates the universalizing arguments underpinning panic-fuelled public discourses, and provides a space for young people to speak about an illicit content that – despite contemporary and historical fears – is very much 'in their hands'.

Speaking back: A new normal?

In the face of contemporary panics, my recent study undertaken with young people in South Australian schools aimed to elucidate how young people negotiate pornification discourses. The project was based in three public, state-funded schools – one occupied a middle-class demographic with a mix of cultural backgrounds, one school was lower middle/working class, and the other working class with a large multicultural cohort. In each school I worked with classes from Year 8 and 9 (age 12–13) and Year 10 and 11 (age 14–16) class for three hour whole-class sessions, in which I presented them with a series of 'pornified' products and debates. The first activity asked them to respond to the Bratz Baby doll, a two-year-old version of the older Bratz doll noted for its pornified appearance. The second activity required them to participate in a debate based on the statement *Young people's access to the internet should be controlled to prevent access to inappropriate content*. The third activity presented them with a series of jeans advertisements – ranging from highly 'pornified' to 'staid' and non-explicit. In groups, they were asked to choose from this set of images to construct their own adverts and associated slogan. Taking the place of the teacher for the sessions (who stayed as observer in the class for duty of care reasons), the sessions ran as open-ended activity-based discussions. I undertook a large-scale discursive analysis of the discussion-based activities which were video and audiotaped. Child and parental consent was obtained from all students participating in the research.[3]

My choice to undertake a discourse analysis in a whole class public classroom environment raised a number of methodological concerns, chiefly focused on the capacity of individual interviews and focus groups to produce a more 'authentic' presentation of the issues. Indeed focus groups or individual interviews would have provided a rich set of responses free of the 'teacher's institutional gaze', and in-class politics of voice, as evidenced by much of the current research in school contexts drawing on a combination of these methods (e.g. Buckingham & Bragg, 2004; Allen, 2005; Renold, 2005; Ringrose, 2012). However, it was precisely the dynamics and performances that constitute whole group naturally occurring spaces that lay behind my decision. Considering how pornified cultures are negotiated *within* naturally occurring spaces such as classrooms is valuable because gender and sexuality is constantly under construction in such spaces (Epstein & Johnson, 1998; Allen, 2005). This works through the ways gender and sexuality are performed and produced, and through the politics of voice and practices of policing to be found there (Renold, 2005). These dynamics are also productive of normative ideas, and in this study I was interested to capture the ways in which a new normal was articulated by young people within public spaces: because the panics pivot on the 'publicness' of explicit sex, the ways in which young people negotiate this in a public context becomes all the more pertinent. As such, focus groups or interviews appeared too limiting, as I did not want to take students out of their familiar contexts to ask specific questions. I was concerned to map the ways in which young people negotiated the 'pornified' within their everyday social worlds. As will be seen, what young people had to say against a public institutional backdrop was complex and surprising.

Porn as 'familiar': The explicit is out to play

First and foremost, the young people described the mainstream presence of pornified culture as part of their social and cultural worlds. From the first activity, the ease with which they invoked the sexually explicit was palpable. When I asked students to write down five words that described their initial reaction to the Bratz Baby doll, within 20 minutes of meeting them the list included hooker, slut, pedobait, whore, dominatrix, slag. Through all the discussions, it was common practice for girls and boys to talk openly (for example) about tits, kink, man-whores, dildos, strip clubs and various porn sites. I was aware that my role as 'teacher but not quite teacher' would allow an openness and permission to speak about issues not usually discussed. However, I still remained part of a backdrop that was 'public' and 'institutional', and thus expected displays of embarrassment and 'showing off'. Indeed, other studies on work with young people have noted this (Buckingham & Bragg, 2004), as has literature on teaching sex education (Allen, 2007). However, the discussions here expressed a different quality: the 'explicit' of sex was talked about frankly, with a degree of familiarity that ran counter to embarrassment. On the whole, it existed as a common-place and regular feature in discussions about popular and media cultures, and was significant for what it signalled in terms of the place of the explicit in public life.

In the second activity, which asked them to debate Internet censorship, the young people expressed a similar ease in conversing about porn, across gender lines and across all the age groups. By way of qualification, the students differed in their willingness to 'talk the explicit' – some talked loud and often, some offered comments here and there, and others remained silent. Indeed, some students expressed more familiarity with sexually explicit and pornographic images than others, and there were gendered and classed differences which I explore in the following sections. As stated above, I aimed to capture the normative voice within a whole class space, and given the scope of the project and the limitations of working in whole class spaces I was not always able to tease out these differences. In addition, given the ethical considerations of working in a large group, I was not able to ask about their specific use of porn or how they 'brought this home' to their sexual practices and identities. However, what was tangible across these lines of difference was its public presence, and their familiarity with the sexually explicit in a public institutional space despite these different engagements. In a *general* sense, I am describing the quality of the relationship to it in the classroom, presented as a routine and habitual aspect of life. In short, it was public.

This familiarity – along with the willingness of young people to 'talk the explicit' – presents a significant challenge to popular adultcentric panics. The young people in this study tell us that explicit representations are very much at home in *public* spaces. In some ways this confirms the claims of pornification panics, which worry that porn has become thoroughly normalized in public life. However, as will be seen below, to say the explicit is familiar and commonplace is *not* to say it is normalized, or that now 'anything goes'.

Porn: LOL

We're not getting off on it, we just think it's hilarious.

(Girl, aged 15, School 1)

As noted above, the panic-induced pornification rhetoric expresses serious concerns. In the face of this seriousness, a striking characteristic of young people's engagement with porn was humour. From the first, it seemed to me this humour indicated something very important in terms of rebordering the normal, as indicated in Kehily and Nayak's classic study (1997). Countering the claims of pornification panics, what spoke loud and clear from listening to young people laugh at porn was the way in which humour was used to keep porn aloof, at arm's length. While they were at pains to stress the generational misunderstandings surrounding porn, arguing it was 'no big deal', when porn was referred to in peer-to-peer discussions, or called on in various whole class activities, the general tone was Laugh-out-Loud (LOL). The following conversation – again exemplifying the kinds of conversations I permitted as 'teacher but not quite teacher' – represents the ways in which porn was simultaneously familiar and hilarious *(Year 11, aged 15–16, School 1)*:

> Me: So it is really easy to access. Would most people access it?
> Girl 1: Yeah!
> Class: All nod.
> Me: So is it seen as, like, weird-arse[4] if you do? Or is it, like, normal?
> Boy 1: It is pretty accepted at this point.
>
> *All laugh*
>
> Boy 2: I think a lot of people use it for humour.
> Girl 1: It's just hilarious.
> Girl 2: It is quite funny.
> Girl 3: I watch porn a lot.
> Girl 1: We're not getting off on it, we just think it's hilarious.
>
> *All laugh*
>
> Me: So it's the LOL factor is it?
> Girl 4: Yeah, it's just humorous.

What this humour points to is an interesting flirtation with familiarity and distance. While porn may function as a familiar feature of cultural life, as noted above, porn is not normalized in ways suggestive of complete normalization, or lack of detachment – it is humorous and caricatured. The following excerpt sums up the use of humour to distance in candid terms. When I asked for further clarification of what might be taboo now, given that 'anything seems to go', the discussion was illuminating *(Year 11, aged 15–16, School 1)*:

> Me: What is the new taboo now? Like you say there's just normal porn, and there's....
> Boy 1: Wacky porn.
> Me: Yeah.
> Girl 2: Maybe to be serious about watching porn.
> Me: So you all laugh about it?
> Girl 2: If someone went home and got off on it, I'd be like...
> Girl 3: That's sick.

Me: So it's kinda normal if it's seen as a joke.
Boy 2: Yes.
Me: But people wouldn't be openly...
Girl 2: Like if someone said I got off on this, I'd be like, ahhhh!

Throughout many of the conversations across different classes and ages, 'wacky porn' was decidedly 'out'.[5] However, as revealed in this excerpt, the ways in which the young people distance themselves from porn in general as an aid to pleasure is revealing. Porn is positioned as something you laugh at, as a publicly known 'illicit', not a publicly professed script for sex and pleasure as put by pornification panics.

In a similar turn, the way in which young people parodied porn represents a significant moment of 'speaking back' to the claims of adultcentric popularized porn panics. In many conversations, panics about porn and pornified culture were referred to by sending up the panics, often in intelligent and insightful ways. Some interesting examples of parody were some very conscious choices of image and slogans for the advertisement construction in session three. In one advert *(Girls, aged 15, School 2)*, the slogan 'If you want dick you will wear this' was set against the advert of a girl on all fours. Another advert announced 'Because you're never gonna look like this anyway!' *(Girls, aged 15, School 1)*.

Emphasizing the funny, shocking and hilarious aspects of porn has the effect of sending up community fears, and can be read as a 'fuck you' to adult panics. I would argue that porn's hilarity and spectacle were marked out to satirize the straightforward sense in which adults interpret its role in young people's lives. This is not to say that young people do not uncritically internalize and construct identities around the limited and limiting gendered and sexual identities made available in mainstream pornified culture, albeit in different ways with different levels of resistance. Indeed, as I argue extensively elsewhere (Mulholland, 2013), limited space is given in classroom spaces to critically unpack the pornography that circulates their worlds. In many ways, as will be seen below, despite the humour and perhaps because of it, gendered and heteronormative conventions are reinforced. However, this said, through the 'whole package of humour' which ran through discussions of porn – casting it as funny and not harmful – young people were reclaiming an agentic relationship to these images, and negotiating the pornified in ways that maintained a distance.

Respectable versus trashy raunch

It's about being raunchy in the right places.

(Girl, age 13)

In addition to humour and parody, another flirtation with distance and familiarity was at work in relation to how publicly explicit representations were bordered. The young people in this study made clear distinctions about what representations were possible 'to bring home' and what were to be kept at a distance owing to their indecency and impropriety. Here again, contra to pornification 'panics', this tells us that 'anything does not go'. Throughout all the activities, historically familiar notions of respectability were utilized to make this distinction. In the first activity, the term 'slut' was often used to describe the Bratz Baby doll. When I questioned what they meant by this term, the conversation moved to a distinction between 'slut' and 'hot'. 'Slut' was articulated through terms such as Fake, Too much make-up, In your face, Attention seeking, Over the top/too much, Try Hard, No standards, Trashy and Dirty.

In the following conversation, references to class and slut were presented in very blatant terms *(Year 11, School 1)*:

Girl 1: A lot of times if you see someone and call them a slut, they're generally trashy. They just look dirty. They look like somebody that would walk across the street and you'd be like OK right you know that's someone who's from Elizabeth or something.[6] Like you can smell smoke, and crack on them, and they haven't brushed their teeth. It's just dirty.

Me: Would people agree with that?

Most: Yep.

Me: Does slutty verge on trashy? What is trashy?... like could you look slutty in Burnside?

All: Yes!

Girl 2: There are people that try to look slutty that don't even do that much.

Me: They're trying to look trashy?

Girl 2: They're just perfect. They have this ideal image in their head that they have to have perfect clear skin, amazing gorgeous eyes, bleached pathetic dead hair.

Girl 1: Yes, but to achieve this they put on six layers of make-up and straighten their hair till it falls out of their head.

As argued above, the notion of respectability was integral to set bourgeois sexualities apart from corruptible others, marked as pathological, deviant, out of control and potentially dangerous. The terms and characteristics employed by young people to describe 'slut' represents a continuation of this tradition. The girl who talks about sluts as 'from Elizabeth' characterises this state as 'natural', a clear example of the 19th-century classing gaze which marked the working classes as 'naturally' degenerate (Skeggs, 1997). In contrast, if you are 'from Burnside' you are *trying* to look slutty, compared to those who are seen as naturally and inherently slutty because of their class position. Indeed, they are clear expressions of how pornified representations operate along class lines, as noted in other important works (Arthurs, 2003;

Skeggs, 2005; Attwood, 2007; Egan, 2013). Indeed, Ringrose and Renold's (2012) recent analysis of 'slutwalks' as a strategy to resist slut-shaming cultures highlights the continued significance of the classing gaze in teen girl cultures.

In contrast to 'slut', the young people indicated forms of representations that could be marked as respectable, despite an explicit display of sex. Hot, as compared to 'slutty', was signified by terms such as Good looking, How you present yourself, Being yourself, 'Normal', Original, Natural, Talented, Longer-lasting relationships, Professional. Throughout a bulk of the discussions, they at pains to stress that what matters is not the explicit, or lack of 'clothes', or fleshy sexualized expressions. As stated by one boy (aged 15, Year 10), 'both categories might dress the same, but the behaviour matters'. When I asked the young people to further explain why certain celebrities could be viewed as respectable 'while not wearing very much', the following comments exemplify the connection between behaviour and respectability *(Year 10, School 2)*:

> Me: Some of you have Jessica Alba. But I've seen Jessica Alba not wear very much. Why is that different? Cause you know how you've said slutty is not about wearing very much? Or is it not so much what you wear but how you wear it?
> Girl 1: How you wear it.
> Me: Tell me more.
> Girl 1: How you pose yourself. How posy you are.
> Me: So if you're kind of out there . . . in your face . . .

As Strathern argues (1992: 130), public expressions of an internal and individualized 'goodness' and 'civility' defined respectability in the 19th century. It was an inherent *behaviour* that structured bourgeois markers of respectability and civility (Strathern, 1992), and as such this contemporary focus on *behaviour* represents a continuation of this trademark of respectability. The following excerpt, again relating to Jessica Alba, makes similar claims about respectability, behaviour and civility *(Year 8, School 1)*:

> Girl: She doesn't present herself like she's gonna go out and have sex.
> Me: Like she's hot.
> Girl: She's controlled.
> Me: So is it partly about control that is this distinction between hot and slutty?
> Girl: There are a lot of celebrities that are out of control. And then they get a reputation as well.

As noted by Skeggs (1997), an important marker of bourgeois respectability is control, connected to the disciplining, policing and regulation of women's bodies. Across all ages, references to female celebrities that 'go too far', 'don't know when to stop' and 'too in-your-face' were plentiful. Walking the line between 'classy/control' and 'trashy/slutty' is a weighty exercise for girls if they want to maintain the privilege of respectability.

Professionalism and natural talent were also significant factors in the distinction made between slutty and hot. Within historical trajectories of sexuality, Strathern (1992) argues that respectability is achieved through a bourgeois sense of entitlement to individuality and worthiness, distinguished from the 'massified' working classes. The ways in which young people express 'hot' as professionalism, talent, and naturalness can be seen as an example of such a claim to individuality/worth. As can be seen in the following discussion, the identification of individual talent and worthiness as respectable marks a continuation of classed bourgeois constructions of 'good sex', and bourgeois femininity and sexuality in particular *(Year 11, School 1)*:

Me: What would you say is the difference between slutty and hot?
Boy 1: Slutty is fake perfection, hot is natural perfection.
Boy 2: Hot generally means you have some respect for the person.
Me: As in they present themselves respectfully, therefore they get respect.
Boy 2: Yeah, so generally they present themselves respectfully. But like with slut you have zero respect for them at all.
Boy 3: They look good, and their personality is good as well. The person.
Boy 4: Slutty is just an overdone image. Alien compared to real people who are just naturally amazing.

What was also clear through all of the activities was a focus on girls as signifiers of 'hot' or 'slutty'. Boys were never mentioned in discussions about what marked out the 'slutty' from the 'hot/respectable'. Indeed, when I asked the classes why male 'celebs' were absent from their discussion, and if boys can be 'slutty', the following excerpt was indicative of the kinds of discussions across the board *(Year 11, School 1)*:

Me: Isn't it interesting that when we put up that list of Hot and Slutty, no one put boys.
Girl 1: I did.
Me: Can boys be slutty?
Girl 2: They can but no one cares.
Boy 1: Technically, yes, but socially I don't think so.
Girl 2: Different rules apply for girls than boys.
Girl 3: Yeah.

On the one hand, the acceptability of 'hot', respectable raunch points to a shift whereby for girls respectability *can* mean displays of sexuality. Indeed, as noted in post-feminist literature, it has become a cultural imperative (Gill,

2009; McRobbie, 2009; Ringrose, 2012). On the other hand, notions of freedom and empowerment are limited, especially in terms of the continued policing of female bodies in relation to slutty (Renold & Ringrose, 2012; Egan, 2013).

Conclusion

This chapter paints a picture of the familiarity with which young people deal with the sexually explicit in general, and the pornographic in particular. However, as I argue throughout, this does not substantiate the key claim of popularized pornification panics that porn is thoroughly accepted or unproblematized by young people. Young people negotiate the discourse of pornification in complex ways. On the one hand the pornographic features in the cultural landscapes of young people as an entirely familiar representation of sexuality (not forgetting there were a variety of readings and interpretations that could not be teased out in this chapter). However, to say the explicit is familiar and public does not overturn its historical function to be kept at arm's length, as the Other to good sex. Through a complex flirtation with familiarity and distance, a fascinating picture emerges in the course of young people's negotiations with the sexually illicit. Raunch and explicit sex per se were not in question, nor were they necessarily in opposition to the respectable. Rather, though the use of humour and parody, porn and the pornified aesthetic are kept at a distance. In addition, young people use historically persistent and familiar signifiers of respectability to mark out the acceptable from otherwise.

The urgent desire from young people to participate in critically engaged discussions presents a stark challenge to adultcentric panics to listen differently: despite the concerns, young people are not 'normalizing' the pornified as claimed. However, while young people express an agency in relation to the issues, they are simultaneously reproducing conventional gender and heteronormative frameworks in their reading of the pornified. This has implications for future research agendas, and for those working with young people in educational and community settings. Despite the limitations of what can be 'said' in a public large group environment (most especially how differences within the class cohort can be teased out), whole class discussions are useful for the ways they shed light on how normative ideas are produced, along with a space in which to critically deconstruct these ideas. Methodologies such as the one employed in this study (coupled with multi-methods which can ascertain more personalized readings and differing engagements) could be integrated into engaging and sophisticated pedagogies, allowing space for young people as sexualized, knowing subjects to interrogate the *assumptions* and *stereotypes* they draw on in their reading of pornified cultures, along with providing a more complicated reading of issues.

Notes

1. This chapter is an abridged and condensed version of my book *Young People and Pornography: Negotiating Pornification*. The arguments and themes that form the basis of this chapter are explored in more detail in this work.
2. Elsewhere I explore the debates (and the nuances and differences within and between them) within the Australian context, mapping out the discourses on pornification across media and popular texts, child psychology and advocacy experts and policy documents.
3. The research received full ethical approval from The Flinders University of South Australia and the South Australian Education Department (Department of Education and Children's Services). Child and parental consent was obtained to use anonymized data generated in the project for reports and publication.
4. Slang for 'weird'.
5. 'Wacky porn' referred to porn genres, tastes and fetishes that fell outside of mainstream hetero-porn. It also referred to violent porn and child porn.
6. Elizabeth is a suburb of Adelaide, South Australia, a lower socio economic area often stereotyped as a 'ghetto' and 'lower class'. Burnside is an area that is solidly middle class.

References

Allen, L. (2005) *Sexual subjects: Young people, sexuality and education*. New York: Palgrave Macmillan.

Allen, L. (2007) Pleasurable pedagogy: Young people's ideas about teaching 'pleasure' in sexuality education. *Twenty First Century Society*, 2 (3), 249–264.

Aries, P. (1962) *Centuries of childhood: A social history of family life*. Translated by Robert Baldick. New York: Random House.

Arthurs, J. (2003) Sex and the city and consumer reading: Remediating postfeminist drama. *Feminist Media Studies*, 3 (1), 83–98.

Attwood, F. (2006) Sexed up: Theorizing the sexualisation of culture. *Sexualities*, 9 (1), 77–94.

Attwood, F. (2007) Sluts and riot grrrls: Female identity and sexual agency. *Journal of Gender Studies*, 16 (3), 231–245.

Attwood, F. (Ed.) (2009). *Mainstreaming sex: The sexualisation of western culture*. London: I.B. Tauris.

Berlant, L. (2102). *Desire/Love*. Brooklyn, NY: Punctum Books.

Buckingham, D., & Sara, B. (2004) *Young people, sex and the media: The facts of life?* Basingstoke: Palgrave Macmillan.

Butler, J. (1990) *Gender trouble: Feminism and the subversion of identity*. New York: Routledge.

Dines, G. (2010) *Pornland: How porn has hijacked our sexuality*. Boston, MA: Beacon Press.

Egan, D. (2013). *Becoming Sexual: A critical appraisal of the sexualisation of girls*. Cambridge: Polity Press.

Egan, R. D., & Hawkes, G. L. (2008a) Endangered girls and incendiary objects: Unpacking the discourse on sexualisation. *Sexuality and Culture*, 12, 291–311.

Egan, R. D., & Gail, H. (2010) *Theorising the sexual child in modernity*. New York: Palgrave Macmillan.

Epstein, D., & Johnson, R. (1998) *Schooling sexualities*. Buckingham: Open University Press.

Foucault, M. ([1976] 1990) *The history of sexuality, volume 1: An introduction.* Translated by Robert Hurley. London: Penguin.

Gill, R. (2009) Beyond the 'sexualisation of culture' thesis: An intersectional analysis of 'Sixpacks', 'Midriffs' and 'Hot Lesbians' in advertising'. *Sexualities,* 12 (137), 137–160.

Gilman, S. (1985) *Difference and pathology: Stereotypes of race, sexuality and madness.* Ithaca, NY: Cornell University Press.

Hunt, L. (1996) Introduction: Obscenity and the origins of modernity 1500–1800, in L. Hunt (Ed.) *The invention of pornography: Obscenity and the origins of modernity 1500–1800.* New York: Zone Books.

Jackson, S. & Scott, S. (2010) *Theorising sexuality.* Berkshire: Open University Press.

Kehily, M. J. & Nayak, A. (1997) Lads and laughter: Humour and the production of heterosexual hierarchies. *Gender and Education,* 9 (1), 69–87.

Kendrick, W. ([1987]1996) *The secret museum: Pornography in modern culture.* Berkeley: University of California Press.

Lindsey, Jo. (2005). Don't panic: Young people and the social organisation of sex, in G. Hawkes, & J. Scott (Eds.) *Perspectives in Human Sexuality.* Oxford: Oxford University Press.

McNair, B. (2002) *Striptease culture: Sex, media and the democratisation of desire.* New York: Routledge.

McRobbie, A. (2009) *The aftermath of feminism: Gender, culture and social change.* London: Sage.

Mulholland, M. (2013) *Young people and pornography: Negotiating pornification.* New York: Palgrave.

Paasonen, S., Nikunen, K., & Saarenmaa, L. (2007) *Pornification: Sex and sexuality in media.* Oxford: Berg.

Paul, P. (2005) *Pornified: How pornography is damaging our lives, our relationships, and our families.* New York: Owl Books.

Renold, E. (2005) *Girls, boys and junior sexualities: Exploring children's gender and sexual relations in the primary school.* London: RoutledgeFalmer.

Renold, E. (2014) Too much too soon?: Girls and boys speak out. Research project to inform the National Assembly of Wales cross-party group on 'Children, Sexualities, Sexualisation and Equalities'.

Ringrose, J. (2011) Are you sexy, flirty or a slut? Teen girls navigating sexual commodification and pornification on social networking sites, in R. Gill, & C. Scharff (Eds.) *New Femininities: Postfeminism, Neoliberalism and Subjectivity.* London: Palgrave.

Ringrose, J. (2012) *Post-feminist education? Girls and the sexual politics of schooling.* London: Routledge.

Ringrose, J., & Renold, E. (2012). Slut-shaming, girl power and 'sexualisation': Thinking through the politics of the international slutwalks with teen girls. *Gender and Education,* 24 (3), 333–343.

Rubin, G. (1984) Thinking sex: Notes for a radical theory of the politics of sexuality, in Carol, V. (Ed.) *Pleasure and danger: Exploring female sexuality.* Boston, MA: Routledge and Kegan Paul.

Skeggs, B. (1997) *Formations of class and gender: Becoming respectable.* London: Sage Publications.

Skeggs, B. (2005) The making of class and gender through visualising moral subject formation. *Sociology,* 39 (5), 965–982.

Smith, C. (2010) Pornographication: A discourse for all seasons. *International Journal of Media and Cultural Politics,* 6 (1), 103–108.

Stoler, A. (1995) *Race and the education of desire*. Durham, NC: Duke University Press.
Strathern, M. (1992) *After nature: English kinship in the late twentieth century*. Cambridge: Cambridge University Press.
Tankard-Reist, M. (2008) The pornification of girlhood. *Quadrant Magazine*, 52 (7–8) 10–16.
Vares, T., Jackson, S., & Gill, R. (2011) Preteen girls read 'Tween' popular culture: diversity, complexity and contradiction. *International Journal of Media and Cultural Politics* 7(2): 139–154.
Weeks, J. (1986) *Sexuality*. London: Tavistock.

21
What Is Self-exploitation? Rethinking the Relationship between Sexualization and 'Sexting' in Law and Order Times

Lara Karaian

Introduction

Since the early 1990s 'sexualization' has emerged as a 'social problem' whereby children, particularly white, heterosexual, middle-class girls, are purportedly being mal-socialized to deny their natural 'innocence', to prematurely embrace and express the characteristics of adult sexuality and to engage in 'self-sexualization' (APA, 2007; Smith & Attwood, 2011; Duschinsky, 2013a; Egan, 2013). In and around the same time as the public opprobrium about sexualization reached its pinnacle in the US and the UK, between 2006 and 2011 (Egan, 2013: 3–4), the West was also witnessing the rise of another representational practice, that of the sexy 'selfie' – semi-nude and sexually explicit self-portraits, taken at arm's length or in a mirror, using a cellphone or digital camera, and then posted to social networking sites such as Facebook, Instagram or Tumblr. Also referred to as 'sexts' by academics and those in the media, although not typically by youth themselves (see Karaian, 2012; Ringrose et al., 2012; Albury et al., 2013; Peskin et al., 2013; Strassberg et al., 2013), sexy selfies have met with a great deal of international attention, if not enthusiasm, by parents, pundits, legal scholars, childhood sexualization critics, child protection and policing agencies, many of whom cite an increasingly sexualized culture as a key cause of the practice (Hasinoff, 2014). The Canadian context is no exception. Members of the Canadian Senate have expressed concerns about the links between 'the social realities that drive the hyper-sexualisation of girls in modern culture' and the sexual exploitation of youth via the creation of child pornography (Jaffer & Brazeau, 2011: 4). Canadian documentaries – such as *Sexy Inc. Our Children Under Influence* (Bissonnette, 2007) and *Sext up Kids* (Palmer, 2012) – warn against Western mainstream media's sexualization of young people and its negative effects on girls' self-esteem and their sexual health; the latter goes so far as to advance the claim that sexualization works in conjunction with easy access to Internet pornography to 'force' teenage girls to self-sexualize and to expose their semi/naked bodies using digital technology, 'often with grave consequences' (Palmer, 2012).

In the midst of this purportedly 'pornified' context (Paul, 2005), a range of adult responders have explicitly and unsurprisingly rejected the possibility that teenage sexting may in fact be consensually chosen by, and a beneficial self-expressive practice for, many teens.[1] Instead, organized responses to teenage sexting in the Canadian context have gone so far as to construct consensual sexting as 'self-exploitation' necessitating a child protectionist and criminal law response (Canadian Centre for Child Protection, 2012; OPP, 2012).[2] And yet, to date there has been little consideration of what 'self-exploitation' entails and no critical deliberation on its potential effects. Thus, in this chapter I consider the relationship between consensual sexting, childhood sexualization discourses, and the structural elements and legal effects of the 'self-exploitation' discourse for Canadian youth. Adopting Alan Wertheimer's contention that 'exploitation claims are meant to have some definable content...they are not merely a rhetorical placeholder for expressing disapproval' (1996: 5), I begin by drawing on political philosophers' assessments of the criteria required for a claim of exploitation to exist.[3] To better make sense of the self-exploitation claim I then consider how it is implicitly given meaning by anti-sexting legal scholarship, case law and child protection initiatives, as well as self-objectification discourses discussed within childhood sexualization literature. I suggest that the purportedly causal relationship between sexualization, consensual sexting and 'self-exploitation' begs further consideration and ask: What exactly does self-exploitation mean with respect to the consensual sexting context? Is the self-exploitation claim structurally sound? What relationship, if any, exists between the practice of self-exploitation and the claim that girls are self-objectifying within a sexualized culture? Ultimately, I suggest that a further theorization of 'self-exploitation' is necessitated by right-wing efforts to co-opt sexualization discourses (Duschinsky, 2013b) in order to advance a conservative law and order agenda which seeks to criminalize youth as a means of 'protecting' them from themselves and others (Salter et al., 2013; Karaian, 2014).

Sexting and self-exploitation in Canada

Unlike in the UK and Australia, the prosecution of Canadian youth for consensual sexting has yet to occur. The criminalization of teens for consensual sexting is nevertheless well documented in the US.[4] Recent studies of arrest trends for child pornography possession and production in the US have found that child pornography possession and production arrests grew significantly between 2000 and 2006 and again in 2009 (Wolak et al.,

2012), and that a large segment of the population being criminalized was minors. While the lack of prosecutions in the Canadian context may be due, in part, to police and prosecutorial discretion and constraint when choosing whether to enforce child pornography statutes, it is also a likely result of the Canadian Supreme Court's finding that privately captured sexual images exchanged via technology between minors who are intimate partners for their mutual enjoyment are exempt from our child pornography laws (R. v. Sharpe, 2001).[5] Notwithstanding this 'private use exemption', the criminal prosecutions of Canadian youth who consensually sext remains a technical possibility in those instances wherein privately captured images are exchanged between individuals who are not 'intimate partners'; when it is determined that adequate steps were not taken to maintain the images as private; or when the courts *determine the production of the image to be exploitative* (R. v. Sharpe, 2001. Emphasis mine). In actual fact, the exemption is narrow and various popular consensual sexting scenarios are subject to prosecution. Indeed, reasons to be concerned about prosecution exist, particularly given Canada's historical criminalization of 'obscenity' on the basis of its 'communicative harm' to women's equality (Karaian, 2009)[6] and, most importantly for my purposes, in the light of the net-widening effect that I suggest the rise of the 'self-exploitation' discourse may have on courts' determinations of the 'exploitative' nature of an image's production. Further cause for concern is raised by Hasinoff, who notes that despite the fact that child pornography laws were not designed to apply to the consensual sharing of private personal sexual media among teenagers, legislators do not want to be perceived as decriminalizing child pornography in any form, and as such most new sexting misdemeanor laws fail to distinguish consensual sexting from the nonconsensual production, distribution, and possession of private images and also criminalize a wider range of images than do child pornography laws (2015: 17).

In this context, teenagers who actively choose to create and share nude or sexually explicit images, for whatever reason, outside the confines of a private and intimate relationship, are increasingly constructed as unable to consent to such behaviour given the purportedly inherent and self-exploitative nature of the practice (Goldstein, 2009; Karaian, 2014). This construction has already found favour in the US, where the conflation of volitional 'sexting' and 'self-exploitation' is most clearly associated with Mary Graw Leary's 2008 article entitled 'Self-produced Child Pornography: The Appropriate Societal Response to Juvenile Self-Sexual Exploitation'. In it, Leary raises concerns about 'Minors, [who] without the grooming or coercion of adult offenders are *voluntarily* creating and distributing self-produced child pornography' (2008: 4–5. Emphasis added). Leary goes on to claim:

> This social phenomenon of self-exploitation by minors is both expanding and novel. It is modern and the behavior lacks a clear definition. As a general matter, this activity is the creation by a minor of visual depictions

of that minor and/or other minors engaged in sexually explicit conduct, including the lascivious display of genitals.

(2008: 20)

Leary does not blame mainstream media's sexualization of children but rather the 'sexualisation and eroticization of children by child pornography'. Nevertheless, her description of this practice as 'modern' engenders a reading of causality that extends beyond increased access to Internet porn and digital technology, and towards the mainstreaming of sex or the pornification of culture more broadly. Leary suggests that 'juvenile prosecution is a befitting response' to this practice (2008: 39), and concludes with the following claim:

> [T]he crime [of self-produced child pornography] is that much more complex because of the nature of the minors *exploiting themselves* in their criminal acts. *The fact of self-harm, alone, however, cannot justify a refusal to prosecute juveniles for self-exploitation.* Once those images are created, they create vast social harm as they are used by offenders to sexually assault children, they aid in the creation of juvenile sex offenders, and they further support the sexualisation and eroticization of children.
>
> (2009: 50. Emphasis mine)

Within the Canadian context, 'self-exploitation' only emerged as a serious 'problem' and a 'serious crime' in 2012 when the Department of Justice announced that it was providing funding for the Canadian Centre for Child Protection (CCCP) – and its subsidiary, Cybertip.ca, Canada's national tipline for reporting the online sexual exploitation of children – to expand its mandate and improve its ability to address the reporting of youths' 'peer- and self-exploitation' (Department of Justice, 2012). In its press release the Federal government claimed that such funding would allow the CCCP to better respond to 'emerging sexual exploitation issues' and to '[move] forward with child protection projects that will focus on protecting the most vulnerable members of our society – *young victims of serious crime*' (2012. Emphasis added). One month later, the Ontario Provincial Police's (OPP) Child Sexual Exploitation Unit released a 'Warning for Teens on Dangers of Irresponsible Texting' wherein they claim: 'Teens frequently engage in relationships with peers through the use of their mobile devices and computers that lead to "self-peer exploitation" (also known as sexting)' (OPP, 2012).

On the heels of these developments the Canadian Centre for Child Protection released its federally funded *Self/Peer Exploitation Resource Guide: School and Family Approaches to Intervention and Prevention*, a tool 'for families, schools and law enforcement to effectively respond to this emerging child exploitation issue' (2012). In the guide, the CCCP writes: 'self/peer-exploitation...coined in the media as "sexting," is generally defined as youth creating, sending or sharing sexual images and/or videos with peers via the Internet and/or electronic devices' (2012: 3). The term 'self/peer exploitation,' according to the CCCP, 'includes both the original trans- mission (one to one) and further distribution (to many) of the content' (2012: 3). Although the CCCP does not actively distinguish between con- sensual and non-consensual, as well as peer and self-exploitation, the above definition implies the existence of a difference between the two wherein the original consensual transmission (one-to-one) of a youth's volitionally pro- duced sexual imagery constitutes 'self-exploitation,' and distribution of the original content to others, presumably without the consent of the image's creator, constitutes 'peer-exploitation' (2012: 3). This differentiation is rein- forced by the guide's acknowledgement of a range of sexting scenarios that identify three categories of participants, the most relevant of which for our purposes is the category dubbed 'Affected Youth': 'Youth whose image/video has been taken and or distributed whether *by themselves* or someone else' (2012: 3. Emphasis added).

Canadian courts have already expressed concerns about peer-exploitation, if not self-exploitation, stemming from volitional sexting. In *R. v. Schultz* (2008), 22-year-old Schultz posted nude photographs of his 16-year-old ex- girlfriend on his Nexopia profile. He was subsequently charged with the distribution of child pornography under s. 163.1(3)(a) of the Canadian *Criminal Code*.[7] Schultz then launched a constitutional challenge arguing that the mandatory minimum sentence of a year's imprisonment as well as the requirement that he register as a sex offender under the *Sex Offender Information Registration Act*, S.C. 2004, c. 10 (SOIRA) constituted cruel and unusual punishment contrary to s. 12 of the *Charter of Rights and Freedoms*. Drawing on hypotheticals in an effort to determine whether the minimum sentence was grossly disproportionate, Schultz raised the example of 'an underage girl who has taken nude pictures of herself and distributed them to friends over the Internet' (2008: para. 122). Following the Supreme Court of Canada's reasoning in *R. v. Sharpe* (2001) – wherein the court, faced with a constitutional challenge to the criminalization of the possession of child pornography as set out in s. 163.1(4) of the Canadian *Criminal Code* held that 'no one denies that child pornography involves the exploitation of children ... possession of child pornography contributes to the market for child pornography, a market which in turn drives production involving the exploitation of children' (2001: para. 28) – Madam Justice J. E. Topolniski of the Alberta Queen's Bench dismissed Schultz's claim. Acknowledging that an underage girl would be subject to reduced penalties under the *Youth Crimi- nal Justice Act*, Topolniski nevertheless claimed that even if the girl was 18 when she voluntarily transmitted the photos of her younger self, she would still find the minimum sentences in s. 163.1(3) to be constitutionally sound (2008: para. 129). Topolniski arrived at this decision based on her contention that the hypothetical girl 'contributes to harmful attitudinal shifts, fuels fantasies, and provides material that may be used to exploit and trauma-tize future victims. By distributing her self-created materials, it was argued, she causes the same societal harms as if she had distributed pornographic materials involving other children' (2008: para. 132). Thus, by finding that the 'prevent[ion] [of] "attitudinal harm to society at large"' and the 'prevent[ion] [of] harm to children' flow as equally from the consensual actions of the hypothetical teenage girl as they flow from the non-consensual scenario in the case before her, Topolniski, like Leary, constructs the consensual female sexter as essentially *the same as* an abusive ex-boyfriend or a hypothetical male sex offender. Taken out of context, her image is construed as inherently harmful. Taken in a context, where the potential benefits of the image to her and others are never considered, the girl is implicitly construed as *more* responsible for child sexual exploitation than the hypothetical paedophile who will use her image for nefarious purposes given that presumably without her there would be no crime (Karaian, 2014). Implicit in this analogy are troubling conflations, slippages and erasures – between notions of sexual expression/sexual abuse, victim/perpetrator, self/peer, consensual/nonconsensual, pleasure/harm and image/reality. These conflations, I argue, work in tandem with sexualization discourse – which blames girls for perpetuating sexualization while also casting them as its victims. Together, they bolster the 'self-exploitation' discourse which, potentially, extends the application of child pornography laws to consensual teen sexters.

Self-exploitation, sexualization, and sexual subjectification in law and order times

Concerns about sexualization and its relationship to self-exploitation have been traced back to feminist media critics who, Duschinsky notes, have claimed that the media's sexist and commercialized cultural representations are 'contaminating the sexual subjectivity and values of young people, encouraging self-exploitation and the re-embedding of patriarchal forms of gendered power', thus requiring psychological oversight and state intervention (Duschinsky, 2013a: 147; see also Egan, 2013). While an increasing number of scholars have critiqued these sexualization discourses for conflating sexuality with sexualization (Egan, 2013), for denying girls' agency (Egan & Hawkes, 2009) and for advancing an overdetermined relationship between sexualization and sexting (Hasinoff, 2014), none to date have considered the relationship between sexualization, consensual sexting and 'self-exploitation' discourses specifically. Indeed, although Duschinsky uses the language of self-exploitation in his summary of feminist media critics' concerns, none of the sources that Duschinsky cites reference the term 'self-exploitation' explicitly, but rather exploitation more generally. And herein lies the issue; the concept of 'self-exploitation' is increasingly used as though its meaning is obvious and its effects are largely descriptive. It has yet to be defined by any agency or academic responding to sexting or childhood sexualization discourses (apart from the CCCP and the OPP who, as noted above, merely conflate the term with a whole host of undifferentiated teenage sexting practices). This begs some critical questions, including what exactly self-exploitation means; whether the self-exploitation claim is structurally sound; and what relationship, if any, exists between the practice of self-exploitation and the claim that girls are self-objectifying within a sexualized culture.

In the following sections of this chapter, I consider answers to these questions by drawing on Alan Wertheimer's book *Exploitation*, in which he describes exploitation as a relational transaction wherein 'A takes *unfair advantage* of B' (1996: 208) and wherein A is always cast as the exploiter and B the exploitee. Following Wertheimer's line of thinking, I suggest that the supposition that a teenage girl self-exploits when she voluntarily takes and shares a sexually explicit image of herself appears to rest on the assumption that the teenage girl is *unfairly using herself for her own ends* – 'A takes *unfair advantage* of A', within our sexualized culture. Structurally, this appears to be the most accurate representation of the notion of 'self-exploitation', although, as will be discussed below, it is quite likely that those who deploy the term may be using it to refer to a girl's unfair facilitation of her own exploitation (by others) in a way that provides *another* with an *unfair benefit*.

If we accept the above noted starting point, then the consensual sexter is cast as *both* exploiter and the exploitee. This seemingly odd set of affairs appears, at first glance at least, to map neatly onto childhood sexualization critics' framing of girls as self-objectifying, and as both the victims and perpetrators of a sexualized culture (Lamb, 2010). However, self-*objectification* in a sexualized context, according to its critics, refers to a process whereby A 'becomes more concerned and engaged with how [A's] body is perceived by *others* while *deemphasizing [A's] own subjective feelings, and internal awareness*' (Papadopolous, 2010: 56), or as a 'process whereby [A] learn[s] to think of and treat ['A's'] own bod[y] as [an] object of *others' desires*' (APA, 2007: 17). These descriptions are important as they point to the need to consider the differences between self-exploitation and self-objectification, and the potential consequences of using the terms interchangeably, the effects of which are considered at a later point in this chapter.

According to Wertheimer, taking 'unfair' advantage can be understood in two ways. First, it may refer to 'some dimension of the *outcome* of the exploitative act or relation', meaning that the transaction is substantively unfair 'because it is wrong for A to *benefit* at all from his or her act (e.g. by *harming* B) or because A's benefit is excessive relative to the benefit to B [or in our case A]' (1996: 17). Second, the purported unfairness 'may imply that there is some sort of *defect in the process* by which the unfair outcome has come about or the formation of the agreement between A and B [in our case A], for example, that A has coerced or defrauded or manipulated B [A]'

(1996: 16). Let's focus for the time being on outcome, or the 'undue bene-fit' to A and the relationship of A's undue benefits to the harms to A in the volitional teenage sexting scenario.

Those concerned with 'self-exploitation' appear to understand this claim in two key ways, both of which I suggest actually undermine the claim's structural integrity. First, they might suggest that there is *no* advantage to A in the volitional sexting scenario, in which case the elemental require-ment of an 'undue benefit' to A has not been met. Here, critics would be using the term 'self-exploitation' incorrectly to refer to what they believe is some other form of wrongdoing, such as age or gender discrimination and/or self-objectification. Alternatively, however, critics might argue that the advantage to A exists, but that it is so *minimal* that it does not out-weigh the effect on A (e.g. harm to A), and, as I discuss shortly, her peers). In both of these instances the term 'self-exploitation' is being used incor-rectly given that normative exploitation claims rest on the belief that the benefit to A must be *excessive* relative to the effect on (e.g. harm to) A. If this standard were actually met (i.e. if the gain to A outweighed, even minimally, the potential harm to A), then a claim of self-exploitation would appear to fail, substantively if not procedurally, because if A is 'better off' after having sexted than she is prior to having sexted (i.e. if the 'net effect' of harm to A is in the negative), then presumably harmful exploitation is not a fitting descriptor for A's transaction with herself. But it is here that the distinction between outcome and process begin to blur. Those who would deny that in the consensual sexting scenario A's use of her 'self' as a means to her desired ends is anything other than 'fair' presumably suggest, as was the case in *R. v. Schultz*, that she cannot experience more benefit than harm from her actions because ultimately it's not *really* her desired ends that are being met, as she believes them to be. Rather, the unfair 'net gains' are reaped by the 'paedophile', whom she has provided with the tools to sexually abuse soci-ety's youth; the porn industry who will profit from her imagery; or even the broader sexualized and patriarchal capitalist marketplace that profits from 'corporate pedophilia' (Rush & La Nauze, 2006).

From here, then, we may want to turn our attention to whether the self-exploitation claim rests on the assumption that there exists a *defect in the process* by which A enters into an agreement with herself. That is, whether there exists a defect in A's *ability* to enter into such a negotiation with herself. Indeed teens' status as minors and their purportedly limited mental capacity is often held up as proof of teens' inability to understand the negative con-sequences of consensual sexting, thus invalidating their ability to 'choose' to sext. However, of greater interest to me is how childhood sexualization discourses come into play here to reproduce a contextual framework within which the alleged defect in process has less to do with age and limited mental capacity and more to do with a sort of false consciousness that is reminiscent of the feminist sex wars of the 1980s and 1990s, which questioned women's ability to consent to sexual relations in a sexist culture within which porn was classified as the theory to which rape was the practice (MacKinnon, 1989). This notion of communicative and social harm – including harm to men's attitudes towards women and harm to women's dignity and their equality – as Calder and Beaman note, is a vestige of the claims regarding the communicative and social harms of pornography stemming from the victory of dominance feminist arguments in *R. v. Butler*. In *Butler,* the Supreme Court of Canada accepted that pornography and obscenity might give rise to social harm of a form cognizable by the criminal law; thus producing a 'legal recognition *as real* of something whose metaphysical status was deeply contested – a certain form of harm' that has long buoyed the criminal law (Calder & Beaman, 2013: 79). I contend that a similar notion of false consciousness and communicative harm is explicit in the hypothetical referenced in *R. v. Schulz* as well as in the claim that girls who volitionally sext are self-exploiting. In our current context, however, proponents of communicative harm see it as flowing from sexualizing media and from the girls who uncritically adopt its messages, thus rendering A's ability to choose to sext inherently defective. Once again, the desires that may have informed a girl's decision to sext, and any excessive pleasure the girl may believe she derived from the practice, are rendered a symptom of a sexualized culture 'organiz[ing] [young] women's pleasure so as to give [young women] a stake in [their] own subordination' (MacKinnon, 1989: 6), returning us to a place where girls' sexual subjectivity and agency are largely disavowed and wherein girls are required to 'reject[]the personal pleasure, privilege, and safety that embodying sexualization and femininity might provide in some contexts' (Hasinoff, 2014: 109). To the extent that such discourses extend dominance feminists' claims about the 'indirect injury' caused to women by the consumption of porn,[8] and cast teenage girls' as prior to sexual consent (Duschinsky, 2013a), or, as I have suggested, as suffering from false consciousness, they render girls' expressions of their sexuality or desire problematic.

This reification of the sex wars, wherein girls' legitimate choices are wholly circumscribed, or restricted to pre-approved sexually normative choices such as abstinence from sexting or 'choos[ing] to participate in [one's] own sexual exploitation' (Opplinger, 2008: 205) brings with it a new dimension – the potential criminalization of girls who apparently perpetrate the culture whose harms they embody. This then extends and complicates Duschinsky's claim about the co-opting of sexualization discourses by the neo-liberal 'responsible right-wing' who – in an attempt to control female sexuality and justify neo-liberal economic policies – problematize sexualisation as a matter of 'girls' using their freedoms irresponsibly thus necessitating the need for *adults* to ' "return" to fiscal and familiar "responsibility" ' (Duschinsky, 2013a: 137). In his genealogy of sexualization as a social problem, Duschinsky suggests that this neo-liberal co-option was facilitated in part by a politics of sexual purity wherein 'the figure of the innocent girl stands as the constitutive outside of the self-reliant citizen, responsible for himself without any need of welfare state protections' (2013b: 366). This, he argues, evidences feminist media critics' utilization of a 'liberal loophole' wherein it is presumed that each citizen should make choices for themselves and be responsible for those choices *unless they are minors* in which case they can legitimately be excused from such responsibility given that their 'individual volition is uncoupled from socially and legally recognized consent, such that they do "not have consent to give or withdraw"' (2013c: para 2.3). And yet, as demonstrated above, youth have been, and are further poised to be, subject to the twin processes of responsibilization and criminalization across the US, Australian and Canadian legal contexts (Salter et al., 2013; Karaian, 2014). Indeed, Leary goes so far as to insist that: 'If we are to combat the sexual objectification of children, we need to prosecute, regardless of the age of the creator' (2008: 41–42). Here, sexual objectification and sexual exploitation are conflated. Sexual objectification, which at one point in time gave rise to questionable effects requiring a concerted, but not legal, response now infuses or stands in for sexual exploitation so thoroughly that it grounds youths' criminalization under our child pornography laws, laws which do not distinguish between those who took the picture and those who appear in it, and where distinctions based on the age of the image's creator and distributor are similarly ignored (*R. v. Schultz*, 2008). It is in this legal context then, that a child who self-exploits by producing sexual imagery of themselves can be prosecuted under the same statute that would define them as 'compliant victims' (Lanning, 2005).

Conclusion

The invalidation of girls' ability to consent to creating sexual images for *themselves*, and to share these with others for *themselves*, not only denies girls their right to be seen as and to see *themselves* as desiring sexual subjects – as someone who 'who feels entitled to sexual pleasure and sexual safety, who [can] make ... active sexual choices, and who has an identity as a sexual being' (Tolman, 2002: 5–6) – such constructions may be co-opted by the right wing to develop a 'discursive coalition', an 'ensemble of narratives that contain assumptions which permits them to mesh together to shape a particular problematization of a policy issue' (Duschinsky, 2013b: 151). Along the lines of those who have already critiqued critics of child sexualization for wrongly conflating objectification, self-objectification, sexual objectification and for limiting their applicability to girls and sexuality (Lerum & Dworkin, 2009a: 257; 2009b), a concerted focus on the structural elements, contextual framework and legal effects of self-exploitation rhetoric exposes the potential limits and harms of its conflation with self-objectification, given the different legal implications implicit in these concepts; namely, the fact that child-exploitation discourses may have a net widening effect on determinations of what contexts may be deemed 'exploitative' and thus subject to child pornography prosecutions. This has developed in a context which focuses on the ways in which girls can change their belief systems and behaviours (Zurbriggen, 2008), and by advancing preventative education which preaches self-respect and self-censorship (CCCP, 2012). Thus sexualization and anti-sexting discourses can be seen as intersecting, not only to responsibilize girls – particularly 'respectable' white, middle-class, heterosexual girls (Karaian, 2014) – for preventing their own and others' sexual corruption (Egan, 2013), but also their own, and their peers, criminalization as child pornographers (Karaian, 2014).

In her now decade-old critique of the Supreme Court of Canada's decision in *R. v. Sharpe*, Lise Gotell asks a question that I have adopted and repurposed here: 'What' she asks, 'would happen if we allowed the child pornographer to speak?' What would happen if we were forced to interrogate the proposition that self-produced 'child pornography' stemmed from girls' sexual desires and their sexual subjectivity and in turn does not necessarily and inherently constitute and cause sexual abuse? (2001). Although some qualitative research with teenage girls has sought to answer questions about the potentially positive implications of self-produced and shared sexual imagery for youths' self-actualization and the role of sex-positivity for combating slut-shaming and what some have deemed 'rape culture' (Ringrose & Renold, 2012; Albury et al., 2013), more qualitative work in this area is necessary. Until then, however, adult responders might do well to reflect on how the corrective to girls' purported false consciousness, namely, ' "right consciousness" ... imposed from the outside by "right thinking" feminists who know what [girls] want' affirms rather than challenges the degraded status of those on whose behalf they speak thus 'perpetuating the cycle it tries to break and, ironically, reinforces the intractability of [girls'] position in society' (Cornell, 1998: 169). Indeed, as Cornell suggests, if the goal is to address child sexual exploitation on the larger scale, early adopters of the consensual sexting = 'self-exploitation' claim might consider how political and ethical struggles to make the 'imaginary domain' accessible to girls (1998: 169) and to acknowledge how the potential expressive interests that youth have in their self-produced sexual imagery may engender 'enabling conditions' (Correa & Petchesky, 1994: 95). These are conditions embedded in the 'structural social conditions of safety, resources and social norms that make [girls' sexuality development and] well-being possible' (Tolman, 2012: 750) and which confront a neo-liberal law and order agenda within which minors are criminalized for their volitional expressive practices.

Notes

1. As William Eskridge notes, the meaning of sexual consent has changed over time and in response to women's and queers' increased power (1995, 48). Consent is not

a simple volitional category but rather is inherently concerned with legal status and social policy (55). That is, the recognition of a valid choice cannot be separated from the *status* of the chooser(s) and the chosen (55). The legal meaning of the same act may differ depending on one's status as a minor or an adult. However, as Eskridge notes, 'status and consent are both conceptions serving a larger cultural script ... [which is] socially regulatory' (55). There are limits to relying on one's status as a 'child' to deny their ability to consent to sexual relations and expression. Given that one's agency is always partial and constrained by internalized norms and structural constraints (for both adults and young people), in this chapter I thus start from the position that consensual teenage sexting is a possibility that can be acknowledged as a valid choice in and by law despite one's status as a minor and notwithstanding our so called sexualized context.

2. This notion of 'self-exploitation' seemingly applies only to youth who engage in consensual sexting.

3. A small and disparate body of literature examines 'self-exploitation' in relation to self-employed cultural entrepreneurship.

4. In 2009, 23% of people arrested for child pornography production were 17 years old or younger (Wolak et al., 2012b: 2). Approximately one-third, or 134, of these young people created these images 'in the context of romantic relationships or for sexual attention-seeking' (Wolak et al., 2012b: 2). According to another US study of arrests, of the cases involving 'youth-produced sexual images' that constituted child pornography in 2008 and 2009, 33% were classifiable as 'experimental' or those which 'did not involve adults or appear to include any intent to harm or reckless misuse' (Wolak & Finklehor, 2011: 3).

5. As our Supreme Court of Canada suggests:

> [A]uto-depictions; that is, visual recordings made by a person of him- or herself alone, held privately and intended only for personal use ... may be of significance to adolescent self-fulfilment, self-actualization and sexual exploration and identity .... Such materials could conceivably reinforce healthy sexual relationships and self-actualization. For example, two adolescents might arguably deepen a loving and respectful relationship through erotic pictures of themselves engaged in sexual activity. The cost of including such materials to the right of free expression outweighs any tenuous benefit it might confer in preventing harm to children.
>
> (*R. v. Sharpe*, 2001: para. 109)

6. Canada's porn wars saw the Women's Legal Education and Action Fund (LEAF) (with the aid of Catherine MacKinnon), intervene on behalf of the Canadian federal government where they successfully argued in support of the state censorship of pornography on the grounds that it constitutes a form of sex discrimination that poses a danger to all women and their equality in *R. v. Butler* (1992).

7. Section 163.1(3)(a) of the *Criminal Code* provides that: Every person who transmits, makes available, distributes, sells, advertises, imports, exports or possesses for the purpose of transmission, making available, distribution, sale, advertising or exportation any child pornography is guilty of (a) an indictable offence and liable to imprisonment for a term not exceeding ten years and to a minimum punishment of imprisonment for a term of one year.

8. Dominance feminism, which gained prominence in the 'sex wars' of the 1980s, is defined by Kathryn Abrams as a 'strand of feminist (legal) theory that locates gender oppression in the sexualized domination of women by men and the

eroticization of that dominance through pornography and other elements of popular culture' (1995: 304). I refer to it as influential because even though dominance feminists' anti-porn ordinances were struck down as unconstitutional in the US, Catherine Mackinnon's work informed the feminist legal facta advanced in *R. v. Butler* and which shaped Canadian obscenity law as well as the cultural terrain within which it is applied.

References

Albury, K., Crawford, K., Byron, P., & Mathews, B. (2013). *Young people and sexting in Australia: Ethics, representation and the law.* April 2013. ARC Centre for Creative Industries and Innovation/ Journalism and Media Research Centre, the University of New South Wales, Australia.

American Psychological Association [APA] (2007) *Report of the APA task force on the sexualisation of girls.* Retrieved from http://www.apa.org/pi/women/programs/girls/report.aspx

Bissonnette, Sophie (Director) (2007) *Sexy Inc. Our children under influence* [Video]. National Film Board of Canada. Retrieved from http://www.nfb.ca/film/sexy_inc /?hc_location=ufi

Calder, G., & Beaman, L. G. (2013). *Polygamy's rights and wrongs: Perspectives on harm, family, and law.* Vancouver: UBC Press.

Canadian Centre For Child Protection (2012) *Self/peer exploitation resource guide: School and family approaches to intervention and prevention.* Manitoba, Canada, 1–52.

Cornell, D. (1998) *At the heart of freedom: Feminism, sex and equality.* Princeton, NJ: Princeton University Press.

Correa, S., & Petchesky, R. (1994). 'Reproductive and sexual rights: A feminist perspective', in G. Sen, A. Germain, & L. C. Chen (Eds.) *Population policies reconsidered: Health, empowerment, and rights.* Boston, MA: Harvard University Press, pp. 107–123.

Department of Justice (18 January 2012) Government announces support for children's protection programs. Retrieved from http://www.justice.gc.ca/eng/news-nouv/nr-cp/2012/doc_32694.html

Duschinsky, R. (2013a) The emergence of sexualisation as a social problem: 1981–2010. *Social Politics: International Studies in Gender, State and Society,* 20 (1), 137–156.

Duschinsky, R. (2013b) Childhood, responsibility and the liberal loophole: Replaying the sex-wars in debates on sexualisation? *Sociological Research Online,* 18 (2). Retrieved from http://www.socresonline.org.uk/18/2/7.html

Egan, R. D. (2013) *Becoming sexual: A critical appraisal of the sexualization of girls.* New York: Polity Press.

Egan, D. R., & Hawkes, G. (2009) The problem with protection: Or, why we need to move towards recognition and the sexual agency of children. *Continuum: Journal of Media & Cultural Studies,* 23 (3), 389–400.

Friedman, J., & Valenti, J. (Eds.) (2008) *Yes means yes! Visions of female sexual power in a world without rape.* Berkeley, CA, Seal Press.

Goldstein, L. (2009) Documenting and denial: Discourses of sexual self-exploitation. *Jumpcut* 51. Retrieved from http://www.ejumpcut.org/archive/jc51.2009/goldstein/

Hasinoff, A. A. (2014) Blaming sexualization for sexting. *Girlhood Studies,* 7 (1), 102–120.

Hasinoff, A. A. (2015) *Sexting panic: Rethinking criminalization, privacy, and consent.* Illinois Champaign, IL: University of Illinois Press.

Jaffer, M., & Patrick, B. (2012) *Cyberbullying Hurts: Respect for Rights in the Digital Age*. Canada: Standing Senate Committee on Human Rights, 1–126.

Karaian, L. (2009) 'The Troubled Relationship of Feminist and Queer Legal Theory to Strategic Essentialism: Theory/Praxis, Queer Porn, and Canadian Anti-discrimination Law', in M. A. Fineman, A. Romero, & J. Jackson (Eds.) *Feminist and Queer Legal Theory: Intimate Encounters, Uncomfortable Conversations*. Burlington, Vermont, USA: Ashgate Press, pp. 375–394.

Karaian, L. (2012) Lolita speaks: 'Sexting', teenage girls and the law. *Crime Media Culture*, 1 (8), 57–73.

Karaian, L. (2014) Policing 'sexting': Responsibilisation, respectability and sexual subjectivity in child protection/crime prevention responses to teenagers' digital sexual expression. *Theoretical Criminology*, 18 (3), 282–299.

Lamb, S. (2010) Feminist ideals for a healthy female adolescent sexuality: A critique. *Sex Roles*, 62, 294–306.

Lanning, K. V. (2005) Compliant child victims: Confronting an uncomfortable reality', in E. Quayle, & M. Taylor, L. Regis (Eds.) *Viewing Child Pornography on the Internet*: Understanding the Offence, Managing the Offender, Helping the Victims. Russell House Publishing, 2005.

Leary, M. (2008). Self produced child pornography: The appropriate societal response to juvenile self-sexual exploitation. *Virginia Journal of Social Policy and the Law*, 15 (1): 1–50.

Lerum, K., & Dworkin, S. L. (2009a) 'Bad girls rule': An interdisciplinary feminist commentary on the report of the APA Task Force on the sexualisation of girls. *Journal of Sex Research*, 46 (4), 250–263.

Lerum, K., & Dworkin, S. L. (2009b) Toward an interdisciplinary dialogue on youth, sexualisation, and health. *Journal of Sex Research*, 46 (4), 271–273.

MacKinnon, C. (1989) Sexuality, pornography and method: Pleasure under patriarchy. *Ethics*, 99 (2), 314–346.

Ontario Provincial Police [OPP] (28 February 2012) *Warning for teens on dangers of irresponsible texting: Long term danger of damage to reputation and identity*. Retrieved from http://www.newswire.ca/en/story/929039/opp-issue-warning-for-teens-on-dangers-of-irresponsible-texting

Opplinger, P. (2008) *Girls Gone Skank*. Jefferson, NC: MacFarland and Company Press.

Palmer, M. (Director) (2012). *Sext up kids* [Video]. Canada: CBC.

Papadopolous, L. (2010) *Sexualization of young people review*. London: Home Office.

Paul, P. (2005) *Pornified: How pornography is transforming our lives, our relationships, and our families*. New York: Times Books.

Peskin, M. F., Markham, C. M., Addy, R. C., Shegog, R., Thiel, M., & Tortolero, S. R. (2013) Prevalence and patterns of sexting among ethnic minority urban high school students. *Cyberpsychology, Behavior, and Social Networking*, 16 (6), 1–6.

R. v. Butler, [1992] 1 S.C.R. 452.

Renold, E., & Ringrose, J. (2011) Schizoid subjectivities?: Re-theorizing teen girls' sexual cultures in an era of 'sexualisation'. *Journal of Sociology*, 47, 389–409.

Ringrose, J., Gill, R., Livingstone, S., & Harvey, L. (2012) *A qualitative study of children, young people and 'sexting'*. London: NSPCC. Retrieved from http://www.nspcc.org.uk/inform/resourcesforprofessionals/sexualabuse/sexting-research-report_wdf89269.pdf

Ringrose, R., & Renold, E. (2012) Slut-shaming, girl power and 'sexualisation': Thinking through the politics of the international slutwalks with teen girls. *Gender and Education*, 24 (3), 333–343.

Rush, E., & La Nauze, A. (2006) *Corporate paedophilia: Sexualisation of children in Australia*. The Australian Institute, Discussion Paper Number 90, 1–72.

Salter, M., Croft, T., & Lee, M. (2013) Beyond criminalisation and responsibilisation: Sexting, gender and young people. *Current Issues in Criminal Justice*, 24 (3), 301–316.

Smith, C., & Attwood, F. (2011) Lamenting sexualisation: Research, rhetoric and the story of young people's 'sexualisation' in the UK Home Office Review. *Sex Education*, 11 (3), 327–337.

Strassberg, D., McKinnon, R. K., Sustaíta, M. A., & Rullo, J. (2013) Sexting by high school students: An exploratory and descriptive study. *Archives of Sexual Behavior*, 42 (1), 15–21.

Tolman, D. (2012) Female adolescents, sexual empowerment and desire: A missing discourse of gender inequity? *Sex Roles*, 66 (11–12), 746–757.

Tolman, D. L. (2002) *Dilemmas of desire: Teenage girls talk about sexuality*. Cambridge, MA: Harvard University Press.

Wertheimer, A. (1996) *Exploitation*. Princeton, NJ: Princeton University Press.

Wolak, J., & Finklehor, D. (2011) Sexting: A typology. *Crimes Against Children Research Centre*, 1–11. Retrieved from http://www.unh.edu/ccrc/internet-crimes/papers.html

Wolak, J., Finkelhor, D., & Mitchell, K. (2012). Trends in Arrests for Child Pornography Production: The Third National Juvenile Online Victimization Study (NJOV3). *Crimes against Children Research Center*, Retrieved from http://www.unh.edu/ccrc/pdf/ CV270_Child% 20Porn%20Production%20Bulletin4-13-12.pdf

Wolak, J., & Finkelhor, D. (2013). Are crimes by online predators different from crimes by sex offenders who know youth in-person? *The Journal of Adolescent Health: Official Publication of the Society for Adolescent Medicine*, 53, 736–741.

Zurbriggen, E. L., Collins, R. L., Lamb, S., et al. (2007). *Report of the APA task force on the sexualization of girls*. Washington, DC: American Psychological Association.

22
Sexting, Ratings and (Mis)Recognition: Teen Boys Performing Classed and Racialized Masculinities in Digitally Networked Publics

Laura Harvey and Jessica Ringrose

Introduction

This chapter responds to the construction of teen boys and masculinity as predatory and hypersexualized in implicitly classed and racialized ways in the popular press and reporting on 'sexting' (Karaian, 2013). We argue that the practices of sexual communication that are often mobilized in debates about 'sexting' need to be understood as part of wider social practices of identity formation that work in relation to local norms of gender, race and class and wider popular cultural representations of ideal masculinities (e.g. pop music, advertising). We examine these practices in our empirical data which explores young people's negotiation of digital sexual cultures and new economies of self-representation on social networking platforms. While the young people in our study did not use the term 'sexting', our research found a range of different communication practices that could fall under this umbrella term (see Ringrose et al., 2012). In this chapter we examine the production, circulation, tagging and commenting upon images via Blackberry Messenger (BBM) and Facebook by working with and building on Paechter's (2010) notion of culturally specific ideals of masculinity(ies), Skegg's (2001, 2004) analysis of value and recognition, and Butler's (1993) framework on performativity. Drawing these tools together we explore how teen boys develop practices of sexualized, raced and classed recognition through performances of masculinities via digital display and commenting online.

Sexualization, 'sexting' and essentialized masculinity

Concerns about girls' bodies, clothing and experiences as 'prematurely sexualized' have dominated headlines and the numerous reviews on 'sexualization' commissioned by the UK government and internationally in recent decades (Barker & Duschinsky, 2012). Numerous scholars point out how concern about the 'sexualization of girls' in the media typically has surrounded white, middle-class girls becoming tainted by working-class associations with sexualized femininity (Egan, 2013; Ringrose, 2013; Lamb, forthcoming).

In contrast to the attention to young femininity in policy and media discourses on sexualization we do not often see boys as the main subject of enquiry. As with much talk about youth sexuality, the voices of boys themselves are often missing from debates about the sexualization of culture. When boys do appear, they tend to be positioned as problematic subjects in relation to the consumption of pornography or as having uncontrollable sexualities (Mulholland, 2013). Boys are often talked about as an essentialized grouping, which is classed and racialized in relation to negative stereotypes around crime and violence. These constructions of masculinity do not critically examine the role of wider power relations or more mainstream discourses of sexism (Gill, 2011).

One of the recent areas of panic over youth sexualization relates to online and mobile technology and practices of youth 'sexting'. The debates on sexting as problematic 'sexualized' practice have constructed young girls as primarily the victims of an assumed predatory and unremarkable culture of masculinity (Albury & Crawford, 2012; Harvey et al., 2013). In the USA and Australia, it is white boys who have been the focus of several high-profile sexting legal cases. However, in the UK context, and more specifically in the more metropolitan city centres, representations seem to implicitly reflect wider narratives of a 'crisis in masculinity', in which working-class, black and Muslim boys are positioned as 'problems' within policy rhetoric, particularly in relation to education and employment (Archer et al., 2010). For example, the most-used anti-sexting film resource in the UK, the CEOP film *Exposed*, profiles a young black man who passes an image sent of his mixed race girlfriend to his friend network. The assumption built into the representational discourses of this film is that in the UK context sexting is more of a problem for black or mixed race teens than white teens (who are not central to the storyline of the film). The development of these dominant discourses on youth sexting can be understood as part of an intersectional process of 'racialization' and 'sexualization', in this case where ideas about digital technologies and young masculinities, social class, ethnicities and sexualities are culturally (re)produced (Harvey et al., 2013).

Theoretical framework

Theoretically this chapter is interested in new economies of self-representation that constitute young people's digitally networked sexual cultures (boyd, 2014). However our interest is in the performative *gendered practices* of online display and representation, which is largely absent from research accounts of social networking practices (Van Doorn, 2010). Whilst in previous research we have explored digital practices of constituting ideal femininities (Ringrose et al., 2013), in this chapter we wish to focus on the digitally mediated practices of performing local and embodied masculinities.

We draw upon sociological research on youth culture, masculinity and education, which shows that young masculinities are complex and shifting, constructed through multiple sites, including friendships, locality, family, school and cultural consumption (Archer et al., 2010). In their research with 14–16-year-olds in London, Archer and colleagues (2010) argued that many of their participants from different ethnic backgrounds constructed their identities as entangled with black Caribbean and North American styles, echoing earlier work on young urban masculinities (Back, 1996; Frosh et al., 2002; Nayak, 2003). The performance of a 'cool' masculinity, particularly within educational contexts, has been theorized as in part a response to racism and the devaluing of working-class and black masculinities (Majors, 1990; Archer et al., 2007). Young people's ability to perform such masculinities without risking conflict with school or harassment from police is differentiated by social class and race (Skeggs, 2004; Gunter, 2010).

We also draw upon new media research, which illustrates how 'gender scripts' are performed through digital display online (Van Doorn, 2010). Siibak (2010) explored how young men on the Estonian social networking site *Rate* performed their masculinities through images of idealized bodies. Manago (2013) focused on how young men take up or subvert hegemonic masculinity in sexual displays online on MySpace. Mowlabocus (2010) has explored the performance of non-heterosexual masculinity online. O'Neill (2014) has explored how members of the Pick Up Artist (PUA) community negotiate masculinity through the online posting of videos of pick-ups and dates. However, none of these studies explored younger teen boys and digital performances specifically in relation to localized young peer norms of social class and race.

We seek to explore the performance of local teen masculinities on social networking sites, drawing upon Connell's (2005) influential theorization of 'hegemonic masculinities' as developed by educational scholars, to think about masculinity in the plural and how different ideals of masculinity are constructed in relation to different communities of practice (Paechter, 2010). This allows us to see how masculinities are differentiated according to race, class and cultural location. Importantly, the forms of masculinity that gain hegemony in any given context are locally specific, and subject to continual negotiation and challenge (Connell & Messerschmidt, 2005; Paechter, 2010; Pascoe, 2012).

We are also interested in how dominant heterosexual masculinity operates around practices of homosociality (Sedgwick, 1985). This concept has been taken up in research on masculinities to explore social relationships between men. In particular, research has examined how gendered power works through such sociality, exploring its role in sustaining hegemony for particular kinds of masculinity and in maintaining gender inequality (e.g. Bird, 1996).

We seek to contribute to this literature on masculinity to think about how practices of identification are situated in visual and embodied hierarchies of value, through practices of *recognition*. Beverley Skeggs's work has usefully combined insights from Foucauldian (e.g. 1979) approaches to discourse and power, with Bourdieu's (1986) analysis of cultural, economic and social capital and Fraser's (1995) work on the politics of recognition, to theorize how gender, 'race' and class are constructed socially. Skeggs (2001) theorizes recognition and misrecognition as social processes in which individuals and groups are evaluated and categorized by each other. She argues that this occurs as part of social practices of evaluation, in which particular forms of capital, such as access to economic resources, cultural knowledge and social networks enable people to be recognised as 'legitimate' or 'authorized' in relation to others. Frith et al. (2014: 10) have pointed to the embodied nature of such practices of recognition. For Skeggs (2004), cultural capitals are context specific – some forms of capital for example are recognized in more marginalized contexts while denigrated by more powerful groups in society. Skeggs and Wood (2012) have also analysed how these notions of value and recognition work in relation to visual economies.

We are also using recognition as a concept derived from psychoanalytical frameworks and discourse analysis to think about practices of legitimation around identity. Butler (1993) develops the idea of recognition to think about how people inhabit 'legitimate' subject positions. Educational scholars such as Youdell (2006) have drawn on Butler and Bourdieu to consider how these identity practices work performatively, examining how boys become characterized as failing at school because they lack the racialized cultural, bodily capitals of 'ideal' [white] learners. Performativity adds a critical dimension to understanding recognition in that it is the space of subjective interaction between discourse and embodied action (Butler, 1993). Pulling all of these theoretical tools together, our chapter seeks to work with these concepts of hegemonic masculinity, homosociality, recognition and value to explore how boys perform idealized forms of culturally specific masculinities online.

The role of social networking within the peer group provides a new space through which young people can negotiate recognition among their peers. Contemporary mobile and online technologies enable many young people to communicate to mass audiences, and 'archive' their friendships, feelings, thoughts and changing identities as they grow up (Robards, 2012). In particular, the ability to be able to interact, 'like', comment and circulate content on mobile devices and online constructs a particularly visual and fluid form of recognition, in which the merits of particular content can be actively negotiated by peers over time. In addition, the possibility to capture content through screen shots (or 'munch screens' on Blackberry messenger) enables young people to collect 'evidence' of conversations and images as part of the messiness between the online, offline, public and private performance of identities. We are particularly interested in how gender, class, race and sexuality are constructed through these practices, and how different images of bodies work in these hierarchies of legitimacy. We show how these online performative practices are affective (Skeggs & Wood, 2012), charged with energetic and emotive dimensions of desire around fulfilling norms of idealized recognition – having value and thereby gaining 'ratings' in the peer network, as we will go on to explore.

Methodology: Researching young people's digital sexual communication

This chapter draws on data from an NSPCC-funded research project about young people's digital sexual communication and 'sexting' practices conducted in 2011 (Ringrose et al., 2012).[1] Much existing research has tended to examine sexting in relation to measuring categories such as gender differences (Livingstone & Gorzig, 2012) although some quantitative studies refer to questions of race and ethnicity (e.g. Fleschler et al., 2013). We would argue that to understand digital sexual communication, we also need contextualized, qualitative analyses of young people's experiences of online communication, particularly in terms of exploring some of the complexity of race, culture and class in young people's digital sexual cultures. Increasing numbers of qualitative research projects are emerging in the UK, US and Australia (Ringrose et al., 2012; Albury et al., 2013; Harris et al., 2013). However, much qualitative research has also not explicitly located and accounted for the cultural and socio-economic background of the participants.

Our research explored the experiences of 35 young people aged 12–15 in two London state schools between June and August 2011. The sample consisted of 18 boys and 17 girls, of whom 23 were from black and minority ethnic backgrounds and 12 were from white backgrounds; 18 participants were aged 12–13 and 17 were aged 14–15. We conducted focus group interviews, then invited young people to connect with us on Facebook for a three-month period, during which we conducted ethnographic observation of young people's online interactions.[2] We followed up with individual interviews with 22 young people, in which we discussed the online interactions we had observed, in addition to following through themes which had emerged in focus groups, such as the popularity system of 'ratings', discussed below.

The schools were located in two different inner-London boroughs, serving students from a range of socio-economic backgrounds. One school was slightly larger than average, while the other was slightly smaller. Students at both schools were from a wide range of ethnic backgrounds. The largest groups of students at the bigger school were from White British, Black African and Bangladeshi backgrounds, while at the smaller school the largest ethnic groups were White British, Black Caribbean, Black African and Other White backgrounds.

Ratings: Navigating recognition and masculinity

Students at both schools discussed their feelings of safety within their peer groups and local streets, including talking about navigating potential theft, harassment and violence. Students in the smaller school discussed this in more detail, relating travelling safely in their local area to being known or popular, wearing the 'right' kinds of clothes and knowing which areas to travel in (Harvey et al., 2013). While young people discussed this in relation to school rivalries and potential gang locations, one young person also framed this explicitly in relation to his ethnic background, describing his tendency not to travel in a nearby area because 'they don't like Albanians' (Kaja, 14–15). Thus acquiring locally recognized cultural capital was important for some of the boys as they navigated their peer groups and local area (Harvey et al., 2013).

'Ratings' was the term used by young people to describe a system of popularity and respect. Wearing particular brands and showing skill or power in football, computer games and fighting were all useful. There were experiences of street violence, and being able to protect yourself and your belongings was important:

> You can't just, if you're nobody you can't just walk past that you wouldn't have any ratings, like people are going to ask you questions where you from, who are you? They ain't heard of you, they take your phone, they'll take whatever nice stuff you've got.
>
> (Adam, 14–15)

Ratings can be understood as a form of social and cultural capital, which enabled boys to move safely and develop networks of friends in their schools and localities. Ratings could circulate online, but also related to offline resources and experiences such as branded commodities (Harvey et al., 2013), and as we explain further below, proof of access to 'real' sexual experiences and bodies (or at least their potential). Particular performances of masculinity, as physically fit, tough, known and heterosexually desirable, were all markers of hegemonically masculine success:

> For example there is like a fight yeah. Like there is three boys versus one boy but people you know are watching the fight and one boy fights all

of them and is not scared, they will go, 'Oh he gets ratings because he's brave'... Like people will say, 'Oh I rate him because he gets girls and that', or gets money and things like that.

(Kamal, 12–13)

Kamal's comment highlights the relational nature of ratings – to be 'rated' is to be recognised as popular by one's peers, and to be seen as inhabiting a particular form of high-status masculinity. While there was much talk about boys' ability to gain ratings, this was less straightforward for girls, who seemed only able to trade on looks in relation to the masculine ratings game (Ringrose et al., 2013). Boys, however, were able to negotiate recognition and value through visual performances of masculinity that included not only displays of their own bodies and other kinds of masculine 'successes', but also the exchange of visual representations of their interactions with girls, including possessing sexual images and talking about their sexual experiences, which we will explore in following sections.

'I've got 42 likes': Recognition and gendered bodily display

The first digital performance of masculinity we want to explore is the posting of idealized images of boys' own bodies. While much of the mainstream news and policy focus of sexualization is concerned with girls' bodies, relatively little attention is paid to images of boys' bodies. Recent masculinities scholarship has explored the increasing visibility of boys and men's bodies, particularly in relation to dominant gendered and racialized notions of physical appearance, such as muscularity (Gill et al., 2005; Kehler & Atkinson, 2010; Drummond, 2011). Young people generally positioned the display of boys' bodies in topless images of 'six packs' and back muscles as fairly ordinary. For example, Kamal (12–13), explained that 'most boys have pictures of their six pack on Facebook'.

Despite the apparent ordinariness of such images, in order to 'successfully' claim value from images, boys needed to navigate gendered and racialized norms of bodily display, particularly in terms of fitness and muscles:

I: Do you ever put picture like that of muscles and things like that?

Daniel: Nah nah nah. For me to do that I would have to be completely big. I'd wanna be proper big to do that. I wouldn't want to do some little half, got a little pack there, little pack there. I'd want to be fully big. And I wouldn't do it in the mirror. I'd get someone to take it of me. Outside or something, not in my house, in the gym...

I: So why do you reckon the guys are putting those kind of pictures up then?

Daniel: 'Cause girls are attracted to guys, a lot of girls are attracted to guys that are ripped, have a good body.

(Daniel, aged 14–15)

Boys posting topless images therefore have the potential to signify a physically powerful masculinity, a 'ripped' body that is 'worked on' at the gym and is perceived to signal heterosexual desirability. The images that boys post, and consequently the recognition they receive, can be understood as always in negotiation – there is an ongoing possibility of comments and 'likes' beyond the moment at which the image is shared. Such interaction poses a potential risk for boys. Daniel's unwillingness to post an image unless he is 'fully big' highlights the potential to be *mis*recognized, or fail to gain ratings for an image.

Kamal, a younger boy (12–13), had posted several topless images on Facebook over the previous year. The most recent image, of his flexed back muscles, had received positive interactions from his friends:

I: Do you get ratings if lots of people like the picture?

Kamal: Yeah right now I've got 42 likes on the picture and lots of comments.

I: So you know how many likes you have got?

Kamal: Yeah.

I: And do people ever write mean things under the picture?

Kamal: Yeah, but only like your friends, like they would say something like, say you are trying to put a picture of a six pack up and it is not like quite a six pack, they will say, 'Keep trying harder until you get like me' and lots of people will start laughing.

Kamal is aware of the popularity of the picture, remembering the number of 'likes' and comments. The comments and 'likes' below the image thus form part of the local, peer-negotiated construction of masculinity. For example, one of the comments below the image describes Kamal's body as 'the best I've seen',[3] highlighting Kamal's success in being recognized. In contrast, Kamal posted an image of his 'six pack' in the previous year, which had only received 2 'likes'. While the image was older, a girl had recently added the first comment on the picture, several months after it was first posted. Such durability (boyd, 2014) of images highlights the complex temporal construction of recognition online.

The visual and archiving capabilities of social networking sites enable the construction of young identities in new ways. Images posted and recirculated not only mark leisure activities, style and consumption, but can also map bodily changes, whether to facial hair, breasts or muscles. Such images could be understood in some senses as commodities or a process of commodification of the self through emergent properties of sexualized embodiment, appearing alongside images of branded trainers or designer labels as part of the classed and racialized performance of 'swagger' (Harvey et al., 2013).

The boys who talked about and performed swagger were from a range of different ethnic and national backgrounds, some of whom performed complex and locally informed versions of 'Black cool' (Archer et al., 2010). Understanding how power works in these performances of embodiment is crucial to understanding the relationship between masculinities and sexting. Facebook likes, comments and threads are new digital affordances that are *negotiated*. They are sites of struggle over meaning – to be 'recognized' as appropriately gendered, classed, racialized, requires access to knowledge (both locally specific and more globalized cultural norms), and for this to be authorized through interactions with others.

Capturing commodities and bodies

The second digital performance of masculinity we want to explore is the request, tagging and circulation of images of girls' bodies, typically cleavage, often with the name of a boy written across in marker pen. We have discussed this practice elsewhere (Ringrose & Harvey, 2015); here we want to develop our analysis in relation to its position in the negotiation of recognition around masculinity and homosociality.

The young people in both schools presented successfully requesting receiving and collecting a range of pictures of girls' bodies, as a way for boys to gain ratings. The images could be used as a form of 'evidence' of a boy's ability to persuade a girl to send a picture:

> Look what you are capable of doing, making a girl take a picture of her breasts and give it to you and stuff
>
> (Boys focus group, 14–15)

While many such images would be circulated via BBM, some images circulated on Facebook, which we were able to observe as part of our online ethnography, and discuss with the young people. For example, Kaja (14–15) had two pictures of a girl with 'Kaja owns' written across her cleavage in marker pen. In the individual interview, Kaja explained that these were from an older girl (18 or 19) who lived far away and had tagged him in them.

Both images were 'headless' shots, one of the strategies that some girls had developed to avoid being identified. One image attracted positive comments and laughter from Kaja's friends, including a friend exclaiming the congratulation 'went in Kaja' and another saying 'someone gets gassed'.[4] The other image is a much closer shot of cleavage. However, in contrast, this image attracted jokes from his friends, with one describing the image as 'a fat man'. Kaja's ability to claim recognition from the images is complicated. The jokey exchange on the close-up, in which it is more difficult to see the shape of the girl's body and her breasts, calls into question Kaja's ability to prove value and heterosexual desirability through 'owning' the breasts in the image – both devaluing the sender and receiver of the image it would seem because the breasts are not clearly visible enough.

Images of girls' bodies, therefore, have the potential to form part of the digital material through which value circulates in the peer network, and through which recognition of hegemonic masculinity is negotiated by some boys. However, such images do not unproblematically enable boys to claim recognition, particularly it seems if they have been sent unsolicited. The ambiguity of this image, and Kaja's ambivalence to it was clear during the interview, as he distanced himself from the sender of the images, both morally and physically, as 'some girl' who 'is from far' and 'has no shame'.

Munch screens: Proving heterosexual desirability

While online content is frequently presented as transient and temporary, images and text are often archived both on social networking sites and communication platforms, and can be captured and saved through screen shots and used as 'evidence'. Adam, a Year 10 boy, explained how messages could be captured, stored and circulated:

> Adam: Like say for example a boy is talking to a girl and the girl says yeah, I'll meet up with you and I'll have sex with you or whatever, the boy will end up like, the boy will probably end up munch screening it and he'll go show his friends that yeah this is what the girl said to me.

In the context of the local peer group, sexual activity with girls signified a high-status masculinity. While the performance of heterosexual masculinity through stories about sexual experiences certainly isn't new (Holland et al., 1998), we would argue that social networking sites bring new processes of mediating gendered recognition, which must be negotiated. In particular, smartphones and social networking sites provide the ability to be able to *prove* that sexual experiences have (or might) take place, through the capturing of text or images:

> I: do you get ratings for saying you've done this and that with girls, or?
> Adam: Nah, you get ratings for what you've, what girls have done to you.
> I: Like what kind of thing?
> Adam: You've had sex with a girl, she gave you a blowjob. Like whatever.
> I: And do people like someone was telling using munch screen to prove stuff like ... ?

Adam: Yeah, like yes, to prove that this girl sent me this, that I can get girls so she said this to me, she said, yeah.

Conversations about sexual experiences appear here as one way in which boys can gain value in the peer group, with munch screens providing a form of tangible evidence for this. Ratings can be gained from being recognized as a boy who can 'get girls'. The distinction Adam makes about the importance of 'what girls have done to you' is particularly significant in terms of the gendered relations of these practices of exchange. Conversations about sex, and sex itself, appear here as something from which boys can extract and exchange value. Even if the sex does not happen, the articulation of its possibility can potentially be exchanged for ratings within the peer group.

In Paechter's (2010) terms, the sharing of images is produced by, but in turn produces, the local communities of practice within the peer group, as the images and discussion around them become sites for peer recognition of hegemonic masculinity. Within this context, there is an additional hierarchy of recognition, in which images of *particular* girls or *particular kinds of bodies* were more valuable than others. We noted in the previous section that Kaja's ability to claim value from cleavage images was complex, relating to norms of desirability and gendered bodily display, which were negotiated in the comments below the image. It was not enough to obtain images or have sex with *any* girl. In order to gain recognition and be 'rated', they needed to be the *right* kind of girl (and have the 'right sort' of body/breasts as explored above).

For example, Kaja explained that to persuade 'a popular girl ... that looks like one of those girls who wouldn't do it then it would make me look even better'. Such discourses of the 'market value' of girls and women's bodies echo O'Neill's (2014) findings in her research about the male Pick Up Artist community. 'Success' in the terms of the PUA trainers, involved successfully 'picking up' and having sex with 'quality' women, including 'proving' this with video evidence. Importantly, the marker of 'quality' for Kaja above, is the scarcity of the particular woman's body, and thus we would argue the implied achievement of the boy in persuading someone who would not be *expected* to send an image. Such evaluations rest on well-worn sexist hierarchies of sexual availability and feminine respectability, but are also importantly locally negotiated in the peer group through conversations about the 'value' of particular girls or images.

These conversations thus produced the norms through which locally valued hegemonic masculinity could be performed and recognized. The dialogic nature of recognition and misrecognition can be observed in the interactions on Facebook. Through likes and comments young people recognize a picture, a performance, as 'good' or 'bad'. Such archived interactions share much with the verbal interactions of everyday life, but with the temporal difference of conversations circulating and recirculating over extended periods of time, as with Kamal's earlier six-pack picture, posted several months before the first comment was posted below it.

It is impossible to get someone naked

While some boys talked of collecting multiple images of cleavage and screen shots (see Ringrose et al., 2013), it is also vital to note the multiple and contested nature of masculinities. Some of the boys we spoke to were critical of, and less concerned about, gaining ratings. Many of the boys we spoke with talked about not being directly involved in requesting, receiving or creating 'sexual' images or text. Sexual communication was not the central feature in all of the boys' Facebook pages or discussions about their use of mobile and online communication. However, as Connell (2005) has argued, lower status masculinities are constructed in relation to hegemonic masculinity in any given context, even where such masculinities reject or do not achieve *dominant markers of masculinity*.

Hierarchies of masculinity also intersected with gendered norms within the peer group, including narratives of growing up and 'appropriate' sexual experience, particularly among the younger cohort (12–13).

> I: We were talking a bit about flirting and stuff, do people send like pictures of naked people around?
> R: No, it is impossible to.
> R: It is impossible, number one, to get someone naked. And then number two to actually send it.
>
> (Boys, 12–13)

The extract above interrupts the familiar story told about 'sexting' of predatory, over-sexed boys, but also highlights something important about the role that 'sexting' practices play both in practice but also in the stories circulating among the peer group about what 'other' people are doing. 'Getting someone naked' is positioned as something impossible, both in practice for these boys, but also in terms of the perceived regulation of the technology. It also tells us something about this practice as fantastical and desirable if unattainable. This crucially points to the potential for images and text to be used as 'material evidence' of desirability and desire, through proof of the ability to achieve the potentially 'impossible' task of getting someone naked.

Conclusion

It seems that fresh rounds of panic in the commentary and debates on the topic of 'sexting' emerge repeatedly (e.g. Angelides, 2013; Stubbs, 2014). We have sought to intervene in these debates, arguing that a contextualized understanding of young people's everyday digital peer cultures is needed.

We have argued that the interactional, archival nature of social networking sites provides space through which young people negotiate local gender norms and their own recognition within these. Through likes, comments and the dynamic temporal possibilities of visual capture, archiving and recirculation, young people navigate their status within the peer group. In this context, the adoption of high-status masculinities, through a system of 'ratings', can be part of how young people gain value in their local peer groups and areas, including as part of a local strategy to remain respected and safe.

Within the local peer cultures discussed above, images and captured text can be understood in some senses as commodities, which can be exchanged for value and recognition. Thus images of girls' bodies form part of a messy entanglement of different forms of 'evidence' in performances of masculinity. While these hierarchies of recognition are negotiated among the peer group, they also importantly draw on globalized norms of gendered embodiment and sexuality, including heteronormativity and racialized norms of idealized bodies circulating in mainstream popular culture and advertising.

We share with Skeggs a concern with 'how certain performances become legitimated and authorised, whether institutionally, discursively or through practice' (2001: 297). Our chapter has highlighted the legitimation of a particular form of masculinity within two London schools. It is important to stress, that while such performances could gain young people status within the peer group, this could not be equally exchanged in other contexts, particularly those in which the young people were marginalized. As we attempt to make sense of young people's digital sexual cultures, we need to develop methodologies and theoretical frameworks that can map how these practices operate and frame how young people live and explore their sexualities.

Notes

1. The research team for this project was Jessica Ringrose, Rosalind Gill, Sonia Livingstone and Laura Harvey, see Ringrose et al. (2012).
2. For an extensive discussion of the methodology and ethics involved in this research project, including the process of how we gained school, parental and participant consent for interviews and friending of school participants on Facebook, please see Ringrose et al. (2012). All of the names used in this chapter are pseudonyms.
3. Some of the wording of posts and comments quoted in this chapter have been edited and changed slightly to convey the meaning of the statement but protect the anonymity of the participant.
4. Jodie, a 13-year-old participant defined 'gassed' as meaning that someone is 'lying' to themselves. An entry on Urbandictionary.com (2014) defines it as 'when one's head has been filled with so many compliments, or has been hit on so much that their mindstate is erred with the belief they're better than everyone else ... especially girls'. http://www.urbandictionary.com/define.php?term=gassed

References

Albury, K., & Crawford, K. (2012) Sexting, consent and young people's ethics: Beyond Megan's story. *Continuum*, 26 (3), 463–473.

Albury, K., Crawford, K., Byron, P., & Mathews, B. (2013) Young people and sexting in Australia: Ethics, representation and the law. ARC Centre for Creative Industries and Innovation/Journalism and Media Research Centre, University of New South Wales, Australia.

Angelides, S. (2013) 'Technology, hormones, and stupidity': The affective politics of teenage sexting. *Sexualities*, 16 (5–6), 665–689.

Archer, L., Hollingworth, S., & Halsall, A. (2007) 'University's not for me- I'm a Nike person': Urban, working class young people's negotiations of 'style', identity and educational engagement. *Sociology*, 41 (2), 219–237.

Archer, L., Hollingworth, S., & Mendick, H. (2010) *Urban Youth and Schooling*. Maidenhead: Open University Press.

Atwood, F., & Smith, C. (2011) Lamenting sexualisation: Research, rhetoric and the story of young people's 'sexualisation' in the UK home office review. *Sex Education*, 11 (3), 327–337.

Back, L. (1996) *New ethnicities and urban culture: Social identity and racism in the lives of young people: Racisms and multiculture in young lives*. London: Routledge.

Barker, M., & Duschinsky, R. (2012) Sexualisation's four faces: Sexualisation and gender stereotyping in the Bailey Review. *Gender & Education*, 24 (3), 303–310.

Bird, S. (1996) Welcome to the men's club: Homosociality and the maintenance of hegemonic masculinity. *Gender & Society*, 10 (2), 120–132.

Bourdieu, P. (1986) 'The forms of capital', in *Handbook of Theory and Research for the Sociology of Education*. New York: Greenwood, pp. 241–258. Retrieved 3 October 2012 from http://www.marxists.org/reference/subject/philosophy/works/fr/bourdieu-forms-capital.htm.

boyd, d. (2014) *It's complicated: The social lives of networked teens*. New Haven: Yale University Press.

Butler, J. (1993) *Bodies that matter: On the discursive limits of 'sex.'* New York: Routledge.

Connell, R. (2005) *Masculinities*. Berkeley: University of California Press.

Connell, R. W., & Messerschmidt, J. (2005) Hegemonic masculinity rethinking the concept. *Gender & Society*, 19 (6), 829–859.

Drummond, M. (2011) Reflections on the archetypal heterosexual male body. *Australian Feminist Studies*, 26 (67), 103–117.

Egan, D. (2013) *Becoming sexual: A critical appraisal of the sexualization of girls*. Cambridge; Malden: Polity Press.

Fleschler, P., Markham, C. M., Addy, R. C., Shegog, R., Thiel, M., & Tortolero, S. R. (2013) Prevalence and patterns of sexting among ethnic minority urban high school students. *Cyberpsychology, Behavior, and Social Networking*, 16 (6), 454–459.

Foucault, M. (1979) Discipline and punish: the birth of the prison. Harmondsworth, Middlesex: Penguin Books.

Fraser, N. (1995) From redistribution to recognition? Dilemmas of justice in a 'postsocialist' age. *New Left Review*, 212, 68–93.

Frith, H., Raisborough, J., & Klein, O. (2014) Shame and pride in how to look good naked. *Feminist Media Studies*, 14 (2), 165–177.

Frosh, S., Phoenix, A., & Pattman, R. (2002) *Young masculinities: Understanding boys in contemporary society*. Basingstoke: Palgrave Macmillan.

Gill, R. (2011) Sexism reloaded, or, it's time to get angry again. *Feminist Media Studies*, 11 (1), 61–71.

Gill, R., Henwood, K., & McLean, C. (2005) Body projects and the regulation of normative masculinity. *Body & Society*, 11(1), 37–62.

Gunter, A. (2010) *Growing up bad: Black youth, road culture & badness in an east London neighbourhood.* London: The Tuffnell Press.

Harris, A., Davidson, J., Letourneau, E., Paternite, C., & Miofsky, K. T. (2013) *Building a prevention framework to address teen 'sexting' behaviours.* Boston: University of Massachusetts Lowell.

Harvey, L., Ringrose, J., & Gill, R. (2013) Swagger, ratings and masculinity: Theorising the circulation of social and cultural value in teenage boys' digital peer networks. *Sociological Research Online*, 18 (4). Online. Retrieved from http://www.socresonline.org.uk/18/4/9.html

Holland, J., Ramazanoglu, C., Sharpe, S., & Thomson, R. (1998) *The Male in the Head. Young people, heterosexuality and power.* London: Tufnell Press.

Karaian, L. (2013) Policing 'sexting': Responsibilisation, respectability and sexual subjectivity in child protection/crime prevention responses to teenagers' digital sexual expression, Theoretical Criminology. doi: 10.1177/1362480613504331.

Kehler, M., & Atkinson, M. (Eds.) (2010) *Boy's bodies: speaking the unspoken.* New York: Peter Lang.

Lamb, S. (forthcoming) What's sexy? Gender and Education.

Livingstone, S., & Görzig, A. (2012) Sexting, in S. Livingstone, L. Haddon, & A. Görzig (Eds.) *Children, Risk and Safety on the Internet: Research and Policy Challenges in Comparative Perspective.* Bristol: The Policy Press, pp. 151–164.

Majors, R. (1990) Cool pose: Black masculinity and sports, in M. Messner, & D. Sabo (Eds.) *Sport, Men and the Gender Order.* Champaign, IL: Human Kinetics Books.

Manago, A. (2013) Negotiating a sexy masculinity on social networking sites. *Feminism & Psychology*, 23 (4), 478–497.

Mowlabocus, S. (2010) *Gaydar Culture.* Farnham, Surrey, England; Burlington, VT: Ashgate.

Mulholland, M. (2013) *Young people and pornography: Negotiating pornification.* New York: Palgrave.

Nayak, A. (2003) *Race, place and globalization: Youth cultures in a changing world.* Oxford: Berg.

O'Neill, R. (2014) Presentation at *Mediated Intimacies.* London: Open University, 30 July 2014.

Paechter, C. (2010) Tomboys and girly-girls: Embodied femininities in primary schools. *Discourse: Studies in the cultural politics of education*, 31 (2), 221–235.

Pascoe (2012) *Dude, you're a fag: Masculinity and sexuality in high school*, 2nd edn. Berkeley: University of California Press.

Ringrose, J. (2013) *Postfeminist education?: Girls and the sexual politics of schooling.* London and New York: Routledge.

Ringrose, J., Gill, R., Livingstone, S., & Harvey, L. (2012) *A qualitative study of children, young people and 'sexting'.* London: NSPCC. Retrieved from http://www.nspcc.org.uk/Inform/resourcesforprofessionals/sexualabuse/sexting-research-report_wdf89269.pdf

Ringrose, J., Harvey, L., Gill, R., & Livingstone, S. (2013) Teen girls, sexual double standards and 'sexting': Gendered value in digital image exchange. *Feminist Theory*, 14 (3), 305–323.

Ringrose, J., & Harvey, L. (2015) Boobs, back-off, six packs and bits: Mediated body parts, sexual shame and gendered reward in teens' networked images. *Continuum Journal of Media and Cultural Studies* 29 (2), 205–217.

Robards, B. (2012) Leaving MySpace, joining Facebook: 'Growing up' on social network sites. *Continuum*, 26 (3), 385–398.

Sedgwick, E. K. (1993) *Between men: English literature and male homosocial desire*, Revised edn. New York: Columbia University Press.

Siibak, A. (2010) Constructing masculinity on a social networking site the case-study of visual self-presentations of young men on the profile images of SNS rate. *Young*, 18 (4), 403–425.

Skeggs, B. (2001) The toilet paper: Femininity, class and mis-recognition. *Women's Studies International Forum*, Local/Global IDs: Materialist Discursive Feminism, 24 (3–4), 295–307.

Skeggs, B. (2004) *Class, self, culture*. London: Routledge.

Skeggs, B., & Wood, H. (2012) *Reacting to reality television: Performance, audience and value*. London: Routledge.

Stubbs, G. (2014) Schoolgirl given police caution after 'sexting' explicit selfie to boyfriend. *Mirror.co.uk* 22 July 2014. Retrieved 1 August 2014 from http://www.mirror.co.uk/news/uk-news/schoolgirl-given-police-caution-after-3896649

Van Doorn, N. (2010) The ties that bind: The networked performance of gender, sexuality and friendship on MySpace. *New Media and Society*, 12 (4), 583–602.

Youdell, D. (2006) *Impossible bodies, impossible selves: Exclusions and student subjectivities*. London: Springer.

Index

Note: Locators followed by 'f' and 'n' denote figures and notes respectively.

Printed and bound in Great Britain by
CPI Group (UK) Ltd, Croydon, CR0 4YY